PATERNOSTER THEOLOGICAL M

Making Disciples

The Significance of Jesus' Educational Methods for Today's Church

PATERNOSTER THEOLOGICAL MONOGRAPHS

A full listing of titles in both this series and
Paternoster Biblical Monographs
appears at the end of this book

PATERNOSTER THEOLOGICAL MONOGRAPHS

Making Disciples

The Significance of Jesus' Educational Methods
for Today's Church

Sylvia Wilkey Collinson

Foreword
by
Brian Hill

Copyright © Sylvia Wilkey Collinson, 2004

First published 2004 in Paternoster Biblical and Theological Monographs
by Paternoster

Paternoster is an imprint of Authentic Media,
9 Holdom Avenue, Bletchley, Milton Keynes, MK1 1QR, U.K.
and
P.O.Box 1047, Waynesboro, GA 30830-2047, U.S.A.

09 08 07 06 05 04 03   7 6 5 4 3 2 1

The right of Sylvia Wilkey Collinson to be identified as
the Author of this Work has been asserted by her in accordance with the
Copyright, Designs and Patents Act 1988.

All rights reserved. No part of this publication may be reproduced, stored in a retrieval system, or transmitted in any form or by any means, electric, mechanical, photocopying, recording or otherwise, without the prior permission of the publisher or a license permitting restricted copying. In the U.K. such licenses are issued by the Copyright Licensing Agency, 90 Tottenham Court Road, London W1P 9HE.

British Library Cataloguing in Publication Data
A catalogue record for this book is available from the British Library

ISBN-10 1–84227–116–4
ISBN-13 978–1–84227–116–2

Printed and bound in Great Britain by
Nottingham Alpha Graphics

PATERNOSTER THEOLOGICAL MONOGRAPHS

Series Preface

In the West the churches may be declining, but theology—serious, academic (mostly doctoral level) and mainstream orthodox in evaluative commitment—shows no sign of withering on the vine. This series of *Paternoster Theological Monographs* extends the expertise of the Press especially to first-time authors whose work stands broadly within the parameters created by fidelity to Scripture and has satisfied the critical scrutiny of respected assessors in the academy. Such theology may come in several distinct intellectual disciplines—historical, dogmatic, pastoral, apologetic, missional, aesthetic and no doubt others also. The series will be particularly hospitable to promising constructive theology within an evangelical frame, for it is of this that the church's need seems to be greatest. Quality writing will be published across the confessions—Anabaptist, Episcopalian, Reformed, Arminian and Orthodox—across the ages—patristic, medieval, reformation, modern and counter-modern—and across the continents. The aim of the series is theology written in the twofold conviction that the church needs theology and theology needs the church—which in reality means theology done for the glory of God.

Series Editors

David F. Wright, Emeritus Professor of Patristic and Reformed Christianity, University of Edinburgh, Scotland, UK

Trevor A. Hart, Head of School and Principal of St Mary's College School of Divinity, University of St Andrews, Scotland, UK

Anthony N.S. Lane, Professor of Historical Theology and Director of Research, London School of Theology, UK

Anthony C. Thiselton, Emeritus Professor of Christian Theology, University of Nottingham, Research Professor in Christian Theology, University College Chester, and Canon Theologian of Leicester Cathedral and Southwell Minster, UK

Kevin J. Vanhoozer, Research Professor of Systematic Theology, Trinity Evangelical Divinity School, Deerfield, Illinois, USA

Contents

Foreword	xi
Acknowledgments	xiii
PART 1 – Introduction and Background to Discipling	**1**
Chapter 1	
Introduction	**3**
Why focus on discipling?	3
Working definitions	4
Aims and methods of investigation	5
Limits of inquiry	7
Sequence of argument	9
Notes to Chapter 1	10
Chapter 2	
Background to the Concept of Discipling	**11**
Educational practices in the Ancient Near East	11
Educational practices in Ancient Israel	14
Conclusions	23
Notes to Chapter 2	24
PART 2 – Discipling in the Gospels	**27**
Chapter 3	
Discipling in Mark's Gospel	**29**
The discipling relationship	30
A new discipling community	33
The discipling model	35
Conclusions and re-examination of working definition	41
Notes to Chapter 3	42
Chapter 4	
Discipling in Matthew's Gospel	**45**
The discipling relationship	46
The discipling model	50
Conclusions and re-examination of working definition	55
Notes to Chapter 4	56

Chapter 5
Discipling in Luke's Gospel — 58
Women in the disciple band — 58
The discipling relationship — 64
The discipling model — 68
Conclusions and re-examination of working definition — 73
Notes to Chapter 5 — 74

Chapter 6
Discipling in John's Gospel — 79
Distinguishing between term and concept of 'disciple' — 79
The discipling relationship — 82
The discipling model — 86
Conclusion and re-examination of working definition — 91
Notes to Chapter 6 — 92

Chapter 7
Conclusions and Provisional Expansion of Definition — 96
The role of Jesus, the 'discipler' — 96
Expectations of disciples in the Gospels — 98
Working definition revisited — 99
Personal reflections — 103
Notes to Chapter 7 — 104

PART 3 – Discipling in the Apostolic Era — 105
Chapter 8
Discipling in the Acts of the Apostles — 107
Changes in the understanding of discipling — 107
Elements in revised working definition — 111
Discipling methods — 116
Conclusions — 119
Notes to Chapter 8 — 120

Chapter 9
Discipling in the Epistles and Revelation — 122
Elements in a revised working definition of discipling — 123
Conclusions — 136

Spiritual gifts and discipling	137
Notes to Chapter 9	138

PART 4 – Evaluation of Discipling as an Educational Practice for Today's Church — 143

Chapter 10
Refining the Definition — 145

Exploration of teaching	145
Schooling or formal education	148
Life related, informal education	148
Definition of discipling	161
Review	164
Notes to Chapter 10	164

Chapter 11
Congruence with the Christian Faith — 168

Core beliefs of the Christian faith	168
Congruence of discipling	174
Conclusions	175
Notes to Chapter 11	176

Chapter 12
Congruence with Findings of Present Day Religious and Educational Research — 178

Research into learning in Australian church life	178
The schooling model	182
Alternatives to the schooling model	189
Conclusions	202
Notes to Chapter 12	203

Chapter 13
Congruence of Discipling with Educational Theories in Today's Church — 208

Christian education	208
The small group movement	219
Theological education	226
Summary of findings	233
Notes to Chapter 13	234

Chapter 14
Conclusions   **240**
The initial research question   240
Findings and definition   241
Congruence with core values and beliefs of Christian faith community and with contemporary educational theory and practice   243
Main conclusions   244
Recommendations for future research   244
Recommendations for future church practice   245
A personal concluding comment   247

Bibliography   **249**
Index   **273**

List of Tables
Table 1: The discipling relationship   100
Table 2: The discipling model   101

Foreword

Two of the things that have needed re-assessment in the field of Christian Education have been its heavy reliance on the schooling model and the lack of clarity in popular references to discipling, a concept which might otherwise have served as a more biblical corrective to the first. Now a remedy is available.

After teaching in primary schools for several years, Sylvia Wilkey Collinson moved into teaching Biblical Studies and Christian Education in higher educational institutions. At one point, she was Vice-Principal of a Bible College. She has also had an enduring commitment to those who teach in voluntary youth organisations and cross-cultural mission situations. On the way she acquired higher formal qualifications in these areas, culminating in the doctoral study which became the basis for the present book. Her range of experiences has fitted her admirably to undertake such a study.

The attachment of the various Christian traditions ever since the fourth century to the schooling model has been rather curious, given that there are no biblical precedents for this approach to teaching and learning. That is not to say that the Christian church has been ill-served by adopting it. It has been a cultural practice worth baptising. Schooling has been put to good use by the church, both in nurturing its own people and training its leaders, and in expressing the compassion of Christ in the many cultures to which it has taken the Gospel.

But an increasing number of writers have been suggesting that the church may have overplayed its hand in this regard, and needs to review the diversity of ways in which people learn. Schooling is, after all, a rather tightly controlled form of education, from which a degree of limitation of personal freedom is never entirely absent. It needs to be complemented by other approaches which reflect more centrally the relational focus and emphasis on responsible personal choice of biblical precedents.

Instruction and example in the home, exhortation and faith-sharing in the faith community, interpersonal discipleship, and public witness in word and by life-modelling: all these are patterns of education and evangelism that play a big part in the New Testament. The present study focuses on discipling, and has much to contribute to current rethinking on this topic.

The author's literature review shows that though discipling is often referred to, in passing, in popular Christian writing, there has been a paucity of systematic studies explaining how it actually works. The model needs clarification, because not all biblical uses of the term "disciple" are applied in the same way, nor are all examples of discipling in the Bible identified by use of the term itself. Then it needs contextualisation, to see to what extent it continues to have something to offer in the vastly different world of today.

Sylvia Wilkey Collinson has the skills to perform these tasks. She has done so in a wonderfully clear and practical way. Leaders in Christian education at all levels will benefit from giving this book sustained attention. Youth leaders and adult educators alike may learn much from it. It is theoretical, in the sense that it supplies biblical, theological and pedagogical underpinnings. But ultimately, and for this reason, it is highly practical, making many valuable suggestions as to how discipling may be done well. In the current climate of suspicion of authorities and relationships in confusion, it is wonderfully timely.

Brian V. Hill
Murdoch University,
January 2004

Acknowledgments

I am deeply indebted to many people who have made both the undertaking and the completion of this study possible. They include my parents, Arthur († 1988) and Rene Wilkey, through whose love, godly nurture and wise counsel I was first discipled; my family and friends, too many to mention, whose input into my life encourages me in the life of a disciple of Jesus; and my students whose special friendships caused me to begin to question the meaning of discipling.

My thanks also go to the Council of the Bible College of South Australia which granted a Sabbatical leave to enable this project to be commenced and to the Rev Dr Bryan Hardman and Dr Allan Harkness who kindly read and critiqued my writings. This would however, never have moved to completion without the invaluable guidance of Professor Brian Hill of Murdoch University, Western Australia, whose patience, clear-thinking questions, and theological and academic insights turned my first vague thoughts into an exciting exploration of discipling. I also acknowledge with gratitude the help which Yvette Stanton, my graphic designer and John, her husband, offered in preparing the manuscript for publishing.

Most of all I thank Gavin, my husband, soul-mate, fellow-disciple and partner in learning who has constantly loved, supported and encouraged me over this time of writing. I owe more to him than I could ever express, and to our faithful and wonderful God.

Sylvia Wilkey Collinson
January 2004

PART 1

CHAPTER 1

Introduction

Why focus on discipling?

An African student had returned to his home country after completing five years of Bible and theological college education in Australia. Two years into an exciting church planting program he wrote to me, "Thank you so much for being my teacher, mother, sister and friend."

An Anglican priest had returned from a difficult experience in a third-world country involving considerable corruption within both the church and the society. She had many questions about the value of what was being done in the name of 'mission'. She, too, had been one of my students who had become a friend. She wrote in response to my letter at that time, "Thanks for all the love and support you have given me over the years. I have appreciated it far more than you probably realize."

Was this discipling? Certainly I had been their teacher, confidant, encourager and friend, but I was uncertain how to describe the nature of our relationship with its previously strong learning component and its continuing supportive and advisory element. Had I unwittingly 'discipled' them? My concept of 'discipling' was what happened when an older Christian met with a new Christian to tell them how to pray and read the bible and to monitor their spiritual growth, or when a stronger personality attracted a weaker Christian into his or her field of influence in order to assist or direct their spiritual development. I felt uncomfortable with the notion, and certainly did not want to damage my friendships with these students by what seemed to me to be slightly predatory behaviour.

The problem was, what did Jesus mean when he commissioned his disciples to "go and make disciples" (Mt. 28:19)? What did he mean by 'discipling' and was I, or should I, be doing it? My dilemma was not easily resolved.

'Discipling' is recognized as a valid model for teaching within various communities of faith or among some groups holding to particular ideologies. The Christian faith community understands its prime directive from Jesus to be the making of disciples. It holds this model of teaching in high esteem because it was the specific form favoured by him in developing the leaders who would proclaim his message to humanity and establish his church across the Roman Empire. However in present day church life, it appears the dominant models of teaching rarely include it. When people refer to teaching and learning they usually have in mind a schooling model. Protestant circles have largely ignored discipling. Where it has been practised, it has sometimes been misused or left mainly to a well-meaning but untrained laity.

When 'discipleship' is discussed the word is used (1) to encourage a particular lifestyle or (2) to refer to the relationships between Jesus and his disciples and to construe similar actions as appropriate for followers today or (3) to help establish new believers in the faith by the exercise of Christian 'disciplines'.[1] However, it seems that more searching theological, philosophical or educational questions about discipling have rarely been asked.

How does discipling differ from 'teaching'? What activities or methods could be described as discipling? Is every interaction between the teacher and the disciple classified as discipling? How many people can be discipled at the same time? Can a person disciple someone who is absent? When does discipling end? What did Jesus mean when he told his followers to go and make disciples? Whose disciples did they make, his or theirs? (Is there a difference?) Is his directive still relevant today? Is discipling a spiritual gift? How does it differ from pastoral care? What is there within the discipling model which would cause us to recommend it as a teaching method for use today? This research will attempt to answer some of these questions.

Working definitions

In common parlance the term 'discipling' may be broadly used for any activity which produces growth or learning in the life of disciples or followers of Jesus Christ. However within this study we intend to examine the more specific model of teaching which may technically be described as discipling. Because discipling comes within the wide range of activities which are classified as teaching it is necessary to define teaching briefly at the outset, without pre-empting the more detailed discussion later. We thus refer to the term 'teaching' as, *an attempt by one person (a teacher) to cause another person or persons to learn.*

Discipling then is a particular mode or 'model' of teaching, as distinct from other models such as 'parenting' or 'schooling'. Each model has a consistent approach to teaching different from the other models, so that while all may use the same wide variety of teaching methods, they do so in a way which is subject to the conditions of the model. A discipler may utilize any number of different methods in the teaching process including narrative, explanation, discussion, instruction, preaching, question and answer, demonstration, modelling, practice, small groups or action-reflection, but he or she will use them within the context of a discipling relationship. The nature and qualities of this relationship will be considered more fully in later chapters, but at the outset of this study we propose as a working definition,

> *Discipling is a voluntary, personal relationship between two individuals, in community or alone, in which the disciple commits him or herself to learn from the other, by imitation, oral communication and sharing in the life and work of the discipler.*

There is also a need to establish from the beginning the difference between discipling and discipleship. The term 'discipleship' is commonly used to describe the way of life expected of all believers in Jesus Christ. They are disciples of Christ, in that they are called to follow him, but the following of that path, while related to discipling, is not the same as the methods of teaching which are used in its promulgation. Discipling is but one method of many used. Maybe if Jesus had not used this method of teaching, the Christian walk would not have been called discipleship. It is the method itself which is the concern of this research, not the life of discipleship.

Aims and methods of investigation

In this study an inquiry will be made into the nature of discipling and its congruence as an educational strategy with the objectives of modern Christian faith communities. It is our contention that discipling, as exemplified in, and endorsed by, the New Testament, warrants greater attention in the church than it is currently getting, in contrast to the priority accorded to practices derived from the schooling model.

This theory will be tested by an investigation into the essential nature of discipling as a model of teaching: by contrasting it with other models of teaching; by finding the degree of support for its effectiveness in present day educational research; and by assessing its relationship to relevant educational theories and practices in the Christian community of faith today. Questions will be asked concerning the discipling relationship – how it commences and is maintained, its duration, and what activities, conditions and qualities are involved.

Part One of our inquiry will investigate the origins of discipling as an educational methodology, which may be as old as humanity itself. The Western world traces discipling back to the cultures of the Ancient Near East and more particularly those of Greece and Israel. *The Oxford English Dictionary* states that the terms 'disciple', 'discipling' and 'discipleship' have come into regular English usage through their New Testament associations.[2] Therefore the Bible, and more especially the four Gospels, will be used as a major source of information. It is recognized that these documents were not primarily written to provide a handbook on discipling methodology. Given that one of Jesus' main tasks was to disciple his followers and his prime directive to his followers was to "make disciples of all nations", then it may be deduced that the discipling methods which he used provided an example for them and subsequent generations of disciplers to imitate. Thus in Part Two of our investigation the discipling activities of Jesus, in particular, will provide significant data.

The motifs of 'disciples', 'discipleship' and 'discipling' within the biblical texts will be examined to clarify our understanding. In our collection of data there will be instances when the term 'disciple' is not specifically applied to a particular person or persons, but the texts provide a description of a learning relationship between two or more persons which leads us to believe that it fulfils the same requirements as those of a discipling relationship. Sufficient of the essential qualities and conditions necessary to define a relationship as discipling, are present. These occurrences of the 'concept' of discipling as we have defined it, will also form part of our study. Conversely, there may be occasions when the word 'disciple' is present but its context demonstrates that the writer is using it in such a way that it does not encompass what we have defined as the minimal requirements for a relationship to be considered as 'discipling'. Such cases will be noted but set aside in our compilation of evidence.

A study will be made of the meaning and impact of the biblical texts themselves. Questions of a critical literary-historical nature will not be pursued at length because the centre of our interest is the transmitted text, which has been accepted for much of the life of the church. However some elements of the reader-response method will be utilized. The linguistic and literary nature of the text will be examined in our interpretation and we will attempt to understand the historical and cultural background, grammatical use of the Greek or Hebrew terms, theological milieu, author's intention, themes and original readers' understanding. Unless otherwise stated all Scripture references quoted are from the *New Revised Standard Version*[3] and the Greek text is based on the 21st edition of Eberhard Nestle's *Novum Testamentum Graece*.

We will not follow in detail critical methods, which seek to discover the emphases of the communities or documents behind the texts.[4] Nor will the historicity of the events narrated be discussed. However some use will be made of the Narrative Critical approach[5] in researching the Gospel materials. That is, an attempt will be made to enter and experience the stories themselves. Actions will be observed and dialogues between Jesus and his disciples listened to, in order to help understand the processes involved in their discipling relationships. Each Gospel will be explored separately, looking for connecting links in the mind of the author which give some indication of the message he was conveying concerning the discipling acts of Jesus and implications for the lives of his implied readers. In the light of the Gospels our working definition will be re-examined and any provisional expansions made.

Part Three of our inquiry will focus on the Acts of the Apostles and the Epistles and Revelation, before refining our definition. A study of the book of Acts will provide the necessary understanding of the transition of the disciples from their role as learners, assistants and companions, to evangelists and leaders. Any changes in the discipling process, once Jesus' immediate presence was removed, will be noted. The problem of the absence of the word 'disciple' from the Epistles will be addressed and questions asked concerning possible reasons. By entering the 'narrative world' of each epistle and examining the nature of relationships and interactions between individuals and groups, an attempt will be made to find evidence of the concept of discipling even when the word is not expressly mentioned.

Within the Christian faith community today, Jesus' teaching continues to be regarded as containing principles relevant to the current age and his directive to make disciples of all nations is considered as carrying authority, therefore we will endeavour to discover whether discipling as a model of teaching has some validity today. We will seek to draw out the principles, which underlie the discipling method as practised in New Testament times and attempt to translate them into contemporary terminology.

In Part Four we will seek to evaluate discipling as a model of teaching consistent with the core beliefs of the Christian faith. And then it will be examined in the light of current educational research and by referring to principles of Christian education as understood by the Christian faith community. Questions as to how to implement it in terms of the teaching processes of the life of the faith community will be addressed. In the light of our findings, the writings of some significant educationists in the fields of Christian education, Small Group theory and theological education will be appraised to discover whether they accommodate the values of the discipling model as a means of transmitting the faith and enabling growth in spiritual maturity. Finally recommendations will be made concerning its more effective utilisation within the theory and practice of Christian education. Some implications for theological education will also be noted.

Limits of inquiry

While the main focus of our biblical research will be on the teaching practices of Jesus, the formal teaching methods which he used when instructing the crowds will only be mentioned in passing. Many scholars and Christian educationists have devoted considerable attention to the spoken teaching methods of Jesus (e.g. parable, illustration, question and answer, discussion, explanation). Our purpose is not to replicate their studies, but to explore the predominantly informal processes of teaching which are possible within the discipling relationship. The content of Jesus' teaching, especially as it relates to the life of discipleship, will only be mentioned if there is particular need to comment on such in the light of his discipling methods.

In our study of the Gospels, we have not gone behind them to the communities (such as the community of the Beloved Disciple) which may well have been responsible for the final redacted editions of these writings. While the first intention of some, if not all, of the evangelists was to bring their readers to belief (Jn. 20:31), the contribution of their writings to the teaching and discipling of believers is undisputed. In their selection of materials concerning the disciples, the writers were endeavouring to portray concepts of faithful discipleship to encourage members of the specific communities of believers to whom their writings were addressed. Interesting though a study of these communities may be, in both the Gospels and the Epistles, our focus will be on the meaning of the received narrative.

Because our task is to examine the notion of discipling and its congruence with the objectives of Christian faith communities, our research has concentrated on the discipling model as it has arisen predominantly within the Christian tradition. Similar teaching practices of other world ideologies or religions, both now and in the world of the Ancient Near East, while containing much of interest, have not been considered.

The limits of the present study do not permit extending our research into an examination of the discipling model as it has been implemented in various traditions throughout the history of the church. Nor will reference be made to the model as it applies specifically to women or children.

In finding support for the discipling model within the modern church, our aim has not been to make an exhaustive study of every possible model of teaching. Our references to parenting, mentoring, spiritual direction, pastoral care, counselling and psychotherapy have been at best cursory. Even in those fields which have received greater attention (e.g. Christian education, small groups, theological education) it has been necessary to limit our attention to the writings of a small number of theorists. Those who have been chosen are, however, those who have had significant influence on the whole field of study or writings which have been perceived as being representative of a much wider group.

The recommendations, which will be made at the conclusion of our work, will suggest possible ways forward for the faith community. Questions concerning preparation of detailed curricula and associated issues remain for later research to address. Our aim has been to reinstate discipling as a valuable agenda item for the attention of the Christian faith community in the 21st century.

Sequence of argument

In Chapter Two a study is made of the background to the concept of discipling as it was understood in the time of Jesus. Antecedents to the idea, in Ancient Near Eastern literature are examined and the classical Greek and Hellenistic use of the term *mathētēs* (disciple) are considered. Because Hebrew has no equivalent for the Greek *mathētēs*, the Old Testament is explored for evidence of other learning communities or discipling-type relationships. Jewish literature from the Dead Sea Scrolls, rabbinic writings and other sources are briefly surveyed for discipling practices during the Intertestamental Period and the first century of the Christian era.

Chapters Three to Six analyse each of the Gospels, to discover the techniques, which Jesus used in teaching his disciples, and the nature of discipling interactions and relationships. The particular perspective of each Gospel writer is noted and implications for the discipling model drawn out. The roles of the Twelve, of Peter and of the women followers receive special focus, and the success or otherwise of Jesus' discipling is considered. Criteria are established for deciding which of the persons whom Jesus encountered could be considered as disciples. Chapter Seven seeks to develop an integrated analysis of discipling from this material. Before turning to discipling as practised by the early church, our earlier definition is revisited in the light of the Gospel record, to ascertain if further expansion is necessary.

Chapter Eight examines the period of the Acts of the Apostles when the apostles and leaders of the primitive Christian community were beginning to respond to Jesus' commission to make disciples of all nations. Their transition from being his close associates to disciplers and leaders of his discipling community is observed. Changes to the practice of discipling, once Jesus' physical presence was removed, are noted. Chapter Nine searches for evidence of discipling relationships within the world encompassed by the Epistles and Revelation and examines the churches represented, in order to ascertain something of their function as discipling communities.

In Chapter Ten a variety of popular and scholarly sources are consulted to clarify the term. It is contrasted with other models of teaching and located within an educational framework, in order to understand more fully its distinctive contribution to the teaching process.

Chapter Eleven looks at core values and beliefs of the Christian church which have particular relevance to the discipling model. Their agreement with the basic premises and mode of operation of the model is determined.

Chapter Twelve examines statistics from various church life surveys in Australia, and seeks to establish what are the participants' perceptions of factors, which have contributed to their own spiritual development. Then a critique is made of the schooling model as it has been used in both secular and faith communities and attention drawn to the need for alternative models of education, especially in the formation of attitudes, values, beliefs and behaviours. Various informal, life-related models are considered and compared with discipling. These include the family, close personal relationships, apprenticing, mentoring, voluntary groups, learning communities (both short and long term), adventure education, collaborative and small group learning. The principles of adult education and their applicability to the discipling model are considered.

Chapter Thirteen turns to contemporary educational endeavours in the church of the Western world. First, we examine the theories of three leading Christian educationists who hold different theological perspectives but each endorse the value of informal models of teaching. The relationships between their theories and the discipling model, as we have defined it, are explored. Next the Small Group Movement and development of house and cell churches are investigated and their value as a medium for growth and development of the church is established. Then a number of strategies for renewal or re-envisioning of theological education are considered and recommendations made for future directions. Finally, we seek to clarify how, in general, the discipling model may be applied in modern church life and offer a number of general guidelines for its operation.

Notes to Chapter 1

1. E.g. Richard Foster lists the Christian disciplines as meditation, prayer, fasting, study, simplicity, solitude, submission, service, confession, worship, guidance and celebration. (Foster, R., *Celebration of Discipline*)
2. Simpson, J.A. and E.S.C. Weiner, *The Oxford English Dictionary*, 733,734
3. Holman Bible, *New Revised Standard Version Bible*, 1989
4. E.g. Source, form and redaction criticism
5. Powell, M.A., *What is Narrative Criticism? A New Approach to the Bible*

CHAPTER 2

Background to the Concept of Discipling

The primary source of our understanding of discipling will be the practice of Jesus himself as recorded in the Gospels. However before proceeding to study the concept of discipleship held by Jesus and members of the early church, a brief review will be made of the background educational practices in the Ancient Near East. Relevant Egyptian, Assyrian, Babylonian and Greek educational practices will be considered. These will be determined in the most part by a study of the secondary sources. Then a more detailed examination of evidence from Hebrew sources will be made. Old Testament terminology applied in learning situations will be discussed. Possible individual or community learning relationships will be explored within the literature of the Jews. The synagogue and rabbinic movements will also be examined and a brief study will be made of the literature from the Intertestamental Period and first century CE.

Educational practices in the Ancient Near East

In the ancient world the initial education of every child was in the home. As children progressed towards adulthood, they followed the occupation of their parents, learning the skills and knowledge required in an apprentice-style work situation. However when reading and writing skills developed in Mesopotamia some time before 3000 BCE, the educational structures necessary to enable succeeding generations to acquire these skills began to develop, and thus the first formal schools came into existence.

From Sumeria there is evidence of a 'tablet house' where reading and writing were taught and a family-like hierarchy of relationships prevailed.[1] Both Babylon and Assyria had a form of elementary education and there was a 'house of wisdom' where higher education was given to younger members of the upper class. "There, presumably, the youthful aspirants for a learned career, seated on benches of stone without backs, studied mathematics and astronomy, medicine, magic arts and theology and all the varied branches of 'the learning and tongue of the Chaldeans' (Dn. 1:4)."[2]

Scholars speculate that apprentice-style learning functioned in the royal courts of the important Mesopotamian cities among sons of the priestly class, to prepare them for leadership in their society. However Crenshaw writes that "only three Mesopotamian kings boasted literacy… and their boasts seem empty",[3] so this education may not have been as extensive as one might at first imagine. Scribal schools may have existed among the Hittites and at Ugarit but little information exists.

Ancient Egyptian education began in a village elementary school followed by a provincial school.[4] For those proceeding to higher education, further study was conducted in a government office associated with the royal court where future courtiers were tutored by senior officials in the real-life situations which arose. This involved business and legal work, and the learning of appropriate behaviours and knowledge required for solving complicated political and administrative problems.[5] The educational process was extended for those who became physicians, architects or priests by further apprentice-style learning. Crenshaw mentions the existence of a royal school about 1900 BCE.[6] McKane adds that there were schools associated with the temples which were not purely for religious purposes, but also for the apprenticing of those who would be associated with the production of the wisdom literature.[7]

The position of women in ancient Egypt allowed some opportunities for daughters of the aristocracy or the royal household to be educated by a private tutor in skills beyond those required for domestic duties. This was, however, rare in the ancient world. Most girls were married at puberty and began bearing children soon after. Their education was within the home and was confined to the skills required for the performance of their household duties.

In the world of classical Greece, Athenian boys were involved in formal schooling from the age of seven but only the sons of the elite in their twenties and thirties were able to progress to advanced studies under the great philosophers.[8] It was these learning relationships of young adult males with older philosopher-teachers which began to be designated as disciple-master relationships.[9]

The term 'disciple' (*mathētēs*) was first used by Herodotus in the fifth century BCE and appears frequently in classical Greek. It is derived from the verb to learn (*manthanō*), and in the learning context it was used by a wide variety of authors in a number of different ways.[10] Rengstorf provides a comprehensive summary of *mathētēs* and the different uses of the word in the ancient world.[11] He proposes that in Greek literature *mathētēs* could denote,[12]

- A man[13] who was engaged in learning specific knowledge or conduct from another person with whom he had a personal relationship. This process of education was intentional and according to a set plan.
- An apprentice or person who was committed to a relationship in which he received instruction in technical or academic information or a particular skill, from another who possessed superior knowledge. The learner was unable to dissolve the relationship, but did retain his personal dignity and some independence.
- An intellectual link between two persons considerably removed in time whereby one seeks to imitate the other. It referred to an inner fellowship

between two persons and the practical effects of such a relationship. It could also be used in a specialised way to refer to a pupil in a particular philosophical school, especially the Sophists.

Thus the emphasis was on a relationship in which a teacher (*didaskalos*) imparted his superior knowledge over an extended period of time and the learner imitated him, much as an apprentice would today.[14]

This learning relationship was usually expressed in communal living. The Greek philosopher, Pythagoras (c.580 BCE) founded learning communities amongst aristocrats in Italy. They preferred to use the term 'brotherhood' to describe their relationships, but the concept of discipleship did operate within these communities. Members learnt the philosophy of Pythagoras and followed his prescribed way of life which included special dietary rules and sharing of property.

Many would consider that the relationship between the great Athenian philosopher, Socrates (c.470-400 BCE) and his students is best described as that of a master to his disciples. His teaching activities attracted young men seeking for knowledge and truth. However Rengstorf claims that Socrates refused to be called a teacher or to allow those under his tuition to be referred to by the term '*mathētēs*'. He felt it did not sufficiently encompass the idea of the fellowship experienced by those who were striving together for a common goal of learning. Socrates taught that persons had to discover what is the nature of things for themselves and that the master's role was more like that of midwife assisting in the bringing forth of truth. He condemned the Sophists who had paying disciples, because he did not believe that virtue could be taught and concluded that the Sophist teachers were therefore charlatans.[15]

Wilkins strongly disagrees with this viewpoint claiming that Plato's Socrates was only against the word 'disciple' when the Sophists were being referred to, but he used the word positively in other contexts to describe "one taken into the tutelage of a master in order to learn a skill".[16] Socrates (and later Plato's Academy) replaced the rational, professional learning relationship of the Sophists with an "ideal fellowship between the one who gave out intellectually and those who received intellectually".[17] It was a fellowship of life as well as intellect, with the director as first among equals. In his *Memorabilia*, Xenophon writes of the relationship between Socrates and one of his disciple-companions. "Euthydemus guessed that he would never be of much account unless he spent as much time as possible with Socrates. Henceforward, unless obliged to absent himself, he never left him, and even began to adopt some of his practices."[18]

In their teaching, Plato and Aristotle both followed Socrates in his practice of sharing common meals. They encouraged learners to be with and observe the teacher in the normal routines of his life, so that a whole philosophy of life and behaviour was communicated. Aristotle refers to the master-disciple relationship as a "moral type of friendship, which is not on fixed terms: it makes a gift, or does whatever it does, as to a friend".[19]

In the fourth century BCE, the Cynic philosopher, Diogenes, attracted a number of disciples who imitated his lifestyle. Of these, Crates, was known for his peripatetic preaching, voluntary poverty and peace-making efforts. A formal school was not established but those who adopted a similar unconventional lifestyle were known as disciples of the Cynics, and their peripatetic teaching throughout the Mediterranean world became a common feature of Greco-Roman life.[20] From the fifth century BCE to the second century CE itinerant philosopher-teachers and their disciples were familiar figures in Mediterranean life.

Epicurus (c.340-270 BCE) may have been the first Greek philosopher to found a school as an institution. However the teacher-disciple concept was still present, even though his followers honoured him as a god and memorized his sayings at his command. He was the only philosopher of note who welcomed women as his followers. However one questions if the intent of their inclusion was educational or otherwise, considering his emphasis on pleasure and ready fulfilment of sensual desires.

Relationships among the disciples of the great classical, philosophical teachers were so firm that when the teacher died these groups did not disintegrate. Sometimes the leader would appoint his successor,[21] or at other times one would emerge from among the followers. However, the members totally identified with the common cause and teaching, doing everything in their power to communicate them to others. Thus the communities of disciples were maintained and traditions were developed to preserve the life of the group. Even when new teachings arose, they were presented as being a natural development of the doctrines of the founder (even if they were not!).[22]

In the Greco-Roman world of the first century CE the concept of discipleship was similar to that of the classical period. The exact nature of the discipling relationship was determined by the individuals involved, rather than the word itself dictating the terms and nature of their interaction.[23]

Educational practices in Ancient Israel

Terminology in the Old Testament

At first sight the concept of 'discipling' appears to be missing from the Old Testament record, however closer study reveals some clues to the existence of relationships bearing 'master-disciple' qualities. The Hebrew language does not have an equivalent term for 'disciple' and the Greek, *mathētēs* (disciple) only appears in the Septuagint translation of the Old Testament in alternative readings of Jeremiah 13:21; 20:11; 26:9. Unfortunately none of these readings is of use in our study of the term or the concept.

In his article in the *Theological Dictionary of the New Testament*, Rengstorf argues that the 'ideal' of discipleship in the Old Testament is that between the nation and Yahweh. And thus for any person, be they prophet, priest or king, to be teacher would usurp God's place as master and differentiate the person from other members of the elect community.[24] Others disagree. Wilkins states that while the primary relationship of those gathered round a 'teacher' would always be with God, there was a second level of discipleship of individuals committed to learning from that other person. He comments further that individuals can be disciples of Yahweh and his prophets at the same time. "The function and kind of discipleship are different…but both relationships can be designated discipleship nonetheless."[25]

Wilkins then examines two Hebrew expressions similar to 'disciple', *talmîdh* (taught one) and *limmûdh* (taught). *Talmîdh* appears only once, as a designation among the temple musicians for a pupil or novice, in contrast with a teacher or master (1 Ch. 25:8). Some conclude on this evidence alone that a formal school existed in Jerusalem for their training,[26] but it could mean no more than that the musicians were involved in a learning process.

The passive participle, *limmûdh* is used six times in the prophets. When it occurs in Isaiah 8:16 (NRSV) it is translated 'disciples'. They may be God's disciples, but the majority of commentators interpret this as Isaiah's prayer concerning his disciples.[27] In Isaiah 54:13 instruction by Yahweh is featured. Twice in Isaiah 50:4 the speaker emphasizes that his relationship with Yahweh is like that of a disciple to his master. He is equipped to see and hear, like 'the taught ones'. Some conclude that there is an allusion to a school of disciples. At the very least it points to a concept, familiar to the readers, involving the prophet and a group of closely associated learners.

Possible discipling relationships

Some have suggested that the relationship between Moses and Joshua was that of a master to his disciple. Joshua was a younger man who accompanied Moses in his national leadership responsibilities as an "assistant" (Ex. 33:11; Dt. 1:38). Their relationship is never described as having a teaching intent. Joshua had tribal leadership responsibilities (Nu. 13:8) and had proven to be a successful military commander (Ex. 17:10-13). He was present during some of Moses' experiences of the presence of God (Ex. 24:13; 33:11) and exhibited his own faith when he returned after spying out the promised land (Nu. 14:30). Joshua came under Moses' authority. The older man prayed for him, sent him out, heard his reports back and encouraged him in his leadership tasks (Ex. 17:9; Nu. 13:16-20; 14:36-38).

Moses shared a close personal relationship with Joshua for almost forty years and during that time the younger man observed at close quarters the example of the life of the "prophet… whom the Lord knew face to face" (Dt. 34:10). Joshua grew in his leadership skills and his relationship of faith in the Lord and is described as being "full of the spirit of wisdom because Moses had laid his hands on him" (Dt. 34:9). He could not but have learned from the example and words of the older man, who in God's name commissioned him as his successor (Nu. 27:18-23; Dt. 31:23). Thus, although the term 'disciple' is not used of this relationship, the concept of discipling seems to be present. Undoubtedly learning occurred.

Learning communities in the Old Testament

Recent studies have suggested a number of different groups within the nation of Israel which may have formed learning communities encompassing discipling relationships. Evidence for these is not conclusive but may be found both in the writings of the Old Testament and in other Jewish literature. We will examine these theories to see possible precursors to the educational situation in the time of Jesus and the early church.

AMONG THE PROPHETS

During the time of Samuel, bands of prophets emerged in the life of Israel (1 Sa. 19:18 – 20:1). E. J. Young conjectures that Samuel brought them into being in an attempt to check the declining religious life of Israel.[28] Samuel had his own house in Ramah, so did not live in these communities but he was their head (1 Sa. 19:20). From a study of the term *nawôth* (camp area) used of these groups, it is assumed that they lived in shepherd camps pitched outside the city.[29] Members of these groups were designated prophets who were appointed by God's Spirit. However Samuel's authority over them probably implies he had the role of a mentor who taught or guided the less able. On two occasions King Saul joined these groups of prophets when the Spirit of the Lord came upon him. He prophesied and entered into their ecstatic experiences (1 Sa. 10.5-10; 19:20-24).

In the Northern Kingdom persons called 'sons of the prophets' appeared at the time of Elijah and Elisha.[30] There were large numbers of prophets at this time and these possibly formed themselves into professional groups usually associated with a sanctuary (1 Ki. 18:4; 13:11; 2 Ki. 2:1,4,5). They seem to have had some structural organisation and communal practices. These groups either lived together under Elisha (2 Ki. 6:1-3) or he visited them (2 Ki. 4:38). By the use of the term 'son', we may infer that close, personal relationships with the leading prophets of the day, Elijah and Elisha, are intimated and disciple-type relationships between them and the group is a possibility.[31]

The prophets, Elijah, Elisha and Jeremiah all had assistants whom some have concluded were disciples. Rengstorf considers these assistants were little more than servants who looked after them.[32] However Elisha's relationship to Elijah has the marks of a disciple. The Lord commanded Elijah to anoint Elisha as his successor and by casting his mantle upon him, signified the beginning of the relationship (1 Ki. 19:16,19-21; 2 Ki. 3:11). Rengstorf does not do justice to the text by asserting that this was just the entrance of Elisha into Elijah's service and that nothing happened until Elijah left the scene (2 Ki. 2:9-12). The whole tenor of the call narrative suggests much more than a glorified servant, although there is no record of Elisha acting as a prophet until after Elijah had gone. Baruch performed a number of roles in the service of Jeremiah, including that of messenger (Je. 32:12-14), scribe (Je. 36:4-8,32; 45:1-3) and spokesperson (Je. 43:3). Even the king saw him as a threat to national security in his own right (Je. 36:26), but Rengstorf claims he was no more than an assistant or interpreter, because we hear nothing about him once Jeremiah had gone.[33]

Commenting on the Elisha incident of 2 Kings 9:1, Josephus concluded that the individual who ran an errand for Elisha was a 'disciple'.[34] Hengel interprets the sons of the prophets sitting before Elisha as disciples in a teacher-pupil relationship (2 Ki. 4:38).[35] Wilson suggests that these were prophets in their own right who joined together under the leadership of Elisha for mutual support, and encouragement in their task because of the negative attitude to them by the leaders of the nation. He considers that the Elijah-Elisha relationship served as a model for the others. Wilson also speculates that these sons of the prophets may have been responsible for preserving the Elijah-Elisha stories.[36] Goppelt sees these relationships as providing a new model for discipleship, that of prophetic activity arising out of the context of fellowship.[37]

Wilkins however believes that these conclusions go further than the text permits.[38] The sons of the prophets were already in existence before Elisha began his separate prophetic ministry (1 Ki. 20:35). Although some respected and joined him, they were not in a trainee relationship. They continued to carry on their own prophetic ministry while following his lead.

The evidence that these bands of prophets were discipleship groups is not absolute. Considering that they lived together and that they were under the authority of a leading prophet, it seems probable that the learning which occurred was intentional. This could still be the case even if they gathered as the Spirit of God came upon them (1 Sa. 10:10-13).

Many suppose that the great writing prophets had 'schools' of followers who gathered around them to be taught. They suggest that these 'disciples' memorized the words of the prophets and transmitted them orally to others before finally collecting the traditions and committing them to writing. There is no evidence for this theory apart from the existence of the prophetic writings themselves, but it is not improbable that this occurred.

SCRIBAL TRAINING

The Hebrew, *sōpher* (scribe) is used for a variety of positions for which literacy skills were important.[39] However, our interest is predominantly in its use as it relates to those versed in the law of Moses (Ezr. 7:6; Ne. 8:1).

Before the Exile, families of scribes preserved the art of reading, writing and transcribing the law. A group of Kenite families lived at Jabez (1 Ch. 2:55). They transmitted their skills to succeeding generations and to princes, priests and Levites. These in turn were expected to instruct the people (2 Ch. 15:3; 17:7-9) and make legal judgements based upon the law and traditions. The association of scribes, priests and Levites occurs a number of times in the pre-exilic period (Dt. 17:18; 2 Ki. 12:10; 1 Ch. 24:6; 2 Ch. 34:13). There are no references to scribal schools, but these may well have emerged as skills were nurtured first within the family[40] and later on a wider scale as specialized training at the national and international level was required (1 Ch. 27:32; 2 Ki 10:6).

From earliest times priests were entrusted with the responsibility for teaching Israel concerning the law of God (Dt. 33:10). Thus they were trained first within the family and then later in the Temple porches or wherever numbers of priests gathered. In early Israel, tuition may have been on an individual basis, but Von Rad suggests the later possibility of a number of specialized schools for scribes, priests, Levites and royal officials. "Questions of ritual and the complex distinctions between clean and unclean will have been taught in priestly schools."[41] By the eighth century BCE, the priests had failed miserably in their teaching responsibilities. Hosea, and later Malachi record the Lord's accusation against them (Ho. 4:4-9; 5:1; Mal 2:7).

Thus when the law became increasingly more important than cultic practices during the exile, the "great period of the *sopherîm*"[42] began when Ezra returned to Jerusalem (c.398 BCE). He was a skilled scribe, priest, teacher and political leader (Ezr. 7:6,10-26) who was endorsed by a Persian royal decree to centralize Jewish education and study of the law. This did much to reinforce the position of scribes and to give status and credibility to their profession. At this time they took over the priestly role and became spokespersons for warning and exhorting the people (Ne. 8:1-8; 13:13).

Literacy was clearly evident in Israel from early in her history,[43] but the first reference to an actual school (*bêth midhrash*) in Jewish literature occurs around 180 BCE in the writings of Ben Sirach (Sir. 51:23) when he invites the untaught to his school.[44] During the Intertestamental Period the emphasis changed from hearing the voice of God in the prophets, to finding new truth in the old Scriptures. The Talmud looks back to this period. "Be patient in [the administration of] justice, rear many disciples (*talmîdhîm*) and make a fence round the Torah" (Aboth 1:1).[45] Later rabbinic literature sees Ezra as a beginning point for their heritage.

It cannot be conclusively proved that schools for the education of the scribes existed. However Wilkins postulates that once a scribe had been trained and taken his position among the class of scribes, the "older, more outstanding scribes would provide guidance for the others, and this certainly could be considered as a type of master-disciple relationship."[46] Those who proved exceptional would be used in national and international positions of influence.

The Wisdom movement

In Jeremiah 18:18 the prophet appears to be referring to three categories of leaders in Israel – the priests, the prophets and the wise or elders (Ezk. 7:26). This latter group gave counsel. Sirach 39:1-11 shows that wise men were competent in the law and had a teaching role.

Many scholars believe that the wisdom literature as it occurred in the Ancient Near East was a product of formal, institutional, master-disciple relationships. The existence of wisdom schools in Mesopotamia, Egypt and the Levant is proven beyond doubt.[47] In Israel true wisdom was considered to begin with the fear of the Lord (Pr. 1:7) and to be his gift, but this did not rule out attempts to develop it in the young. Von Rad postulates that the earliest wisdom literature was intended to develop and educate young men in 'wisdom'. It originated in the royal court, promoted strongly by the kings Solomon and Hezekiah, and was designed to build up a competent body of future leaders and administrators.[48] It was 'school wisdom' with elders transmitting to younger men how decisions of national, social or judicial consequence were to be made. However it was not totally confined to the royal courts and as the literature indicates, it dealt with life questions asked by the middle classes and landowners. Von Rad therefore concludes that "wisdom centres" must also have existed.[49]

A second theory concerning the wisdom tradition in Israel suggests that it was a developing oral tradition within families and clans starting with short proverbial sayings, and that it gradually permeated the full strata of the society and related to the whole of life. Parents instructed children in the wisdom of life (Pr. 1:8; 31:1).[50] Terrien and Lindblom both postulate a class of 'the wise' who were influenced by the wisdom outlook of surrounding nations and gave oral teaching to groups of disciples and to the people at large.[51] The existence of such a class of both men and women has some supporting evidence in the Old Testament record (Jdg. 5:29; 2 Sa. 14:2; 16:23; 1 Ki. 2:9; Is. 19:11,12), however more recently Whybray, through his study of 'the wise one' (*chakham*), has discounted the whole idea.[52] McKane and Wilkins both believe that they were not necessarily a separate class, but that the term designated people in a variety of professional classes, including the scribes, prophets, priests, elders and nobles who possessed the quality of wisdom (Je. 8:8,9; 18:18; Pr. 22:17).[53]

It is difficult to know what the situation really was. Wilkins concludes, "Something was out there of an institutional kind behind the clearly recognisable body of wisdom writings, with its own language and ideology."[54] Thus we may say that a master-discipleship type of training for the wise men could have been possible.

The synagogue and the Rabbinic movement

After the Babylonian exile the focus of the faith of Israel shifted to some degree from the Temple and its cultus, and began to include the synagogue as the centre of social and religious life in each Jewish community.[55] In the synagogue, every Sabbath the Law and Prophets were read and expounded to the people within the context of worship, prayer and praise. The chief function of the synagogue became education, so that they acted as "popular universities, a kind of extra-mural department of the main university, which was the newly built

Temple at Jerusalem".[56] With the desire to teach the people reinforced by the Hellenistic emphasis on education, the number of scribes increased and the more prominent became rabbis.

Rabbinic schools formed in a synagogue or in the temple porches for the purpose of studying the Scriptures, especially the Law.[57] Younger men[58] gathered in an attitude of reverence and respect to learn as disciples. They were known as *talmîdîm* (apprentices).[59] Wilkins made a careful study of the rabbinic use of *talmîdh* (taught one) and deduced that the basic concept refers to persons training to be rabbis. This meant that they were professional students of the Torah (particularly the oral Torah), the Scriptures and religious traditions of Israel. The term also covers followers of a cause (not necessarily religious) and it is in this way that rabbinic writings refer to Jesus' disciples.[60]

Students of the rabbis served them as slaves and obeyed them totally, even if it meant going against the authority of their own fathers.[61] They came to the rabbi requesting permission to be his disciples. They often lived in close community with him and one another looking after the practical needs of the rabbi, while he expounded the Law as it impinged upon people's lives and relationships with God and one another. The rabbi lectured and allowed opportunity for questions and some discussion. Learners were required to listen and learn his rabbinic pronouncements by rote so that they became bearers of the tradition.[62] Rabbinic guidance was considered indispensable for anyone wishing to study the Scriptures, because a long period of training was considered essential to true understanding. By the time of Christ rabbis had greater influence on the people than the priests, although it is thought that numbers of priests were also trained as scribes or rabbis.[63]

Scribal training took many years. Once a person was ordained at forty he became an 'ordained scholar' and could officially be called a rabbi.[64] There were some teachings which were considered so holy that a teacher would only speak of them in private with his most intimate students. The more sacred a truth the smaller the number of people to whom he could speak.[65]

At the time of Herod the Great young Jews came from as far away as Babylonia, Media, Asia Minor and Egypt to study at the feet of famous rabbis. Josephus describes young men gathering around the rabbis like an army.[66] Hillel had eighty pupils[67] and Gamaliel II (100-130 CE) is said to have had over a thousand at one time. They learned from the master in daily life as well as through lectures, which were often open to the public. The decisions and teachings of the rabbi were communicated to others by the chain of tradition.[68] In the Pharisaic scribal communities unconditional obedience was required and these groups encouraged the Pharisaic influence over other people in Jewish society. Ordinary folk held the scribes in very high esteem, even greater than that for the high priest. On occasion scribes even dared publicly to call the priests to repent of their ways.

Rabbinic students learnt the oral Law, which could not be committed to writing but was very important in interpreting the Scriptures. Hillel taught seven basic rules for interpretation.⁶⁹ Rabbis thus repeated the oral Law on a number of occasions for the learners to memorize its content. This further cemented the master-teacher relationship. Students were classified at several levels. A beginner studied scribal materials, a distinguished student began to learn independently by questioning the master. A senior student was associated more closely with the rabbi and stood with him at prayers. The highest level was a person who was qualified to become the intellectual equal of his teacher. After ordination he became a rabbi.

A large body of rabbinic literature exists which was compiled c.200-500 CE. Much of this material contains traditions which go back centuries. However none of the evidence can be used conclusively to elucidate the concept of discipleship at the time of Christ, because it is uncertain exactly when such practices came into operation.

Intertestamental and first century CE literature

Neither the Jewish Apocrypha (c.250-50 BCE), nor any known pseudepigraphic writings (c.200 BCE-150 CE) have yet been discovered which include the word *mathētēs* (disciple).⁷⁰ However as has already been noted *bêth midhrash* (school) first appears around 180 BCE, and there is plenty of evidence that learning, instruction, teaching and education were occurring.

The strict ascetic community at Qumran (c.150 BCE-70 CE) although not using the term '*mathētēs*' for any of the teaching relationships which developed,⁷¹ did have a 'disciple' concept in their community. Its founder, the Teacher of Righteousness, attracted people to him who left their employment, homes and families in order that they might study the Torah and obey God better by living a strictly communal life isolated from the rest of their nation. He and his successors guided the community's study in master-disciple type relationships, and led them to discover what they believed was the true meaning of the Torah. La Sor states there is no indication that the Teacher of Righteousness had any kind of close fellowship with a smaller special group within the community, as Jesus did with the Twelve. A "council of twelve" existed but their role was that of administration, and there is no evidence that they received any special instruction.⁷² Culpepper suggests that there was a school which had special responsibility for writing and collecting the Dead Sea Scrolls. In them they recorded the teachings of their founder, his interpretations of Scripture and tradition, and guidance for the community in its daily life.⁷³ However he concludes that at Qumran the basic idea of discipleship was seen as relating the follower to Yahweh.

In the extant writings of the Alexandrian Jew, Philo (c.25 BCE-50 CE), the word *mathētēs* occurs fourteen times. He used the teacher-disciple pattern of Abraham, Isaac, Jacob, Moses and Rebecca, referring to their being disciples of God or as teaching others by their example as recorded in the books of Moses.⁷⁴ Wilkins states that Philo uses the term with various shades of meaning connected with the idea of a person's reaching full maturity, perfection (*teleios anēr*).[75] He believes Philo uses the term to refer to a learner who is instructed by a teacher until he advances to perfection; an advanced learner who teaches others but has not yet fully achieved the goal; one taught by God himself, not needing human instruction, and who is now fully perfect. This latter category is a change from the Classical or Hellenistic Greek use of the word which required a human teacher (living or dead).

In the extensive writings of Josephus (c.37-110 CE), the word '*mathētēs*' is used fifteen times. His use gives some indication of the meaning of the term in the time of the Gospel writers and the early church. These meanings include: a learner and imitator of another person (e.g.Lot of Abraham); a disciple-master relationship with a lifelong commitment (e.g.Joshua and Moses, Elisha and Elijah, Baruch and Jeremiah. Josephus has put his own interpretation on the relationship in these cases); one who follows the teachings of a person or group, often removed in time from that person; or a member of a school or movement.

Jewish practices found in the Gospels

The Gospels reveal that the Pharisees had disciples who were concerned about fasting (Mk. 2:18) and the legality of Jews paying taxes to Caesar (Mt. 22:16). Josephus says that the Maccabean ruler, John Hyrcanus, was a '*mathētēs*' of the Pharisees.[76] Thus Albright and Mann suggest Pharisaic disciples were "those who were being instructed in, and who were assimilating, the teachings and practices of the Pharisees".[77] This would involve the formal academic learning of the Torah and tradition in order to produce legal adherence. They probably followed outside the party, in contrast with the "'scribes' of the Pharisees" (Mk. 2:16) whom Wilkins suggests were the interpreters of the Law within the party.[78]

John the Baptist gathered a group of disciples, who were interested in Jewish matters of purification (possibly baptism), fasting and prayer (Mk. 2:18; Jn. 1:35-37; 3:22-26). They served John by conveying messages from and to him while in prison (Mt. 11:2-7; Lk. 7:18,19) and burying his body (Mk. 6:29). They may have assisted him in baptising, as did Jesus' disciples (Jn. 4:1,2). He taught them to pray (Lk. 5:33; 11:1). Little else is known of their activities. However, Bornkamm and Wilkins agree that "the disciples of John represent the closest analogy to the disciples of Jesus, even though they are not exactly parallel."[79] They were unique in that, though committed to John, there was no great emphasis on intellectual study. They followed John's teaching concerning repentance and the Coming One, which led them to Jesus and to a life of righteousness in preparation for the coming kingdom.

A further New Testament use of the word is in reference to the "disciples of Moses" (Jn. 9:28). Here the Jews were claiming to have a direct line between them and God's revelation to Moses. They were claiming Moses' authority for themselves and their actions. They saw discipleship in this context as referring to commitment to a type of teaching, nothing more.

Thus it is evident that 'disciple' was a general term for a follower. It encompassed a number of different types of followers who committed themselves whole-heartedly to a teacher or a belief system. It usually involved changes in their lifestyle and the adoption of special behaviours.

Conclusions

In the civilisations of the Ancient Near East a variety of learning relationships between the generations existed. Early education was always in the home and family. In most societies it was rare for any but the children of the wealthy to have formal elementary schooling. Young people took their place in the family business or occupation and learnt the necessary knowledge and skills on the job in apprentice-like relationships. However as literacy skills developed and in the context of the development of a leisured class each society's demand for education became more specialized. Select young men from upper class families joined themselves to a master, teacher or philosopher in a school, academy or a loose confederation of learners to acquire the knowledge or conduct needed for their future role in society. A wide variety of learning practices resulted. These were more dependent on the individual teacher than on some preconceived form of education.

Learning relationships involved close, personal family-like commitment of both teacher and taught to one another, for a significant period of time. It usually entailed communal living. Learners observed and imitated their teachers as they pursued their daily occupations and assisted them in performing their duties. The way of life was prescribed by the master who often commanded obedience. Together they believed in and worked towards common goals.

In ancient Israel the worship of Yahweh brought an extra dimension to learning relationships. His people were considered primarily to be his disciples, but this did not preclude other secondary discipling relationships. Some conclude that the use of the words *talmîdh* (taught one) and *limmûdh* (taught) shows that the master-learner relationship between prophet and followers was a familiar one. Others conclude that the presence of these words is evidence for the existence of formal schools in which young men were prepared for their roles as prophets, priests, Levites, scribes or the wise. However the first mention of a school in Israel is not until 180 BCE.

No specific instances of discipling are spelled out in the Old Testament, but learning relationships between older experienced leaders and aspiring young men were more than likely. The servants or 'sons of the prophets' appear to have learnt from the great prophets as they participated in their life and work. Younger men probably gathered around elders in wisdom 'schools' in order to learn the conduct of ordinary life, and how to make decisions of national, social or judicial importance. As priestly leadership was taken over by scribes and rabbis, a community gathered around them to learn the Torah and traditions.

Intertestamental and first century CE literature uses the concept of discipleship on numerous occasions. At Qumran followers of the Teacher of Righteousness lived in a strict, ascetic community to give themselves to the study of the Torah and following Yahweh with undivided allegiance. Philo described those who were progressing to greater maturity as 'disciples'. Josephus used the term to refer to those who were learning from and imitating another person in a lifelong relationship.

Apart from the disciples of Jesus, the Gospels refer to disciples "of the Pharisees" who received Pharisaic formal academic instruction, and "of Moses" who followed the law and claimed they possessed Mosaic authority. The disciples of John the Baptist did not appear to have the same academic emphasis as others, but they served him and possibly shared in his ministry.

Thus in the ancient world, the concept of discipleship covered a very wide range of learning activities and relationships involving a master and learner or learners. It entailed the learners committing themselves to the authority of the master for an extended period of time, and usually occurred in a community of fellow learners. It sometimes implied formal academic learning, but more usually involved the impartation of knowledge, skills and conduct in informal situations as the master went about his daily occupation. The term allowed teachers to give to each discipling relationship the qualities which they considered to be of greatest importance.

Notes to Chapter 2

1 The master teacher was referred to as 'father', tutors as 'older brothers', fellow students as 'brothers'. (Crenshaw, 1985, 608)
2 S.R.Driver as cited in McKane, 1965, 39
3 Crenshaw, 1985, 608
4 Laurie, 1907, 42
5 McKane, 1965, 45
6 Crenshaw, 1985, 607
7 McKane, 1965, 36
8 Castle, 1961, 83
9 The master-disciple concept was not used to refer to intergenerational family learning, nor was it used for children learning from adults. It was applied only to an educational situation, between two or more adults which extended beyond the mere learning of factual information.
10 Plato of Athens, Xenophon of Athens, Aristotle of Stageiros, Aristophanes of Athens, Isocrates, Demosthenes (Wilkins, 1988, 22-32)
11 Rengstorf, 1967, 416-26
12 Rengstorf, 1967, 416,417
13 All references are to males, because apart from the Epicureans, women disciples were extremely rare.
14 Rengstorf cites instances of this usage for those learning rhetoric, Sophist philosophy,

Background

weaving, to play the flute or be a doctor. (Rengstorf, 1967, 416)
15 Rengstorf, 1967, 417,418
16 Wilkins, 1988, 18,19
17 Rengstorf, 1967, 419
18 Xenophon *Memorabilia* 4.2.40 as cited in Robbins, 1984, 86
19 Aristotle as cited in Illich, 1973, 102
20 Ferguson, 1987, 276-7
21 Rengstorf, 1967, 423
22 Rengstorf, 1967, 425
23 It was used for learners of a skill, adherents. Occasionally kings are referred to as disciples or emulators of a god, a technical term for intimate relationship involving imitation, learning and zealous following of the master. (Wilkins, 1988, 33-41)
24 Rengstorf, 1967, 426-431
25 Wilkins, 1988, 49
26 Wilkins, 1988, 46
27 Wilkins, 1988, 47
28 Young, 1955, 91
29 Wilkins, 1988, 55
30 1 Ki. 20:35; 2 Ki. 2:3,5,7,15; 4:1,38; 5:22; 6:1; 9:1
31 Young, 1955, 93
32 Rengstorf, 1967, 428. Elijah's servant checked the weather (1 Ki. 18:43); Elisha served Elijah (1 Ki. 19:19-21; 2 Ki. 3:11); Gehazi served Elisha by delivering messages (2 Ki. 4:12,25,38: 5:20; 6:17; 8:4,5).
33 Rengstorf, 1967, 429
34 Josephus, 1980, 202
35 Hengel, 1981, 17,18
36 Wilson, 1980, 202
37 Goppelt, 1981, 209
38 Wilkins, 1988, 59,60
39 These include officer or overseer (Ex. 5:6), the seventy elders (Nu. 11:16), administrative officers in the army (Dt. 20:5), magistrates (1 Ch. 23:4), the royal private secretary (2 Sa. 8:17), and the military scribe (Je. 37:15). (Hillyer, 1978, 478)
40 There appears to be a long line of scribes within Shaphan's family (2 Ki. 22:3; Je. 36:11,12; 40:9). Baruch and his brother, Seraiah, were possibly also scribes (Je. 32:12; 51:59-64).
41 He finds evidence of deductive questioning typical of a school situation in many Old Testament passages (e.g. Pr. 6:27,28; 23:29,30; Jb. 8:11; Is. 28:23-29; Ezk. 15:1-3; Am. 3:3-8). (Von Rad, 1972, 18)
42 Hengel, 1974, 79
43 Dt. 24:1,3; Jos. 18:9; Jdg. 8:13-17; 2 Sa. 18:17; Jb. 31:35-37; Pr. 3:3; 4:1-9; 7:3; 8:32-36; 17:16; Is. 8:16; 10:19; 29:11,12; Je. 8:8; 32:12; Hab. 2:2.
44 Wilkins, 1988, 96
45 Wilkins, 1988, 71
46 Wilkins, 1988, 71
47 Wilkins, 1988, 85
48 Von Rad, 1972, 9,15; Goldsworthy, 1987, 78
49 Von Rad, 1972, 17
50 Gerstenberger as cited in Wilkins, 1988, 75

51 Terrien and Lindblom as cited in Wilkins, 1988, 75,76
52 Whybray as cited in Wilkins, 1988, 79
53 Wilkins, 1988, 80-88
54 Wilkins, 1988, 88
55 The first inscriptional evidence for a synagogue is third century BCE in Egypt. (Culpepper, 1982, 25) By the second century BCE synagogues were in existence in all the cities throughout the land. It took a further two centuries until the villages had them also. (Laurie, 1907, 87) The elementary school did not become firmly established in synagogues until after 200 CE. (Culpepper, 1982, 25)
56 Castle, 1961, 166
57 Paul, the apostle, studied at the feet of Gamaliel (Acts 22:3).
58 Women were considered to be on a lower level than men in religious matters and were not permitted either to learn or teach. (Rengstorf, 1967, 433)
59 Kaiser, '*Talmîd*', 1980, 480
60 Wilkins, 1988, 118
61 Rengstorf, 1967, 434
62 This explains the response of Jesus' hearers to his different approach in teaching, "He taught them as one having authority, and not as the scribes." (Mk. 1:22)
63 Jeremias, 1969, 234
64 Jeremias, 1969, 235,236
65 The vision of God in Ezekiel was considered so holy that the rabbi would only speak softly to one student with both their heads covered as a sign of reverence. (Jeremias, 1969, 237,238)
66 Wilkins, 1988, 119
67 Some estimates are much higher. The World Book Encyclopedia sets the number at more than a thousand. (Olmstead, 1976, 220)
68 Jeremias, 1969, 242,243
69 Longenecker, 1975, 34,35
70 Wilkins, 1988, 96,97
71 No technical terminology for 'disciple' is used because they considered themselves as a brotherhood.
72 La Sor, 1972, 217
73 Culpepper as cited in Wilkins, 1992, 88
74 Robbins, 1984, 94
75 Wilkins, 1988, 100-104
76 Josephus, 1980, 281
77 Albright and Mann, 1971, lxxvi
78 Wilkins, 1988, 107
79 Wilkins, 1988, 105 (See also Bornkamm, 1960, 145)

PART 2

CHAPTER 3

Discipling in Mark's Gospel

Having briefly surveyed the concept of 'discipling' as it was practised throughout the world of the Ancient Near East before the time of Christ, we now turn to an examination of the discipling methods used by Jesus as described by the four Gospel writers. Each writer had a particular body of intended hearers or readers to whom they brought their own perspective on the great events. By examining each one separately, an attempt will be made to discover the distinctive characteristics of the portrayal of the discipling ministry of Jesus in each Gospel. A composite picture will thus be constructed giving a greater understanding of Jesus' discipling aims and methods.

Mark's Gospel will be explored first because of the widely held belief that this Gospel was the first to be written. We will then turn to Matthew and Luke's accounts particularly noting Luke's portrayal of the place of women among the disciple band. The Gospel survey will be concluded by an examination of John's unique contribution to the subject.

In this chapter Mark's Gospel will be examined in the light of the working definition proposed in Chapter One[1] in order to determine the nature of the discipling model used by Jesus as portrayed by Mark. The text will be studied to determine which persons may be designated as making a voluntary commitment to learning from Jesus, the nature of their relationship with him and their involvement in his discipling community. Having determined the particular scenarios which Jesus employed in his discipling model, we will then explore the different teaching methods he used. Evidence will be gathered of his formal teaching of both the disciples and the crowds. His modelling of the life of faith will be examined, and the service rendered to others by members of the discipling community will be studied. The processes of action and reflection, which Jesus encouraged among his followers, will be noted and his use of the lives of others as demonstrations of his teaching will be observed. The occasions when he allowed his disciples the freedom to fail and then receive further teaching will also be studied.

Finally we will raise the question of how adequate our working definition has been in enabling us to portray Mark's contribution to the discipling model employed by Jesus.

The discipling relationship

A voluntary commitment to learn from another

As was noted in the previous chapter the Jews regarded the ideal of discipleship as the relationship of the nation with Yahweh, their master and teacher. Robbins sees Jesus as recorded in Mark's Gospel adopting a role similar to that of God, in the Old Testament. He issued commands, directions and explanations with God's sanction (1:11; 9:7), but without needing any prior divine instruction. His own authority and "knowledge of the gospel of God allows him to take over Yahweh's role of calling, teaching and commissioning."[2] Robbins continues that the disciples function in a way similar to the prophets of the Old Testament. They were called and commissioned by Yahweh to say and do certain things. However, in the comparison Robbins makes no mention of the primary role of disciples which is to learn from their master. In fact they do not receive a compelling revelation to speak the message from the Lord. Rather they voluntarily choose to commit themselves unreservedly to being learners and followers of Jesus.

The disciples were an important group in Mark's Gospel. The word, *mathētēs* (disciple), is used 46 times.[3] It first appears in 2:15 when Jesus and his disciples were at dinner in Levi's house. Mark adds the explanation that "there were many who followed him". The noun *mathētēs* and verb *akoloutheō* (to follow) and their derivatives are used throughout this Gospel to convey discipleship.[4] Mark first records the calling of four fishermen followers (1:16-20) and later Levi, the tax collector was added to the band (2:13,14).[5] Mark cites these as examples of how the followers were enlisted. He was adopting a practice common in ancient literature of rehearsing the initial moment of the call to discipleship to show the characteristics of the relationship involved.[6]

Jesus took the initiative in calling his disciples. This was different from the common practice of the day. Learners usually came to teachers requesting the privilege of being their disciples. Mark 1:14,15 may be a summary statement of what was to follow,[7] or it may indicate that there was a period of time in which Jesus moved around the province of Galilee proclaiming the coming of the kingdom of God before he called his disciples (1:16-20). They may well have responded to him as someone whom they already knew and whose message was familiar.[8]

The fishermen were called in pairs. These partnerships were already firmly established by both family and business ties. Encased in the call was the promise that Jesus would make them "fish for people" (1:17). He was outlining his teaching plans for them, in language readily understandable to fishermen. They were not called simply for their own learning. Right from the beginning there was an expectation that they would be involved in bringing others to Jesus. His call to follow took them away from their home and families, but it is interesting to note that, initially, they invited Jesus into their homes to meet their extended family and friends and to assist in meeting their needs (1:29-34). As the discipling community grew, its members were also included in the hospitality extended to Jesus by the newcomers (2:15-17).

Jesus called followers to him from among the crowds on a number of occasions, summoning them to a life of faith and self-denial, but few were prepared for the level of commitment required. The rejection of the rich young man demonstrated that commitment and a willing response to his call was expected of all who became his disciples no matter what their social standing (8:1,34-38; 9:35; 10:21-22,42; 12:43). Mark places three of the occasions when Jesus called his disciples immediately after his three passion predictions.[9] This seems more than coincidental. It appears that Mark, at least, believed that the disciples of Jesus should expect their lives to follow a path of suffering similar to that of their master.

Twelftree points out that in Jesus' calls there is often "an initial aorist followed in most cases by a present setting out what lies ahead."[10] Thus, in Mark 8:34 the aorist tense which indicates a once-only action in the past is used for 'come' (*elthein*), 'deny' (*aparnēsasthō*) and 'take up' (*aratō*), but the tense changes to the present imperative for 'follow' (*akoloutheitō*). He concludes that Mark is indicating that the initial group of verbs were a series of once-only acts which then led to the on-going process of following. Thus the text indicates that the disciples made a conscious decision to follow Jesus.

From the wider group of "many" followers (2:15) Jesus appointed twelve men whose names are listed (3:13-19), however they were not the only ones who received the teaching designated for the inner circle. "Those who were around him along with the twelve asked him about the parables" (4:10). Munro notes that Mark uses *tois idiois mathētais* (to his own disciples) forty three times to indicate this group in contrast with only ten uses of the Twelve.[11] This wider group probably also included the women from Galilee whose discipleship was indicated only at the end of the Gospel (15:40,41,47). Mark describes their following using the imperfect tense. *Akolouthoun* (a continuing action) which implies they were a continuing part of the discipling community. Munro suggests that the woman who anointed Jesus at Bethany was a disciple who was travelling with him or a member of the family showing him hospitality (14:3-9).[12]

Mark describes Jesus as preparing the "way" (*hodos*) and the disciples as being "on the way" (1:2; 8:27; 9:33,34; 10:32).[13] Many have inferred from Bartimaeus' *akolouthei* (following) Jesus "in the way" that he too became a disciple (10:52). Mark does not record any other recipients of healing who followed Jesus, but the Gadarene demoniac begged to "be with him" (5:18,19) although his request was refused. Mark may be indicating his discipleship apart from that of the accepted group, because he obeyed the commission of Jesus by returning to his home and friends and proclaiming God's mercy. Twelftree comments that his desire to be with Jesus was the appropriate response, but that others who were healed were not recorded as doing so.[14]

Thus Mark designates as disciples or followers of Jesus a disparate group of individuals, each of whom had encountered Jesus personally, responded to his call and voluntarily committed themselves to learning from him. They included the Twelve, a number of women from Galilee and a wider group of others, possibly including Bartimaeus, many of whom were unnamed.

A close personal relationship

The disciples were called by Jesus to follow him. This involved accompanying him on his travels and being in his presence. Their lifestyle was closer to that of the peripatetic philosophers and teachers of the Greco-Roman world than that of the Jewish rabbinic schools. Learning occurred as they responded to Jesus' needs, modelled themselves on his way of life, assisted in his public teaching and ministry to the crowds and received private tuition as a group.

The Twelve were specially called so that they "might be with him". Best's point that "being with Jesus" was unimportant to Mark because it is referred to only one time,[15] seems to ignore the general thrust of the Gospel. The Twelve were with Jesus continually, except for the time of their mission to the villages (6:6-13), until his arrest in the Garden of Gethsemane when they deserted him (14:50). He directed and shaped the course of their lives over that time in a close personal relationship. This was not distance education or Theological Education by Extension.[16] The presence of Jesus was vital to the concept of discipleship presented in Mark. Mark includes no references to any activity of Jesus involving his absence from his followers, except for times of prayer (1:35; 6:46; 14:32,35,39).

Trocme claims that their first responsibility was to be Jesus' attendants and only secondarily were they to be recipients of his teaching.[17] However the predominant designation for the group was *mathētēs* (disciples), not *diakonoi* (servants) or *douloi* (slaves). This infers that their relationship to Jesus was one in which teaching and learning were predominant.

As teacher and protector, Jesus committed himself to his followers. He promised to teach them to fish for people. He defended his disciples against the criticism of the religious leaders on three occasions when their behaviour was questioned.[18] He cared for their physical well-being and safety (4:38-40; 6:51) and ensured that they had sufficient rest and recreation (6:30). But there were also times when he rebuked them because of their failure or lack of faith and understanding,[19] and when he was indignant with them concerning their treatment of children (10:14).

Those who followed Jesus committed themselves to him and to his teachings. They came under his authority and usually carried out his commands to the best of their understanding (6:12,39,45; 8:6; 9:10; 11:4; 14:16). Rigma comments, "Discipleship is a quality of life, and important to that lifestyle is the quality of faithfulness".[20] Jesus expected his followers to show faithfulness in relationships even if adverse circumstances arose. This he demonstrated in his teaching on marriage and divorce (10:1-12). Only those disciples who at the end of their lives were still faithful to him would know salvation (13:13).

Mark portrays all the disciples as failing to remain consistently faithful in their relationship with Jesus. Their desertion comes at the climax of his Gospel. They were grief-stricken when Jesus told them that one of their number would betray him (3:19; 14:18-21,41-45). Peter protested he would never deny Jesus, but later three times he denied knowing him (14:26-31,54,66-72). They all protested loudly that they would be faithful to death, when Jesus warned them that they would be scattered as sheep, but in the end they fled (14:27-31,50). Yet there is no hint that desertion stopped their discipleship or that the relationship was destroyed. Malbon writes "fleeing indicates that the disciples are fallible, not that they are non-followers".[21] Maybe by warning them before their failure took place, Jesus was enabling them to see God's work in spite of their weakness. Perhaps Peter's tears signified his repentance (14:72). At the close of his Gospel Mark records the message of reconciliation from Jesus: "Go tell his disciples and Peter that he is going ahead of you to Galilee." (16:7)

The betrayal of Jesus by Judas Iscariot is constantly in the mind of Mark (3:16; 14:10,11,18-21,43), but as Best comments, "...unlike Matthew and Luke he does not recount Judas' death and so leaves open the possibility of his repentance". He continues that "...curiously Judas is not excluded from the message of 16:7".[22] We conclude that Judas was the one who put himself outside the possibility of forgiveness and discipleship. If Judas had been willing, he could have been reconciled after failure.

There was a group of women followers who did not desert, but watched the crucifixion "from a distance" (15:40-41). However Malbon comments that they also failed because they were not close.[23]

In this Gospel both men and women disciples failed to follow consistently. Some deserted Jesus in his darkest hour. Some were too afraid to pass on his message. But failure did not exclude them from being his disciples. The relationship was not severed.

A new discipling community

The call of Jesus required his disciples to leave their homes, families and employment in order to be part of the discipling community who travelled with him. By leaving their normal routines they had opportunities for fresh experiences which they had never before encountered. This new community replaced in some way the natural family with its brothers, sisters, mother, father and children and incorporated a hundredfold more of brothers, sisters, mothers and children (3:31-35; 10:29,30).[24]

Following Jesus involved self denial, not for the sake of it, but that there be no hindrances to learning and service within the new community. The fishermen left their nets. Levi left his tax booth. The Twelve left everything, in comparison with the rich young man who could not pay the price and went away grieving (10:22,28). Jesus taught that the value of the kingdom far outweighed anything they could give up, even if it was life itself (8:34-9:1; 10:28-31, 42-45).[25]

Twenty three times Mark draws a contrast between 'insiders' (*hoi peri auton*) and 'outsiders' (*ekeinois tois exō*), from whom the truth may be hidden (4:10,11). Outsiders included those who did not believe in him or refused to follow him or tried to take him away from his ministry. Among these were his family (3:21 literally – those with him, *hoi par' autou*) and residents of his home town (6:4). Jesus claimed as his true family those who do God's will (3:35), or those in the parable of the sower who "hear the word, accept it and bear fruit" (4:20). The disciples were not however to regard themselves as an exclusive group. Believing in Jesus and doing God's will, or lack of belief caused the division between outsiders and insiders, not actually being present with the group all the time. Jesus showed this truth by his acceptance of the ministry of the unknown exorcist (9:38-41). He enabled his followers to see that there were others who also believed in his name and did God's will who were not among their group, but who were on the same side in the conflict against evil. Some of the women who followed Jesus may not have been continually present but as the crucifixion and resurrection narratives demonstrate, they were an integral part of the wider discipling community.

Communal living produced its own challenges to learning. Their arguments, grasping for positions of greatness and angry reactions to one another and to people coming to Jesus, provided opportunities for him to bring further teaching (9:33-37; 10:13-15,35-45). Jesus' widespread popularity as teacher, preacher and healer led to their observation of, or participation in a wide variety of unusual situations, which led to further lessons. And their subsequent conversations and discussions facilitated reflection, questions and learning from one another and Jesus himself.

Jesus' healing of the paralysed man demonstrated that forgiveness was his prerogative (2:9-11). The word *aphiēmi* (send off, let go, release) used in 1:18,20 to refer to a disciple's leaving to follow, also appears in 2:5,7,9,10 for forgiveness involving the paralysed man. This interesting variation has led Twelftree to suggest it may indicate "…that Jesus releases people from things they find difficult to leave behind so that they can follow".[26] It seems that there is a very close connection in Mark with the concepts of 'following' and 'forgiveness'. "Repentance for the forgiveness of sins," was the message proclaimed by John the Baptist, Jesus and his disciples (1:4,15; 6:12). Forgiveness is available for the *polloi* (many), including the disciples, through the pouring out of Jesus' life as a ransom (10:45; 14:24). What better way to display forgiveness to others than by living in a close, discipling community of forgiven people!

The group into which Jesus called his disciples was to be centred on him with its members committed to learning from him and one another as they developed close personal relationships with him and fellow members. He committed himself to them to teach them in community and as part of the wider crowd to which he ministered. He expected them to put the demands of family, possessions and employment in second place to their faithful following of him.

The discipling model

Formal teaching

Jesus believed that his words of teaching were of vital importance and repeatedly stressed to his hearers the need to listen (4:3,9,23; 7:14; 8:18). In this Gospel approximately one sixth of all the verses contain his general teachings to the crowds. The disciples were present for this, but they also received more specialized explanations and revelations when they were alone with him (4:10,34; 7:17-23; 10:10). Words to his disciples constitute another one sixth of this Gospel, which means that fully a third of Mark contains the verbal teachings which the disciples heard.[27]

However this Gospel does not record long teaching passages like the other Gospels,[28] apart from the parables in chapters 4 and 12 and the 'Little Apocalypse' of chapter 13.[29] Most of Jesus' verbal teaching came as a result of the criticisms or questions of others (2;6-10,18-22,24-28; 3:22-29; 7:6-23; 9:11-13,38-50; 10:2-12,17-31; 11:27-33; 12:13-40) or unusual happenings among the crowds or the disciple band (3:32-35; 8:15-21; 9:14-29; 10:14,15; 11:22-26; 12:43,44; 14:6-9). He did spend some time preparing and teaching his disciples concerning the way of discipleship (6:10,11; 8:34-9:1,33-37; 10:35-45), and on three occasions he attempted to teach concerning his coming suffering, but the disciples' understanding was limited (8:31; 9:30-32; 10:32-34).

Thus, in Mark, the vast majority of Jesus' recorded words of teaching occurred within informal situations, in everyday conversations or in response to the questions of those whose curiosity was aroused by the actions of himself or his followers. His skill as a teacher lay in being ready with the right comments when situations provoking interest arose. The openness of the public, itinerant lifestyle of Jesus and his disciples, actually promoted greater opportunities for his response.

Modelling

Jesus modelled the life of faith for his disciples. In every aspect of their communal life he demonstrated the principles that he wished to impart. His life showed that greatness in God's kingdom is radically different from the world's concept of greatness. Mark depicts the disciples as desiring to '"save their lives' 8:35, 'acquire the world' 8:36, 'be great' 9:35 and 'exert authority over' or 'lord it over' others 10:43-44".[30] Jesus taught that true greatness lies in self-denial (not asceticism) and humble acceptance of the lowliest position (9:33-37).

Malbon believes that the women disciples found this role easier to adopt than the men because of their inferior status in that society.[31]

He modelled an attitude of servanthood by caring for the physical, emotional, social and spiritual needs of the crowds, his disciples and the most insignificant members of their society. His treatment of children was in marked contrast to the prevailing practice of the day where they were considered to be unworthy of public attention. He picked them up in his arms, blessed them and defended them, warning his hearers of the severe consequences for any who might cause them to sin (9:36,37,42; 10:13-16).

Jesus openly acknowledged his deeply troubled feelings in Gethsemane and modelled faithfulness through costly obedience (14:33-41). This was supremely demonstrated in his sacrificial death on the cross when he fulfilled the Isaianic prophecies of the suffering servant of the Lord.[32] It is obvious from the proportion of material which Mark devotes to the suffering and death of Jesus that he believes Jesus cannot be understood apart from the cross, and he uses the suffering servant image as the primary means of depicting the mission of Jesus.[33] By implication, it is also the vocation of the disciple.

Establishing a serving community

In the ancient world disciples were expected to serve their master. As they shared in the life and work of the master they performed servant tasks within his discipling community. Thus they imbibed the beliefs, attitudes and values of the community and its master. The discipling community which Jesus established was also a serving community, but Jesus radically departed from tradition by also serving his disciples. Indeed the purpose of his coming was "…not to be served but to serve, and to give his life a ransom for many" (10:45). In his three passion predictions he endeavoured to prepare them to see his death in terms of God's suffering servant giving his life (8:31,32; 9:31,32; 10:33,34). He taught that true greatness was found in servanthood (9:35; 10:43).

Mark's Gospel records Jesus assigning tasks and communal responsibilities for his disciples to perform. Their assistance was often helpful although sometimes they were over-enthusiastic and the service they offered was inappropriate. This was so when Peter went to look for Jesus (1:36) and when he offered to build booths on the mount of Transfiguration (9:5), or when the disciples forbade the unknown exorcist to work in Jesus' name (9:38), or rebuked those who brought the children to Jesus (10:13). Malbon comments "their exuberance must often be redirected by Jesus… The disciples intended to assist Jesus' ministry; they were surprised to learn their actions displeased Jesus".[34]

They also served by managing and feeding the crowds, providing transport by boat and donkey and by preparing the Passover meal (3:9; 4:1; 6:41; 8:7; 11:7; 14:12-16). Their service was never performed alone. They shared it with one another and, as Malbon noted, acted on behalf of others.[35] Schweizer summarizes, "…according to Mark, there are different tasks for different disciples:

not all of them are obliged or allowed to be with him in a bodily way. Some, inside and outside of the group of the Twelve, are sent to preach, some to heal, some to other tasks".[36]

Mark's Gospel, however, only uses *diakoneō* (to serve) for the actions of Jesus or the women and angels. This may indicate some failure on the part of his male disciples. Jesus reminded them that service was to be to all. Even the least significant of children, or weak unimportant brothers and sisters, were to be received, welcomed and cared for by the community, as if they were Jesus himself (9:37).

In commenting on the servanthood of women in this Gospel, Selvidge writes, "Most of the women are nameless, but their characterisations by Mark serve as very important examples of serving followers".[37] Peter's mother-in-law was the first to be mentioned as serving Jesus and his four disciples. This was her natural response to Jesus' healing (1:29-31). The women from Galilee who were present at the crucifixion had served him (*diēkonoun autō*). By providing "for him" and not "for them" (the male disciples) Mark is conveying their discipleship (15:41). They anticipated that their final service would be anointing Jesus' body for burial (16:1). Gill comments, "at the climax of his Gospel (Mark's) four leading women, rather than four leading disciples, are said to have ministered to Jesus."[38]

Action and reflection

Discipleship as portrayed by Mark always involves activity. Jesus' disciples were not like the disciples of the rabbis whose learning centred on formal studies of the Torah. They were not called to be passive learners but were given tasks to perform which required the development of new skills and understandings. All disciples had service responsibilities to fulfil although they were not all the same. Practical learning was usually undertaken in collaboration with at least one other disciple and was under the supervision of Jesus.

Mark is the only evangelist who outlines the threefold purpose in the selection of the Twelve. They were "…to be with him, and to be sent out to proclaim the message, and to have authority to cast out demons" (3:14,15). The most notable instance of active ministry which the Twelve were required to perform in this Gospel was their mission to the villages of Galilee (6:7-13,30). Mark reports that they went out in twos preaching the message of repentance.

Between the call of the Twelve and their being sent out, Jesus structured four major lessons for them to grasp. First, he explained the parable of the sower, thus helping them to understand the responses to be expected when his word was preached (4:1-34). Second, he demonstrated his power to protect them, by stilling the storm (4:35-41). Third, he used three major miracles to show his power to heal and exorcize evil spirits (5:1-43). Fourth, he visited his home town where he was received with unbelief (6:1-5). Each of these lessons was imperative for the Twelve to learn if they were to fulfil his mission and realistically be prepared to face the variety of responses to their message. Finally, he gave them his authority over the unclean spirits and told them what to take, and how to deal with rejection (6:7-11). Mark subsequently records their return and reports their successful fulfilment of his commission (6:13). The message of repentance was proclaimed, the sick were healed and they cast out many demons.

On a later occasion Jesus inferred that they would also be among those proclaiming the good news to all the nations and, even though it would not be easy, the Holy Spirit would be with them (13:10,11). Thus, he was envisaging that the ministry begun by his disciples when they were sent out would be of a continuing nature.

In these early chapters of Mark Jesus used a 'shared praxis' approach. He successfully established a pattern of learning by outlining for the Twelve what they would be doing in the future and preparing them by giving them opportunities for observation, action and reflection. After they returned they reported to Jesus "all that they had done and taught" (6:30), which no doubt provided further opportunity for reflection.

The journey of Jesus and the disciple band out of Israel's territory into Iturea and the villages of Caesarea Philippi may have been undertaken to provide a break midway through the pressurized public ministry of Jesus (8:27-33).[39] The time taken in travel and the peace of the beautiful mountainous area[40] provided an ideal opportunity for a major reflective period on all that had occurred previously. By questioning the disciples concerning his identity, Jesus was leading them to form their own conclusions concerning all that they had seen, heard and experienced with him. After Peter's confession of him as the Messiah, Jesus began to prepare them for his suffering and death. Thus the journey provided opportunity for consolidation of what had been previously learned, and enabled further teaching to take place before the final journey to Jerusalem.

Jesus appeared to time the activities involving his disciples in such a way that between periods of intensive ministry he structured opportunities for quiet reflection and discussion with himself and others of the company. This sharing of praxis enabled consolidation of learning before they embarked on new situations with further demands and further opportunities to make new discoveries.

Demonstration

Through his healing, teaching and other miraculous activities, Jesus demonstrated the power of God as the kingdom began to break through to them. Jesus expected his followers to be characterized by active faith in every aspect of their lives, but they seemed slow to learn (5:40; 8:17-21; 9:19). On many occasions it was the crowd, rather than the disciples, who expressed amazement at what Jesus said and did (1:22,27; 5:20; 6:2; 7:37; 9:15; 11:18).

He drew attention to the faith of others in order to demonstrate the response he required. He made a special point of speaking with the haemorrhaging woman whose healing took place because she took the initiative of putting her faith into action (5:25-34). Through his granting of sight to the blind Jesus was seeking to demonstrate his ability to bring spiritual sight (8:22-26; 10:46-52). Some see in the two-part healing at Bethsaida the two-part process of spiritual sight coming to the disciples and Peter.[41] During Jesus' ministry they struggled between commitment and incomprehension (8:32,33; 9:32; 10:35-41), and it was only after the resurrection that their understanding clarified. O'Grady writes, "...when someone discovers the significance of the passion of the Lord, that person 'sees'; his blindness is removed".[42]

They had to learn that their lives would involve suffering or death as Jesus had demonstrated. "If anyone would come after me, he must deny himself and take up his cross and follow me" (8:34). This new set of values was totally different from those of their society.

The service offered by both Jesus and the women was often self-sacrificial, but not necessarily menial. Twice, Mark contrasts female self sacrifice with male greed. The generosity of the poor widow at the temple treasury who gave all her living, *bios* (life), is contrasted with the scribes who "devour widows' houses" (12:40-44). The woman who spent a fortune anointing Jesus' body for burial is contrasted with Judas who betrayed him for the price of a cheap slave (14:1-11). Jesus used these women as examples of service for all his disciples.

Many of Jesus' actions were demonstrations of his teachings. By drawing attention to qualities within the lives of people they encountered, Jesus was providing his followers with concrete illustrations of the life of faith and self-sacrifice to which he was calling them.

Allowing freedom to fail and receive further teaching

Mark often depicts the disciples as ignorant and slow to understand the teaching of Jesus, but the very process of the recognition of their weaknesses facilitated their learning, and their failures were never regarded as irreparable.[43] Sometimes Jesus allowed his disciples to begin to implement their learning even though he knew they would not immediately succeed. Their failure to deliver the epileptic boy from demon possession (9:19) resulted in further learning. Cranfield writes, "Apparently they had taken it for granted, on the strength of past success (6:13,30), that they would be successful again, and it seems that it was in this 'taking for granted' that their lack of faith lay."[44]

The disciples were slow to discard their old values. They valued popularity (1:36,37), power and position (10:35-41), competitiveness (9:33,34) and belief in the value of wealth (10:24-26) and were slow to change. But Jesus enabled them to identify their attitudes and provided corrective teaching.

On a number of occasions Jesus rebuked or questioned his disciples concerning their lack of faith and understanding in order to point out their weaknesses, bring new teaching into the situation and provide direction for the future (8:32,33; 10:14,15). Sometimes he could not contain his amazement.

"Do you still not perceive or understand? Are your hearts hardened? Do you have eyes and fail to see? Do you have ears, and fail to hear? …Do you not yet understand?" (8:17-21)

He sought to develop their faith and trust in him after their fear in the storm (4:40) and on the lake (6:50) displayed their weaknesses. Cole points out that it was the disciples' idea that they were perishing, not the Lord's.[45] As Jesus' death approached, their fears for their own safety increased (9:32; 14:50,66-72; 15:40). Selvidge recognizes that fear can be a part of discipleship (10:32). It does not stop their following, but shows that their faith needs to increase.[46]

When they forgot to bring any bread it has been suggested that Jesus reproved them for their lack of faith in his provision after the miraculous feedings of the Jewish multitudes (8:14-21).[47] Gibson, however, suggests that the rebuke was because the disciples had wilfully neglected (*epilanthanomai*) to bring the bread. He noted that Jesus had just indicated his intention to travel to Gentile territory and concludes that the disciples did not want the Gentile multitudes to be fed by him, nor did they wish that he would offer salvation to non-Jews.[48] They failed to understand he had come for all, not just the Jews.

When Peter tried to divert Jesus from the cross and its suffering, Jesus sternly rebuked him as speaking words from Satan himself (8:33). Cranfield seeks to explain Peter's reaction. The "…idea of a Messiah suffering at the hands of Israel's enemies may not have been strange, but at Israel's leaders' hands would be shocking".[49] The disciples repeatedly failed to understand his passion predictions. And in the Garden of Gethsemane, though requested to watch and pray, Peter, James and John slept during Jesus' time of turmoil seemingly unconcerned by his grief or his rebuke for their lack of prayer (14:32-42). Finally all his disciples deserted him and fled (14:50)

Mark also depicts the failure of the women who had been given the commission to pass the resurrection message on to his disciples and Peter (16:7,8). The majority of scholars believe that Mark fully intended his ending to be 16:8, "They said nothing to anyone, because they were afraid".[50] Malbon observes however, that they must have told someone or the narrator would not know.[51] She believes that they acted in fear, but their failure did not exclude them from being disciples.

Malbon suggests that chapter 16 be interpreted in the light of Jesus' words describing future persecution of the disciples (13:9-11), and infers that by speaking to them concerning a time beyond his death and resurrection, the text implies that they would be reinstated as disciples in spite of their failure. The resurrection message to the disciples supports her view by nominating them as disciples even after they deserted him in Gethsemane. "Go tell his disciples and Peter that he is going ahead of you to Galilee; there you will see him, just as he told you" (16:7).

Mark does not leave us with a sense of the disciples' failure. Jesus' rebukes were used as a means by which new and further teaching was introduced. Forgiveness and restoration were part of Jesus' message for them concerning his kingdom. The disciples were never considered hopeless. "The failure of the disciples shows God's strength."[52]

Conclusions and re-examination of working definition

Jesus called the crowd and the disciples to himself and taught them using a variety of methods. The group who committed themselves to learning from him in exclusive disciple-master relationships was composed of twelve men whom he specifically called to be with him throughout his public ministry and a wider group of women and men who followed and came under his authority. All made a voluntary commitment to him and his way of life, leaving everything else which prevented their complete devotion. They expected to learn from him and to be involved in his mission to bring others to him.

They entered into a close personal relationship with Jesus who also committed himself to them. They served him and other members of the discipling community who gathered around him as they participated in his life and work and learned from his teaching. Their commitment to him was to be a lifelong experience, however there were times when fear, misunderstanding and lack of faith prevented their wholehearted following. Their failures were not regarded as precluding them from discipleship, but as opportunities for further growth and learning.

Jesus established a discipling community whose members related to one another closely as brothers, sisters, mothers and children. All who followed him were considered 'insiders', part of the disciple band, even though it seems as if it was only the Twelve whose presence was continuous over the whole period of public ministry. Some growth experiences arose from the community itself, others were nurtured within it.

The discipling model depended to some degree on formal verbal teaching and oral communication and this element was frequently present in Jesus' teaching, but he supplemented it to a large degree by many informal teaching methodologies.

Jesus provided an example for his disciples to imitate. He was the faithful servant of Yahweh and his leadership modelled the kingdom values which he taught, including those of humility, servanthood and self denial. Their close personal relationships with him enabled them to observe his private and public life and to enjoy the benefits of his honesty and openness to others.

By establishing a serving community, Jesus set up opportunities for his followers to work together in partnership with one another away from the responsibility and familiarity of home, family and employment, so that their learning was not distracted by other matters. He gave them varying ministry tasks to perform with one another and with him.

In the midst of his busy, public ministry Jesus provided opportunities for the disciples to withdraw from the crowds in order to have time to reflect and learn from their experiences before moving on to further ministry. Thus their learning came from the cycle of action and reflection established. He gradually increased the responsibilities he entrusted to them, and built on previous learning before proceeding to more difficult concepts and expectations. He gave them his authority and supported, encouraged or rebuked them as was appropriate.

Jesus used his own actions and the lives of others to illustrate his teaching and demonstrate its practical outcomes. And he allowed his disciples the freedom to implement his teaching and fail. Thus they were enabled to learn from their own imperfect attempts, identify their weaknesses and receive his further teaching.

In the light of Mark's portrayal of discipling we have found little evidence for teaching relationships between two individuals alone. Mark records no conversations between Jesus and one other disciple. All take place within the community or in a small group.

There was an expectation that the discipling relationship with Jesus would be a lifelong commitment to himself and to the discipling community. The concept of discipleship allowed for periods of failure in persons' lives, but those who did not persevere to the end would not be regarded as part of the community.

The discipling methods used by Jesus certainly included the methods listed in our definition but it has been established that further methods were also employed. These included learning through shared action and reflection and being given freedom to act and fail. No failure of a disciple was to be regarded as beyond forgiveness or as unable to be used as an opportunity for further learning.

Thus the working definition requires refinement, but it would be premature to attempt this until we have applied the same kind of analysis to the testimonies of the other Gospels. We move on, therefore, to the Gospel of Matthew.

Notes to Chapter 3

1 Discipling is a voluntary, personal relationship between two individuals in community or alone, in which the disciple commits him or herself to learn from the other, by imitation, oral communication and sharing in the life and work of the discipler.
2 Robbins, 1984, 119
3 Aland, 1978, 172
4 A discussion of the use of these two terms will be included in Chapter 4 on Matthew's Gospel.
5 The call of Levi presents some problems. On the basis of comparison with Matthew 9:9,10, Levi is frequently taken to be another name for Matthew and thus he is seen to be part of the Twelve. Others, including Eduard Schweizer, believe that he is outside the Twelve and his call is included to show "that it is not only the twelve that are called to follow Jesus in a literal sense". (Schweizer, 1978, 391)
6 Robbins, 1984, 93
7 Guelich, 1989, 41
8 His call may not have been the 'bolt from the blue' that Schweizer has suggested. He maintains that, "They are in no way prepared for this call. They are not in a holy state;

they are doing their everyday work of fishing or mending the nets or calculating taxes… His word hits them unprepared, but it hits them like the call of the creator who 'calls and there it is' (Ps. 33:9). It creates their obedience." (Schweizer, 1978, 390) It is more plausible to suppose that they had some understanding of Jesus and his message prior to his call.
9   Mk. 8:31; 9:30,31; 10:32-34
10 Twelftree, 1990, 6
11 Munro, 1982, 229
12 Munro, 1982, 240
13 The 'Way' was the name adopted by the infant church in early descriptions of itself. (Acts 9:2; 19:9,23; 22:4; 24:14,22)
14 Twelftree, 1990, 7
15 Best, 1977, 381
16 Theological Education by Extension (T.E.E) originated in the 1960s and was designed to provide training for pastors and church workers mainly in 'Third World' countries without a large financial outlay and without taking them away from their homes or communities. Studies are provided by correspondence for individuals working alone or in small groups. Personal contact with teachers is limited to brief visits or short residential courses. (Ferris, 1990, 13-15)
17 Trocme, 1963, 182
18 When they were criticized for not fasting and for picking corn on the Sabbath (2:18-28), and eating with ceremonially unclean hands (7:1-8).
19 These will be discussed at length when we consider the teaching purposes of his rebukes.
20 Rigma, 1989, 6
21 Malbon, 1983, 49
22 Best, 1977, 387
23 Malbon, 1983, 43. Munro questions the normal translation of this passage and offers the possibility of *apo makrothen* (from a distance) as referring to the women's place of origin, because the phrase is placed immediately after *gunaikes* (women). The translation would then read: "But there were even women from afar watching". (Munro as cited in Selvidge, 1983, 399)
24 The omission of 'father' from this list leads to the suggestion that there would only be one Father in the new community, God himself. (Munro, 1992, 228)
25 Schweizer comments that Jesus "becomes so important that our ego comes to an end, as far as it is not directed towards him, and receives from him a value and an importance that surpasses all previous value and importance." (Schweizer, 1978, 392)
26 Twelftree, 1990, 6
27 Mark's Gospel contains 666 verses (NRSV) of which 90 verses contain the direct words of Jesus as he taught the crowds or spoke to the Pharisees in the presence of his disciples. Another 16 verses are unclear as to who is being addressed. Jesus' specific teaching of his disciples, by themselves, accounts for 114 verses.
28 e.g. Matthew's sermon on the mount (Mt. 5-7), Luke's sermon on the plain (Lk. 6:17-49) or John's teaching in the upper room (Jn. 13-17).
29 Cole, 1961, 197
30 Rhoads, 1993, 358
31 Malbon, 1983, 43
32 This mysterious figure features in Deutero-Isaiah (Is. 42:1-4; 49:1-6; 50:4-9; 52:13-53:12) and was seen by Israel as depicting her own sufferings.

33 Selvidge, 1983, 397
34 Malbon, 1986, 119
35 Malbon, 1986, 109
36 Schweizer, 1978, 391
37 Selvidge, 1983, 398
38 Gill, 1987, 15
39 The place of this journey and the chronological order of Mark's pericopes within the structure of the book are outside the scope of this study.
40 Lane, 1974, 289
41 Best, 1978, 549
42 O'Grady, 1980, 83
43 Kebler, Wrede and others consider that Mark is seeking to attack the disciples for their blindness, misunderstanding of discipleship and eventual abandonment of Jesus. (Kebler as cited in Malbon, 1993, 91-92. Wrede as cited in Twelftree, 1990, 5) However many scholars including Malbon, Tannehill, Reploh and Best propose that the disciples are being used as models, admittedly weak ones, for the readers and that Mark is addressing the disciples' failure in such a way that it would encourage the community to which he was writing when they failed to understand or to follow faithfully. (Best, 1977, 377-401; Twelftree, 1990, 5; Malbon, 1993, 91-92)
44 Cranfield, 1959, 301
45 Cole, 1961, 96
46 Selvidge, 1983, 400
47 Kingsbury holds the view that Jesus was rebuking the disciples for still thinking in human, not divine, terms. He believed that unless overcome, their incomprehension would destroy their commitment to him. (Kingsbury, 1989)
48 Gibson, 1986, 36
49 Cranfield, 1959, 280
50 A discussion of the textual problems associated with the ending of Mark's Gospel is beyond the scope of this thesis. For a detailed discussion of textual evidence for this ending see Guthrie, 1975, 76-79.
51 Malbon, 1983, 45
52 Best, 1977, 399

CHAPTER 4

Discipling in Matthew's Gospel

We now turn to a study of discipling as it is portrayed by the Gospel writer, Matthew. Most modern scholars hold the view that Mark was written prior to Matthew and was one of Matthew's sources.[1] Of Matthew's 1,068 verses about 500 contain Marcan material.[2] Therefore a degree of repetition of materials may be expected. For the purposes of this study we will refrain from repeating discipling issues covered in the previous chapter and confine our remarks to any different emphases or additional materials in Matthew. His purposes in writing and the intended recipients are quite different from those of Mark. Consequently Jesus' discipling relationships are portrayed from a different perspective.

Many consider Matthew is, "in its entirety, a didactic paradigm, a Gospel written for teaching and making disciples".[3] We would therefore expect to find much here to assist in our search for understanding of the discipling role of Jesus and his training of his followers to be disciple makers.

We will now seek to ascertain whether the elements of the working definition of 'discipling' which has been proposed are present in Matthew's Gospel. The roles of Jesus in the lives of his followers and as leader of the group will be studied. As with Mark, the call narratives and naming of the Twelve will be explored to determine the discipling expectations of both Jesus and his disciples. The degree of Jesus' emphasis on learning will be assessed. The lives of persons who encountered Jesus will be examined in order to determine which actions and characteristics are essential to the concept of discipleship, whether the term 'disciple' is used to describe the relationship or not.

Particular attention will be given to the nature and duration of the discipling relationship. The formation, composition, structure and functions of the discipling community will be considered. A summary will be made of the various methods used by Jesus in promoting learning. Finally, Jesus' commissioning of his followers for the on-going task of making disciples will be examined. In the light of our discoveries conclusions will be drawn and suggested alterations to the working definition noted.

The discipling relationship

A voluntary commitment to learning from another

After introducing Jesus and the beginnings of his public ministry, Matthew follows Mark's sequence and records the initial call of the four fishermen disciples (Mt. 4:18-22). In addition to what has already been noted, Matthew informs his readers that Jesus had previously moved from Nazareth to live in Capernaum, the town of the four (4:13). This would seem to indicate that these men had already encountered Jesus on other occasions before they responded to his call. They would thus have been better able to assess the cost involved in their personal lives before making their decision to follow him.

The call of Matthew, the tax collector, was some time later (9:9-13). His call bears such striking resemblance to that of Levi in Mark's Gospel[4] that many have concluded that both narratives refer to the same person. Being a tax collector, Matthew was not a popular or exemplary member of society. His appointment to the disciple band, and the company Jesus therefore kept, was immediately criticized by the seemingly pious Pharisees. However Jesus defended his association with Matthew and indicated that he had not come for the outwardly righteous, but for those aware of their need for forgiveness. Commitment to Jesus, rather than legalistic righteousness was a prerequisite for discipleship.

In comparison with Mark, Matthew gives the Twelve greater prominence than the wider group of disciples or the crowds (*ochloi*). Very few others are described as being "with Jesus" or he "with them". However scholars are divided concerning his use of *mathētēs* (disciple) as a technical term for the Twelve.[5]

Matthew does not repeat Mark's threefold commissioning of the Twelve (Mk. 3:14,15), but his content closely parallels it. Jesus summoned them (literally, called to himself, *proskaleō*). This is similar to Mark's statement that they were "to be with him". Mark continues, they were "to be sent out to proclaim the message and to have authority to cast out demons." Matthew announced that Jesus "gave them authority over unclean spirits… disease and every sickness" and charged them to proclaim the Kingdom (10:7).

Matthew's Gospel has an additional emphasis on the Kingdom of God. By initiating the call, Jesus was making a statement about the Kingdom. He came in weakness and in a manner which opened himself up to the possibility of rejection. He maintained his vulnerability within the discipling relationship. In this way he showed that the kingdom he was instituting would not involve force or coercion and none of the outward demonstrations of earthly power expected from this world's rulers. Other teachers of his time expected prospective disciples to request permission to follow. The teachers themselves would never expose their vulnerability or risk being rejected.

Jesus' disciples were also different from other disciples in the ancient world because there was no expectation that they would eventually progress beyond their teacher to having their own disciple band. Jesus taught that no authority would ever supersede his (28:18-20). He would always be Lord, and his followers were called to commit themselves to him as lifelong learners.

The choice to come under his authority in a discipling relationship was completely voluntary. Although he issued the call, there were those whom he actively discouraged from following because he believed they had not sufficiently weighed up the sacrifice involved. Jesus demanded all or nothing. Before they made their decision they had to be aware of the deprivations and priorities expected of his disciples (8:19-22).

Even though Jesus' demands were so stringent, this Gospel demonstrates that when his disciples did fail in the Garden of Gethsemane (26:56) their discipleship continued. Judas, the betrayer, was the only one who excluded himself from the possibility of restitution by taking his life (27:3-5). Even Peter's denial seemed to place no ultimate obstacle to his continuance as a disciple (26:69-75). Matthew does not describe how their desertion and betrayal were resolved, but by going to the mountain in Galilee to which Jesus had directed them, the disciples demonstrated that they were still his followers (28:16-20). Jesus signified their restoration by his words of commission.

Thus their voluntary commitment to Jesus was clear, but not all scholars believe that learning was the intended outcome. Rengstorf claims that because Matthew only uses *manthanō* (to learn) three times and the other Gospels use it even less, Jesus' main concern was not to teach, but to awaken unconditional commitment to himself.[6] He suggests that the Gospel writers prefer *akolouthein* (to follow) to describe the disciples' true intention. Wilkins, however, disagrees and notes that Matthew's emphasis on understanding and learning is a key to Jesus' teaching intention (9:13, 11:29).[7] Rengstorf's evidence does not make a strong case.

While *manthanō* may rarely be used, *mathētēs* (disciple) appears 72 times in Matthew.[8] If the disciples had a role other than as learners, it would be expected that Matthew would also use other titles to refer to them, such as *diakonos* (servant, helper). This does not happen. In playing down learning as a function of the disciples, Rengstorf ignores the sixty per cent of this Gospel which contains Jesus' oral teaching of his disciples.[9] Additional evidence also exists that Jesus utilized a wide variety of informal teaching methods. Many of his miracles were performed with a learning intention as part of their function. A case could be made that Jesus' major intention in both public ministry and private relationship with his disciples was to teach. Only the intention of the cross was greater.

Thus for Matthew the disciples were a small group, usually the Twelve, who had their faults and failures but acknowledged Jesus' authority in their lives, and set themselves to learn from their close association with him as teacher and master. Their voluntary commitment was to following Jesus wholeheartedly whatever the cost.

A close personal relationship

The nature of the relationship between Jesus and his disciples has been the topic of some debate. A number of scholars question whether Matthew uses *akolouthein* (to follow) in a purely literal sense, or as a technical word to describe the life of those belonging to the disciple group.

Both Strecker and Betz claim that Matthew consistently uses *akolouthein* to signify discipleship.[10] Other scholars suggest that the context is important in determining the matter and thus insist that the two blind men whom Jesus healed became disciples (20:34).[11] Kingsbury examines the call narratives which clearly indicate that a life of discipleship is intended in 4:20,22. He postulates that discipleship is intended if the dual motifs of 'personal commitment' and 'cost' are present in an *akolouthein* passage (e.g. 8:19,22; 9:9; 10:38; 16:24; 19:21,27,28).[12] He excludes the crowd and many recipients of miracles. Thus, "…being the recipient of a miracle of Jesus… is not a sufficient basis for becoming his disciple: one must instead be summoned by Jesus to come after him and emboldened to endure the cost of discipleship."[13]

The concept of 'following after' was never used to refer to the life of pupils in rabbinic schools.[14] Their primary task was to learn the Torah. The teaching methods which Jesus used were different from those of other Jewish teachers of his day. Formal learning was part of his disciples' experience, but they also learnt from their personal experiences in observing and imitating Jesus, following his itinerant lifestyle, joining in his ministry and relating closely to him.

Matthew waited until the end of his Gospel to mention a wider circle of faithful followers beyond the Twelve (27:55-61). These included a group of "many women" who had "followed" Jesus from Galilee and watched the crucifixion from a distance. Matthew does not use the term 'disciples' to refer to them, but as we have already indicated, their 'following' and costly commitment qualifies them as those who demonstrated discipleship in their lives. The discipleship of Joseph of Arimathea also became apparent when he took the body of Jesus and placed it in his own new tomb.

Matthew was indicating that the circle of disciples which would be the focus of ministry was extending beyond the Twelve to a much larger group of men and women. They would however be distinguished by their commitment to following Jesus and their relationship to him as master no matter what the cost.

A new discipling community

Once called, the disciples immediately came into a community relationship centred on Jesus but in company with one another. Matthew's call was followed by a dinner with his tax-collector and sinner friends, at which Jesus and other disciples were present (9:9-13). The group of twelve were committed to Jesus for the whole period of his public ministry.

His relationship with the Twelve receives greater prominence than any association with an individual disciple or particular subgroup. The learning relationships which Jesus established with the Twelve seem rarely to involve a one-to-one dimension. Matthew only records one private conversation between Jesus and a disciple, when Peter took Jesus aside and rebuked him for predicting his suffering and death (16:22-24). Other conversations recorded between Peter and Jesus occurred among the Twelve with Peter acting as their leader or representative spokesperson (15:15; 17:24-27; 18:21; 19:27). Peter's confession of Jesus as the "Messiah, the Son of the living God" (16:16) was part of a conversation involving all the disciples.

When Matthew lists the Twelve he inserts *kai* (and) between the names in such a way that he appears to be indicating the existence of subgroups within the community (10:2-4). Peter and Andrew and James and John are linked, and within that subgroup he indicates the pairs of brothers. The remaining disciples appear in pairs, Philip and Bartholomew, Thomas and Matthew, James son of Alphaeus and Thaddaeus, Simon the Cananaean and Judas Iscariot.[15] As with the brothers, at least some of these subgroups may have existed long before Jesus arrived. He appealed to them as partners and as a small group (4:18-22). These partnerships and subgroups do not play a major role in Matthew but some are mentioned.[16] Jesus may have given them special discipling activities, but evidence for such in this Gospel is scanty.

Although it might appear that the disciple band was a closed group of only twelve men, the passion narratives reveal that there were other functioning members who also formed subgroups (27:55-61). One of these consisted of at least three women who provided for (*diakonousai*) Jesus. It included Mary Magdalene, the mother of James and John who earlier had requested favoured positions for her sons in the kingdom (20:20-28) and Mary, the mother of James and Joseph, who were known to the community.

Other members of the disciple band included Joseph of Arimathea who took the body of Jesus and prepared it for burial. He appears acquainted with the women who observed. The woman who anointed Jesus in Bethany displayed spiritual insight greater than all the other disciples (26:6-13).[17] On the resurrection morning both an angel and Jesus himself commissioned Mary Magdalene and the other Mary to tell the good news to the men,[18] and issued the command to go to Galilee where they all[19] would see Jesus (28:1-10). While only Joseph of Arimathea is nominated by Matthew as a disciple, the women were obviously vocal, active participants in the disciple band and members of the learning community.

Thus in Matthew, Jesus discipled the Twelve by calling them into a small communal group committed to him as master and teacher for the whole period of his public ministry. As part of the process each member of the Twelve formed a partnership with another member (or brother). Smaller subgroups also performed specific tasks. After his resurrection Jesus delivered the commission to make disciples of all nations to his established discipling community of eleven (28:16-20).[20] But already that community had expanded to include family members and others with spiritual insight who were prepared to serve him. They were all part of the growing, discipling community who were about to become a disciple-making community.

The discipling model

Formal teaching

Jesus employed a wide variety of methods to teach his disciples. We have already seen that the verbal teaching which he delivered to them privately or in the presence of the crowds constitutes more than half of this Gospel. On occasions he deliberately adopted the formal sitting posture of a rabbi (5:1). Matthew records five great discourses (5:3-7:27; 10:5-42; 13:3-52; 18:1-35; 23:2-25:46). When the disciples were ignorant, unbelieving or in opposition or conflict with Jesus, Matthew portrays Jesus using it as an opportunity to teach. In doing so the disciples are presented in a more favourable light than in Mark.[21]

Jesus was not a domineering or indoctrinating guru. Instead of demanding unquestioning obedience, he endeavoured to increase the understanding of his disciples by explanations and providing opportunity for discovery learning which promoted both retention and understanding. Gerhard Barth lists understanding as the essence of being a disciple.[22] *Suniēmi* (to understand) occurs frequently in Matthew (e.g. 16:12; 17:13) and is seen as an essential prerequisite for the word of God to be fruitful (13:1-23,51). However it comes as a gift from God, not through human endeavour alone.[23] Jesus' disciples were blessed because they had knowledge of the secrets of the kingdom of heaven, in contrast with earlier prophets and righteous men for whom the kingdom had not yet arrived and the crowds who were incapable of understanding.

Mark frequently notes the disciples' lack of understanding, but in parallel passages, Matthew either omits it (14:31-33; 17:9,23), or sees it as a temporary matter to be corrected (13:51; 16:12; 17:13). When they were slow to grasp Jesus' teaching he questioned them, "Are you… still without understanding?" (15:16). It was important that the disciples should understand, otherwise they would not be able to carry out his commission to teach the nations.

Modelling

While Matthew contains much of Jesus' formal teaching, Jesus also taught by modelling in his own life the qualities he sought to inculcate. The Sermon on the Mount taught the life characteristics of 'the blessed' which were displayed clearly in Jesus' life (5:2-12). Because his disciples were with him for the extended period of his public ministry they, particularly, were able to observe him in both public and private situations.

Religion in Jesus' day held three basic acts of piety – alms giving, fasting and prayer. Jesus was criticized by various groups because his practices were different (9:14-17). He taught that a basic attitude of humility before God was much more important than mere outward acts of piety (6:1-18). His life continually demonstrated a close communion with the Father in prayer (11:25-27; 14:23; 26:36-44; 27:46).

A distinctive Matthaen expression for disciple is *mikros* (little one). In Matthew, people's own righteousness is insufficient. Jesus taught that only the childlike and meek will receive God's righteousness required for them to enter the kingdom (5:3-6; 18:3-5). Those qualities were also displayed to his disciples in his own life. They, too, were to care for the needs of one another (10:42), seek the lost, restore the straying, nurture the weak and forgive with overwhelming generosity no matter what the personal cost (18:10-14,21-35). They were to root out the causes of sin in their own lives, forgive one another and offer to others the assurance of forgiveness when they turned from wrongdoing (16:18,19; 18:6-22).

Matthew saw the humble example of Jesus as the fulfilment of Isaiah's prophecy concerning the servant of the Lord. "He will not wrangle or cry aloud, nor will anyone hear his voice in the streets. He will not break a bruised reed or quench a smouldering wick until he brings justice to victory" (12:19-20).

As opposition to Jesus grew and he moved towards the cross with its suffering, mockery and humiliation, he began to prepare his disciples for the persecution and suffering which would come to them as his followers (10:16-24,38). He modelled what it would mean for them to take up the cross and follow.

Establishing a serving community involving small groups

Following Jesus was not a comfortable matter. Not only did it lead to persecution and suffering but it called for a level of insecurity considered offensive to Jews of his day. rabbinic schools provided a peaceful, secure atmosphere[24] but the conditions for Jesus' disciples were diametrically opposed. They were called to follow him as first priority and if necessary to abandon home, shelter, family responsibilities and even life itself (8:20-22; 10:37-39; 16:24-27).

Family was extremely important for every Jew and a father's authority was unquestioned. For a son or daughter to put responsibility towards another person before family responsibilities was "completely unthinkable to Jewish sensitivities. It was a purely sacrilegious act of impiety."[25] Jesus taught his disciples that their basic allegiance was to be to him and the Father in heaven, and then to their earthly family members. He demonstrated the commitment required when his own earthly family visited. Though some may consider he was harshly rejecting his family by asking who they were, he was really extending the circle of his family to include his new community. "Whoever does the will of my Father in heaven is my brother and sister and mother" (12:50). He upheld the high ideals of the Old Testament law concerning family responsibilities (5:17;

15:4-6), but taught that family responsibilities must not take precedence over doing the will of God.

The disciples were members of Jesus' family. In it God was Father (23:8) and other disciples were brothers, sisters and mothers (12:46-50; 25:40; 28:10). France comments "This is not merely the language of camaraderie; the basis of their brotherhood is that they are first of all brothers of Jesus."[26] The pattern for their community relationships was seen in that of Jesus with his Father. The disciples were called to relate without anger, criticism or bitterness (5:22-24; 7:2-5). Error, resentment or sin were to be dealt with in such a way that restoration was achieved (18:15-18).

Mutual love, care and forgiveness were expected (18:35). As Jesus demonstrated loyalty to his disciples when he defended their actions against legalistic criticism by others, they were to display family loyalty to one another (12:1-8; 15:1-9). The joy of belonging to this new community was likened to guests at a wedding experiencing joy in the bridegroom's presence (9:14-17). No other experience of life could outweigh its worth (13:44).

The community did not exist for its own sake, but for the sake of others. While it provided support and encouragement, the lives of the disciples were to be focussed outward towards serving others. Jesus told them to pray "the Lord of the harvest to send out labourers" (9:37,38). Immediately following that statement Matthew recorded Jesus' conferral of authority on the Twelve and then listed their names, nominating them as *apostoloi* (sent out ones) and stating, "These twelve Jesus sent out" (10:1-5). It seems they were to answer their own prayers.

Learning and mission were integrally related in the life of discipleship. When Jesus called the fishermen it was to follow him and learn to "fish for people" (4:19). Jesus' discipling was different from his public teaching ministry. Only disciples were sent out to fish or harvest, to draw others into the kingdom of heaven. In Matthew, disciples hear, understand and live by the teachings of Jesus and do God's will.

Although Matthew's Gospel records Jesus' instructions to his disciples in preparation for their mission to "the lost sheep of the house of Israel" (10:5-42), he does not actually mention the pairs or their going out or returning. The other Synoptics supply this information. This seems to indicate that the authority was for their everyday work as disciples which Jesus expected them to perform, not just for a specific time of mission. Matthew's overall focus was on their world-wide mission which included Jews and Gentiles, and for which they were commissioned by Jesus after the resurrection (28:18-20).

Action (possible failure) and reflection

The mission of the disciples to the villages of Israel was an important illustration in the other Synoptics of Jesus' teaching by action and reflection, but

Matthew appears more interested in Jesus' instructions for mission than its actual fulfilment.

He does, however, include other occasions where action was followed by reflection and learning occurred. Jesus sought to develop their faith by a process of shared praxis as the disciples observed and shared with Jesus in his ministry. Though their faith was greater than the unbelief of many of their generation (13:58; 17:17; 21:32), Jesus described it as *oligopistos* (little faith). On four occasions Matthew records Jesus rebuking the inadequacy of their faith (8:26; 14:31; 16:8; 17:20). He was seeking to gradually increase their belief in him to the next level which he described as "faith as small as a mustard seed" or "undoubting faith" (17:21; 21:21) which was demonstrated by prayer. They possibly only achieved this level of faith after the resurrection, but even then some doubted (28:17).

The evangelist shows a growth in their faith as they encountered life-threatening situations and later reflected on them. A major crisis occurred for the disciples when, as a result of following Jesus, they were caught in a sudden, life-endangering storm (8:23-27). They cried out to him for deliverance and the first thing he did was question their fear and rebuke their "little faith". Then he calmed the storm. This miracle which saved their lives provoked them to reconsider Jesus' identity.

In Matthew's narrative of the walking on the water he emphasized Peter's response (14:22-33).[27] Jesus seemed to be encouraging quite bizarre behaviour by calling Peter to come to him on the water, but the event was a master stroke he used to enlarge the faith of Peter and the other disciples in a situation involving possible danger – a forerunner of modern adventure education? Held suggests this scene shows Peter as "a disciple on the way to discipleship",[28] learning and growing in response to Jesus' revelation of himself. This incident enlarged the disciples' understanding of Jesus' power and authority, which he had previously given them to enable them to heal, raise, cleanse, exorcize and perform other mighty works.

On a number of occasions the disciples were asked to perform supernatural actions. However, more often than not, they failed. Matthew shows how their deficiency led to a willingness to learn from Jesus and to move on to further opportunities for service. Thus when the disciples were unsuccessful in casting out the demon from the epileptic boy, they questioned Jesus privately as to the reason and he used their failure to encourage them to exercise greater faith in God demonstrated by prayer, so that they would regard nothing as impossible (17:14-21).

When the five thousand were in need of food, Jesus said to his disciples, "You (*humeis* emphatic) give them something to eat" (14:13-21), but their faith did not stretch beyond the five loaves and two fish. Consequently Jesus himself met the people's needs, and allowed the disciples to witness his miraculous provision. However they seemed slow to learn from the experience and when Jesus again expected the disciples to provide for the four thousand they failed for the second time (15:32-39). It was only when Jesus guided their reflection on these two incidents and rebuked them for their little faith that they finally understood (16:8-12). Wilkins comments that they "become examples of imperfect followers of Jesus, who are taught and who advance to understanding and solidarity with Jesus."[29]

Demonstration

As was observed in our study of Mark, Jesus was quick to recognize the faith and trust demonstrated in the lives of others who were not disciples and to hold them up as examples for the encouragement of his followers. France comments that Matthew's miracle stories "provide models of how a disciple may relate to and depend on his Lord in the crises of life".[30] Matthew 9 includes a series of miracles which illustrate the faith in action of the friends of the paralysed man (v.2), the woman with the haemorrhage (v.22) and the two blind men (v.28). No disciple was ever praised by Jesus for having "great faith". Jesus only commended two people in this way. Both were Gentiles, a Roman centurion and a Canaanite woman (8:10; 15:28).

Training to carry out the discipling role with others

Jesus was providing his disciples with an effective teaching model for them to utilize in their future role as leaders of his church. However his primary concern was that they would understand the nature of God's kingdom and his position as God's anointed One. At the close of his ministry, when his role as teacher was finished they finally understood who he was and worshipped him (28:17).

Jesus authorized Peter and the rest of the disciples to deal with members of the church who sinned (18:15-22). He gave them the power to "bind" and "loose" (16:19; 18:18) which Heirs suggests conferred on them authority over demonic powers and probably also the authority to resolve whatever problems or issues might arise within the church they would lead.[31]

The climax of Matthew's Gospel records Jesus' final commission to his disciples (28:18-20).[32] These words form a bridge between the discipling role which Jesus had performed among them and their future role. Jesus proclaimed that the ultimate authority in heaven and earth was his. In the light of that truth he commissioned his disciples for their task of making disciples. The verb *mathēteusate* (make disciples) is in the imperative and it is the main verb of the sentence. Thus their calling and the task of the church was to make disciples. They were to make others into what they were themselves. These would not be their own disciples, but people who also freely chose to come under the authority of Jesus who had promised to be with them always.

Within the same sentence there are three participles which elucidate the disciple-making process. They are dependent on the main verb but in such a construction the participles themselves commonly assume the force of an imperative.³³ The first participle, *poreuthentes* (having gone, or as you go) indicates that wherever they went on earth, they were to be carrying out this task. Jesus had confined himself primarily to the "lost sheep of Israel" (10:6), but they were to make disciples of "all nations" and fulfil the prediction of Jesus that "many will come from east and west… in the kingdom of heaven" (8:11). The second participle *baptizontes* (baptising) refers to the public act by which those who believed in Jesus would identify themselves with him, the Father and the Holy Spirit and with the community of his followers. It showed their incorporation into the discipling community. The third participle *didaskontes* (teaching) affirms the teaching role of the community of believers. Jesus said they were to teach others to "obey everything that I have commanded". The verb *tērein* (to obey) conveys the idea of observing or paying attention to.³⁴ It may well be a reference to the responsibility of Jesus' disciples to provide in their own lives worthy models of the fulfilment of Jesus' commands. Previously they had not been authorized to teach, but now their understanding had increased they were ready to fulfil this role. Their teaching was to include right belief, as well as the right way of acting, living and dying.³⁵

As Jesus discipled the Twelve, they were to continue the process wherever they went among the nations, incorporating those who responded, into discipling communities and teaching them everything they knew. In this Gospel, Matthew himself appears to be continuing that process by formulating a discipling manual to be used among the nations for teaching all that Jesus had commanded.

Conclusions and re-examination of working definition

Matthew focuses on the learning relationships which Jesus had with the Twelve, sometimes as a whole or in smaller subgroups. He shows how they responded to the call and voluntarily committed themselves to following Jesus for an extended period of time, learning from him and holding to his teachings even though there was considerable cost to them personally. Large sections of Matthew's writing contain Jesus' formal teachings and many instances may also be seen of his more informal interactions which resulted in learning.

Jesus structured their lives and activities in such a way that they were constantly being challenged to question and learn from a multiplicity of informal situations. These included the new thoughts, attitudes and values which came as they left the familiarity of their homes, families, occupations and cultural norms and moved into a community composed of fellow learners, from a variety of backgrounds, moving around the provinces of Galilee and Judea.

The disciples came into a close, personal relationship with him as teacher and master. The community they joined also formed close, family-type relationships where nurture occurred. Their attitudes, values and behaviours were challenged as Jesus modelled, in his daily life and interactions with large numbers of different people, the life of the 'blessed' – a life of humble service and self-giving sacrifice. They also saw faith in action in the lives of those who came to him with their needs.

They learned new skills and behaviours as Jesus led them into demanding or life threatening circumstances which stretched their little faith to its limits, and beyond. When they failed, appeared ignorant or lacked the required faith to act with the authority Jesus had given them, he rebuked them and then led them into greater understanding. Finally they received Jesus' commission to go out to make disciples of all nations.

This study of Matthew's Gospel has resulted in the further discovery of three important facets of discipleship. First, the intention of discipling was not for them to learn more and more for their own satisfaction and growth in learning, but that their learning would enable personal growth in faith and trust in Jesus and the Father. Second, discipling relationships occurred primarily in community or in small groups and rarely in one-to-one relationships. Third, the focus of discipling was outward, seeking to serve others and to make disciples of all nations.

The disciples of Jesus would never progress to being teachers and masters. They would not gather their own disciples one day. Jesus would always be the one with authority. They would, however, become disciple-makers who would serve God and enable others to commit themselves to faithful following in the community of God's people wherever they were. This would take place through baptism and incorporation of others into the faith community, and through teaching everything which Jesus had communicated to them. The methods outlined in our definition form part of that teaching process, but additional discipling methods including small groups, collaborative learning and adventure education have also been shown to make a valuable contribution.

Further adjustment to our working definition is therefore required, but this will not be attempted until our study of all the Gospels has been completed.

Notes to Chapter 4
1 For a detailed discussion of Marcan priority see Guthrie, 1975, 133-143.
2 Bruce, 1960, 31
3 Arias, 1991, 411
4 Matthew adds an extra sentence to the conversation (Mt. 9:13).
5 Donaldson believes it generally refers to the Twelve. (Donaldson, 1996, 32); Albright and Mann, and Pesch assert that *mathētēs* and *dōdeka* (twelve) are used synonymously by Matthew. Others including Hengel and Przybylski acknowledge that *mathētēs* is not so exclusive. (Wilkins, 1988, 167)
6 Rengstorf, 1967, 406
7 Wilkins, 1988, 160-164
8 Aland, 1978, 172
9 Matthew has 1071 verses. Of these 295 contain teaching directly for his disciples and a further 300 verses are addressed to the crowds with his disciples also hearing. In a small number of these passages, e.g. the Sermon on the Mount (5:1; 7:28), it is unclear as to

which group Jesus was addressing. But which ever group it was, the disciples received the teaching anyway. In these calculations we assigned unclear passages to the crowds.

10 Kingsbury, 1978, 57
11 Kingsbury, 1978, 57
12 This he describes as personal sacrifice and single-hearted devotion to God.
13 Strecker and Betz as cited in Kingsbury, 1978, 68,73.
14 Hengel, 1981, 32
15 By comparing the four lists of the Twelve and their variations in order and composition, it may be deduced that each pair belonged to a small group of four with Peter, Philip and James the son of Alphaeus as leaders. (Bruce, 1971, 36)
16 Two disciples found the donkey (21:1,2) and three of the fishermen brothers featured in the Transfiguration and Gethsemane narratives (17:1-13; 26:37-46).
17 She is identified in John's Gospel as Mary of Bethany (Jn. 12:1-8).
18 "The Holy Spirit made Magdalene the apostle to the apostles." This quote by Augustine led to her being known as *apostola apostolorum*. (Augustine as cited in Moltmann-Wendel, 1982, 64.)
19 *Opsesthe* (You {plural} will see him) implies the women will also be present.
20 It is assumed that Judas had already committed suicide (27:5).
21 "He avoids reporting what is unfavourable to the disciples, by toning it down, passing over it or simply twisting it round." (Barth, 1963, 118)
22 Barth, 1963, 105
23 Barth, 1963, 110
24 Hengel, 1981, 14
25 Schlatter as cited in Hengel, 1981, 14
26 France, 1989, 264
27 Mark's record focused on the disciples' terror, hardness of heart and lack of understanding (Mk. 6:45-51).
28 Held, 1963, 205-6
29 Wilkins, 1988, 169
30 France, 1989, 263
31 Hiers, 1985, 250
32 Many scholars have questions as to the authenticity of parts of this passage. Leon Morris comments, "the arguments are all subjective: there is nothing else with which to compare the passage, and textually it is well attested." (Morris, 1992, 744)
33 This explains why the TEV, NJB and other modern translations make all the verbs into imperatives. (Newman & Stine, 1988, 913)
34 Arndt & Gingrich, 1957, 822
35 Morris, 1992, 749

Chapter 5

Discipling in Luke's Gospel

Luke's Gospel is the third Synoptic Gospel on which we focus our attention. Materials common to these Gospels are generally thought to have originated from Mark. Of Luke's 1149 verses, 350 are paralleled in Mark.[1] However Matthew and Luke share an additional body of common information[2] consisting of approximately 250 verses.[3] Almost half of Luke's Gospel is unique to him. Thus while there will inevitably be matters in Luke which we have already covered, new insights into the discipling relationship will be gathered from the fresh data and from his different perspective on what are common materials.

The relationships of Jesus with his women followers will be specially examined and their inclusion and possible roles within the disciple band will be discussed. Any differences in Jesus' approach to, or expectations of women and men disciples will be addressed.

Luke's perspective on learning intentions, relationships involved and the nature of the discipling community will be studied. Aspects of the discipling model as it appears in this Gospel will be determined. Evidence for formal teaching, modelling, community, action and reflection and demonstration will be gathered and any further teaching comments will be made. Then conclusions will be drawn. Finally the working definition will be reconsidered and any necessary adjustments suggested, before completing our investigation of the Gospels with the subsequent study of the Gospel of John.

Women in the disciple band

Before proceeding further, it is important to give special consideration to the nature of the relationship between Jesus and the women known to be closely associated with him and his mission. Women feature more prominently in Luke's Gospel than the other Gospels, and although in previous chapters we have already commented on their presence, a more detailed discussion would be helpful at this stage.

Were there women disciples?

At the outset it is important to note that nowhere in the Gospels was a woman designated by the term *mathētēs* (disciple). However if the argument from silence was used to conclude that there were no women disciples, then on the same grounds, "the seventy" who were sent out on mission would also be excluded (10.1-20).

There were no women in the Twelve.[4] However a small group of women were associated with Jesus in his inner circle of disciples. "The twelve were with him as well as some women…" (8:1,2). In the Gospels they were frequently mentioned by name in groups of two or three (24:10)[5] with Mary Magdalene's name first.[6] Some suggest that they parallel the three male disciples closest to Jesus[7] or the recognized male partnerships. Grundmann proposes that the naming means they "appear on the same level as the men."[8]

Some of the women were clearly relatives of male disciples. A few modern scholars have traced possible family connections among Jesus' disciples and early followers. They have noted all the possible overlapping of names and conclude that Jesus' early followers were a small group of family members and close friends.[9]

The term *mathētēs* in Luke encompasses a seemingly larger group than either Mark or Matthew has indicated. There was "a great crowd of his disciples" (6:17, see also 19:37). Seventy were appointed and sent out on mission. And there were "many other" women (8:3). Therefore it seems highly likely that within the larger group which Luke nominates as disciples, a number of women could have been present.

In Mark and Matthew the verb *akoloutheō* (to follow) and its derivatives are used to convey discipleship. Both Gospels describe the women who watched the crucifixion as 'following' him from Galilee (Mk. 15:41; Mt. 27:55). To ensure that their following was not interpreted as a physical matter only, both synoptists add that they ministered to (*diakoneō*) Jesus. They seem to be trying to ensure that their readers understand the role of these women as active, serving, followers of Jesus.

Luke also describes the women who watched the crucifixion as having followed along with (*sunakoloutheō*) Jesus from Galilee (23:49).[10] They remained faithful and watched from a distance. Presence 'with' Jesus was a distinguishing mark of the Twelve and the women (8:1,2).[11] Martha and Mary appear to be exceptions to the practice of following (10:38-42). They remained in their own home and offered hospitality to Jesus and his followers when required and yet they appear to be part of the discipling circle.

Akouē (hear) is used 65 times in Luke[12] and is a key concept in understanding Jesus' purposes for his disciples. Jesus taught that the primary response to him was to hear the word of God and obey it (8:21). Those who did so, whether female or male, were considered as his 'mother' or 'brother', and objects of his blessing. His response to the woman in the crowd who called down a blessing on his mother reinforced his message. Hearing and obeying were more important than motherhood, no matter how important that role might be (11:27,28). Disciples were people who had responded to his call, and embarked on a life of hearing and obeying, irrespective of their gender.

Thus the test of discipleship in Luke's Gospel was hearing and obeying. We can assume that even though there is no mention of women disciples there were a number of women who were faithful hearers and doers and were in essence disciples of Jesus.[13]

The conversation between Jesus and Martha leaves no doubt that Jesus fully intended that women should learn from him. In the privacy of her home, Mary adopted the traditional learning posture of a disciple at the teacher's feet. This was revolutionary in the culture of the day because women's education was limited to the domestic arts.[14] Judaism exempted them from studying the Torah.[15] No rabbi would speak to a woman, even a family member, in public.[16] Martha resented Mary's behaviour but Jesus pointed out that he would have preferred for her to be a learner also.[17]

The men in dazzling clothes on the resurrection morning expected the women to "remember" Jesus' passion predictions which he had given to his disciples (24:6-8). If the women were not considered as disciple-learners then they could not reasonably be expected to remember. Jesus expected women to know. If Cleopas' companion was a woman (perhaps "Mary, the wife of Clopas" Jn. 19:25), then she was taught by Jesus along with her husband (24:13-35).

We therefore conclude that there were women closely associated with Jesus and his disciple band, although there were none among the Twelve. They were known by name and formed smaller subgroups. While the Twelve saw their responsibility to be 'with' Jesus, it may be that his women followers were more closely involved in the care of children or other family members, or had other reasons for remaining at home. Their ministry included offering hospitality. Others were free to leave home to be with him, although at least some of these did so with their sons or male relatives who were also followers. Jesus expected all his followers to hear God's word and to put it into practice. He gave no specific teaching to men and not to women. His teachings were for them all. The fact that the word 'disciple' was not used for women, does not mean that they were not his faithful learner-followers who heard and obeyed his teachings as the will of God. Thus while the term 'disciple' was not applied to them, they did fulfil the concept of discipleship in their lives.

What did the women do?

Jesus' disciples learnt as they shared in Jesus' servant ministry and as they went out to towns and villages in his name. The nature of the involvement of the women is not always clear. Some believe that "the roles that are offered to women in Luke-Acts present a very limited and conventional scope for their activity,"[18] however that is not necessarily so.

Luke 8:1-3 appears to be a summary statement of the involvement of the Twelve and "some women" during Jesus' Galilean ministry. The women are described as *diēkonoun* (serving, ministering to, providing for) them out of their resources (8:3). The imperfect tense of the verb "...describes a prolonged situation or portrays an event as happening repeatedly within an indefinite period of time."[19] This verb "has the special quality of indicating very personally the service rendered to another".[20] *Autois* (to them, masculine plural) means that they were serving Jesus and the Twelve.[21] Many believe that this involved financial help or domestic duties (4:39; 10:40),[22] however there is no necessity to limit the verb in this way.

Diakonein (serve) is frequently used in the New Testament. It applies to activities of waiting at table (Lk. 17:8), hospitality, assisting and visiting the needy (Mt. 25:42-44), fulfilment of apostolic responsibilities (2 Cor. 3:3), collecting for saints (2 Cor. 8:19) and prophecy (1 Pet. 1:10-12). Timothy and Erastus were *diakonountēs* (assistants/helpers) of Paul in preaching (Acts 19:22). In this Gospel Jesus was regarded as "one who serves" (22:27). Thus *diakonein* is used for a wide variety of activities carried out by Jesus, his apostles and other believers. The word itself certainly is not restricted to imply that the service which these women offered to Jesus and his band, only included a limited range of actions.

However the phrase *ek tōn huparchontōn autais* (out of their resources[23]) describes the service in greater detail. Whatever they had they used for Jesus. The source of these resources is uncertain, because only a small number of women had anything like economic independence.[24] They were probably responding to Jesus' teaching, to sell all and give to the poor (12:33; 14:33). Jesus' family and neighbours in Nazareth opposed his public ministry and the male disciples left everything to follow Jesus, consequently their need for support was crucial and these women would have provided substantial assistance to meet these needs.

Martha's service was also out of her resources (10:38-42). She offered hospitality (food and accommodation) to Jesus and his followers in her home in Bethany (10:40). Of recent years there has been much debate over this pericope. Some see it as supporting women's traditional roles in preparing of food and offering of hospitality.[25] Others use it to argue for the liberation of women from a domestic role to that of diligent learners.[26] Davies gives little credence to it as evidence for Jesus' sympathy with or encouragement of women's ministry and sees its value only as an illustration of Luke's desire to engage the attention of his audience in which women were numerous.[27]

Elizabeth Schussler Fiorenza adopts a different perspective again. In her book *In Memory of Her* she argues that Luke is seeking to perpetuate women's submissive, passive role. By comparing Luke 10:38-42 with Acts 6:1-4, she separates *diakonia* (ministry) into 'waiting on tables', possibly including eucharistic ministry (by the seven) as a lesser ministry, and 'of the word' (by the apostles) as a greater ministry.[28] She considers that Luke subordinated both Martha and

Mary by implying that Martha's table service was not as valuable as the ministry of the word. And Mary, she believes was even discouraged from table service, so that she performed no active Christian ministry at all. "It is even more important that Mary does not engage in ministry at all… but rather acts as the faithful but silent disciple."[29] Later in *But She Said* (1992), Fiorenza revised her interpretation of Martha's service and claimed she was "actively occupied in preaching the word in the house church, while Mary listens passively".[30] However, while Fiorenza has been influential, her interpretations seem precariously based on scant evidence and tend to disregard the basic hermeneutical principle of looking for the plain meaning of the text within its context.[31] Similar situations are not unknown, but it seems unlikely that its meaning has been obscured from all others until Fiorenza discovered it, to the advantage of her larger thesis[32].

The women followers of Jesus served as they were able, using whatever resources of time and possessions they had at their disposal to support and further his purposes. Full details of their activities are not available but rather than seeing their service as being restricted to financial and domestic roles, it is possible to view them in a variety of different situations offering ministry, both spiritual and physical, to Jesus and his band.

The women followed, travelled and witnessed (23:49,55,56). They are described as accompanying Jesus from Galilee. As has been already noted *sunakolouthousai* (follow along with) is a technical term describing their discipleship. It is a present participle showing that their 'accompanying' had not finished. They had been part of the disciple band as it went through cities and villages (8:1) both within Galilee and on the road to Jerusalem (9:51). In Galilee some may have used their own homes as a base or been dependent on local hospitality in the villages they visited.

Sim proposes that "the majority of these women were single"[33] and cites as evidence the shame and outrage incurred if any woman left her husband in that male-dominated society. However, if they were relatives of the other disciples, the problem would not arise.[34] It is possible that they were even among the seventy sent out by Jesus, travelling in partnership with a son, husband or other relative (10:1).[35]

There is no way of knowing if they healed or proclaimed the good news of the kingdom as did the male disciples. It would have been culturally unacceptable for them to preach in public.[36] Opportunities probably arose for them to speak to other women or in the homes where they stayed. Some testified to the healing or deliverance which Jesus had brought to their own lives.

They witnessed the crucifixion and burial. Luke is the only writer who mentions "all his acquaintances"[37] watching the crucifixion, but among them he emphasizes the presence of the women. Witherington notes the feminine participles in the passage. He comments that the long standing of the women as followers accredited and authenticated their witness because they could relate what they were *horōsai*[38] (seeing) at the cross to what they had known before.[39]

Their witnessing of the burial ensured that the possibility of mistaking the tomb early on the Sunday morning was eliminated.

Three women are named[40] and others were present to attest to the empty tomb and receive the resurrection message from the men in dazzling clothes (ch.24). Unlike the other Gospels, Luke does not record a resurrection appearance to the women or their commissioning to go and tell the disciples. They were reminded of Jesus' prediction of his death and resurrection, "Then they remembered his words". This implies more than an ordinary recollection of past events. It shows a transformation taking place in them and their understanding, and moves them to faith that Jesus had been raised from the dead.[41]

In Jewish legal cases it was necessary to call for a minimum of two or three witnesses (Dt. 17:6; 19:15). The Old Testament does not stipulate that the witnesses must be male, but by the first century CE the witness of women was regarded as being admissible only in very exceptional cases. Jews widely regarded women as liars.[42] The women (whose trustworthy characters we may presume were already known to the apostles) returned with the resurrection announcement, however "their words seemed to them like nonsense".[43]

'Three' was regarded as a complete, finished, definitive number. Thus the women performed a significant role as the three witnesses to the three great events of the crucifixion, burial and resurrection of Jesus. Ricci writes, "Luke, by using three names, produces the double effect of emphasising the veracity of the episodes concerned, by giving them three witnesses, and of stressing the importance of the persons listed, who form a salient group."[44]

The apostles only believed after Jesus appeared to Simon, to the Emmaus travellers and finally to the gathered group in Jerusalem.[45] In Luke's last scene Jesus commissioned all present as "witnesses of these things". "Repentance and forgiveness of sins is to be proclaimed in his name to all nations, beginning from Jerusalem." That was the task of all those, both men and women, who followed him.

Thus there is no indication in the words or teaching of Jesus that the expectations of the women members of the disciple band were any different from those of the men. Though they were not described as 'disciples' they were expected to do what the disciples did. That involved following him, learning, hearing God's word and obeying it and serving him and others using whatever means were at their disposal. Cultural norms certainly placed restrictions on the women's freedom of movement and expression of service, but there are no constraints implicit in the text as to how they should or should not go about fulfilling their responsibilities. They were expected to know and learn in the same way as the men. Their lives and the witness of what they had seen and heard showed to the world Jesus' work of salvation, healing and restoration. Their faithfulness to him enabled them to receive the great resurrection news, and to convey it to others with the conviction of their own personal experience. They too were "witnesses of these things". Therefore we can conclude that the concept of discipleship may be applied to the women in the same way as it is applied to those faithful men who followed, learned, heard, obeyed, served and witnessed.

The discipling relationship

We now return to an examination of the discipling relationship as it was outlined in the working definition.

A voluntary commitment to learning from another

Luke uses the term *mathētēs* (disciple) 37 times[46] but it is far less precise in his Gospel. Sometimes there seems to be little difference between Luke's 'disciples' and the crowds. His term refers to those who followed Jesus and heard his words. Jesus entered Jerusalem with a "whole multitude of disciples" (19:37). However the commitment of many of them had not been tested. Obedience to the words they heard[47] and perseverance in following (8:15) were proof of genuine discipleship. Only "his acquaintances" (*hoi gnōstoi autō*, the ones known to him) remained with him to watch the crucifixion from a distance (23:49). Even among the Twelve the discipleship of Judas Iscariot was found to be spurious.[48]

The intention that Jesus would be involved in teaching those whom he called, is clearly implied in Luke. Before the disciples began to follow, Luke records Jesus' repeated practice of teaching – in the synagogues of Galilee and Judea (4:14,15,44),[49] on the Sabbath (4:31,32) and in the open air (5:1,3). In the synagogue at Nazareth (4:16-27), the description of his teaching posture and his distinctive '*Pesher*' (fulfilment) interpretation of the reading from the Prophets, was typical of rabbinic practices of his day.[50] He was a widely recognized teacher before he called his followers and they would have expected to learn from him as they participated in his ministry.

The inner core of his disciples came to him in response to his call. As with the other Synoptics, the call narratives play an important part in understanding committed discipling relationships in Luke. In ancient literature call narratives required an "immediate, unconditional commitment of the disciple to the teacher entailing a departure from previous life activities".[51] Teachers might even issue radical demands requiring prospective disciples to obey them even if that involved a complete disregard for social convention.

Jesus also required an unconditional commitment from his disciples, which sometimes involved a disregard for social convention. He expected them to give priority to following him, and to regard family responsibilities or their own lives as having less importance. They were to weigh up the cost involved before they became his disciples. This is more obvious in Luke's Gospel because Luke locates the call narratives after a period of public ministry (5:1-11). Jesus had already become a popular, Spirit-filled teacher (4:14,37). He had performed healings and exorcisms and even visited Simon Peter's home in Capernaum

(4:23,31-41). He had involved himself in the fishermen's business affairs in such a way that they recognized that he was no ordinary person. Peter first regarded Jesus as *epistata* (Master, a term denoting authority), but after the miraculous catch he recognized him as *kurie* (Lord).[52] Thus their decision to follow was both informed and voluntary.

In his call Jesus promised, "from now on you will catch men".[53] It was in effect a command. *Zōgreō* (catch, to take alive) occurs in the Septuagint referring to saving persons alive from danger.[54] Jesus was implying that those whom he called would be shepherds, carers and rescuers of God's people. Luke is thus portraying their discipleship as having a positive impact on the lives of others.

Levi's call followed two more miraculous healings (5:27-32). Luke uses the word *thesomai* (a strong verb indicating to see/observe/look at)[55]. This suggests that Jesus singled out Levi in particular and called him to follow. He immediately left everything. *Katalipōn* (abandoning, aorist participle) stresses Levi's single, decisive break with his old life.[56] *Akolouthei* (followed, imperfect indicative) shows his continuing life of discipleship. As we noted in an earlier chapter, his discipleship involved a conscious response to a known person, a break with his old life and the beginning of a continuing relationship.

Before calling the Twelve, Jesus spent the night in prayer. This indicates their special role within the large group of disciples. He called them by name,[57] and designated them as *apostolous* (apostles) (6:12-16). In using this term more than the other Gospel writers,[58] Luke is showing that they were fully accredited representatives of Jesus with a specific commission.[59] Implicit in their appointment was their future task of leadership within the church.[60]

There is no record of Jesus calling or commissioning any of the women. Some responded to him after he healed or delivered them from evil spirits (8:2,3). There was a close connection between Jesus' healing ministry and the response of faith to his proclamation of the kingdom (5:31,32; 9:1,2).[61] As noted earlier, the desire to be with Jesus was the appropriate response to his work of healing or exorcism. But not all who were healed made that response.

Jesus issued the call to discipleship to "all", but they had to fulfil his requirements. Jesus said, "Let him *arnēsasthō* (deny, aorist middle imperative) himself and *aratō* (take up, aorist imperative) and *akoloutheitō* (follow, present imperative) me" (9:23).[62] Denying self and taking up one's cross was a single decision and daily commitment to obedience. Following was a continuous, costly discipline. Flender writes, "to be a disciple is not an inalienable right but a privilege to be constantly renewed in obedience."[63] Seccombe comments, "'his own cross' implies Jesus is carrying a cross with the disciple following behind bearing his. The whole party is being led together to public crucifixion."[64] The true disciple must be like the master, ready for suffering or death (14:25-27). Fear or persecution is no excuse (12:4,8,9; 21:12-19).

Commitment to Jesus might involve renouncing employment, possessions or family (18:28-30). No other relationship in the disciple's life, even that of wife, was to be more important (14:26).[65] Some say this displays a "dim view of marriage",[66] or sexual asceticism,[67] but it seems simply that the priorities of the kingdom were to be paramount.

No rabbi expected such radical demands of his disciples. Some who came to Jesus considered the cost was too high. The rich ruler could not give up his wealth (18:18-25). And three would-be disciples decided that the physical privations, family renunciation or immediate requirements were too demanding (9:57-62). But for his true disciples the mission to which they were called far outweighed any sacrifice they made (12:13-21; 16:1-13). God's fatherly provision could be trusted (12:22-34; 22:35).

A close personal relationship

It seems difficult to see how the considerable number of 'disciples' mentioned by Luke (6:17; 15:1,2; 19:37) were able to form close personal relationships with Jesus unless we conclude that there were many among them whose discipleship had not yet been tested by obedience and perseverance. However there were at least seventy genuine followers who obeyed Jesus and went out on mission (10:1,17). It would seem that close, personal relationships with all seventy may be impossible, but Jesus' words imply quite the contrary. "He who listens to you listens to me; he who rejects you rejects me." (10:16). Jesus, himself, was to be considered as being present with them and working through their words and ministry. That denotes a very close relationship! He acknowledged that they were in a privileged position which many in the past had longed to share (10:23,24).

The relationship which Jesus had with his disciples was one which would continue into the kingdom. Jesus promised that those who were faithful to him in his trials would share in table fellowship with him in his kingdom and be in positions of power judging the twelve tribes of Israel (22:28-30).

Jesus also enjoyed close, personal relationships with women as they travelled with his band and in their family surroundings. He received their service to him and his followers (4:39; 8:1-3). He conversed freely with them and defended their rights to learn (10:38-42). Ricci describes his relationships as having "deep understanding – sharing… mutual exchange and acceptance".[68] His attitude of complete chastity toward them and the similar requirement of his followers allowed the women a freedom and safety which was not always accorded them in those days.[69]

In Luke, the disciples accompanied Jesus on his travels in Galilee and on the road to Jerusalem (9:51; 17:11).[70] As they approached Jerusalem he began to prepare them to understand his suffering and death (9:22,44,45; 18:31-34) and the glory involved (9:31,32). Although the disciples were fearful, Luke moderated some of the events recorded in Matthew and Mark to enable his characters, "especially Peter, to remain noble".[71] He writes of Jesus' praise, "You are those who have stood by me in my trials" (22:28) and his prayer for Peter that his faith would not fail (22:32). Luke does not mention the disciples' desertion, but records a group "of all his acquaintances [who]… stood at a distance, watching" the crucifixion (23:49).

Luke does not use *mathētēs* (disciple) from the end of the Gethsemane story (22:45). Rengstorf concludes that this is because, "the behaviour of the disciples of Jesus during the passion is equivalent to a breach of the relationship by them, and that it is the task of Jesus to gather disciples afresh after his resurrection".[72] Certainly after the resurrection Jesus renewed table fellowship with his disciples (24:30,43). By this act he demonstrated that the relationship severed by death and any faltering in their commitment was fully restored.

The close personal relationships which our working definition lays down as necessary for 'discipling', are clearly seen in this Gospel. Although the number of persons included in Luke's use of the term *mathētēs* is larger than the other Synoptics, the text implies that those whose commitment to him was long-term enjoyed close, personal fellowship with him.[73] Opportunities for developing relationships were enhanced in the disciple band as its men and women members lived, worked and travelled together with Jesus. Even when the other Synoptics record the faltering of the disciples, Luke minimizes their failure and shows them after the resurrection in renewed fellowship with Jesus.

A new discipling community

All who responded to the call of Jesus and who heard God's word and put it into practice (8:21) became members of a new family-style community,[74] with Jesus as the central authority figure. He was never classified as "one of the boys". He was always apart and yet with them. There were no earthly father-figures in his family. Fiorenza suggests that this implies that "in the messianic community all patriarchal structures are abolished".[75] Servanthood, not authority, power or status demonstrates greatness in the new community (22:24-27).

In Middle Eastern culture eating together is an important expression of relationship and community. The disciples frequently ate together but their company was never exclusive. At times it included tax collectors and sinners and the five thousand (5:30; 7:36; 9:17; 11:37; 14:1; 19:7). Not all these occasions expressed community, for Jesus was the guest of a Pharisee on more than one occasion in this Gospel. The most significant meal which the disciples and Jesus shared was the Passover in which he instituted the means by which they would remember his sacrifice for them (22:14-20). However their expression of relationship was marred by the disciples' dispute concerning greatness and Jesus' prediction of Peter's denial and his own imminent betrayal (22:21-34).

Because of the multiplicity of relationships within the wider discipling community smaller groups of two or three individuals formed. Greater intimacy and opportunities for service, learning and development were fostered within these closer, supportive groupings. Individual differences were also catered for more easily. Luke's list of the Twelve does not indicate any pairing (6:14-16), but the seventy formed partnerships for mission (10:1), two were sent to fetch the colt

(19:29)[76] and Jesus taught two on the road to Emmaus (24:13-35). The three closest to Jesus were mentioned together on several occasions.[77] The existence of these subgroups within the community meant that learning, encountering the presence of God, serving others and proclaiming the message of the kingdom, were enriched by the presence of others who shared the same experiences. The learning impact of these events was enhanced as the participants reflected together on their encounters.

The discipling model

Formal teaching

Forty three percent of Luke's Gospel is devoted to transmitting the words of Jesus' teaching.[78] In the majority of these situations the teaching was not primarily directed to the disciples, although they were present and listening. Much of Jesus' teaching arose informally throughout his ministry when his actions provoked questions or his opponents gathered against him. There were however some elements of a formal approach present.

The synagogue and Temple courts provided a 'classroom' setting. In Nazareth Jesus delivered his mission statement in the synagogue (4:16-30). After presenting the reading from the Prophets, he adopted the traditional posture of the teacher and sat down to expound Isaiah's words, applying them to himself.[79] During the final week in Jerusalem Jesus taught daily in the Temple courts in the formal manner of a rabbi, questioning and being questioned (19:47-21:38). All the people were spell-bound, returning early each morning so as not to miss any of his teaching.

In the Sermon on the Plain (6:20-49) and other public teaching occasions (8:4-8; 11:29-36; 14:26-35; 20:9-18), he appeared to be teaching according to a predetermined plan. The different settings which Matthew and Luke give for the same teaching probably indicate that it was repeated on several occasions.[80]

The parables at first appear to have emerged spontaneously within everyday situations, however the parabolic form is notoriously difficult to construct.[81] It would have been most unusual for one to spring to mind naturally without a certain amount of forethought. Consequently we have grounds for assuming that Jesus intentionally prepared his parables for teaching purposes, using the resources of his culture, current affairs and everyday life in Palestine. Then he introduced them when an appropriate formal or informal occasion arose. Sometimes he may have structured situations which led to their presentation.

In the specialized teaching he presented to his disciples he appeared to have some kind of curriculum in mind. They were privileged recipients of the secrets of the kingdom of God (8:10; 10:21-24) and would eventually be commissioned as his witnesses to proclaim repentance and forgiveness of sins to all nations (24:46-49). He consciously prepared them for future ministry situations they would encounter and for their leadership and pastoral responsibilities within the church (6:39-42; 9:3-5,48; 10:2-16; 16:1-13; 17:1-10; 18:16-17; 24:48). He also warned them of the judgement they would experience if their leadership was found wanting (12:48). His questions enabled assessment of progress in learning to be made. Some teaching was only introduced after they grasped more basic understandings (9:18-23).[82]

Thus Luke provides good evidence that Jesus made some use of elements of formal education (use of a building, large groups of learners, prepared curriculum, assessment procedures and practices common to professionally trained rabbis) in order to provide his followers with a number of different learning experiences.

Modelling

Disciples were expected to imitate their master. Luke provides his readers with frequent examples which show how Jesus modelled the behaviours he was promoting in his verbal teaching (6:29-35). He describes how Jesus faced and overcame temptation (4:1-13). He shows Jesus' strong example of prayer, especially before each of the major events in his life (11:1-4).[83] The impact of this was reinforced by encouragement to pray (10:2) and teaching concerning perseverance in prayer (11:5-12; 18:1-8). Jesus' non-retaliation (9:51-56), love and forgiveness of enemies (23:34) provided an outstanding model for his disciples when they, also, were regarded with disfavour by his opponents (6:1-5; 19:39; 21:17).

Jesus seemed intentional in his use of modelling as part of the discipling process. He anticipated that the lives of his followers would be like his in helping others to seek for purity of life (6:40). He used the image of a lamp and light (11:33-36) to encourage "children of light" (16:8) to be like him and allow his light to shine through their "whole body so that it is full of light and has no darkness in it".[84]

Luke is the only Gospel writer to describe the way of the cross (23:26-32). Some interpret Simon of Cyrene as a model of the ideal disciple because he carried the cross behind Jesus.[85]

Establishing a serving community

Jewish rabbis demanded that their disciples learn their lessons by rote. To them memorisation was of utmost importance. Within the teachings of Jesus evidence also exists that his structures helped to facilitate rote learning, by repetition (6:20-26) and chiastic arrangement of materials (e.g. ch.18).[86] But serving others was much higher on Jesus' agenda for his disciples. They were commissioned (5:10) and empowered for ministry, first in Israel (9:1; 10:19) and then amongst all nations (24:47-49). They were always to be ready and watchful, like servants accountable to their master, not knowing when he might appear (12:35-40).

Jesus' discipling community did not exist for its own benefit, even though its members did support, offer hospitality to and pray for one another. They were to be like Jesus. He came into the world as Saviour and Messiah (2:11), "a light for revelation to the Gentiles and for glory to... Israel" (2:32). So he sent them out into the world, to bring healing and deliverance and to proclaim the beginning of his kingdom evidenced by all that they had seen, heard and learnt from their time with him.

Action and reflection

Luke's account of the action-reflection cycle which Jesus used to develop his disciples is similar to what has already been noted in the Gospels of Mark and Matthew. Jesus' disciples were called to "catch people" (5:10). Like every Jewish male learning a trade they were expected to observe and learn from working with Jesus. They were apprentice-proclaimers of the kingdom, bearing testimony to Jesus. "Discipleship as Jesus conceived it was not a theoretical discipline, but a practical task to which men were called to give themselves and all their energies. Their work was not study but practice."[87]

The report of Jesus' public announcement of his 'mission statement' at the commencement of his ministry is unique to Luke. Jesus identified Isaiah's words as encapsulating the focus of his own ministry. In the power of God's Spirit he would "preach good news to the poor... proclaim freedom for the prisoners and recovery of sight for the blind... release the oppressed... proclaim the year of the Lord's favour" (4:18,19). These same activities were the basis of the disciples' ministry. They were to 'preach', 'proclaim' and 'release'. This was especially evident when he sent them out on mission.

Luke records two missions of the disciples, first with the Twelve and later with a larger group of seventy.[88] After a period of observation and listening the Twelve were given authority and sent to drive out demons, cure diseases, preach and heal the sick (9:1-6). This is similar in all the Synoptics. He gave them instructions concerning their lifestyle and message and what to do when people were not receptive. Jesus deliberately allowed for a period of quiet reflection and reporting back on their return (9:10). However it was not long before they were again plunged into the demands of his busy public ministry (9:11).

Luke is the only Gospel writer to include the sending out of the seventy (10:1-16). He indicates that they went in pairs in a way similar to the mission of the Twelve recorded in Mark (Mk. 6:7). They cured the sick and proclaimed the kingdom. They were to be regarded as messengers and fellow workers with Jesus. Those who listened to or rejected them would actually be regarded as doing it to Jesus, himself. This was similar to the rabbinic concept of the '*shaliah*'. These were authorized persons, commissioned with distinctive tasks (often legal rather than religious), which took them some distance from the one who sent them. They represented in their own person the rights of the other. "The one sent by a man is as the man himself."[89] Rengstorf comments that they were not sent out alone, but usually had two or more together.[90] The word is also used in the Old Testament for Moses, Elijah, Elisha and Ezekiel who under God's authority performed tasks which were usually attributable to God himself.[91]

Luke gives greater attention to Jesus' instructions for mission than to recording what actually happened. But when they returned they reported all that had happened to Jesus, who then used the occasion for further teaching (10:17-24). They rejoiced that God's power was working through them, but Jesus reminded them that their motivation for mission was to be the greater joy which comes when people turn to God (10:20; 15:7,10,32). In his post-resurrection commission to them Jesus reminded them of their ongoing mission to proclaim his message among all nations (24:46-49). And we may assume that the action reflection pattern which he established with them would continue into their worldwide mission.

Throughout this Gospel the action-reflection cycle is repeated. By living closely with the disciple band Jesus was able to use their sharing of experiences to bring further teaching. He then gave them greater tasks using their increased understanding. This led to further growth. It is interesting to note that this pattern of action and subsequent reflection was one which Jesus probably first observed in the life of his own mother (2:19,51).

Demonstration

Jesus was aware that his life and deeds clearly demonstrated the message of his words and undeniably revealed his true identity to people with open minds. The news of what he did spread widely (5:15) and many responded in amazement and gave praise to God (5:26; 7:16; 18:43). "A whole multitude of disciples" recognized God's power demonstrated in Jesus' miracles (19:37). When the disciples of John the Baptist came to Jesus, instead of directly answering their inquiry he allowed his deeds and words to bear witness to his identity as "the one who is to come" (7:18-23).

Healing the demon-possessed was a prominent part of Jesus' ministry from the very beginning (4:31-36,41). This clearly demonstrated his authority over Satan's domain and the superiority of God's power at work through him (10:18). But when his opponents attributed his deeds to Beelzebul, the ruler of demons, Jesus revealed the inadequacy of their logic. However, they refused to listen (11:17-23).

This Gospel is structured so that Jesus' early ministry of healing, deliverance, miraculous signs[92] and public proclamation of the kingdom (4:14-9:50) provides a strong demonstration of his identity. Once his disciples believed he was the Christ the focus of his ministry changed. In the 'journey narrative' which followed (9:51-19:44) Jesus began to prepare them for his death and resurrection (9:21,22, 44,45; 18:31-34).

The passion and resurrection of Jesus was the final irrefutable demonstration that Jesus was God's anointed, the one to whom Moses and the prophets looked (24:1-12,26,27,44-46). The two men in white at the empty tomb, the grave clothes, his conversation on the road to Emmaus, breaking of bread and his invitation to look, touch and watch provided ample supporting evidence (ch.24).

Enabling the development of maturity

Kingsbury suggests that in Luke the disciples are portrayed as spiritually immature.[93] They were fearful (in the storm), impertinent (Peter with haemorrhaging woman), perplexed (as to how to feed the crowd), dull (heavy with sleep on Mount of Transfiguration), ineffectual (healing the demon possessed boy), status conscious (wanting to be the greatest and refusing children access to Jesus), exclusive (stopping the strange exorcist), vindictive (wanting to call fire from heaven) and had misplaced joy (in subduing demons).

While agreeing with the judgement concerning their immaturity, O'Toole makes a case for Luke's portraying them as more than ignorant failures. He notes that Luke frequently omits or modifies unfavourable perspectives on their behaviour in the Marcan record. He does not blame them for their lack of understanding but shields them by explaining or softening the culpability. Peter also appears in a much more favourable light in Luke than the other Synoptics.[94]

Jesus was seeking to enable his disciples to develop to maturity and to learn to think for themselves. They had the potential to develop into "good soil" by hearing the word of God, holding it fast and bearing fruit (8:5-15). The two disciples on the road to Emmaus were reminded that Jesus' teaching was built on the truth already revealed in part through the writings of Moses and the prophets, but it was not immediately obvious. On their own they were foolish and slow of heart to believe (24:25).

Enlightenment came with Jesus' presence after the resurrection. The women "remembered". The eyes of the two on the road to Emmaus "were opened". He appeared to the disciples in Jerusalem and "he opened their minds" (24:8,31,45). Before they could preach the message of repentance and forgiveness of sins, they had to understand it from the Scriptures and then in their own experience. Jesus then declared them to be witnesses. In effect, Jesus was declaring them to be spiritually mature.[95]

In his portrayal of the disciples Luke patiently allowed them to move from immaturity to maturity. When they received the full revelation of Jesus as resurrected Lord all that had previously been unclear came into focus and they saw and believed. They became the eyewitnesses of "the events that have been fulfilled among us" (1:1,2, see also 24:48).

Conclusions and re-examination of working definition

It seems clear that in this Gospel and the other Synoptics both men and women were significant members of the discipling community around Jesus. Though the number of disciples in Luke seems to be larger the same commitment to learning, remembering and maturing in understanding was expected. Some disciples were called, others responded to Jesus' work in their life. Some left all to follow, others offered hospitality or used what possessions they had to generously support his work.

The close personal relationships which Jesus developed with his male and female followers were obvious. Without any hint of sexual impropriety Jesus sustained a wonderful family love and loyalty with people of all ages. He mixed easily with them and showed deep understanding of them. He accepted women as full members of the community and received their ministry to him as he taught and served them. Possibly only the apostles were present with Jesus for the full time of his public ministry, but provided others were hearers and doers of the word of God, their membership of the disciple band seems assured.

Jesus engaged in formal teaching practices with his disciples and the crowds, but he also structured learning situations for them within the community and as they shared in his ministry to others. As he announced his mission of deliverance, healing and proclamation of the good news, his followers also became involved in service modelled on his. They responded to what limited understanding they had and in doing so progressed to greater. By committing themselves to him they experienced more of his power and understood more of his teaching as he revealed the secrets of the kingdom.

All were expected to be witnesses to what Jesus did in their lives and to what they knew of him. When he sent them out on mission they proclaimed the kingdom of God, and exercised the power which he had given them for the healing of diseases and exorcism of evil spirits. If women disciples went out on mission they would have done so in a manner appropriate for their culture. The cycle of action and reflection, between partners and in the community as a whole, with Jesus was important in enabling further learning.

After the resurrection his disciples finally remembered his previous teaching and understood. All the different strands of his teaching came together. Only then did Jesus announce to them, "You are witnesses of these things." They could only perform that task competently when they understood the full picture and after God gave his promised Holy Spirit to empower their work (24:48,49).

From this study of Luke's Gospel the conclusions reached in the other Synoptic Gospels are reinforced. Discipling relationships between Jesus and one other individual are not strongly supported but the other elements of our working definition are clearly maintained and the additions which we have suggested after examining the other Gospels are sustained.

Luke includes women as full members of the discipling community. Within the text there is no implicit restriction on their learning or their service, although there may be some practices considered inappropriate to a culture which placed limitations on them, as indeed it did on men also!

It seems that within the Synoptic Gospels there is a remarkable consistency which we have discovered in the discipling methods used by Jesus. Although some minor differences have been observed between the writers in their portrayal of the discipling model, no contradictions have occurred and the overall picture has been strengthened rather than weakened.

Notes to Chapter Five

1. Bruce, 1960, 31
2. This is usually designated as coming from the Q source (German *Quelle*, source), a hypothetical document widely regarded as underlying the common materials which Matthew and Luke share. (Guthrie, 1970, 130)
3. Bruce, 1960, 31
4. Both theological and cultural reasons have been given. First because "the twelve apostles symbolised the formation of a restored people of God, the true Israel" they should be males to replicate Israel's twelve patriarchs. Second because the witness of women was considered to be culturally unacceptable they would be unable to fulfil the primary apostolic role of witnessing to the life, death and resurrection of Jesus (Giles, 1985, 49-50). This second reason appears slightly incongruous in the light of their place in the narratives of Jesus' death, burial and resurrection.
5. Mary Magdalene, Joanna and Susanna (8:2,3), Mary Magdalene, Joanna and Mary the mother of James (24:10). See also Mk. 15:40; 16:1; Mt. 27:56.
6. Mary Magdalene is the only woman whose name appears in all four Gospels (Mt. 27:56,61; 28:1; Mk. 15:40; 16:1,[9]; Lk. 8:2; 24:10; Jn. 19:25; 20:1,10-18). The mother of Jesus is also mentioned by all four but John does not name her. The prominence of Mary Magdalene has led to the assumption that her position was that of leader among the women, in a similar position to Peter among the men.
7. Hengel has noted a tendency to group women's names into threes as with the three male disciples closest to Jesus. (Hengel as cited in Fiorenza, 1988, 139)
8. Grundmann as cited in Marshall, 1978, 316
9. (Robinson, J.A.T., 1984, 413-430) John Wenham also presents supporting evidence for close family relationships among Jesus' followers. He suggests Salome was sister of Mary, the mother of Jesus, and wife of Zebedee, which makes the disciples James and John first cousins to Jesus. He also posits that Alphaeus/Clopas/Cleopas was brother to Mary's husband Joseph, husband of the other Mary and father of James the Less and Joses. (Wenham, 1984, 34-42)
10. Mk. 15:40,41; Mt. 27:55
11. Mark 3:14 includes "to be with him" as an apostolic responsibility.
12. Aland, 1978, 12
13. Karris, 1994, 10; Ricci, 1994, 58,61
14. Jeremias, 1969, 363
15. "If a man gives his daughter a knowledge of the Law it is as though he taught her lechery." "Better to burn the Torah than to teach it to women." Rabbi Eliezer (c.90 CE) as cited in Jeremias, 1969, 373.
16. Jeremias, 1969, 360

17 O'Toole, 1984, 120; Marshall, 1978, 450-1; Tannehill, 1986, 136
18 D'Angelo, 1990, 448
19 Maria Co as cited in Karris, 1994, 10
20 Beyer, 1964, 81
21 The textual variant *autō* (to him) has equal manuscript support, but the majority of scholars prefer *autois* (to them). Metzger prefers *autois* concluding that *autō* is "a Christological heightening". (Metzger as cited in Marshall, 1978, 317.) Karris believes *autois* is likely to have been changed from *autō* in the light of the experience of Christian community. (Karris, 1994, 6)
22 Witherington is quoted as saying, only "the well-to-do women underwrote the expenses of the group". Of the rest he wrote, "some of these women could give only their time and talents, perhaps in making meals or clothes." (Witherington as cited in Sim, 1989, 56.) Sim comments that the men usually accepted responsibility for preparation, distribution and blessing of food (9:10-17; 22:8-13,17-20; 24:30). (Sim, 1989,58)
23 *Huparchonta* can also mean property, possessions, means, resources at one's disposal. (Arndt & Gingrich, 1957, 845)
24 In New Testament times Jewish women were not all free to possess or dispose of resources at will. What was acceptable depended on marital status. (i) If married women brought possessions into the marriage, they were unable to dispose of them without the husband's permission. If they left the marriage their goods stayed with the husband. (ii) Single women, unless they were minors and were under their fathers, were free to inherit and dispose of goods as they wished, if they had no brothers. The practice would however, be regarded with extreme disapproval by society at large. (iii) Widows had some economic independence, but could not inherit directly from husbands. They were entitled to be maintained by their husband's estate. They also regained control over their own possessions. (iv) Divorcees had the right of dispossession over their own goods and had some entitlement from their husbands unless they were put away for serious transgression etc. (v) Former prostitutes did have personal and financial independence. (Sim, 1989, 54)
25 Witherington, 1984, 126
26 Noted by Davies, 1991, 186
27 Davies, 1991, 190
28 Fiorenza as cited in Koperski, 1999, 522
29 Fiorenza as cited in D'Angelo, 1990, 455
30 Koperski, 1999, 523
31 Fee & Stuart, 1982, 16
32 Reinhartz in Koperski, 1999, 528; Seim recognises problems implicit in Fiorenza's assumptions concerning technical usage of *diakon*-terms. (Seim in Koperski, 1999, 531)
33 Sim, 1989, 53
34 The presence of various mothers of disciples in the disciple band may have been possible because the usual age for marriage of girls was between 13 and 14 years, while husbands were considerably older. If the sons were about Jesus' age then these women may have been widows, or past child-bearing age and therefore freer to travel with their sons as they followed Jesus. (Jeremias, 1969, 365-368)
35 The wives of the apostles, Jesus' brothers and Cephas were known to travel with their husbands, as the missionaries of the early church went out with the gospel (1 Cor 9:5). See also Witherington as cited in Sim, 1989, 62.
36 "Eastern women take no part in public life… A woman who conversed with everyone in the street could… be divorced without the payment prescribed in the marriage settle-

ment." (Jeremias, 1969, 359,360)
37 They were probably Jesus' male friends or relatives.
38 The participles *sunakolousai* (accompanying) and *horōsai* (seeing) are both feminine plural, which means Luke emphasises that the women were the key witnesses. Some have suggested that *pantes hoi gnōstoi autō* (all those who knew him) was added later to a feminine tradition, but no textual evidence exists.
39 Witherington, 1984, 123
40 Mary the mother of James, is inserted in place of Susanna from the 8:1-3 list.
41 Karris, 1994, 15
42 Jeremias, 1969, 374,375
43 Dillon expresses surprise at their unbelief in spite of the facts being given to those most intimately related to Jesus' life and ministry, by women who had participated fully in Jesus' ministry. (Dillon, 1978, 58)
44 Ricci, 1994, 128
45 Was Luke catering for male prejudice, by ensuring the witness of the women was not the only evidence for belief in the resurrection? The witness of women bore very little weight. Josephus wrote, "Put not trust in a single witness, but let there be three or at least two whose evidence shall be accredited by their past lives. From women let no evidence be accepted because of the levity and temerity of their sex" (Antiquities 4.8.15). However a study of the status of women in the Mishnah, lists cases in which their witness was acceptable. These include virginity, when she is sole witness to a man's death, and some property cases. "In accepting a woman's testimony or making her swear an oath, the sages implicitly equate her with a man, for they assume she possesses similar qualities of rational thought and moral choice – two important qualities of personhood." (Wegner as cited in Karris, 1994, 18)
46 Aland, 1978, 172
47 Flender, 1967, 25
48 The life of Judas demonstrated that though he heard the word, it did not bear fruit. Luke passes over his betrayal very briefly in this Gospel (22:47,48) but gives more attention to Judas in Acts 1:16-20.
49 v. 44 Some important manuscripts have *Galilaias* (Galilee) or *tōn Ioudaiōn* (translated as "the land of the Jews").
50 Longenecker, 1975, 70
51 Droge as cited in Butts, 1987, 201
52 It is unclear exactly what he would have meant by use of *kurie* (lord). Marshall comments that the term "presumably has a deeper meaning than *epistata* (Classical Greek: term of respect used for officials. In Luke it appears 6 times as a title addressed to Jesus, nearly always by the disciples) "and is not simply equivalent to 'Sir'". (Marshall, 1978, 204)
53 Marshall, 1978, 205
54 Nu. 31:15,18; Dt. 20:16 etc. Luke has taken away the negative implications of Mark's phrase *aleeis anthrōpōn* (fishers of men) and turned Jesus' call into a positive influence in the lives of those encountered. (Marshall, 1978, 205)
55 Matthew & Mark use *eiden* (saw).
56 Marshall comments that it was likely he first tied up his business matters. (Marshall, 1978, 219)
57 For discussion of lists of names of the Twelve and variations between the Gospels see Marshall, 1978, 239-241.
58 Occurrences in the Gospels: Lk. 6:13; 9:10; 11:49; 17:5; 22:14; 24:10; Mt. 10:2; Mk.

3:14; 6:30; Jn 13:16.
59 See discussion of meaning in Rengstorf, 1964, 424-30.
60 Wilkins, 1992, 113
61 These passages come within a section of Luke containing six healings and three exorcisms (4:14 –9:50). Faith is linked to healing (7:1-10; 4:16-30). (Ricci, 1994, 125)
62 Wilkins, 1992, 215
63 Flender, 1967, 25
64 Seccombe, 1986, 14
65 In omitting 'husband' from the people to be 'hated', "Luke presents the only textual basis for assuming that the Jesus movement was a charismatic movement of wandering men, sons and husbands". (Fiorenza as cited in Ryan, 1985, 56.)
66 Davies supports his belief by showing that divorce was permitted, but remarriage forbidden (16:18). (Davies, 1991, 187)
67 D'Angelo, 1990, 456
68 Ricci, 1994, 112
69 Jeremias, 1969, 376
70 The 'journey' motif is a feature of Luke.
71 Luke omits Jesus' reprimand of Peter after his passion prediction when Peter tried to stop him (Mk. 8:32,33; Mt. 16:22,23). Luke transposes the fear of Peter, James and John at the Transfiguration to when they entered the cloud, so that their fear is more closely connected to the high point of the story, and lessens the attention given to Peter's not knowing what to say (9:28-36). (O'Toole, 1987, 83)
72 Rengstorf, 1964, 447
73 Wagner suggests that the maximum number of persons able to relate to one another in fellowship is 250, and recommends a lower number for most modern church congregations to ensure meaningful relationships. (Wagner, 1976, 105)
74 Ryan, 1985, 57
75 Fiorenza, 1983, 147
76 Also in Mt. 21:1
77 Luke records them at their call (5:3-11), in Jairus' home (8:51) and at the Transfiguration (9:28).
78 Luke contains 1149 verses. 499 verses contain the words of Jesus' teaching heard by the disciples who were constantly with him. 187 verses are addressed to the disciples alone, 212 to the crowds, 78 to teachers of the law, Pharisees or Sadducees, 15 to individuals and 7 are uncertain.
79 It is likely at this time that there was a lectionary for the reading of the Law but the reading of the Prophets may have been the choice of the reader himself. (Edersheim, 1886, 444,448)
80 Much of the material in Matthew's Sermon on the Mount (Matt 5-7) is paralleled in Luke's Sermon on the Plain (Luke 6:17-49).
81 Stein, 1978, 42-43; Snodgrass, 1992, 594
82 Only after Peter identified Jesus as Messiah were they able to receive teaching concerning his death and resurrection.
83 Jesus prayed at his baptism (3:21); before he chose the Twelve (6:12); before questioning the disciples about his identity (9:18); at the Transfiguration (9:28); on the Mount of Olives before his arrest (22:39-46); and on the cross (23:34,46).
84 O'Toole, 1984, 201
85 Marshall, 1978, 862

86 Bailey, 1976, 49-75
87 Manson, 1931, 239
88 "Many good manuscripts read seventy, as NRSV, but there are many also which read 'seventy two' as in the margin. With the evidence at our disposal certainty is impossible (though I think 'seventy two' is slightly more likely)." (Morris, 1974, 181)
89 Rengstorf, 1964, 415
90 Rengstorf, 1964, 417
91 Rengstorf, 1964, 419
92 The large catch of fish (5:4-11), calming the storm (8:22-25), feeding the five thousand (9:10-17) are nature miracles which provide further demonstration of Jesus' true identity.
93 Kingsbury, 1991, 19-20
94 Omitted or modified from Mark: No record of (1) Jesus' rebuke of Peter at Caesarea Philippi Mk. 8:33; (2) disciples not understanding parables Mk. 4:13; (3) disciples' fear in storm Mk. 4:40; (4) apparent disrespect in presence of haemorrhaging woman; (5) discussion about 'rising from the dead' Mk. 9:10; (6) inability to heal boy with evil spirit Mk. 9:18; (7) disciples following although afraid Mk. 10:32; (8) James and John's request concerning positions in kingdom Mk. 10:37; (9) Jesus' request to pray so as not to be tempted Mk. 14:38; (10) Jesus finding them asleep a second and third time Mk. 14:40,41; (11) disciples fleeing from Gethsemane Mk. 14:50.

Explanations or additions to soften apparent failures: They were sleepy 9:32; It was hidden from them 9:45; 18:34; Jesus defended them against Pharisees' criticism 19:40; They followed Jesus to Gethsemane 22;39-46; Were sleeping from sorrow 22:45; Watched crucifixion from afar 23:49.

Peter: Denial introduced earlier in passion narrative than in other Synoptics; No record of Peter cursing or swearing; Jesus is not mentioned by name during denial scene although he is called 'Lord' 22:54-62. Jesus' prayer for Peter is included and he is given the role of strengthening other disciples 22:31,32. (O'Toole, 1984, 178-180)
95 Kingsbury, 1991, 136

Chapter 6

Discipling in John's Gospel

The word *mathētēs* (disciple) occurs 78 times in John's Gospel. This is more than in any other New Testament book.[1] However John uses the term to describe a slightly different group of people from the synoptists. Among the varied groups John refers to as 'disciples' are a 'devil', many who rejected Jesus and some who later tried to kill him, at least one who was afraid to acknowledge him openly, another whose faith was weak and who needed visible proof in order to believe, a group who denied Jesus or were absent when he was on the cross, and those who had faith and remained faithful no matter what the cost. Thus at the outset it will be necessary to examine these people in the light of the working definition established in Chapter One. Then it will be possible to assess whether their lives meet the criteria we have established for genuine discipleship.

A second matter to be addressed concerns the people in this Gospel who are not designated as disciples but who seem to have some kind of close, learning relationship with Jesus. Their lives will also be examined in the light of our working definition to determine if their relationships with Jesus have a discipling intention. Finally, having determined which relationships display the concept of discipleship, we will be able to examine the discipling methods which Jesus used.

Evidence of Jesus' discipling relationships in this Gospel will be compared with the working definition already established. Thus voluntary commitment to learning from another, close personal relationships between teacher and learner and the presence of a discipling community will be explored. Elements of the model of discipling which Jesus used as portrayed by John's Gospel, will be distilled and any additional characteristics will be noted. Finally, we will return to the definition to assess whether this Gospel has any new light to shed on the practice of discipling or its processes.

Distinguishing between term and concept of 'disciple'

For the purposes of this study we are more interested in those people around Jesus to whom the concept of discipleship applies, than in those who were designated by the term 'disciple' but did not embody the concept in their lives.

First, we turn to the Twelve. In the Synoptics they were the inner core of disciples and although Judas finally showed that his discipleship was not genuine the others, despite their failure, remained his followers. In contrast John rarely mentions the Twelve as a group (6:67,70,71; 20:24,25). He includes Peter's denial and reinstatement, but there is no reference to their desertion after Jesus' arrest. All except Judas were faithful. John does not list their names although six (possibly seven) of the Twelve are mentioned.[2] And he continually introduces other people into the inner circle around Jesus thus minimising the emphasis on the Twelve.

Second, there was a wider group of disciples who were committed to Jesus, saw his miraculous signs (2:11; 6:2), joined him in his travels in Judea, Samaria or Galilee (3:22; 4;27; 6:16,19; 11:7,54) and participated in his ministry (6:5-13). Their attachment to Jesus had a learning dimension because John comments on their level of understanding (12:16; 16:17,29) and records their questions (9:2). Their presence probably corresponds to the Seventy mentioned in Luke, and Mark's wider circle. They displayed the characteristics Jesus required as distinguishing marks of genuine disciples – obeying Jesus' teaching (8:31), bearing lasting fruit (15:8,16) and sustaining loving relationships with Jesus and fellow disciples (13:35).

At the crucifixion, burial and resurrection John enables the reader to observe a widening of the inner circle of disciples. These included Jesus' mother and aunt, other women and the Beloved Disciple (19:25-27) who were near the cross, and Joseph of Arimathea and Nicodemus who performed the hurried burial (19:25-27,38-42).

A third and much larger group was also designated disciples. To them, Jesus professed to have come down from heaven, to have a special relationship with the Father, and to be able to give eternal life to those who ate his flesh and drank his blood (6:32-58). He was referring to the vicarious nature of his sacrificial death and his significance as the heavenly Son of Man. This large group had followed Jesus for a time but as his message became clearer they began to complain and finally they completely rejected him (6:60-69). They found his words *skleros* (hard, offensive). It is difficult for the reader to see how these 'disciples' differ from the crowds who listened to Jesus' teachings in the Synoptics.

Schnackenburg comments, "Whenever the disciples are mentioned by the evangelist, it is their faith that is the important issue".[3] In John, true faith in Jesus is necessary for genuine disciples (6:35,37,45),[4] so the departure of this larger group highlights the need for an agreed body of shared beliefs between 'discipler' and disciple. If this is not so, then a discipling relationship is scarcely possible.

Some of those who left were probably among the group of former 'believers' who looked for an opportunity to kill Jesus (8:31,37). Such was their rejection of Jesus and his teaching. Though this may appear shocking, it is similar to the action of Judas Iscariot who betrayed Jesus (18:2-5), even though he was one of the Twelve.[5] He no longer believed and was willing to endanger the life of Jesus for his own financial gain.

It is possible that this large group was attracted to Jesus by his miraculous deeds (7:3-5). While they came to 'believe', their faith did not endure. However lasting faith needed to be based on more than the sensational. Morris comments, "While such faith is better than none it is not the deepest faith".[6] John believed that Jesus "would not entrust himself to them, for he knew all" (2:24). He knew they were not those to whom his cause could be entrusted. They were not fully committed nor did they possess abiding faith (15:6) or bear the marks of genuine disciples. Thus while the term 'disciple' was used of them, their lives did not embody the concept of discipleship and we will discard them from our study.

Fourth, John informs us of a number of people whom he does not designate 'disciples' but who had close, personal learning encounters with Jesus. These people include Jesus' mother Mary, Nicodemus, the woman of Samaria, the man born blind, Mary, Martha and Lazarus, and Mary Magdalene.

In our working definition 'discipling' requires commitment to a personal relationship. Such a relationship requires more than one meeting as it is only built up over a period of time. Thus while the woman of Samaria (4:7-39)[7] and the man born blind (9:1-38) came to faith in Jesus and learnt from him there is no evidence of any continuing contact, so we will not include them in this study.

It is difficult to determine the status of Nicodemus, but the three incidents recorded by John concerning him, relate his willingness to learn from Jesus (3:1-12), his defence of Jesus' cause before the chief priests and Pharisees (7:45-52) and his performance of the disciple's task of burial of the master (19:38-42). Thus his commitment to Jesus continued over a period of time, learning was involved and in the end he seems to have become a functioning part of the discipling community. Those who conclude he was a disciple allow for the possibility of his weakness in remaining secret about his commitment prior to the crucifixion, in a way similar to Joseph of Arimathea.[8] Earlier in this study we suggested that all those, except public figures, whose names appear in the text were possibly members of the early church to whom the Gospels were addressed. The fact of his name being recorded here may be evidence for his discipleship.[9]

Jesus' mother, Martha, Mary and Lazarus[10] and Mary Magdalene all had loving relationships with Jesus over an extended period of time. They were committed to him, obeyed his teaching and in this Gospel are portrayed as part of the close discipling community around Jesus.

To summarize, in examining Jesus' discipling model in John's Gospel we will only use those relationships which embody the concept of discipleship, irrespective of whether the term 'disciple' is applied to them or not. We will draw on materials which include the Twelve, the wider unnamed group of disciples who remained committed to him, his mother, Martha, Mary and Lazarus and Mary Magdalene and the special case of the Beloved Disciple.

The discipling relationship

A voluntary commitment to learn from another

John records five men who began to follow Jesus early in his ministry (1:35-51). Andrew and an unnamed disciple came as a result of the testimony of John the Baptist. Simon Peter and Nathanael came because their brother or friend told them. Each, discovering Jesus, shared his findings with others. Philip was the only one recorded whose call came directly from Jesus (1:43). However Jesus clearly made a choice of all his followers (6:70; 13:18; 15:16). Each one he regarded as entrusted to him by the Father (17:6,9). This element of mutual choice is a necessary component in the formation of all discipling relationships. Both 'discipler' and disciple must voluntarily commit themselves to each other.

Jesus' encounter with this early group of disciples shows a pattern in his discipling.[11] Collins proposes that discipleship begins when witness is borne to Jesus and four actions follow. These are indicated by the verbs, to follow, seek, stay and see (1:35-40).

After hearing John's testimony to Jesus, two of his disciples changed their allegiance and began to follow Jesus. Their following was evidence of the deeper relationship with Jesus which they desired. In our work on the Synoptics we established that the verb *akoloutheō* (follow) is synonymous with discipleship. Jesus frequently used it to describe the life to which he called his hearers (1:43; 8:12; 10:4,27; 12:26; 21:19,20,22). Jesus then asked them, "What are you looking for?" To seek/look for (*zēteō*) is a common motif in this Gospel. It describes the quest of disciples to learn from and about the master.[12] They responded by asking Jesus, "Where are you staying?" To stay/permanently abide (*meneō*) is another Johannine motif and is used to describe committed relationships within the Godhead and between the believer/disciple and Jesus.[13] Finally Jesus invited them to "Come and you will see" (from *horaō* see and understand). When they accepted Jesus' invitation their discipleship and search for understanding began. Collins summarizes, the "...disciple is the one to whom testimony about Jesus has been made, and so he enters into dialogue with Jesus. He addresses Jesus with a faith that is as yet superficial (*Rabbi*) but which will grow to greater fullness by interacting with Jesus. He finally appreciates where Jesus abides and comes to abide with him."[14] They were the foundation members of a quickly growing community of believers committed to remaining with Jesus, living and learning together.

An essential component in any discipling relationship is the learning intention. This is clearly evident in John. Those who followed Jesus are recorded as frequently addressing him as, *Rabbi* or *Rabbouni* (Hebrew for 'teacher', 1:38,49;

4:31; 9:2; 11:8; 20:16). Their relationship with him was in many ways typical of other discipling associations. They spent time with him (3:22; 2:12), listened to his teaching and fulfilled the duties of students towards their master. They bought food for him (4:8,31-33), baptized (4:2), and assisted him with ministry to the crowds (6:5-13). They strongly identified with him even though they did not always understand (4:27,33; 12:16; 16:17).

After the large numbers defected, Jesus questioned the Twelve concerning their commitment to him. Peter's response of behalf of them all was a strong confessional statement. "We have believed (*pepisteukamen*) and have known (*egnōskamen*) that you are the Holy One of God."[15] Their commitment was considered and total. They knew that there was no one else to whom they could go. He was the bringer of "words of eternal life" (6:67-69).

John is kinder than the synoptists in his portrayal of those who were committed to Jesus. He does not dwell on their failures. Opposition from the Jews and the possibility of persecution or death did not appear to daunt them. Thomas voiced their sentiments as they set out for Jerusalem. "Let us also go, that we may die with him." (11:16) John does not record their forsaking Jesus in the garden, but shows Jesus negotiating to allow their freedom (18:8,9). And although the high priest may have been concerned that they were a threat (18:19), in the end only the Beloved Disciple and some women were present at the crucifixion (19:25,26).

Yet despite their commitment they misunderstood Jesus' mission. In the garden Peter attempted to defend his master (18;10,11). Later he denied him three times (18:15-18,25-27). Luthi calls his denial "the death of discipleship".[16] But he did not desert the cause. Later, beside the sea he reaffirmed his commitment and received the commission to care for Jesus' flock (21:15-22).

Genuine disciples freely committed themselves to him even at the expense of their own personal safety. They accepted his teaching and believed in its truth (16:29,30) because they knew his words conveyed eternal life. When they did not understand, Jesus used the opportunity for further teaching.[17] But it was only after the resurrection that the full light dawned.

A close personal relationship

Jesus called the disciples "my friends" (15:14,15), but he was never described as their friend. The relationship between Jesus and his disciples was not an equal, reciprocal one. He always remained the 'Teacher' and 'Lord' (13:13. See also 6:68; 11:32,34; 13:25; 20:2,25; 21:12,21). They would always be his disciples, no matter what their level of maturity. However, that was not to say that there was not a special kind of closeness which they enjoyed. The disciples are referred to as "his own" whom he loved to the end (13:1; 10:3).

More than the Synoptics, this Gospel gives greater insights into the close, personal relationships which Jesus enjoyed with his followers. John enables us to glimpse the love of Jesus in his gentle conversation with Martha (11:5), in his concern for Mary, "greatly disturbed in spirit and deeply moved" (11:33), and in his tears for Lazarus, "he whom you love" (11:3,35,36). We see his special resurrection appearance to Mary Magdalene in her grief (20:11-18). Jesus took the time to recommission Peter for his task of shepherding his flock, and reinstated him to his former position among the disciples which his denial may have threatened (18:15-18,25-27; 21:15-23). Jesus' love for his mother was clearly evidenced in his provision for her future security in the care of the Beloved Disciple (19:25-27). The Beloved Disciple was close to Jesus, although it is difficult to know who this enigmatic figure was (13:23-25; 19:25-27; 20:2-9; 21:7,20-24).[18] His appearance seems brief. He is only mentioned from the Last Supper to the end of the Gospel.

In his teaching, Jesus likened his relationship with his disciples to that of a shepherd with his sheep (10:1-18) and a vine with its branches (15:1-8). He finally demonstrated the full extent of his love by laying down his life for them. He emphasized the necessity for them to listen to his voice and to remain continually in touch with him so that they would lead productive and fulfilling lives.

Committed disciples enjoyed close, personal, loving relationships with Jesus. These were based, not on equality, but on Jesus' total commitment to them and his self-giving, shepherding love.

A new discipling community

The love which Jesus poured out for his sheep resulted in their concern for others, both within the flock and beyond. On occasion Jesus related to individuals on a one-to-one basis,[19] but the pictures he used to describe his relationships were collective images. They were branches on a vine (15:5), or sheep in a fold (10:1-18), or a community of believers centred on him and the Father. A triangle of loving relationships bound them all together (13:31-35; 14:20-23; 15:9-17; 16:27).[20] Community was an essential component of discipleship. The mark whereby others would know that they were his disciples was their love for one another which was modelled on the love which Jesus had for them.

In this Gospel not all those whose lives embodied the concept of discipleship with its communal emphasis left their homes and travelled with Jesus.[21] Mary, Martha and Lazarus never appear beyond Bethany. However this family frequently expressed community, even if it was only for short periods of time, by the hospitality which they extended to Jesus and his disciples (12:1-8, Lk. 10:38-42). They may have even offered accommodation to the group during the Passover Week prior to the crucifixion (Mk. 11:11; 14:3). It is evident that their closeness to Jesus was nurtured during these times of hospitality.

John has portrayed a significant block of Jesus' teaching (ch.13-17) occurring in the context of a communal fellowship meal (13:4). Some scholars hold that this 'last supper' may have included a group wider than the Twelve,[22] and there is nothing in John's account which precludes that, although the Synoptics appear to make the Twelve the focus (Mk. 14:17).[23]

Jesus expressed a concern that the discipling community which he established should continue after he had returned to the Father. He prayed for all his disciples, "those whom you gave me", that they might have the same unity as he enjoyed with the Father (17:9-11). He realized how easily community is destroyed and in his prayer requested that all those, who in future would believe in him, might experience that same unity among themselves (17:20-23).

Community is also maintained by love and concern for others in need, and attention to their pastoral care. The family was expected to assume this responsibility but Jesus extended it to all members of the discipling community. As Jesus provided for his mother's future in the care of his Beloved Disciple,[24] he expected members of the community to care for one another. After the resurrection he specially commissioned Peter to feed and tend his flock (21:15-17).

The community aspect of the discipling relationship is quite apparent in the resurrection narratives. Mary Magdalene and Peter shared the resurrection news with the community gathered behind locked doors. Peter and six others went fishing together and shared an early morning meal with Jesus (20:2,18,19,26; 21:1-14).

Thus the communal nature of relationships between Jesus and his disciples were expressed, not only by travelling together but through giving and receiving hospitality, sharing meals, pastoral care for those in need, prayer, sharing good and bad news and even an all night fishing trip. The love triangle, which was created by the love of the Father and the Son, encompassed the disciples as individuals and as a group. And as they experienced God's love they were able to display it towards others. That was the hallmark of all true disciples. However the prayer of Jesus warned that community might be easily disrupted. Disciples of Jesus must do as Jesus did, praying for and working towards encouraging the maintenance of a unity centred on him.

Shared belief

Discipling is a voluntary learning situation and therefore requires a basic body of shared belief agreed upon by disciple and 'discipler' in order for both parties to consider a learning relationship to be worthwhile. Andrew heard John the Baptist's testimony concerning Jesus and, after spending some time with him, came to the conclusion that he was "the Messiah" (1:35-41). Philip referred to him as "the one Moses wrote about in the Law and about whom the prophets also wrote", and Nathanael confessed him as "the Son of God", "the King of Israel" (1:43-51). Commentators[25] consider it unusual that these men made such bold assertions about Jesus at the very beginning of his public ministry, in contrast with Peter's much later confession in the Synoptics.[26] They could not fully understand the meaning of the titles until after the resurrection, but on the basis of their limited belief they committed themselves to a relationship with Jesus and confessed it to others. In response, Jesus revealed himself to them as the Son of Man who was the ladder-link between heaven and earth (1:51). He would reveal heavenly things and be the means by which God would bring salvation to the earth.[27]

In voluntary learning situations learner-adults continually assess whether it is worthwhile to persevere. New teachings are subjected to scrutiny and accepted or rejected according to their congruence with beliefs already held. If new beliefs are found to be incompatible, then the thinking learner must weigh them up and choose which has the greater validity. When they are found to be wanting, both the teaching and teacher will be rejected. Jesus' genuine disciples accepted his teachings. But we have already noted that there was a widespread disaffection midway through his public ministry. Large numbers of 'disciples' rejected Jesus' teachings and left (6:60-66). They no longer held a shared body of belief. Judas Iscariot demonstrated by his betrayal that he did not believe (6:70; 13:10,11,18-30; 18:1-5), nor did he hold to Jesus' teachings for he was a thief (12:6). His parting from Jesus was inevitable.

The discipling model

Formal teaching

Thirty six per cent of John's Gospel contains the direct words of Jesus' teaching.[28] This includes conversations with a teaching intention which he held with individuals (37 verses[29]), discourses or answers to questions delivered to the Jews, crowds or Pharisees (149 verses), and specific teaching directed to his disciples (132 verses[30]). As with the Synoptics, we may safely assume that the disciples who were with him also heard his words to the crowds. Thus the formal teaching they received was much more than that of the crowds.[31]

Jesus' conversation with the teacher (*didaskalos*), Nicodemus (3:1-21), was conducted using question and answers according to rabbinic tradition. His use of Old Testament typology in connecting the brass serpent in the wilderness with his death would have also been a method familiar to Nicodemus.[32]

The Upper Room discourses recorded in John 13:1-17:26 are probably a combination of various sayings of Jesus from a variety of contexts which were recounted by the early church when they met for the Lord's Supper.[33] They are strong evidence for Jesus' formal teaching of his disciples, although it is unlikely to have all been delivered on the one occasion as it appears in the text.[34] Jesus used his questions (14:9,10,38) and those of others[35] to promote thinking and assess their progress. They found it hard to grasp his origins or understand the ultimate purpose in his coming to earth (13:36; 14:5,8,22) and feared to ask more. However, aware of their problem, Jesus explained things further (16:17-22).

Jesus seemed surprised when his disciples took so long to learn and believe (16:31), but he realized that they would not grasp everything until after his death and resurrection. Only then would the full evidence be available (2:17,22) and the Holy Spirit would be with them to teach and guide (14:26; 16:13, 20:22).

Thus there is evidence here for Jesus' use of formal teaching methods although the settings were informal. In the upper room discourse Jesus took the initiative and taught according to his agenda, making informal assessment as he went along and adjusting his delivery accordingly.

Modelling

John's Gospel gives a greater insight than the Synoptics into the relationship between the Father and Son who provide a perfect model for the disciple's relationship with Jesus. This includes their "mutual love (3:35; 13:3; 15:10), an intimate union (8:29; 16:32; 17:5,21), a complete knowledge of one another (10:15) and a common purpose (5:19-21,26)."[36] As Jesus responded to the Father, the disciple is called to a close relationship of obedience, love and knowledge. As Jesus was sent by the Father, so disciples are sent by him (20:21).

In the Synoptics Jesus sometimes praised the faith of those he encountered or presented them as examples to be followed, but within the discipling community he did not make it a practice of praising one member to the others. Mary of Bethany is an exception. Jesus praised her because she listened attentively to his teaching rather than being distracted by domestic duties (Lk. 10:38-42). There seems to have been a growth in her understanding after her brother, Lazarus, was restored to life (11:28-32). Jesus praised her for a second time[37] when she demonstrated extraordinary spiritual perception by performing an extravagant act of devotion in anticipation of his death and burial (12:1-8).[38] Her action has been described as prophetic.[39] No other disciple displayed such insight into the future course of events. However not all recent scholars agree. Feminist scholars have questioned the traditional interpretation on the grounds that she appears as a passive character who never spoke or questioned and twice had to be defended by Jesus against others who criticized her devotion and desire to serve him.[40]

Readers of the Gospels have found other models of discipleship in John's pages, Jesus' mother, Martha and Lazarus, Mary Magdalene, Peter and the Beloved Disciple. Many scholars consider Mary, the mother of Jesus, as the paradigm disciple because she was willing to be obedient (2:1-5) and remained faithful to him until the end (19:25-27).[41]

Martha's confession, "I believe that you are the Messiah, the Son of God, the one coming into the world" (11:27), parallels Peter's confession of the Synoptics[42] and is seen by some as apostolic in nature.[43] She had obviously received much of Jesus' teaching[44] and, although she may not have completely understood her statement, her faith in Jesus' power which restored Lazarus is an example of her true discipleship (11:1-44). Lazarus has been described as "the type of the Christian disciple",[45] but the response of a corpse can hardly be compared with the obedient faith expected of disciples (11:41-44; 12:1-11).

A special feature of John's Gospel is the resurrection encounter of Mary Magdalene with the risen Lord (20:1,2,10-18),[46] and her commissioning to go to the disciples with Jesus' message.[47] In the New Testament the mark of an apostle was having seen the risen Lord (1 Cor. 9:1). Augustine referred to her as "*apostola apostolorum*" (apostle of [to] the apostles) because she saw the Lord and carried the message entrusted to her to the others.[48] Moloney sees within the narrative evidence of development in her faith. First she considered Jesus as "gardener", then "*Rabbouni*" and finally "Lord".[49] Her faith was transformed as she delivered the message in obedience to Jesus' command, "I have seen the Lord!" Mary also proved she belonged to Jesus in a special way when she recognized her "shepherd's voice" (10:3).

Simon Peter is another who has sometimes been seen as a paradigm disciple. John records his many conversations with Jesus and incidents in his discipleship (6:67-69; 20:3-9). When Simon was introduced to Jesus by his brother, Andrew, Jesus changed his name to *Cephas* (Peter) (1:40-42). Morris explains that when a new name is given by men it shows the authority of the person conferring it but when God renames someone it indicates the new characteristics which that person displays from that time on.[50] Thus Peter was coming under Jesus' authority, but his character was still in the process of developing throughout this Gospel. His growth in understanding through the foot washing incident seems minimal (13:6-10). In five of the six passages containing both Peter and the Beloved Disciple, Peter compares unfavourably. However he finally understood, and his preparation was finished when he met Jesus beside the sea (21:1-22). Jesus reinstated him as leader after the denial (13:36-38; 18:15-18,25-27), and commissioned him as shepherd to feed and care for his followers. He was then ready to follow Jesus into future leadership irrespective of the consequences.

The Beloved Disciple who only appears in John is described as "the disciple *par excellence.*"[51] His love and belief were exemplary.[52] He remained faithful when all the others failed. He was entrusted with the care of Jesus' mother (19:25-27). He was present at the supper (13:23-25), cross, empty tomb (20:2-9) and resurrection appearance by the sea. He possessed a unique ability to discern matters hidden from others (21:7) and a destiny different from Peter (21:20-24).[53] If he was "another disciple" then he also was present with Peter at Jesus' trial (18:15,16). Apart from that we know very little about him or his discipling relationship with Jesus. He does very little apart from appearing in "the dark moments of discipleship"[54] and being a dependable witness. Some see him in the position of leading disciple which Peter holds in the other Gospels. However Brown, Cullmann and others disagree, acknowledging that "they are given different roles: one superior in authority and the other superior in personal relationship to Jesus."[55]

The perfect model of life for all disciples is that shown in the relationship between Jesus and his Father. But there were others within the discipling community who, while nowhere perfect, provided examples of obedience, devotion and faithfulness. Some were examples of the transformation which Jesus worked in people's lives. They demonstrated the development of understanding and growth to maturity which is required of all genuine disciples.

Establishing a serving community

The different expressions of community in this Gospel have already been noted, but the serving nature of the discipling community is not very prominent. In John the disciples were predominantly observers, learners and receivers of the teachings of Jesus. They travelled with him (1:43; 4:3-5; 11:16), joined in social and family commitments with him (2:2) and provided assistance to him in his ministry (4:2,8,31; 6:5-13: 12:20-22).

Jesus taught that there was a harvest to be brought in, but there is no evidence in John that the disciples did anything about it (4:34-38). There is no record of the disciples on mission to Galilee or Judea. The action-reflection process of learning involved Jesus' action, not the disciples'.

However every indication was that the disciples would serve in the future. Jesus used the image of the vine to show that the discipling community was expected to bear lasting fruit (15:1-17). Fruit bearing was one of the authenticating marks of a committed relationship with Jesus. Those who failed to do so would be cut off from the vine and destroyed, and even the fruitful would be subject to pruning so that they might be more productive. Brown comments that "'bearing much fruit' and 'becoming my disciples' are not two different actions, but one is consequent on the other."[56]

It was only after they had received the full revelation of Jesus in the cross and resurrection that the disciples were sent out into the world in the same way as the Father had sent Jesus (20:21). Jesus gave them his Holy Spirit to enable them to proclaim forgiveness or judgement on the deeds of others within the discipling community (20:21-23). Peter was commissioned for his task of pastoral care, feeding and tending Jesus' flock (21:15-17). Others had their destiny to fulfil. The important thing was that they continued to follow their Lord further (21:22). Thus in John's Gospel the serving community would come into focus in the future.

Demonstration

This Gospel records some vivid demonstrations of Jesus' teaching. The seven signs illustrated different aspects of himself and his nature. The miracle of water into wine revealed his glory to his disciples (2:11). Both the healing the official's son and the paralytic at Bethesda were signs of Jesus' life-giving power (4:54; 5:1-9).[57] Feeding the five thousand showed him as Messianic deliverer and illustrated his teaching that he was the bread of life (6:1-15,22-58). Walking on the sea revealed Jesus "as the revelation of God coming to his disciples in distress" (6:16-21).[58] Giving sight to the man born blind illustrated that Jesus was the source of light of all humankind (9:1-41; 8:12).[59] The raising of Lazarus showed God's powerful and compassionate action through the Son. "The sovereignty of God is established in redemptive power for all humanity and the Spirit of the age to come is released for the world." (11:1-45)[60]

Jesus washed his disciples' feet in a deliberate, controversial act (13:1-20). On one level he was modelling servant leadership but within the act and the ensuing conversation was a second deeper level of teaching. The full significance of Jesus' action would be unintelligible to them until after his death. He was offering a superb demonstration of "the greater cleansing that he [is] about to achieve through his redemptive death, by which his disciples… [will] be granted not only remission of guilt, but a part with him in the eternal kingdom".[61] This was a participatory teaching activity to explain these difficult concepts.

The anointing of Jesus' feet by Mary of Bethany (12:1-8) was an act of amazing self-sacrifice[62] by a woman who more than any of the other disciples perceived something of the cost to Jesus of the gift of his life. Her act demonstrated self-sacrificial love, another picture of what Jesus would do on the cross. Matthew's Gospel explains what she had done would be remembered throughout the world wherever the gospel would be preached (Mt. 26:13).

John's Gospel and the Synoptics bear witness to the resurrection of Jesus as a life-changing event in the experience of the disciples and of central importance to the belief of the faith community (2:22; 20:29-31). They firmly held that it was the ultimate demonstration of the veracity of Jesus' claims and the authentication of all his teaching.

Jesus was well aware not only of the importance of teaching by his words, but of also demonstrating in concrete terms the abstract realities which he was seeking to convey. Not only was he showing his superb understanding of the content of his teaching but his insight into the capacities and understandings of his learners.

Pastoral care

Jesus displayed a deep love and gentle concern for his followers. Those who obeyed were his friends (15:14,15). He likened his role in caring for them to that of a good shepherd bringing his sheep to an abundant life (10:1-18). He bore with the weaknesses and inadequacies of those who followed him, while all the time seeking to strengthen their faith and belief, until they themselves reached a point of lasting commitment. The relationship they shared was deeply personal. He provided protection and food for their every need in order for them to enjoy abundant life. He even laid down his life for their salvation. Later Jesus used the shepherd imagery again to describe Peter's role in nurturing the faith community who were Jesus' lambs and sheep (21:15-17).

Jesus prayed for them that they would have his joy and be protected, sanctified and unified (17:6-19). He requested unity for them and for those who would come to faith through their message, so that the world would know where he had come from, and that they were loved by the Father.

The love which was intrinsic within the Godhead undergirded the deep relationship between Jesus and his disciples (14:21; 15:9-17). They were to love one another with the same love that Jesus had for them (13:34). He expressed his love by giving the Holy Spirit as counsellor and teacher forever (14:16-26; 16:7-15). The 'great climax of the Fourth Gospel' and the basis for the disciples' authority in ministry was his breathing on them and imparting the Spirit (20:22).[63]

Conclusions and re-examination of working definition

Not all those nominated as 'disciples' in John displayed the qualities of discipleship. However the record of the first five followers of Jesus clearly shows the intention of discipleship. It was to be a relationship in which Jesus and his followers devoted themselves each to the other in an exclusive commitment. These five came to Jesus seeking to learn from him, stayed with him and saw the truth behind his words demonstrated in his life and actions. True disciples joined in community with other learners, progressed to understand him and bore testimony concerning him to others.

Jesus sought to teach, nurture and increase the faith of those who were following him. Much of his teaching was delivered to the Jews (crowds or Pharisees) in his own defence but his disciples received additional specific teaching. His many miraculous signs displayed different aspects of his divine character and led those who believed to see "his glory, the glory of the one and only Son who came from the Father" (1:14). These were visible illustrations of his words of teaching. Those who saw the signs but disbelieved his authoritative words were not true disciples and eventually withdrew.

John's Gospel provides new insights and fresh information concerning the lives of some of Jesus' closest followers who were only briefly mentioned in the Synoptics. Our understanding of his close personal discipling relationships is thus enriched, and the concept of community is broadened to include the offering of hospitality from one's own home and the sharing of communal meals. Prayer and pastoral care for other community members is encouraged and the understanding that potential members are to be brought to the Shepherd is important.

The most outstanding contribution which John's Gospel makes to our understanding of the relationship between Jesus and his disciples is that their relationship is derived from and should be modelled on the relationship of the Father to the Son. Thus knowledge, understanding, common purpose, unity and love coming from the Father and the Son to all faithful disciples should permeate the whole discipling community, so that all share in it together and the work of Jesus is continued on earth through his people in the power of his Spirit.

Further facets of discipleship have emerged from our examination of John's Gospel. Discipling requires the development of a committed relationship over a period of time. It is valid to teach on a single occasion, but the encounter may only be described as 'discipling' if it continues for an extended period of time. There may be, however, a period of time in which a learner weighs up the validity of the teachings presented until the full extent of the teaching becomes known. If the new teaching is at variance with previously held beliefs, learners have only two choices, either to accept the new, or to reject it and the discipler whose teaching it is. Discipling requires that both parties hold to a shared body of basic beliefs.

The close personal relationship between teacher and disciple is not just an academic relationship. The teacher also cares for the physical, emotional and spiritual well being of learners within the discipling community by praying for them and offering appropriate pastoral care.

Discipling requires that both discipler and disciple be oriented to life beyond the discipling relationship. Disciples not only share in the work of the discipler, but the work itself becomes their work. The mission of the discipler becomes the focus of the life of the learner.

Notes to Chapter 6

1. Aland, 1978, 172
2. They were Andrew (6:8) and Simon Peter (1:40), Philip (6:5-7; 14:8) and Nathanael (1:43,45), Thomas (11:16; 14:5; 20:24-29), the other Judas (14:22) and Judas Iscariot (6:71; 12:4-6; 13:2,26-30; 18:2). There is some debate concerning the identity of Nathanael. He may have been another disciple outside the Twelve. Some identify him with the ideal disciple because his name means "God has given." Others believe Nathanael is another name for Matthew. Morris considers it a strong possibility that he is Bartholomew because of his association with Philip in all three Synoptics and the fact that Bartholomew is not a personal name. He almost certainly had another name. (Morris, 1971, 163-164)
3. Schnackenburg, 1982, 207
4. Quast, 1989, 46
5. Judas is described in John as a "devil" (6:70,71), "a thief" (12:6), not clean (13:10,11), under Satan's power (13:27) and "doomed to destruction" (17:12). In predicting his betrayal and offering him the sop, Jesus was probably causing him to rethink his actions but Judas would not (13:18-30). Culpepper describes him as the representative defector. (Culpepper, 1983, 124)
6. Morris, 1971, 206
7. The leaving of her water pot may be an indication of her discipleship because she left all to follow (4:28).
8. Pryor believes his understanding of Jesus was limited, and that in assisting in the burial "he displays no awareness of the future glory of the 'lifted up' Jesus". (Pryor, 1992, 20)
9. Pamment comments that in the Gospels individuals who are important witnesses are

Discipling in John's Gospel   93

always named, as are those whose relationship with Jesus develops. Evidence would also suggest that people known to the Christian community in later years (e.g. officials or members of the later church) were also named. (Pamment, 1983, 364)

10 By the use of their names and the statement that Jesus loved them the implication is that the three were his disciples. (Witherington, 1984, 108)

11 Collins, 1990, 48-54

12 The Hebrew word to seek (*darash*) can also mean 'to interpret' the Scriptures. Thus by seeking Jesus these disciples were actually seeking out the one to whom the Scriptures point and in whom they are fulfilled. He is the ultimate interpreter (6:31-33) and is addressed by these disciples as *"Rabbi"*. (Collins, 1990, 52)

13 1:32,33 The Spirit remains on Jesus; 12:34 the Christ remains forever; 14:10 the Father remains in Jesus and 15:10 he remains in the Father; 15:5-10 believers remain in Jesus and he in them.

14 Collins, 1990, 54

15 These two verbs are in the perfect tense which indicates a present state resulting from a past action. Morris paraphrases it as "We have come to a place of faith and continue there. We have entered into knowledge and retain it." (Morris, 1971, 390)

16 Luthi as cited in Maynard, 1984, 538

17 The misunderstanding of Jesus' disciples is a recurrent theme in this Gospel. They failed to comprehend his body as a temple (2:20-22), Jesus' true sustenance (4;32,33), the relationship between sin and suffering (9:2), the nature of death (11:7-16), fulfilled prophecy in the entry into Jerusalem (12:12-16). (Culpepper, 1983, 117)

18 Tradition has unanimously identified the Beloved Disciple with the Apostle John. Morris, Bailey, Bernard and Barclay believe "there seems no reason for doubting that it was the apostle John." (Morris, 1971, 625) However many modern scholars do not believe he was one of the Twelve: some believe he was the writer of this Gospel, but not the apostle; others, the unnamed disciple of John the Baptist (1:35-39) (Brown, 1966, 32); Lazarus (Eller, 1987, 334); A fictional, idealised figure to show what true discipleship should be (Davies, 1992, 341); A Jerusalem priest (Bultmann in Quast, 1989, 77); A Gentile (Pamment, 1983, 367)

19 His conversations with Nicodemus, Martha and Mary, Mary Magdalene and Peter all appear to be conducted on a one-to-one basis. Others may have been present but not as active participants.

20 The Holy Spirit was also closely involved among them as the Advocate given by the Father to abide in and with Jesus' disciples to teach and guide (14:16,17,26). Jesus would send him to his disciples to prove the world wrong about sin, righteousness and judgement and to take what belonged to Jesus and declare it to them (16:7-15).

21 Bruce, 1971, 18

22 Lee, 1993, 1-20

23 The problem of John's dating of this meal, in comparison with the Synoptics, becomes obvious here. John has Jesus crucified on the day of Preparation for the Passover (19:31). And thus according to the calendar by which John was operating this meal was not the Passover. That would seem to support the absence from this meal of the whole family including children, who had a special role to play in Passover celebrations.

24 On the basis of the mention of Jesus' aunt and the possible equating of her with Zebedee's wife and Salome, Robinson has suggested that if the Beloved Disciple was John, the son of Zebedee, then he was Jesus' cousin. (Robinson, 1984, 419,420,424)

25 Brown suggests "John has placed on their lips at this moment a synopsis of the gradual

increase of understanding that took place throughout the ministry of Jesus and after the resurrection." (Brown, 1966, 78) Morris explains that though they may have used these phrases as being the highest expressions open to them, they did not reach anything like adequate understanding until a much later date. [Morris, 1971, 160,168] Bultmann sees *su ei ho huios tou theou* (you are the Son of God) as an insertion by the writer (not necessarily Nathanael's actual words) and used with the other titles to bring out Jesus' importance. (Bultmann, 1971, 104,107)

26 "You are the Christ, the Son of the living God." (Mt. 16:16); "You are the Christ." (Mk. 8:29); "The Christ of God" (Lk. 9:20).
27 Morris, 1971, 171
28 Of John's 878 verses (including 7:53-8:11), 318 verses contain Jesus' words of teaching.
29 Nicodemus 17 verses, woman of Samaria 12, blind man 3, Martha 5
30 The high priestly prayer of Jesus (17:1-26) has been omitted from this number.
31 It is also interesting to note that the content of Jesus' teaching in this Gospel is totally different from the Synoptics.
32 Longenecker, 1975, 74,153
33 Beasley-Murray, 1987, 222
34 Morris quotes R.H. Lightfoot who draws attention to the fact that after 13:2 John "avoids mention of any particular place or time in connection with the events and instruction of chs.13 to 17, until 18:1 is reached." (Morris, 1971, 610)
35 Peter, Thomas, Philip, Judas
36 Giles, 1979, 67
37 John does not record Jesus' commendatory statement, "...wherever the gospel is preached in the whole world, what she has done will be told in memory of her." (Mk. 14:9; Mt. 26:13)
38 Schneiders, 1993, 138
39 Witherington, 1984, 124
40 Schaberg, 1992, 289; Brown, 1979, 195; Witherington, 1984, 119
41 Moloney, 1984, 86,90; Brown, 1966, 105; Brown, 1979, 195; Witherington, 1984, 119
42 This shows that "women are able to be fully fledged disciples of Jesus". (Witherington, 1984, 109)
43 In the early church to confess Christ in this way was considered the mark of an apostle. (Moltmann-Wendel, 1982, 25)
44 Evans, 1983, 150
45 Suggit, 1984, 106
46 Matthew and John record her as the first witness to the resurrection. Lk. 24:34 and 1 Cor. 15:5 record Peter as first.
47 A number of scholars comment on her being the primary witness to the resurrection in John's Gospel, in contrast to Peter in the writings of Paul and Luke. (Brown, 1979, 189; O'Collins & Kendall, 1987, 635; Schussler-Fiorenza as cited in O'Collins & Kendall, 1987, 640) Some see the juxtaposition of Peter and Mary in the resurrection narratives of John's Gospel, as acknowledging the witness of the women to be of equal and complementary validity with the men (disciples). (Perkins as cited in O'Collins & Kendall, 1987, 644)
48 Augustine as cited in Moltmann-Wendel, 1982, 64. See also Brown, 1979, 189
49 Moloney, 1984, 81
50 Morris, 1971, 160
51 Brown, 1979, 191

52 Culpepper sees similarities between the Beloved Disciple and the promised Paraclete. (Culpepper, 1983, 123)
53 Minear, 1977, 115
54 Neirynck, 1990, 336
55 Maynard, 1984, 546
56 Brown as cited in Bolt, 1992, 18
57 Beasley-Murray, 1987, 73
58 Beasley-Murray, 1987, 89
59 Beasley-Murray, 1987, 155
60 Beasley-Murray, 1987, 191 (See also 187)
61 Beasley-Murray, 1987, 234
62 The value of the perfume was estimated at three hundred denarii, a year's wages for a labourer.
63 Maynard, 1984, 538

Chapter 7

Conclusions and Provisional Expansion of Definition

In Chapter One we noted that this investigation is of the concept of discipling, not just those instances when the term 'discipling' is actually used. We adopted that strategy because it was anticipated that it would provide more diverse resources for us to investigate in order to develop a theoretical construct for discipling which was characteristically biblical. Using our working definition as a means of entering the Gospels we found that this undertaking enabled the common elements within both term and concept to be extracted, despite variations in terminology.

In the four preceding chapters we have used the Gospels to make an extensive study of the discipling processes which Jesus employed. These findings will be briefly summarized in table form. We are now in a position to draw some overall conclusions concerning the roles and expectations of disciples and of Jesus, the discipler. The discipling model which he used will be further clarified and the working definition proposed in Chapter One will be provisionally amended in the light of discoveries thus far. This has been necessary before moving on to consider discipling in the early faith communities, as portrayed in the book of Acts, the Epistles and the book of Revelation.

Finally I will make some personal reflections on the journey thus far.

The role of Jesus, the 'discipler'

Before proceeding further it seems in order to make some general comments about the role of 'discipler' which Jesus adopted. Jesus was widely recognized as a teacher of considerable note even though he lacked the rigorous formal training customary for the Jewish rabbis (Mk. 1:22; 6:2,3; 12:14; Jn. 7:15). Throughout his public ministry he was referred to as "teacher" (*didaskalos*) 45 times, "rabbi" 14 times[1] and "master" (*epistatēs*) six times.[2] The verb *didaskō* (teach) is frequently used referring to his activity. The Jewish historian, Josephus, later referred to him as "a teacher of such men as receive the truth with pleasure."[3]

We have already seen that in the ancient world many teachers adopted an itinerant lifestyle, speaking to assembled crowds in public and at the same time gathering around them groups of learners who stayed with them for a period of time. Jesus fulfilled both these roles, with the crowds and with his disciples. It is this second role which has formed the basis of our present study.

During the period of his public ministry in Galilee and Judea, Jesus devoted the majority of his efforts to three activities, healing and casting out demons, proclaiming the kingdom of God to the crowds and teaching his disciples. While Jesus never turned away anyone in need, he maintained a definite order of priorities. His proclamation of the good news of the kingdom of God took precedence over healing and exorcism (Mk. 1:38,39). There were many times when he was able to use the platform which his miracles provided to teach the crowds and his disciples the spiritual truths of the kingdom. But when the choice arose as to whom he would teach, we have already established that Jesus sought to devote the majority of his time to his disciples rather than the crowds. It was not that he did not care for the crowds. "He had compassion for them, because they were like sheep without a shepherd." (Mk. 6:34) But for the time of his ministry, discipling was the most important function which he performed. He was laying the foundations of leadership for the faith communities which would be established to take his message to the world.

From this premise we deduce that when Jesus was involved in his healing, exorcism and public teaching ministry he was also conscious of the presence of his disciples. His agenda for their learning was being furthered even when they were not directly regarded as the objects of his particular ministry at that time. Thus as they followed him, remained with him, observed his actions and interactions with others and heard his words, they were being discipled, even if it appeared to be indirectly. Therefore, to nearly everything which Jesus did in the presence of his disciples we have attributed a discipling intention.[4]

Teachers determined what was expected of their disciples according to their own teachings and philosophy of life. The word *mathētēs* was able to become a specialized term for Jesus' followers because the common usage was general enough to hold the specialized connotations the Christian community appended to it."[5] Jesus made particular, unique demands on his disciples. Once they understood and voluntarily accepted his terms there were no negotiations. He maintained full authority and his disciples accepted that or withdrew. His words carried the implicit claim that he had a right to be obeyed (Mt. 7:24; 24:35; Jn. 5:24; 6:63). This authority was derived from his claim to have a unique relationship with the Father (Jn. 12:49; 7:17; 17:8) and was not like that of the rabbis (Mk. 1:22; Mt. 7:28,29; Lk. 4:32). He reinterpreted the Jewish law and commandments making his directives equal with the Scriptures (Mt. 5:21-48).

While Jesus' authority was undisputed by his disciples, his relationships with them were not primarily authoritarian in character. He loved them, shared himself with them, and entrusted them with ministry responsibilities even though they sometimes failed. His disciples retained their individual freedom at all times. They were free to come or go. But those who stayed did so on his terms. Jesus was conscious of their frailty and accepted them as they were, while seeking to develop them further. He knew that Judas would betray him, that Peter would deny him and all the disciples would desert him, but Jesus did not exert his power to overrule their freedom to act as they chose.

Some of Jesus' actions and the discipling methods which he used were unique because they were directly related to his claim to be the Son of God. People could not replicate them. These included the delegation of his authority to the disciples so that they could continue his works of healing, exorcism and ministry; leading them into life-threatening situations in which they needed to put their trust in him; foretelling the future in order to prepare them for the devastating course of events associated with his crucifixion; imparting to them his Holy Spirit as teacher, counsellor, encourager; and giving his life for the forgiveness of sin and their salvation.

In addition to what has already been gleaned from our study of the individual Gospels there is much we can learn from the example of Jesus. He was able to communicate the knowledge of God through his own experience. Prayer was a vital sustaining reality. His awareness of his humanity and his understanding of his unique individuality enabled him to communicate to others with sympathetic understanding and gave him the skills required to maintain constructive, helping relationships.

Not only was Jesus aware of his own being and what was happening in his own life, but he must have shared some of those insights with those closest to him. The Gospel accounts of his temptations must have come directly from him (Mt. 4:1-11). His pattern of openness when he shared his feelings and innermost thoughts made him a role model for those who were closest to him.

His rare use of one-to-one encounters and his preference for relating to others in small groups or community settings circumvented the possibility of Jesus being accused of asserting inappropriate power over weaker individuals against their wills. Nor was there ever a hint by his accusers of any sexual impropriety. The disruption caused to his followers by his withdrawal after his death and resurrection was minimized because the small groups and the discipling community were able to continue. They provided a structure which would enable discipling to continue within the faith community. And the discipling communities in turn were able to welcome, nurture and incorporate into their life, people from all the nations who came to belief in him.

Expectations of disciples in the Gospels

Our study of the Gospels has shown that Jesus called his disciples to abandon their previous lifestyle, denying personal ambition, comfort and safety and, as his followers, to embark on a radically different life within the family of God. Those who were genuine made an informed decision to voluntarily commit themselves to hear and obey his words, and to put him and his kingdom first in their lives. They were primarily learners, who were expected to grow in their knowledge and understanding of God and his kingdom. This would not just be evidenced through academic cognisance but would result in growth in their faith relationship with God affecting their attitudes, values, qualities of character, behaviour and skills for continuing the works of Jesus.

They developed enduring, close, personal relationships with him and with one another in the discipling community. They received his love and nurture. They were learners, open to think and to seek for truth. Their itinerant lifestyle allowed opportunities for both individual and communal reflection as they encountered particular situations and experiences of life. By living with and relating closely to Jesus their learning was greatly enhanced as they observed and actively participated in his life and work. Finally, having received his authority and his Spirit they went out into the world as his faithful witnesses through word and deed. The findings from the Gospels have been briefly summarized and presented in Tables 1 and 2 (see pages 100 and 101).

Working definition revisited

Having examined the four Gospels in the light of our working definition, we are now in a position to further refine it. In Chapter One we proposed,

Discipling is a voluntary, personal relationship between two individuals in community or alone, in which the disciple commits him or herself to learn from the other, by imitation, oral communication and sharing in the life and work of the discipler.

This has provided a common method for analysing data in each of the Gospels, but also has exposed nuances peculiar to each Gospel which has the potential to refine the definition further. Thus we are ready to make some changes.

First, it has become necessary to add to the learning dimension of discipling the intention that learning will take place. Teachers are not always able to bring about learning in the life of pupils, but the intention to do so is sufficient for an action to be classified as teaching. The discipling relationships which Jesus formed in the Gospels had a strong learning intention, although with some, like Judas Iscariot, the results appear to have been limited. Jesus' primary role during his public ministry was that of teacher and, privately among his followers, his recorded words were almost always aimed at their instruction.

The Greek word, *mathētēs*, means a learner, pupil or disciple and is derived from the verb *manthanō* (learn). The Gospels usually referred to the group around Jesus as 'disciples'. This shows that their primary role was perceived to be that of learners. Jesus' teaching plan was to prepare them to "fish for people". The Twelve and others were to be with him, like apprentices learning his trade. They would become teachers, proclaimers and healers, but first they must know, understand and experience him and the kingdom. Immediately before his departure to the Father he commissioned them as teachers to make disciples of all nations. Therefore we have added the concept of 'an intentional learning activity' to our definition which becomes, *"Discipling is an intentional learning activity…"*.

TABLE 1: THE DISCIPLING RELATIONSHIP

MARK	MATTHEW	LUKE	JOHN
Who were the 'disciples'?			
The Twelve, women from Galilee, wider group of others.	The Twelve, later – many women and others (Joseph of Arimathea).	Large group (70+) including women, some were scarcely indistinguishable from the crowds.	'Word' includes a wide group, some who ultimately rejected Jesus. 'Concept' includes others not so nominated.
Characteristics of the relationship: Voluntary commitment to learn			
Jesus called disciples to learn to fish for people. Required them to be committed.	Fishermen disciples responded to Jesus as a resident of their town. Following involved commitment to him, having counted the cost before joining.	Jesus called disciples to unconditional commitment, obedience and perseverance, to be shepherds, carers, rescuers of God's people.	Disciples were to follow, seek, stay and see – to be fully committed. They addressed Jesus as teacher.
Characteristics of the relationship: Close personal relationship			
Jesus committed himself to his disciples, defended them against criticism. They were to "be with him", under his authority. They were not consistently faithful, but their relationship was not severed.	Jesus called followers to himself. There was never any expectation that his Lordship would be superseded.	Disciples accompanied Jesus on his travels. The ministry of the seventy was to be considered to be the same as his. No desertion is mentioned, disciples' failure is minimized.	Disciples were called friends of Jesus (his own), but not in an equal relationship. John gives glimpses into Jesus' discipling-type relationships with a number of different people.
Characteristics of the relationship: New discipling community			
Disciples left home, family and employment to be part of Jesus' travelling community – insiders (not outsiders).	Called into a community involving partnerships and subgroups of family and others with spiritual insight.	Were members of a community with Jesus as central authority figure. Shared table fellowship, but not exclusively (tax collectors and sinners also welcomed).	Relationships between persons of Godhead pattern for disciples. Disciples referred to by collective images (flock, vine). Hospitality and table fellowship important.
Characteristics of the relationship: Shared belief			
n/a	n/a	n/a	Genuine disciples assessed and accepted Jesus' teachings. Others rejected and left.

TABLE 2: THE DISCIPLING MODEL

MARK	MATTHEW	LUKE	JOHN
Formal teaching			
Most of Jesus' teaching was informal, resulting from questions or criticisms.	Five great teaching discourses. Jesus taught for understanding, not indoctrination.	Jesus taught the disciples alone and when he was addressing others they also heard.	Jesus taught through conversations with individuals and lengthy discourses (upper room etc).
Modelling			
Jesus modelled suffering servanthood and respect for children.	Jesus modelled the "life of the blessed", servanthood, meekness and childlike faith.	Jesus modelled how to overcome temptation, the life of prayer.	The Jesus/Father relationship models the disciple/Jesus relationship. Other models also show true discipleship.
Establishing a serving community			
Jesus served his disciples, who served together, sometimes inappropriately. 'Serve' is only used of women and Jesus.	Disciples left security of the familiar to join God's family where love, care and forgiveness operated.	Discipling community existed for ministry first to Israel and later as a light to the Gentiles.	Serving nature of discipling community is not prominent.
Action and reflection			
Disciples equipped for action by Jesus. Observed first, then sent out to preach and exorcize – a collaborative activity. Took time to reflect and report back on experiences.	Jesus sent disciples out to serve, fish and harvest. He used challenging situations to develop their faith. Their failures led to further teaching/learning.	Disciples called to catch people by preaching, proclaiming, healing & releasing. Observation, action and report back cycle was repeated with increased numbers.	Disciples' actions not recorded, but they observed Jesus' actions and reflected on them.
Demonstration			
Faith, generosity, self-sacrifice of others (often women) acknowledged by Jesus for disciples to emulate.	Jesus used faith demonstrated by others to encourage disciples.	Jesus' words & deeds attested to the authenticity of his identity. Healing the demon-possessed showed his spiritual authority over Satanic powers.	Jesus' teaching demonstrated by the seven signs. Foot washing and anointing showed the meaning of the Passion in believers' lives.
Other			
Jesus allowed them to fail, then rebuked, questioned & taught further. All offered forgiveness & restoration, no hopeless cases.	Jesus prepared and commissioned disciples for leadership and to make disciples through going, baptising, teaching.	The failures of the disciples were somewhat excused as they were slowly being brought to greater maturity by Jesus.	Pastoral care of disciples by Jesus and one another is an important role of community.

Second, it has become clear that the discipling relationships which were formed between Jesus and others in the Gospels were rarely one-to-one encounters. Among the Twelve it seems that Philip may have been alone when Jesus called him (Jn. 1:43), and Peter may have had two conversations alone with Jesus, although on both occasions the other disciples were within sight (Mk. 8:32,33; Jn. 21:15-22). All other recorded interactions between Jesus and members of the Twelve took place with all present, or occasionally among one of the subgroups.

Within the wider group of disciples there is a possibility that Jesus conversed alone with Nicodemus (Jn. 3:2), Martha (Jn. 11:20-27) and Mary Magdalene (Jn. 20:14-17), but such occasions were surprisingly rare. The overwhelming majority of discipling interactions happened in small groups, within the community of followers or as Jesus preached, ministered to those in need or interacted with his opponents. Thus we need to broaden our definition from *"two individuals"* to *"…two or a small group of individuals…"*.

Third, the emphasis on the community of learners has been shown to be an integral part of the discipling process, and thus it is important to retain the phrase "in community". However the alternative "or alone" which was in our original definition has so little support that it seems best to omit it and insert *"…typically in a community…"*.

Fourth, as we examined John's Gospel and the large number of so-called 'disciples' who deserted Jesus because of his teachings, it is important to mention the sharing of a body of beliefs between discipler and disciple. We therefore add, *"…holding to the same religious beliefs…"*.

Next, the voluntary commitment required has already been noted, but it is not only from disciple to teacher. In discipling, the commitment must be mutual. Thus *"…a voluntary commitment to each other…"*. Previously we recognized that *"personal relationship"* is essential for discipling, but after our study of the Gospels it seems appropriate to further qualify the relationship by adding *"…close…"*.

The time frame over which a discipling relationship operates has been found to be important. Discipling usually relies on a continuing face-to-face relationship and requires an extended period of time in which to develop. The Twelve were with Jesus for the whole period of his public ministry and though there were failures, all but Judas remained his disciples. The women and others in the disciple band joined him in Galilee and continued following him to Jerusalem. The household of Lazarus, Martha and Mary had repeated close contacts with him. Thus it is important to add *"…for an extended period of time…"*. A unique aspect of the discipling relationships which others had with Jesus was that there was no expectation that his genuine disciples would ever reach a point of moving beyond having him as their teacher. Their commitment to him was lifelong. Even after his death and resurrection, there was no hint that his authority as their master would be replaced by another.

Our original working definition included a number of teaching methods, "... *imitation, oral communication and sharing in the life and work of the discipler*". While the inclusion of these as important discipling methods has been validated, our study has discovered many other methods of teaching which Jesus also used. Those methods of a formal nature often took place in public. The majority of Jesus' informal methods were structured specifically for his followers. Among these were: withdrawal from familiar surroundings and incorporation into a new serving community; small group and collaborative learning; and action-reflection (shared praxis) which also allowed freedom to fail and participation in dangerous circumstances. These methods are not core factors in a definition of discipling and belong more appropriately in an expanded illustrative description. We would however include the phrase "...*largely informal*..." in our definition to indicate the overall scenario in which the majority of the learning activities and methods are used.

Finally we have replaced "...*to learn from the other...*" with "...*to enable the disciple/s to learn from the other*".

Our revised working definition has now become

Discipling is an intentional, largely informal, learning activity in which two or a small group of individuals, typically in a community holding to the same religious beliefs, make a voluntary commitment to each other to form a close, personal relationship for an extended period of time, to enable the disciple/s to learn from the other.

Personal reflections

Having now completed the Gospel survey I have been surprised by the discoveries made. I expected to understand more of the one-to-one relationships through which Jesus focussed on teaching his followers. I had thought that there would be more emphasis on formal teaching methods, and I had not even considered the teaching possibilities provided by a learning community or when Jesus led them into dangerous circumstances or situations of possible failure. The presence of small groups and long-term partnerships between disciples was a pleasant discovery, because I have often experienced the enjoyment of collaborative learning with family or good friends.

The variety of informal teaching methods which Jesus utilized in his discipling has been exciting. The stimulation of learning from close, personal relationships between individuals, partners, small groups and a larger community offers opportunities for learning which appeal to the deep social, emotional and psychological needs of humanity. These strategies bring joy and satisfaction to the learning process, which far surpass those attainable through an exclusive use of the schooling model of learning. The action-reflection method has strongly appealed to the activist in me and provides a solution to every caring teacher's problem, that of encouraging those not gifted academically to learn and operate successfully at their own level of gift-

edness. The possibility of the less privileged having access to long-term teaching has delighted me.

As a believer I have been inspired to continue in my own personal, learning relationship with Jesus, although I am removed in time from him by two millennia. As a woman I have been encouraged to see in Jesus a total disregard for the cultural mores which allowed women no opportunities to be challenged to learn to become strong, spiritual beings and which cared nothing for their holistic development as free, responsible adults. Finally, from my perspective as a teacher, I have glimpsed the superb skill of a Master Teacher who knows and understands the deepest being of those who are his. He meets them in such a way that there is room for all their learning needs and individual differences to be met and fulfilled, and for them to develop towards their full potential as children of the Father.

Notes to Chapter 7

1. Stein, 1978, 1
2. Arndt & Gingrich, 1957, 300
3. Josephus, 1980, 379. There is, however, widespread doubt concerning the authenticity of this particular text.
4. The events associated with his suffering and death had a far greater meaning than just a teaching intention.
5. Wilkins, 1988, 125

PART 3

CHAPTER 8

Discipling in the Acts of the Apostles

In the previous chapter our working definition was refined in the light of discoveries concerning the process of discipling which Jesus adopted with his followers. We now turn to the Acts of the Apostles in order to examine what happened within the young faith community once Jesus, the discipler, was no longer physically present.

The continuing relevance of discipling as a model of teaching will be discussed. And changes to the understanding of discipling by the infant church and the portrayal of those differences by the writer of Acts will be observed. Its practice will be explored and methodologies compared with those of Jesus and with his instructions in the Great Commission. Consistent with our interest in the concept and not just the use of the term, relationships between believers will be examined to ascertain if practices which embodied the concept of discipling as we have defined it, were in evidence even if the writer does not explicitly designate them as such.

Finally a brief comparison will be made between the discipling model and the schooling model, and their suitability for the needs of the early faith communities as depicted in Acts.

Changes in the understanding of discipling

In Luke's two part history of the foundation and early life of the Christian community he discontinues using the word *mathētēs* in his Gospel after Luke 22:45 and only resumes it in Acts 6:1. In the interim, as a result of the events associated with what the Gospels attest as the death, resurrection and ascension of Jesus, momentous changes occurred in the lives of the disciples. They believed Jesus had returned to the Father and sent his Holy Spirit to them at Pentecost. Had the discipling relationship finished or had it remained intact albeit with dramatic changes?

Was discipling still relevant?

In a thought-provoking article the well-known Christian educator, Lawrence Richards, dismisses 'discipling' as a Jewish rabbinic method with no relevance to Christianity beyond the time of Christ and no direct applicability to Christian education.[1] He says the discipling method "can not and must not be adopted by the church".[2] He claims that because it establishes an elite class of believers, Jesus specifically forbade discipling within the body of Christ when he warned against calling another person, 'rabbi', 'teacher' or 'father' (Mt. 23:9-12). He affirms that Jesus' intention was for leaders in the Christian community to serve and shepherd rather than rule over. Therefore he concludes that Christian maturity comes, not from following another, but from commitment to Christ and expression of love towards others in the community and beyond.

Much of what Richards has said is helpful, however his rationale for abandoning discipling as a model of teaching fails to address a number of issues.

- It hinges on Jesus' method of discipling being the same as that of the rabbis, which we have already established, was not the case.
- Even if Jesus' method had been the same, as a skilled teacher he would have been aware of the effect of his modelling on the lives of his followers. It seems illogical that he should use a method to great effect with his disciples in preparing them for a similar teaching ministry, if he had no intention that they emulate his method. When he forbade the calling of someone by a title of authority it seems more likely he was saying something about the nature of the teaching relationship (which we will discuss shortly) than about the method itself.
- If it was not the intention of Jesus that his followers should disciple others, then why did he issue the command to 'make disciples' (*mathēteuō*) (Mt. 28:19)? Richards plays down the importance of the verb because it only occurs four times in the New Testament, in contrast with the noun *mathētēs* which appears 167 times. He says that making disciples is bringing people to full commitment,[3] but he has nothing further to add concerning the Great Commission. The early church must certainly have believed that Jesus was attributing great importance to disciple-making, or Matthew would not have made this command the climax of Jesus' teaching in his Gospel. Early believers acted as if they believed that one of their major tasks was to make others into disciples of Jesus.
- Discipling was a method which Paul and Barnabas used to advantage, on at least one occasion among "many" people (Acts 14:21), without any implicit condemnation.
- By his frequent use of the term 'disciple' in Acts, to designate a believer, follower of or adherent to the way of Jesus, Luke indicates that the early Christians still understood themselves to be disciples of Jesus even in his bodily absence.
- We have no dispute with Richards over Jesus' intention that leadership in the faith community is serving or shepherding, but leadership is not the same as teaching. The strong learning intention of the discipling relationship is different from a pastoral care or service intention.

Thus we will argue that Richards has abandoned a model of teaching, clearly demonstrated to be effective by Jesus, because he has failed to notice the change in focus of 'disciple' and 'discipling' in Acts. It is the nature of that change which we intend to explore in this and the next chapter.

A teaching model with a changed modus operandi

The roles of both Jesus and the disciples changed in the book of Acts. Luke introduced the account of the beginnings of the church by recording the ascension of Jesus (Acts 1:9-11). It is clear that for the disciples their master and discipler had been removed, but in Acts he was never thought of as absent.

Jesus was described by Peter (2:33; 5:31) and Stephen (7:56-60) as exalted in power, with the Father, unseen but not unseeing, vitally involved in the affairs of humans as Ruler, Judge and Saviour, who sent his Spirit to equip them for ministry. He was recognized as the Lord,[4] who still had his disciples (9:1). Their continuing deep personal relationship with him was evidenced by the central position he held in their proclamation,[5] and the record of their frequent prayers in Acts which stands in stark contrast to the Gospels in which there is little mention of their prayers.[6] Indeed Jesus dominated the thinking of all the apostles and believers.

The authority of Jesus, as master, still resided with him, but because he was removed from them, his words as remembered by his followers embodied of his authority. The new faith communities which came into being were accountable to the central group of apostles and the Jerusalem elders who had been with Jesus. Their collective wisdom was referred to for an understanding of how the teachings of Jesus would apply in new situations. This was especially necessary as the gospel extended into Samaritan and Gentile worlds (5:1-11; 8:14,10,11; 15:2-33; 2:20-26). Individual leaders, even Peter and Paul, were held accountable to the wider group for their actions (20:18,19). Later as others grew in their knowledge and understanding of the Way, and were guided by the Holy Spirit, the collective body began to make administrative decisions, advise, send out, decide doctrine and pronounce judgements (13:3; 14:26,27; 15:40; 18:22). Thus the faith community itself became the vehicle for discipling, under the Lordship of the ascended Christ.

The use of the noun, 'disciple', also changed in Acts. *Mathētēs* occurs twenty-eight times in this book,[7] but it is never used to refer to leaders of the church or to the Twelve, even though they were the ones chiefly called 'disciples' in the Gospels. Luke prefers to nominate them as 'elders', 'apostles' or 'the Twelve'.[8] Their two major functions were first, as people commissioned by the risen Christ, to be his witnesses (1:22; 4:33; 22:15; 26:16), to demonstrate God's power by signs and wonders (2:43; 5:12), to evangelize, teach and preach and pray (2:42; 5:29; 6:2,4; 14:4,6,14). Second, they were overseers and administrators of the faith community (4:35,37; 5:2; 6:6; 8:14,18; 9:27; 11:1; 15:2-29). Their role as learners (disciples) was not rescinded, but their primary task now was to make disciples of Jesus through the witness of the community to him. Willimon writes, "Making disciples is the job of disciples in Acts".[9] There was no suggestion that they would be like the rabbis who after a period of instruction, left to make their own disciples. All disciples would still belong to Jesus.

Arndt and Gingrich state that in Acts the term 'disciple' is a general designation, almost exclusively used for members of the new Christian community.[10] It seems to be used interchangeably with 'brethren, friends, saints, righteous, believers, saved, Christians, Nazarenes, Galileans, church, congregation, fellowship, sect and flock'.[11] It is rare in the singular[12] and frequently refers to groups of believers in different places.[13] It included both men and women who were responsible to God for their own actions (5:1-10), took part in major church decisions (6:2), performed acts of service for others[14] and suffered persecution for their faith (9:1,2).

On only one occasion were believers said to be disciples of anyone other than Jesus. They were those who assisted Paul to escape from Damascus (9:25). They were probably individuals who came to belief through his preaching immediately after his conversion. Some may have been servants or fellow-persecutors who were travelling with him at the time of his vision (9:7). The group of 'disciples' (probably disciples of John the Baptist) at Ephesus who knew only John's baptism responded to the message concerning Jesus and the Holy Spirit, seeing it as an extension of what they had already received (19:1-7).

One of the uses of *mathētēs* in Greek literature which Rengstorf notes is that which describes "an intellectual link between those who are considerably removed in time whereby one seeks to imitate the other."[15] This fits well with Luke's use of the term in Acts. However the link which he portrays in Acts between Jesus and "the disciples" is much more than an intellectual link. It is a deep inner relationship of a believer with his or her God, Lord and Saviour. Rengstorf comments that the emphasis "is thus removed from the formal side of the relation between *mathētēs* and *didaskalos* (teacher) to the inner fellowship between the two and its practical effects, and this to such a degree that the latter is basic to the whole relationship".[16]

All believers then continued to be learners and followers of Jesus. They rarely did so alone, but men and women came together under the leadership of those who had been with Jesus, to receive his teachings, to make decisions, to serve, to suffer and to help others to be his disciples also.

Thus in Acts Jesus remained the master and those who responded to him in faith moved into a close, personal inner fellowship with him which had practical effects in their daily lives. Jesus was no longer their immediate teacher. The apostles and others who had heard his teachings passed them on to the community. His words, not the teachers or their words, had the authority. And members of the discipling community became both teacher and taught, disciple-maker and disciple.

Elements in revised working definition of discipling

It is now our task to determine whether 'discipling', as it has been redefined in the light of the Gospels, was a model of teaching demonstrable within the life of the early faith communities. Elements in our revised working definition will be isolated and the text of Acts examined to see how the various components we have specified operated within the life of these communities.

An intentional, largely informal, learning activity

For the members of the faith community to continue being called 'disciples', their role as learners must have been of equal significance with their role when Jesus was with them. Their communal life, summarized in Acts 2:42, focussed on what Marshall suggests were the four essential elements which characterized Christian gatherings: teaching, sharing a fellowship meal, remembering Christ's death and prayer.[17]

Teaching (*didaskō*) was a major task and a primary means of extending and maintaining membership of the church (2:42).[18] It is not used in Acts for proclaiming (*katangellō*) or announcing the good news (*euangelizomai*) about Jesus. It is used for passing on his teaching in a more formal, structured situation. It was an intentional activity which was performed primarily by the apostles and leaders.[19]

In the sharing of fellowship meals and within the everyday life of the faith community, informal teaching opportunities arose and the church was built up (9:31). Learning is implicit in many of Luke's comments about the church. They learnt the importance of complete truthfulness (5:11); that Gentiles were equal inheritors of God's grace (11:18); that God answers prayer (12:16), calls to service (13:2) and guides decisions concerning belief (15:28). Priscilla and Aquila informally explained the way of God more accurately to Apollos (18:26). Paul reminded the Ephesian elders of the example of his life (20:18). Sometimes the informal learning which occurred was an intentional activity. At other times it was a result of reflection on events which appeared to be outside the realm of human planning.[20]

As they gave and received hospitality,[21] shared their possessions and meals, and gladly spent time together (2:42-47), differences in attitudes and life-style became obvious (4:13). Their common life enabled learning to take place formally in structured meetings and informally through good and bad examples, encouragement and rebuke and daily conversations with others. Thus the life of the community itself and its members, became agents for discipling to take place.

Two or a small group of individuals, typically in a community

When Jesus called his disciples to leave close family ties, employment and the comforts of home in order to follow him and be part of a new learning, discipling community, he was providing for the time when his physical presence would no longer be with them.

The numbers of believers increased dramatically (3:41; 4:4; 6:7). Persecution forced many to flee to other places, but they continued to proclaim the good news of Jesus wherever they went (8:1-4). At first this was only among the Jewish communities and within the confines of the synagogue (11:19), however the message soon spread to the Samaritans and Gentiles (8:5; 11:20,21). Through the preaching of the apostles, especially Paul and his associates, Christian faith communities with appointed elders were established in many places (14:21-23). More intimate personal relationships within these communities could be maintained, because they met in homes with limitations on the number of people able to be involved, although overcrowding sometimes caused problems (20:7-11).

Continuing contact was made through repeated visits and letters (15:36; 18:23). But as the life of these groups developed they assumed responsibility for their own growth and pastoral care (20:28-32). Thus individuals within these relatively small groups meeting in homes learned from one another as they gathered together and as they shared their daily lives.

Within Acts there is also evidence for close, discipling relationships among those who travelled with the apostles proclaiming the message of Jesus. Acts particularly focuses on Peter, Philip, Stephen, Barnabas and Paul. These men did not have disciples as Jesus did, but Peter (11:12), Barnabas (15:39) and Paul (13:13; 15:30; 16:3; 18:18; 19:22,29; 20:4; 21:29) had those in an apprentice-type role who assisted in evangelism and building up the infant churches.[22] They were committed to the work and to closely relating to one another. By living, working and travelling with the more experienced leaders, they observed their examples in life and ministry (20:18-35) and heard their teaching even when it was not focussed directly on them (19:9,10). Theirs was an implicit curriculum.

There are numerous examples of partners or small groups in ministry teams who related closely to one another.[23] It seems probable that in the partnership between Barnabas and Paul, Barnabas first discipled Paul and then Paul took over the leadership until Barnabas disagreed with his decision to exclude John Mark from their second missionary journey and they parted (11:25,26; 12:25-13:16; 15:36-41). As these partners or small groups ministered together they learnt collaboratively and from the example, conversation or direct teaching of each other (20:7,11). Their shared experiences, coupled with the responsibility of reporting back to a sending group, meant their joint reflections enabled learning to take place (11:1-18; 14:27; 15:4; 18:22; 21:19). When they failed, some were given the opportunity to learn again (15:37,39).

Teaching and learning the faith was very important in these early communities. And although the initial message of Christ often came from outside the communities, their experience of life together with one another or in small groups resulted in their learning together. Through worship, prayer, fellowship and service, members individually and collectively contributed to the learning scenario of the whole group, formally and informally.

Holding to the same religious beliefs

Those who came to believe in Jesus as Lord and publicly declared their allegiance to him through baptism (2:41; 8:12,38; 10:48), shared the same understandings of the faith, whether they had been Jews or Gentiles previously. Many were prepared to suffer persecution or even death rather than abandon their belief. This consistency of belief was ensured by the authority, which they attributed to the words and teachings of Jesus. Those who had received his teaching were entrusted with its propagation. And thus it was that the apostles and Jerusalem elders supervised the first steps of the faith into Samaritan and Gentile territory (8:14; 10:34-48). They guarded the purity of the original message from syncretistic encroachment by Judaizers (15:1-21) or the polytheistic religions of the Gentile world (17:22-31; 19:9,26). The apostles ensured that a consistent body of beliefs was held by all the faith communities by making follow-up visits and reporting back to the wider group of apostles and elders at the mother churches of Jerusalem or Antioch. The Council at Jerusalem also ensured that its decisions were carefully communicated to all the churches. Paul highly valued his own education as a rabbi (22:3) and Jewish Christians continued to attend synagogues until they were expelled. But there is no hint in Acts that those who did not believe in Jesus had any part to play in teaching the church, nor did anyone seek to be taught by an unbeliever. Indeed the fear of God's judgement ensured that only the genuine joined the community of the faith (5:11) and that they held firmly to the teachings of Jesus.

Make a voluntary commitment to each other to form a close personal relationship for an extended period of time

For a relationship to be classified as 'discipling' in character it must also be voluntary, of a close, personal nature and operate over an extended period of time.

During the period covered by the book of Acts, increasing numbers of people heard the preaching of the good news and voluntarily committed themselves in faith to Jesus (2:41; 4:4; 6:7; 13:48; 14:1,21). Some pleaded to be told what they must do to find forgiveness (2:37-41; 16:30-34). Others saw the signs and wonders done by the apostles and turned to the Lord (9:35,42). On a number of occasions Paul argued for the gospel (18:4; 19:8). Some accepted the truth after persuasion or having examined the Scriptures for themselves to verify what was being preached (17:4,11), but savage persecution and a healthy number of sceptics deterred many from mindlessly following the crowds (8:1; 9:1,2; 17:32). After the Ananias and Sapphira incident people feared to join unless their faith was genuine (5:1-11). There was no coercion. No inducements were offered. Commitment was by free choice.

Those who turned to Jesus demonstrated their decision by baptism and incorporation into the community of faith. We have already noted that, in these communities, frequent prayer and communication about Jesus and his teaching enabled people who had never seen him in the flesh to develop a close, personal relationship with him.

Parallel to the growth of direct relationships with Jesus, the members of the communities developed warm, loving relationships with one another. From the beginning the Jerusalem church were "of one heart and soul" (4:32). They shared all they had with one another and especially with those in need. They joined together at the Temple and in their homes. They prayed, learned, worshipped and ate with one another (2:42-47; 4:32-37; 6:1).

Other faith communities had similar relationships among their members, although there is no record of the sharing of common possessions being repeated elsewhere. Hospitality, care for the destitute, generosity to the needy and concern for the persecuted were regular practices (11:29,30; 16:33,34,40). Strong bonds between members of these communities evoked emotions of great joy or deep sorrow on behalf of one another (8:2; 9:39; 12:14; 15:25; 20:37,38; 21:5,9,13,17). When members moved away they joined new communities of believers in new places, and sustained their previous relationships through visits, messages and letters.[24] Relationships were important and continued for lengthy periods of time. Acts has no record of any believer who withdrew from the faith to return to a previous way of life.

While all who were committed to Jesus became part of one of the faith communities, a select few are recorded as joining teams which travelled to various parts of the Roman empire taking the message of Jesus Christ to those who had not heard. These were specialized teams led by an apostle or one of their associates, and in some ways were a microcosm of the faith communities from which they came. These smaller groups, sometimes consisting of only two or three persons, were voluntary in nature. John Mark was free to leave Barnabas and Paul's team although his decision did not gain him popularity (13:13). Luke joined and left at intervals, as indicated by the 'we' passages (16:10-17; 20:5-21:18; 27:1-28:16). Paul and Barnabas parted company when they could not agree (15:39,40). They were responsible before God to decide their itinerary, methods of evangelism (16:10; 17:14,15; 18:5,18-21; 19:22; 20:4,5) and duration of operations (11:26; 18:11; 19:10; 20:27-31).

While their commitment was primarily to Jesus and to fulfilling his mission of taking the good news wherever they went, they developed close bonds with their fellow team members. Their relationships displayed love and care for the well being of one another[25] even though their relationships were not always free of tension (15:36-41). They shared every aspect of life, travelled thousands of kilometres, and frequently suffered hardships and persecution together.[26] Some like Paul and Timothy or Barnabas and John Mark were almost like father and son (12:25; 13:13; 15:37; 16:1-3).

Thus within the mission teams, within each faith community, and within the whole family of believers there was a primary commitment to relating to Jesus as Lord and a secondary commitment to the development of long-term, close, personal relationships with fellow members of the Christian community of faith.

To enable the disciple/s to learn from the other

Within the book of Acts there is very little direct evidence for one person enabling another to learn in a more personal way. Learning obviously took place but it is not the author's primary interest. The focus of attention is on Peter and Paul and is mainly towards the proclamation of Jesus Christ to those outside the faith community. However glimpses of learning opportunities do occur from time to time.

The group in Jerusalem devoted themselves to the apostles' teaching (2:42). Philip and the Ethiopian (8:26-40) and Peter and Cornelius (10:17-48) had very successful informal teaching sessions, however no evidence exists that they were ever more than single encounters. New believers in Antioch were taught by Barnabas and Paul (11:22-26; 15:35). Mission teams led by Paul encouraged and taught converts (men, women and children) in many of the towns and cities they visited (15:41; 16:5,40; 18:23; 20:1,2,7-12; 21:4-9).

The interaction between Paul and the Ephesian elders gives greater insight into how these groups learned from their personal relationship with him. Paul loved and was dearly loved by the leaders of the Ephesian church (20:17-38). He had taught them formally in public, and in private homes. Informally he shared his own personal struggles and was conscious that the example of his life among them would impact strongly on their own spiritual development. His final words warned them about dangers to their own faith and that of those in their care.

The working relationships within mission teams provided opportunities for the participants to learn from the leader or from one another, although that was not the *raison d'être* for the group. It is probable that Barnabas taught Paul for a time until he was firmly grounded in the faith and his leadership gifts were strengthened (9:27-30; 11:25,26; 13:1-7). Barnabas also encouraged and sought to develop ministry gifts in the young John Mark (12:25; 13:13: 15:37-39). Paul shared ministry with Silas (15:40-18:22), Timothy (16:1-3; 17:14,15; 18:5; 19:22; 20:4), Erastus (19:22) and possibly Sopater, Aristarchus, Secundus, Gaius, Tychicus, Trophimus (20:4; 21:29) and Luke as fellow travellers, learners and assistants in the work.

Conclusion

Thus we have established that all the elements in our revised working definition of discipling were present in the teaching interactions of the early faith communities of Acts. However, while Jesus remained the master albeit in a different form, the concept of discipling changed and two expressions of it emerged.

First there was the faith community itself which by its common life and daily interactions on a variety of levels became a medium for discipling in both formal and informal, intentional learning situations. Then there were smaller travelling teams under the leadership of an apostle or associate who went out to spread the message of Jesus and nurture believers throughout the Empire. These groups were not separate from the faith communities in any way. They operated under the authority of at least one of the communities, being sent out and reporting back to them. Their primary role was evangelism, and operations were similar to the mission of the disciples which Jesus organized. Leaders had recognized teaching gifts and responsibilities, and team members assisted in an apprentice-style role.

Discipling methods

Having established that discipling was a model of teaching present in early faith communities we turn to the only use of the verb 'make disciples' (*mathēteuō*) in the Acts of the Apostles (14:21). The verse and its context will be examined to discover what teaching methods Paul and Barnabas used with the people involved. The methods found will be compared with those outlined in the Great Commission of Jesus (Mt. 28:19,20) and their relationship to the elements of our revised working definition will be noted.

A four-fold process

After Paul and Barnabas proclaimed the good news, they made disciples among those who responded (14:21-23). This was a fourfold process: (1) confirming or strengthening (*epistērizontes*) the souls/minds of the disciples v.22, (2) encouraging (*parakalountes*) them to continue in the faith in spite of persecution v.22, (3) gathering believers into churches over which elders were appointed as teachers and spiritual guides v.23 and (4) entrusting them to the Lord with prayer and fasting v.23.

This process corresponds remarkably closely with Jesus' discipling instructions in Matthew 28:19,20: (1) instruction in the teachings of Jesus, (2) awareness of his presence with them to the end of the age, (3) being publicly incorporated into the body of believers by baptism and (4) identifying with and relating in trust to the three persons of the Godhead. Therefore we may conclude that in Acts the process of discipling consists of four necessary components which follow belief in Jesus as Lord and Saviour. These components appear to harmonize very closely with a number of the elements in our definition.

First, Paul and Barnabas "strengthened the souls of the disciples" and the churches in the faith, by teaching, warning and encouragement (15:36,41;

16:5; 18:23; 20:1,2,30). All these references use the verb *stērizō* (to strengthen, set up, make firm, establish, support).[27] By its repetition and its close conjunction with the 'soul' (*psuchē*, centre of inner life of a person, feelings and emotions[28]) and 'the faith', it is clear that teaching the elements of the faith to new believers, in order for them to understand, feel and to be able to stand firm, was essential to making disciples. New believers "devoted themselves to the apostles' teaching" (2:42). They heard the witness of those who had been with Jesus. This "serving the word" was regarded as the primary role of the apostles (6:4). 'Strengthening' appears to have been directed mainly at imparting beliefs not merely at an intellectual level, but also at the level of feelings. It may have been predominantly formal in character, involving discussion, debate and teaching.[29] Acts 18:23 *dierchomenos kathezēs* (passing through in order) suggests that Paul's approach to strengthening the communities he previously established was planned and systematic.

The teaching of new believers appears to correspond to the more formal teaching sessions of Jesus' ministry. In the early faith communities teaching occurred when they gathered together for worship, prayer and instruction. Luke tells us much more about the evangelistic preaching of the gospel than he does about the content of the teaching. However it probably centred around the person of Jesus, his resurrection and messiahship (4:33; 5:42), and warned about the false teaching of Judaizers (15:1,28,29). We may therefore conclude, in the absence of contrary evidence, that new believers were taught, according to Jesus' instructions, "to obey everything that I have commanded you" (Mt. 28:20). And it seems probable that more formal teaching methods were primarily utilized for this task.

Second, making disciples includes the encouragement of persons to long-term commitment to faith in Jesus. The verb to encourage (*parakaleō*) means 'to call someone to oneself' or 'an admonition to stand firm'. Schmitz refers to it as "oral exhorting of disciples who need strengthening."[30] Barnabas excelled in this. His name means 'an encourager' (4:36,37). New believers particularly needed encouragement and Barnabas offered it to Paul and the recently founded church in Antioch (9:27; 11:23). Encouragement is not a formal teaching activity but in Acts it happened informally sometimes just through a person's presence or by words, visits and letters (15:31,32; 16:40; 20:1,2). Schmitz comments that encouragement in Acts "expresses the divine aid which is already lavishly granted to the members of the suffering community of Jesus by present exhortation and encouraging events."[31] Encouragement equipped new converts to stand firmly in the faith and persevere in spite of suffering or persecution, knowing Jesus' presence was with them.

Third, discipling occurred within a community of faith. Apollos may be the only one who was discipled alone (18:24-26).[32] Those who committed themselves to belief in Jesus declared it publicly in baptism and then they and their households gathered into groups united by their faith, belonging to one another. They met regularly and formed close, personal relationships with one another. They were not haphazard groups of individuals. Leadership was important. In Jerusalem the apostles, James, the brother of the Lord, and the elders had positions of leadership (5:1-11; 8:14; 9:27; 11:1,30; 12:17; 15:2-29; 16:4; 21:18-25). In other places elders were appointed as teachers, pastors and spiritual guides. Paul gave special time to those he appointed, especially the Ephesian elders. He taught them informally through the example of his own life and pastoral leadership and openly shared his own struggles with them (20:18-35).

Fourth, "with prayer and fasting they entrusted them to the Lord". In line with what we have already stated about the Lordship of Jesus, and the primary relationship of every disciple with him, we find that new believers were entrusted to his special keeping. Their personal relationship with God as Father, Son and Spirit was the most important aspect of their discipleship. Paul fasted and prayed for the churches he helped establish, but he commended believers to God, for his nurture, teaching and care (20:32,36). Paul knew he would not always be there for these groups of learners. While he was able, he kept in touch with them. But greater than all human relationships, was their relationship with God. It was foundational to their lives as disciples, and far more enduring and pervasive than anything he or any other disciple-maker could provide.

Thus we conclude that in Acts discipling involved establishing close, personal relationships with those who responded to the message of Jesus and shared the common belief that he was both Lord and Christ. It was a four-fold process with a learning intention in which the teachings of Jesus were transmitted through formal and informal means. Discipling encouraged learners to persevere in their commitment to Christ in spite of difficulties. Through their public declaration of baptism they were incorporated into faith communities where elders and leaders provided teaching, nurture and guidance. And through prayer and fasting they were commended to the Lord whose disciples they really were.

A schooling model?

Having examined this transitional period in the life of followers of Jesus, we note that there was no attempt to set up a school or theological college to carry on the task of teaching those who came into the faith or to train future leaders. No one took on the role of a guru or gathered disciples. There were no buildings set aside for instruction or attempts to formulate a curriculum. The small disciple band who were constantly with Jesus throughout his public ministry (1:21,22) expanded so rapidly that any thought of adopting a schooling model would not have kept pace with the growth.

The discipling community with its commitment to close, personal relationships, small groups and life-related teaching processes was ideally suited to a time when believers were faced with rapid social change. During the Acts period most persecution of the church was from the Jews. Expulsion from their synagogues forced early Jewish believers away from the support of their extended family and their age-old religious practices and dimmed their strong national identity. Persecution by the Roman authorities was increasing. Religion was a life and death affair. Believers were often poor or uneducated or displaced, without the life supports they had previously known. They did not need a school. They needed teaching, but in a family-type atmosphere where opportunity was provided for them to be strengthened in their belief so they could withstand the attacks to their faith. They needed encouragement to persevere, knowing that Jesus was with them continually. They needed to know that they belonged to the community as full members signified by their baptism and that their leaders would teach, guide and pastorally care for them. And they needed a strong personal relationship of trust in their Lord and God.

The discipling community quickly became a diverse grouping of faith communities which gathered in different locations under the leadership of apostles or elders. The task of teaching new believers fell first to the apostles, then to those who were with Jesus and finally to any who "had been instructed in the Way of the Lord" (18:25). They, in turn imparted their beliefs and understandings to others. The close, personal relationships between committed members of each faith community promoted informal learning. Their gatherings became the locus where planned instruction, encouragement, modelling and guidance were shared between members. All learnt and received from one another.

A schooling model of teaching would have severely limited the potential for growth within the faith communities. The discipling model had a capacity for encompassing a wide variety of people from different ethnic, cultural and educational backgrounds. It was not confined by buildings, curriculum or specific methods of teaching. It was ideally suited to the rapidly changing experience of these early communities.

Conclusions

In the book of Acts the 'discipling' process had changed. No one ever graduated beyond being a disciple of Jesus. Those who responded in faith to him and received his Holy Spirit, publicly identified with him in baptism and joined with other believers in smaller caring communities which were part of the much wider group of his followers. They believed Jesus was with them and was aware of the events in each of their lives. They communicated with him in prayer and came under the authority of his words and teaching as conveyed by his apostles.

All believers were considered 'disciples', and within the Christian community could be teachers or learners. Some worked together in small groups and learnt as they went out into the world with the good news and as they reported back to their sending communities. Learning occurred through formal instruction and informal activities whenever members of the communities came together for worship, to encourage one another to persevere through difficult times, to appoint elders who would love, teach and guide those in their care, and to entrust others prayerfully to the Lord to whom they belonged and whose Holy Spirit lived within them. Their close personal relationships and shared common life enabled all members to learn from their Lord and from the lives and examples of others.

Notes to Chapter 8

1. Richards believes that the use of discipling by the rabbis established an elite class whose theological method Jesus condemned, because they cancelled out the intent of God's written word and replaced it by their own oral traditions and personal authority. He continues that Jesus established himself as having full authority and as being the embodiment of God's word. (Richards, 1992, 3-11)
2. Emphasis is his. (Richards, 1992, 9)
3. Richards, 1992, 4
4. Acts refers to Jesus as the Lord (1:6; 2:25,34,36), the Lord Jesus (4:33; 7:59; 8:16; 9:5,17; 10;36 etc.) or the Lord Jesus Christ (11:17).
5. Dodd summarised the content of the primitive *Kerygma* from the speeches in Acts which constitute almost one third of the book. It was centred on Jesus as the fulfilment of prophecy, whose ministry, death and resurrection took place according to God's plan. It portrayed Jesus as exalted with God, sending his Spirit to the church, which looked to his return, and appealed for repentance in order that forgiveness and salvation might be received. (Dodd as cited in Ladd, 1974, 329)
6. In Acts prayers were made by individuals (7:9,60; 10:9), the whole church (1:14,24; 2:42; 4:24-31, 12:5,12) and the apostles (3:1; 6;3-6; 8:15). Paul prayed alone and with others (9:11; 13:3; 14:23; 22:17), at Philippi (16:13), with the Ephesian elders (20:36) and disciples from Tyre (21:5), in prison (16:25), in Malta (28:8) and near Rome (28:15). The frequency of these occasions contrast with the disciples' inadequacies regarding prayer in the Gospels (Lk. 11:1; Mk. 9:29; Mt. 26:40,41).
7. Aland, 1978, 172
8. Elders (*presbuteroi*) occurs in 11:30; 14:23; 20:17; 21:18. Apostle/s (*apostolos*) is used in 1:2,26; 2:42,43; 4:33,35,37; 5:2,12,18,29,40; 6:6; 8:1,14,18; 9:27; 11:1; 14:14. A governing board of apostles and elders is mentioned in 15:2,4,6,22,23; 16:4. The only occurrence of 'the Twelve' is in Acts 6:2.
9. Willimon, 1988, 127
10. Arndt & Gingrich, 1957, 487
11. Jackson & Lake, 1966, 375
12. Only four individuals are nominated as "a disciple" in Acts, Ananias (9:10), Tabitha (The only use of the female *mathētria* 'disciple' in the New Testament, 9:36), Timothy (16:1) and Mnason (21:16, an early disciple).
13. Damascus, Jerusalem, Joppa, Antioch, Lystra, Derbe, Galatia, Phrygia, Ephesus, Tyre, Caesarea
14. Tabitha "was devoted to good works and acts of charity" which included the making of tunics and other clothing for widows (9:36,39). Disciples at Antioch sent famine relief to believers in Judea (11:29). Different groups of disciples were particularly active in ministering to Paul's personal needs (9:17; 14:20) and attempting to ensure his safety (9:25; 19:30; 21:4,16).

15 This enabled Socrates to be called the true disciple of Homer even though he lived 300-400 years later. (Rengstorf, 1967, 416)
16 Rengstorf, 1967, 417
17 Marshall, 1980, 83
18 Kee, 1990, 80
19 *Didaskō* is an activity recorded of many in Acts, the apostles (5:21,25,28,42), Peter and John (4:2,18), Paul and Barnabas (11:26; 15:35), Paul alone (18:11; 20:20; 21:21; 28:31), certain individuals (15:1) and Apollos (18:25).
20 Paul used his suffering to encourage and strengthen the disciples. "It is through many persecutions that we must enter the kingdom of God." (14:22, See also 16:40)
21 Simon the tanner, Cornelius, John Mark's mother, Lydia, the Philippian jailer, Jason, Aquila and Priscilla, Titius Justus, the disciples at Tyre, believers at Ptolemais, Philip, Mnason and Paul himself all offered hospitality to others in their homes.
22 These included Silas, Timothy, Sopater, Aristarchus, Secundus, Gaius, Tychicus, Trophimus, Luke, Priscilla and Aquila and Erastus.
23 Peter & John (3:1-4:31; 8:14-25); Peter & six 'brothers' (11:12); Barnabas & Paul (11:30; 12:25; 13:2-12); Paul & Barnabas (13:13-15:35); Paul & Silas (15:40-17:14); Paul and various named and unnamed companions (20:4), including Luke (the "we" passages 16:10-17; 20:5-21:18; 27:1-28:16); Paul & Trophimus (21:29); Silas & Timothy (17:14,15; 18:5); Barnabas & John Mark (15:39); Ananias & Sapphira (5:1-10); Judas/Barsabbas & Silas (15:22-34); Aquila & Priscilla (18:2); Priscilla & Aquila (18:18,26); Timothy & Erastus (19:22); Gaius & Aristarchus (19:29). The principle of pairing among the twelve could explain Peter's initiative in electing Matthias to fill the vacancy left by Judas Iscariot (1:26).
24 Aquila and Priscilla are known to have lived in Rome, Corinth and Ephesus (18:2,19 See also Rom. 16:3; 1 Cor. 16:19; 2 Tim. 4:19).
25 Believers tried to ensure Paul's safety on a number of occasions (9:25; 17:10,14,15; 19:30; 21:4,12).
26 Travelling teams were driven out of the region (13:50), threatened with mistreatment and stoning (14:6,19), flogged and imprisoned (16:23), narrowly escaped lynching (17:5; 19:30), were plotted against (20:3), and suffered in storms and shipwreck (27:14-44).
27 Luke uses this same verb for what happened to the feet and ankle bones of the crippled man in Acts 3:7 when he was healed and enabled to finally stand firmly on his own. (Arndt & Gingrich, 1957, 775)
28 Arndt & Gingrich, 1957, 901
29 Willimon, 1988, 107
30 Schmitz in Kittel, Vol.5, 1967, 796, 774-776
31 Schmitz, 1967, 799
32 Some may consider Philip's time with the Ethopian eunuch as discipling in intent, however it appears that they only met once. Luke's focus is on the missionary expansion of the church. No patterns of discipling or church planting can be inferred from their brief meeting (8:26-40).

CHAPTER 9

Discipling in the Epistles and Revelation

In the previous chapter we established that after the ascension the whole concept of 'discipling' in the faith community changed. Jesus was still the Lord and his authority continued in his words and teachings. His followers related to him in prayer and worship but the human expression of the disciple-maker became a function of individual members of the community of believers or the community as a whole. There were no gurus with their own authoritative teaching, demanding unconditional obedience to their will. Those who were gifted as teachers were themselves under the authority of Jesus. No one person was always teacher. All community members contributed to the learning of others. New faith communities sprang up in many different places because the number of believers was increasing rapidly through the missionary outreach of the apostles and their associates. Persecutions also forced believers to relocate to different parts of the Empire. Members of these newly formed faith communities committed themselves to Christ and to one another in close, personal relationships in which further discipling took place.

We now turn to the Epistles and Revelation to ascertain whether these new trends continued as the church grew and expanded across the Roman Empire. An attempt will be made to enter the 'narrative world' of the Epistles and to examine the nature of relationships and interactions between the individuals and groups included in these writings.

At first glance it could appear as if the practice of discipling ceased because the Epistles and Revelation nowhere use the words *mathētēs* (disciple) or *mathēteuō* (make disciples) whilst the technical term for following Christ, *akoloutheō*, is absent from all but Revelation 14:4.[1] Giles suggests that "such language would not be properly understood in the Hellenistic world".[2] At that time it was generally used for learners in philosophical schools and was only beginning to be used to describe a follower of a religious figure.[3]

In accord with our previous practice, our task is to see if the concept of 'discipling' was present in the life of the faith communities of the Epistles. If they are not upheld, then we may assume that the concepts of 'disciples' and 'discipling' did not apply beyond the period of Acts and were no longer relevant once the generation of the disciples of Jesus died out. We would also assume that 'discipling' has no continuing relevance for the Christian faith communities of the present day. We therefore turn to our revised working definition to determine if the elements which constitute the practice of discipling were present in the Epistles.

Elements in a revised working definition of discipling

The Epistles and Revelation are a rich source of teaching materials which have been used by individuals and churches down through the centuries. Each was written to bring encouragement or teaching to a particular person or faith community. In this study the texts will be examined, not for teaching content, although shared beliefs will be important, but to ascertain the nature of the teaching-learning activities demonstrated. Evidence will be gathered of any intentional, largely informal, learning activities implicit in the texts. The size of groupings of people engaged in these activities will be established and the nature of their relationships examined. If all or most of the elements of discipling as we have defined it are present, it may be concluded that discipling was a continuing practice of the early faith communities.

An intentional, largely informal, learning activity

Teaching and learning occurred in a number of ways in the life of the faith communities, both when they were gathered formally and when individual members related informally. A brief consideration of three Greek words *didasko* (teach), *oikodomeo* (build up), and *manthano* (learn) in the Epistles will indicate something about these processes. The materials also will be examined for indications of modelling and ministry involving the action reflection process.

TEACHING AND LEARNING IN THE EPISTLES

Didasko (teach) and its derivatives occurs 69 times in the Epistles.[4] It is the general word for intentionally instructing or teaching someone or some thing. It usually refers to the formal imparting of spiritual truths to others. In the gathered faith communities, it was often used to describe an action of someone who possessed a special ability to teach which was believed to be a spiritual gift from God (1 Cor. 12:28,29; 14:6; Eph. 4:11; 1 Tim. 3:2; 2 Tim. 4:2).[5] The content of the teaching was closely associated with the Scriptures (Rom. 15:4; 2 Tim. 3:16), and was believed to be trustworthy and consistent with sound doctrine (Tit. 1:9; 2:1). We have coined the term '*didasko*-teaching' to describe this action.

Didasko-teaching is often mentioned in association with other verbs including 'urge', 'insist on', 'remind', 'convince', 'rebuke', 'encourage' and nouns such as 'revelation', 'knowledge', 'prophecy' and 'traditions'. Members of the community who were regarded as possessing the gift of teaching were expected to use it widely (Rom. 12:7; 1 Cor. 12:29; Eph. 4:11), even though all would teach in some way by their involvement in the faith community.[6] Thus *didasko*-

teaching centred on the knowledge and understandings of the faith as revealed in the Scriptures, and passed down as traditions[7] in a body of doctrinal assertions when the community gathered in a more formal setting.

Oikodomeō (build up) appears 11 times in the Epistles.[8] The church is described as a building[9] being slowly constructed to make a dwelling-place for God (1 Cor. 3:9; Eph. 2:21,22; 1 Pet. 2:5). *Oikodomeō* is associated with the gradual growth of the whole faith community into maturity in Christ (1 Cor. 13:10-12; Eph. 4:15; Phil. 1:6; 3:12-15; Col. 1:28; 4:12; Jas. 1:4). The community was strengthened and established when each member exercised his or her spiritual gifts and enabled each part of the body to work together properly (Eph. 4:16, also 4:12; Col. 2:19). In all of the images which describe the growth of the community, God as Father or Son is vitally involved as foundation, head and source of life (Eph. 5:23; Col. 1:18) or grower. The 'building up' is "simultaneously of the person and the community, but it occurs only when the community of persons is immersed in the living tradition"[10] of the churches under the lordship of Christ.

Paul and his associates exerted every effort in building up the Corinthian believers (2 Cor. 10:8; 12:19; 13:10). While no gift was unimportant, the gifts of apostles, prophets, teachers and interpreters of tongues were given priority because they were directly related to achieving growth if exercised in an atmosphere of love, grace and peace (Rom. 14:19; 15:2; 1 Cor. 8:1; 12:28; 14:3-19,26; Eph. 4:11,12,16,29; 1 Thes. 5:11). There were no passive receivers. All members were "drawn into God's service by receiving a particular charisma- that is a particular type of ministry within the whole body".[11] For this building-up teaching we have coined the term, '*oikodomeō*-teaching'. It encompasses all the formal and informal aspects of the common life of the faith community and is much broader than *didaskō*-teaching.

Manthanō (learn), occurs 18 times in the Epistles.[12] It is the usual term to describe the successful result of intentional teaching, instruction, question and answer, dialogue or some verbal communication such as prophecy (Gal. 3:2; 1 Cor. 14:31,35). The word may also describe informal situations when learning results from the intentional or unintentional example of others (1 Cor. 4:6; Phil. 4:9)[13] or from life's experiences (Phil. 4:11; 1 Tim. 5:4,13; Tit. 3:14). The writer to the Hebrews uses it in this way to describe Jesus' learning obedience through suffering (Heb. 5:8).

From the use of these verbs we may form several conclusions. *Didaskō*-teaching with its knowledge-based learning is similar to the formal teaching which is part of the discipling process. *Oikodomeō*-teaching encompasses many intentional, informal learning activities which take place in the community of faith. Both enabled learning (*manthanō*) to occur and both were important for believers, but the concept of *oikodomeō*-teaching accommodates a greater diversity in the range of learnings produced. These include knowledge, understandings, values, attitudes, skills and behaviours which characterize a person and community growing together in likeness to Christ.

LEARNING FROM THE EXAMPLE OF OTHERS

Learning from the intentional or unintentional example of others has been a learning method recognized from the beginning of human culture and was common among Greco-Roman teachers.[14] In the Epistles believers are encouraged to learn by imitating God, Christ or others in the faith community.

The encouragement to imitate (*mimeomai*) God occurs only in Ephesians 5:1. The concept is not an Old Testament one, but was a common theme in antiquity and familiar in Hellenistic Judaism.[15] It has associations with putting on the new humanity created after "the likeness of God in true justice and holiness" (Eph. 4:24). Wild suggests that being like God is the goal of Christian discipleship. He recognizes the possibility of imitating God directly because the community of believers joined to Christ has direct access to God himself.[16] God's character is being imitated when people are truthful, in control of anger, industrious, love their wives and obey their parents (Eph. 4:25-28; 5:25; 6:1). In Jewish belief God is depicted as the Divine Warrior who fights against evil and brings justice and truth.[17] Believers are specifically encouraged to put on his armour to do the same (Eph. 6:10,11).

Following Christ's example is a common theme in the Epistles (Rom. 15:3,7; 2 Cor. 8:9; Eph. 5:2). Giles suggests Paul uses the "*imitatio Christi*" (imitation of Christ) concept, as a substitute for the life of discipleship depicted in the Gospels.[18] Philippians 2:4-11 and 2 Corinthians 4:10,11 encourage believers to emulate the attitudes of Jesus' humble servanthood, obedience, willingness to surrender rights and to suffer unjustly.[19] Hebrews exhorts readers to look "to Jesus the pioneer and perfecter of our faith" (Heb. 12:2,3). Jesus set the precedent for his disciples to follow by "leaving behind... security, congeniality and respectability" for the reproach of the cross.[20] John encourages walking "just as he walked" (1 Jn. 2:6, see also 3:16).

Peter encourages those about to suffer to follow Christ's example (*hupogrammos*) of innocent suffering without retaliation (1 Pet. 2:18-25, see also 4:1). There is no mention of Jesus as teacher in this letter, but following "in his steps" starts with the call of God (2:21) in a way similar to Jesus' call to his disciples. Elliott comments that Jesus is more than the model as he also enables disciples to be followers.[21] Michaels adds, "Only in community, 1 Peter teaches, is it possible to follow in the path that Jesus walked alone".[22]

Aware of the effectiveness of learning through exposure to good models, Paul was conscious that others would learn from his relationships with others and his attempts to imitate Christ (1 Cor. 4:16; 11:1; Gal. 4:12; Phil. 3:17; 4:9; 1 Thes. 1:6; 2 Thes. 3:7-9). He wanted his conduct to correspond with his teaching. "The life of the teacher is the proof or disproof of what he says."[23] His openness about his past life (1 Cor. 15:9) and present struggles enabled the process of God's transforming work in his life to be seen (Rom. 7:7-25; 15:14-29; 1 Cor. 4:9-13,16). Some writers believe that the imitation of the examples of Christ and Paul are parallel ideas,[24] but Christ alone was the perfect, sinless example (Heb. 4:15). Paul was worthy of emulation only in his attitudes and striving towards the goal (Phil. 3:10; 1 Cor. 7:7,8; 8:13; 2 Cor. 4:2; 6:11; 11:21-12:10; Col. 1:24; 2:1; 1 Thes. 2:1-12). His missionary endeavours also provided a demonstration of methods of spreading the gospel (1 Cor. 2:1-5; 9:15-27; 15:10).

Paul encouraged his readers by praising certain individuals and churches whose examples were worthy to be followed (Macedonians, 2 Cor. 8:1-5; Judeans, 1 Thes. 2:14; Timothy and Epaphroditus, Phil. 2:19-30).[25] His rebukes demonstrated behaviours to avoid (1 Cor. 10:1-11; Phil. 3:2,18,19).

The Pastoral Epistles encourage believers by examples in the writer's life (1 Tim. 1:16; 2 Tim. 3:10,11). Timothy was instructed as a leader to "set the believers an example… that all may see your progress" (1 Tim. 4:12,15). By praising the worthy, or drawing attention to the unworthy, behaviours to imitate or avoid were made known (1 Tim. 1:19,20; 2 Tim. 1:5,16-18). Older women were encouraged to exemplify loving family relationships and good household management (Tit. 2:3-5) for the benefit of younger women. Hebrews invites readers to imitate the heroes and heroines of the faith in the Old Testament, or mature believers known personally "who through faith and patience inherit the promises" (Heb. 6:12; 11:4-12:1; 13:7). Peter advocates that elders be examples to the flock (1 Pet. 5:3). In his third epistle, John dissociates himself from bad examples and fosters imitation of the good (3 Jn. 9-12). In Revelation the example of Antipas (Rev. 2:13) and the martyrs (Rev. 7:14), the 144,000 who kept themselves pure and blameless (Rev. 14:4,5) and the saints in their praying (Rev. 8:4) are all upheld as models of faithfulness to be emulated.

Thus the theme of 'imitation' occurs as an intentional learning activity in the writings of Paul, the Pastorals, Peter, John, Hebrews and Revelation. Believers are encouraged to learn how to live by imitating God's justice and holiness, and by following the suffering servant example of Jesus. Those who observed the examples of previous generations, leaders, the community and one another would learn from them. And secure, loving relationships would be established in the churches as they imitated the example of Paul and all those who were endeavouring to imitate Christ.

Learning while active in ministry

The discipling strategy of Jesus was continued into this period of the early church. Smaller groups of selected individuals formed teams around Paul or others of the apostolic band and travelled to various places introducing people to Christ and strengthening the infant churches. There was no general call for believers to leave home, family, employment or possessions,[26] but many did as a result of persecution or because they joined the teams taking the gospel to new places. Large numbers of individuals are listed as being involved in these teams. Several women's names were also included. It is difficult however to know whether their ministry tasks differed from those of the men. Both men and women were apostles, deacons, evangelists, teachers, prophets, leaders of house churches and influential patrons.[27]

The primary intention of these mission teams was not to teach or disciple their own members but that was an inevitable outcome when more experienced, more mature Christians related closely to committed but younger or less experienced fellow workers for extended periods of time. Putting faith into practice was regarded as a means of its growth (Jas. 2:22). Sometimes the activities of these groups resulted in hardship, persecution or suffering for the faith. They never intentionally endangered lives, but if suffering arose they did not shrink from it because there was a strong belief that through it the gospel would spread and growth in maturity (endurance, character, hope and experience of the love of God) would result (Phil. 1:12-14; Rom. 5:3-5; Jas. 1:4).[28]

Conclusion

In conclusion, while no evidence exists for the schooling-model of teaching being practised by these early faith communities there is evidence for both formal and informal teaching in the Epistles. When the church gathered as a whole those with recognized gifts taught or proclaimed God's message to the assembled whole. This was an important component of its life. Although the discipling model of teaching is not explicitly mentioned, various informal learning processes were evident. These included the exercise of diverse spiritual gifts within the life of the faith community which led to mutual 'upbuilding': *oikodomeō*-teaching. Believers were encouraged to learn by imitating Christ's example and observing the life of faith as it was demonstrated by others. Active involvement in ministry and its accompanying hardships, in fellowship with other experienced and more mature believers led to further learning.

Thus the first condition for discipling, the existence of intentional, largely informal, learning activities has been shown to be fulfilled.

Two or a small group of individuals typically in a community

Of the informal methods listed above it is necessary now to ascertain if the Epistles and Revelation indicate that these were carried out by two or a small group of individuals within a communal setting. Learning relationships between two individuals will be discussed first, before small learning groups are examined. Then the faith communities will be investigated to ascertain if their size permitted them to fulfil the conditions we have established as necessary for discipling.

Learning relationships between two individuals

Is there evidence for learning relationships between individuals? The apostles, Paul, Peter and John probably related to numbers of people who learnt from them like apprentices, but little evidence exists concerning the nature of these relationships, apart from Paul's relationships with Titus and Timothy. Over twenty associates of Paul and members of his mission teams appear in the Epistles. Some he baptized (1 Cor. 1:14-16), advised (Phil. 4:2,3) or regarded as his spiritual children (Phm. 10-16).

Thus Paul's relationships with Titus and Timothy are invaluable for this study. It is inappropriate here to launch into a detailed discussion of the authorship of the Pastoral Epistles,[29] but after consideration of various viewpoints it is believed that the documents reflect a genuine relationship between Paul and his two associates.[30] Thus we will refer to the texts of these Epistles and Acts to examine the intentional, largely informal learning relationships between Paul and these two men.

Titus was probably a Greek believer who was converted under Paul's ministry.[31] He was among those who travelled with him and related closely to him.[32] Four events concerning Titus are noted. First, he was an observer of Paul and Barnabas' private meeting with the Jerusalem church leaders who were testing the accuracy of Paul's gospel message. Though he was a Gentile he was welcomed as their brother (Gal. 2:1-3). Second, Paul sent him and another "brother" to Corinth as his emissaries to deal with problems there (2 Cor. 12:18).[33] His mission was successful and Titus later revisited on his own initiative (2 Cor. 7:6,7,13-16; 8:16-17). Third, Paul left Titus in Crete with his authority to firmly establish the churches, appoint suitable elders, teach sound doctrine, exhort, reprove and model good deeds (Tit. 1:5; 2:1,7,15). Paul continued his support by letter. Titus was last mentioned in Dalmatia where he was working (2 Tim. 4:10).

The relationship between these two was very much that of an apprentice with a master. Titus' initial role was that of a fellow "brother" who observed the private interactions and doctrinal discussions between Paul, Barnabas and the leaders of the infant church. He then was delegated with another brother to attend to a problem situation on Paul's behalf. Later he took the initiative to encourage them. Having successfully completed his assignments, Titus was entrusted with further more demanding responsibilities. Paul continued to offer him support during this time by his letters of advice and encouragement. Finally he was fully equipped to move into an independent ministry, still keeping in touch with the one who had apprenticed him.

The relationship between Paul and Timothy was closer to that of father and son than apprentice and master or rabbi and disciple.[34] Although Timothy was nurtured in his faith by his mother and grandmother (2 Tim. 1:5; 3:15), Paul performed his circumcision (Acts 16:3) and sought to develop the young man to the full potential of his natural endowments and spiritual gifts. Paul shared from his life experiences with Timothy (1 Tim. 1:12-16) provided a godly example to him and immediately involved him in active ministry with him and his co-workers (Acts 16:1-5). After a period of observation he provided Timothy with opportunities to preach (2 Cor. 1:19) and deputized him to pastorally support the young, persecuted church at Thessalonica, strengthening its members in their faith (1 Thes. 3:2-6). Timothy was an assistant to Paul and co-writer of Epistles during his missionary travels and his imprisonment (2 Cor. 1:1; Phil. 1:1; Col. 1:1; 1 Thes. 1:1; 2 Thes. 1:1).

Timothy's natural lack of confidence (1 Tim. 4:12; 5:23; 1 Cor. 16:10) may have led Paul initially to give him less demanding situations than Titus, or to offer more encouragement and guidance (1 Tim. 1:7; 4:14; 2 Tim. 1:6). But with the assistance of others, Timothy ably ministered in Beroea (Acts 17:13-15), Macedonia (Acts 19:22), Thessalonica, Corinth and possibly Philippi (Phil. 2:19-24). In the latter part of Paul's life when Timothy was in Ephesus Paul addressed the Pastoral Epistles to him, instructing, advising, urging and warning him concerning the fulfilment of his leadership tasks. Paul constantly prayed for him (2 Tim. 1:3) and blessed him (1 Tim. 6:20,21; 2 Tim. 1:2; 4:9-22).

Paul did not relate to Titus or Timothy in a formal academic setting like the rabbis with their students. The learning which occurred was very much life and ministry centred. Although Paul's letters to them contained teaching, it arose in response to the situations in which they found themselves, not some pre-determined curriculum. The world was their classroom.

Paul formed long-term, close personal relationships with Titus and Timothy and openly shared his life as an example (Tit. 3:3-7). He treated them as sons and they willingly responded. Many times in the ancient world teaching is compared to paternal duties. Kurz claims, "It envisages not merely formal teaching but the total formation of the disciple".[35] Paul aimed for their holistic development in every aspect of their lives including their growth to maturity in Christ. Paul's teaching strategy was similar for them both. First they joined his band as observers. Then they were given limited responsibilities under his close supervision. Their level of involvement in ministry gradually increased as their knowledge and skills developed. Finally Paul entrusted them with full responsibility for dealing with problems, false teaching and leadership issues in various churches under his care. He regarded them as his trustworthy representatives (1 Tim. 1:3,4; 4:1-3; Tit. 1:5,9). Throughout the process their 'ministry-learning' was faithfully nurtured by Paul who provided opportunity for their reflection, guidance and encouragement as appropriate.

John's second letter "to the elect lady" and third letter "to the beloved Gaius" may have been written to individuals with whom he had close teacher-learner relationships. "The elect lady" may have referred to an older lady who led a house church, but the expression is more likely to be the personification of a church.[36] Gaius[37], however was probably leader of a house church in which John exercised some oversight. They obviously shared a loving, joyful, father-son type relationship. John prayed for him, received news about his spiritual well being, commended him for his hospitality and advised him on various matters. The formal teaching contained in these letters is part of a much broader teaching approach by the apostle facilitating learning in the lives of those whom he loved.

The apostle Peter refers to Mark as "my son" (1 Pet. 5:13) and early church traditions associate Mark's writing of his Gospel with Peter from whom he acquired much of his material.[38] Their relationship must have been close and oriented towards Mark's learning, but no data exists for us to use in this study. The remaining Epistles and Revelation contain no real proof of any close, personal, one-to-one teaching relationships in the early communities of faith. That does not mean that they did not exist, but solid evidence is lacking.

Helpful evidence therefore exists in the Epistles for teaching occurring between some of the apostles and small numbers of other individuals. These relationships were of a close, paternal nature. Their learning included both knowledge and practice of the faith and encompassed imitation and the development of ministry skills as well as their holistic development as persons "in Christ".

LEARNING RELATIONSHIPS WITHIN THE MINISTRY TEAMS

The Epistles also portray close relationships between the small groups of believers who formed mission teams which travelled throughout the Empire with the message of Christ. Informal learning was not the primary object of their interactions, but would have been an important part of the experience. Judge believes these early 'missionaries' were not simple Galileans, but a "very cultivated section of internationalized Jewry"[39] and some Gentiles. Paul gathered groups of fellow workers around him wherever he travelled.[40] Other apostles and their associates did the same. Some were accompanied by their wives (1 Cor. 9:5). Few ministered alone. Fiorenza compares these teams with the mission of Jesus, "partnership or couple-mission, not individual missionary activity, seems to have been the rule in the Christian movement just as in the Jesus movement".[41] Their mission plan was similar to that of Jesus. From the close-knit faith communities selected members went out in partnerships or small sub-teams to bring the gospel to those who had not heard or to encourage newly planted churches.[42]

Thus both the teams and the partnerships provided opportunity for learning and for imitation of others. It is not stated, but we may surmise that collaborative learning took place as they reflected on their shared experiences and ministry (1 Thes. 4:9,18; 5:11). Those who were with the apostles or contemporaries of Jesus would have learnt his teachings directly from them. The more mature would have influenced the development of newer believers. And all who exercised their spiritual gifts would have participated in the growth of others.

LEARNING RELATIONSHIPS WITHIN THE FAITH COMMUNITIES

Even though the number of believers rapidly increased, they gathered in faith communities small enough to enable the development of relationships and provide opportunity for formal and informal learning. Andersen comments that communities "appear first whenever people are connected together by a common purpose or need and secondly when the relations between them are achieved in the manner of self-revelation and other-appreciation".[43] The churches were such communities. They shared their common life in Christ and desire to take his message to the world and their relationships were characterized by openness and mutual love and appreciation. The resultant nurturing environment provided opportunities for all to express their spiritual gifts within the community and in the wider world.

Within a few years numerous faith communities were scattered across the Roman Empire. Believers met in homes and when they outgrew their accommodation they divided and kept on growing.[44] Banks states that some groups were quite small. Even the largest would have included no more than 30-45 adults and children.[45] He argues for occasional 'whole church' meetings of various house groups in cities like Corinth (1 Cor. 1:2,11) although he claims that numbers in Rome precluded this possibility there.[46] He concludes, "Even the meetings of the 'whole church' were small enough for a relatively intimate relationship to develop between the members."[47]

Chapple considers the church at Thessalonica, "was relatively small in size, and its members were involved in the kind of face-to-face interaction that implies a strong sense of solidarity and common purpose."[48]

The Epistles know nothing of 'mega-churches'. It was expected that people in the faith communities would be able to know and care for one another, greet one another warmly (Rom. 16:16), judge those who erred from the way (1 Cor. 5:11-13) and contribute to the common good by exercising their spiritual gifts and actively participating in their gatherings (1 Cor. 14:26-31). Mutual ministry, corporate responsibility and meaningful interactions were only possible if numbers were small. If groups became too large, distributed participation would decrease, quality of interactions would deteriorate and subgroups would appear.[49] Thus the faith communities were small enough to enable meaningful, learning relationships to develop between all the men, women and children. And each member was able to contribute to the building up of others and to reach out in service beyond the community.

Conclusion

Thus evidence has been presented to show the importance of relationships in the early church. It is clear that they frequently resulted in learning between two individuals (as with Paul and Titus or Timothy), or within the mission teams, or as the house-churches gathered for worship and mutual ministry. Thus the second element in our definition of discipling, "two or a small group of individuals, typically in a community" has been demonstrated.

Holding to the same religious beliefs

It was established from Acts that 'disciples' were those who believed Jesus had conquered death and was in the presence of God as their Saviour, Lord and Master. They believed that they could relate personally to him by accepting his salvation in faith, by prayer and by obeying his teachings. Acts does not portray 'discipling' as a teacher or master bringing about learning in a disciple, but as small groups of believers forming close personal relationships, ministering together and learning from one another. It is now necessary to establish if these beliefs and intentions held by the church in Acts were consistent with the beliefs and practices of the writers and faith communities in the Epistles and Revelation.

The writers of the Epistles and Revelation affirm the belief that Jesus was both Lord and Christ, frequently using the terms "our Lord Christ Jesus" and "Jesus Christ our Lord".[50] He was the one who had been among them in full humanity,[51] and they believed was now present with the Father in glory (Rev. 1:13-20), possessing all power and authority, both in the church and in the world.[52] Through his sacrificial death he had brought many people into the family of God, to which they responded by voluntarily submitting to his authority and that of the Father (Rom. 8:15-17; 1 Pet. 1:3; 1 Jn. 2:1-5). Thus their belief concerning Jesus was consistent with his teaching concerning himself as Son of Man in the Gospels, and the dawning belief of his followers in Acts, that he was the universal Lord (Phil. 2:9-11; Col. 1:15-20; Jude 25; Rev. 5:9-14). Their basic creed was "Jesus is Lord" (Rom. 10:9; Phil. 2:11).

Their prime relationship was with Jesus and their lives fulfilled the conditions Rengstorf specifies for the use of the word *mathētēs* (disciple), when persons did not live at the same time as the one whose teachings they followed.[53] As we have previously noted, he points out that *mathētēs* could be used when there was an intellectual link between persons. The teacher's physical presence was not as necessary as the sharing of an inner fellowship which had practical effects in a desire to imitate the master. Thus the Epistles embody this concept of discipleship even though the term is not present. The phrase, 'in Christ', is used as a substitute to convey the concept of the close, personal spiritual relationship between Jesus Christ and his followers (Rom. 16:7-10; 1 Cor. 3:1; 15:22; 2 Cor. 5:17; Gal. 1:22; Eph. 3:6; 1 Thes. 4:16; 1 Pet. 3:16).

As has already been established, no one took over the same discipling role which belonged to Jesus. Christians would have no other Lord. They were his disciples and remained under his authority. Thus it was that the eye-witness accounts of the teaching of Jesus became authoritative and apostles as repositories of his words conveyed something of his authority (1 Cor. 12:28; Eph. 3:5; 4:11; 2 Pet. 3:2).[54] When the generation of witnesses began to die out teachings and writings with apostolic associations were collected into what later became the New Testament canon. These were regarded as revealing the will of God in a manner equal to the Jewish Scriptures (2 Pet. 3:16; 2 Tim. 3:16). The authority of judging between believers, deciding correct doctrines and discerning the mind of God was invested in the faith community as a whole, operating through the Spirit under the authority of Jesus' teachings and the Scriptures (1 Cor. 5:4,5; 6:1; Gal. 1:7-9; Col. 2:6,7; Heb. 4:12; 1 Jn. 4:3).

Teaching was thus seen as having vital importance. The apostles and other writers of the Epistles and Revelation wrote to help establish their readers as mature in the faith (Col. 1:28). They recognized the importance of equipping others as teachers to pass on the faith to future generations (2 Tim. 2:2; 1 Tim. 1:3). Leaders were to be selected according to their teaching ability (1 Tim. 3:2; 2 Tim. 2:24). Titus was encouraged to help the older women to teach "what is good" (Tit. 2:3). The recipients of Hebrews were rebuked because it was expected that they should be teachers, but their progress and learning had been too slow (Heb. 5:12).

False teaching was condemned. The Epistles and Revelation repeatedly warn against false teachers and the stringent judgement they face, because they are accountable for those they lead astray.[55] Paul warned Timothy of the futility of those who tried to teach without full understanding (1 Tim. 1:7). And his prohibition against women teaching is probably to be interpreted situationally in the light of the false, Gnostic-type teaching threatening Timothy's church in Ephesus (1 Tim. 2:12).[56]

The shared belief in the lordship of Christ and the necessity for faith and growth to maturity in him was the basis for the teaching-learning relationships of the Epistles. These relationships ensured the continuing well being of the shared life in Christ of the faith communities and those who mistaught or destroyed these relationships would be subject to severe judgement. The beliefs and intentions of these communities were consistent with those portrayed in the Gospels and Acts. The Gospel concept of 'making disciples' of Jesus is similar to the Pauline desire that people be firmly established 'in Christ'. This is achieved through the ministry of leaders, teachers and the life of the faith community. Those who did not hold to these beliefs were regarded as outsiders, having no part with Christ. They were neither disciples nor disciple-makers.

We have therefore confirmed that the third element in our definition of discipling, "holding to the same religious beliefs" has been strongly re-affirmed in the Epistles and Revelation.

Make a voluntary commitment to each other to form a close, personal relationship for an extended period of time

An examination of the teacher-learner relationships within the Epistles[57] necessitates investigation into the character, duration and voluntary nature of their commitments to one another. Not all individual relationships within the Epistles are able to be examined in this way, however there are some, and there are many general teachings which will also assist our search.

The teaching of the Epistles encourages close, personal relationships between all believers whether in house churches or in relationships with the wider group of all those who put their faith in Jesus Christ. Quality relationships were possible because of the limited numbers able to meet in a home. When they gathered in larger groups or welcomed visitors into their midst there was an immediate love and warmth among them which was fostered by Paul and others who regularly travelled among the churches, and brought news, greetings, encouragements and even practical assistance to them from their brothers and sisters in other places.

Paul encouraged the members of various faith communities to think of themselves as different parts of a body with specific but differing responsibilities, "members one of another" (*allēlous*) (Rom. 12;5; Eph. 4:25), who love, honour, care for and help bear burdens for one another (Rom. 12:10; 13:8; 1 Cor. 12:25; Gal. 6:2). He discouraged the destruction of others (biting or devouring) and advocated forgiveness and harmony, even if it involved persons waiving their own rights (Col. 3;13; Rom. 15:5; Eph. 5:21). However this did not mean that there were no standards, or that love could be equated with indulgent tolerance. Close relationships also entailed responsibility for correcting or teaching one another so that others were not misled into following a false way (Rom. 15:14).

Paul could not have extended a close personal relationship to every member of every church which he established, but he certainly committed himself to a significant number. These included Titus, Timothy and all his fellow workers (Rom. 16:9; Phil. 2:25-30; Col. 4:7-13 etc). He acknowledged a daily concern for the churches (2 Cor. 11:28) and encouraged members to commit themselves to one another. Warm relationships between Peter and Mark, John and Gaius have already received comment. John's rich love to the recipients of his letters is obvious throughout his writing by his repetition of such phrases as "my little children" (1 Jn. 2:1) or "beloved" (1 Jn. 4:7). He saw God's love outworking in the shared love within the community (1 Jn. 2:10; 3:10,11,14; 4:7,8,11,12,20; 5:1,2).

Peter emphasized the care which Jesus as the shepherd gives to his sheep (1 Pet. 2:25, Jn. 21:15-17), and encouraged leaders to tend the flock in their charge (1 Pet. 5:2). Young people and those who were older should have a mutual respect for one another (1 Pet. 5:5). Their love should involve commitment to pastoral care and concern for others. Hebrews exhorted believers to encourage one another in such a way that love and good deeds result (Heb. 10:24,25).

All these references describe relationships which believers should enjoy with one another.[58] Although some relationships were short passing encounters, within the faith communities there was a long-term commitment of members to one another. Paul's commitment was lifelong (2 Tim. 4:7-22), but those on his mission teams were committed to him for varying periods of time, some for a year or two, others long-term. Fellowship between those separated by distance was maintained by visits, prayers,[59] envoys and letters.

The voluntary nature of these relationships is seen in a few instances when free choice was involved. Titus "of his own accord" planned to revisit Corinth (2 Cor. 8:17). Demas after a time with Paul (Col. 4:14; Phm. 24), deserted and went to Thessalonica (2 Tim. 4:10). All Paul's companions left him at his first defence in Rome (2 Tim. 4:16). At other times people came and went under Paul's direction (1 Cor. 4:17; 2 Cor. 9:3-5; Eph. 6:21,22; Phil. 2:19; Col. 4:7,8 etc) but there seems no reason to doubt that the choice was theirs. Members of the churches were under no compulsion to belong, but were bonded by their common belief. Some drifted away from Christ and withdrew from fellowship (Heb. 2:1; 10:25). Those who were not genuine did not continue indefinitely (1 Jn. 2:19). But those who persevered to the end in spite of hardships proved the sincerity of their faith (Rev. 2:7,11).

We may therefore conclude that the Epistles and Revelation give numerous examples of persons and groups who voluntarily committed themselves to maintaining close, personal relationships with each other for extended periods of time. Thus the fourth condition for discipling, "a voluntary commitment to each other to form a close personal relationship for an extended period of time" is present in these writings.

To enable one to learn from the other

From the earliest days of the church, the apostles conveyed Jesus' teaching to others (Gal. 1:11,12,18; 2:1-10). Paul's encounter with Jesus and his rabbinic training set him aside as both apostle and teacher (1 Cor. 15:8,9; Rom. 1:1; Phil. 3:5,6). However as numbers increased apostles were not always present in every faith community. Those who had the spiritual gifts of prophecy, teaching and interpretation of tongues were therefore encouraged to exercise them in the body: *didaskō*-teaching (Rom. 12:7; 1 Cor. 14:12).

However all the gifts were given so that all might be built up (*oikodomeō*-teaching) and the message of Jesus made known to the world (Eph. 4:11-13). Thus teaching was not just confined to verbal instruction but extended to example and active ministry, so that all members, men, women or children taught others on occasion.

For much of the life of the church it has been considered that women should not teach men in matters of faith on the basis of 1 Timothy 2:12.[60] In the light of our present study this poses a very difficult problem. If, as has been stated already, upbuilding results from the healthy operation of the whole of the life of the faith community, then everything which believers do will enable others to learn. This will include informal modelling, active service, words of encouragement, not to mention any formal teaching in which they engage. If women are part of the discipling community, it is inevitable that others, including men, will learn from them.

From 1 Corinthians 11:5 it is clear that women contributed to the upbuilding of the faith community by their prayer and prophecy. Paul prescribed that when they did so they were to act in a culturally appropriate manner. He also encouraged all members of the church to strive for the gift of prophecy because it was most effective in building up the church (1 Cor. 14:1-5). It is therefore difficult to know what he was prohibiting when he said he did not permit women to teach or have authority over men. Powers holds that women were not to teach husbands.[61] Evans believes Paul was prohibiting the women (or wives) of Ephesus "from usurping an authority that was not rightly theirs and from domineering over the men by their teaching".[62] "It is not the question of instructing or teaching him but the manner of doing it."[63] Kroeger and Kroeger maintain that Paul was forbidding the women from perpetrating a Gnostic-type heresy common around Ephesus, which taught that woman was the originator of man.[64] Whatever was the exact nature of Paul's prohibition, it seems that it was not an all encompassing one which applied in all situations. As full members of the community of faith, some women would have been involved in formal teaching through prophecy, and others in informal teaching as they exercised their spiritual gifts which enabled learning to take place in the lives of other members, men, women and children. The leadership positions which women held in various house churches bears this out.[65]

The corporate life of the faith communities gives us every indication that teaching covered a wide range of different activities. Learning occurred in many different situations as formally and informally believers in Christ related to one another as individuals and in small groups, in worship, ministry and the daily functions of life. Opportunities abounded for intentional and unintentional learning to take place between men, women and children enabling the fifth condition for discipling to take place, "to enable one to learn from the other".

Conclusions

Thus the five conditions which we stipulated in our revised working definition as essential to discipling have been found to be present in the world of the Epistles and Revelation. We therefore conclude that the concept of discipling was a common practice evident in the teaching and learning encounters of the early faith communities in the period in which these documents were written, even though the term itself is nowhere used.

Within the living, growing, working, faith communities three different situations in which discipling operated were evident. It was present in master-apprentice or parent-child type relationships between two individuals when one person who was seen to have greater knowledge, maturity or skills worked alongside and lovingly nurtured another, resulting in their learning. It occurred among members of the mission teams as they went out together with the message of Christ on behalf of the faith communities, and sought to nurture those newly established in the faith. In these small teams, leaders and members were seen as examples, teachers, proclaimers of the faith and encouragers of the work of ministry. Finally, discipling occurred within each local faith community as individual members exercised their spiritual gifts within the loving, caring body of believers. While some accepted greater responsibility for teaching and building up the body, no one member was always teacher or always learner. Men, women and children learnt from one another as they shared their lives in worship of God and participated in his mission to the world.

Thus intentional, largely informal activities abounded, in which two or a small group of individuals typically in a community, and holding to the same beliefs, voluntarily committed themselves to each other to form close, personal relationships for an extended period of time, to enable one to learn from the other.

Spiritual gifts and discipling

The gift of teaching/teachers (*didaskalous*) appears in the 1 Corinthians 12:28 list of spiritual gifts, third after apostles and prophets. Elsewhere it is in association with prophecy and service (Rom. 12:6,7), preaching and apostleship (1 Tim. 2:7; 2 Tim. 1:11) and pastoring (Eph. 4:11). Paul classifies it as one of the higher/greater (*meizona*) gifts to be desired (1 Cor. 12:29-31). Its prominence may suggest that it was a gift associated with leadership and more formal teaching situations.

Nowhere is a gift of discipling mentioned. We may therefore assume that it probably involved the gift of teaching when either *didaskō*-teaching or *oikodomeō*-teaching took place. However the ones who exercised other spiritual gifts which resulted in the upbuilding (*oikodomeō*-teaching) of the community as a whole may also be described as involved in the activity of discipling.

Those who exercised a direct intentional teaching role with individuals, small groups and the faith community would frequently have been leaders (a spiritual gift, Rom. 12:8) or more mature believers. Ability to teach was regarded as a qualification of leaders, elders or bishops within the faith community (1 Tim. 3:2; 5:17; 2 Tim. 2:24; Tit. 1:9). They also were entrusted with the responsibility of equipping others to teach (2 Tim. 2:2). Thus it may be deduced that many of the leaders of the faith communities had the requisite gifts to enable them to disciple both individuals, small groups and the whole faith community.

Leadership in the Christian community was to be patterned on the servanthood of Jesus (Phil. 2:5-8). It was to involve pastoral care of the members of the community like that of a shepherd with his flock. In the Old Testament shepherds were responsible to provide nourishment, strengthen the sick, weak and injured and restore the lost and straying (Ezk. 34:2-4). Jesus nurtured those in his care, brought others to himself and gave himself for their salvation (Jn. 10:14-16). Teaching feeds, nurtures and sustains. Peter who had been specifically commissioned to a shepherding role among Jesus' sheep exhorted his fellow elders to do the same (1 Pet. 5:2-4). This explains why the gifts of pastor and teacher are mentioned together. They are however two different, but related functions. Tidball summarizes Paul's pastoral strategy as being encouragement, enabling, exposition, example and exhortation.[66] Pastoring encompasses more of the general overall care for the health and safety of individuals within the larger flock and the seeking of those who stray or have not yet come into the fold. This has many elements in common with discipling and *oikodomeō*-teaching, but less overlap with *didaskō*-teaching.

Earlier it was suggested that *didaskō*-teaching was closely related to formal teaching which is frequently equated with the schooling model of teaching. It is certainly part of discipling but is limited in all that it is able to convey of the Christian life and experience. *Oikodomeō*-teaching is much broader in range and ability to influence change, growth and development. It is the result of all the members of the faith community exercising their gifts for the common good (1 Cor. 12:7) that all will grow to maturity, to the full stature of Christ (Eph. 4:13).

We are now ready to move from the biblical evidence into a study of discipling as a model of teaching in modern educational research. We will seek to reach a satisfactory definition of discipling which will include the biblical elements discovered and we will attempt to express them in terms relevant for Christian education in the church of today.

Notes to Chapter 9

1 The only occurrences of *akoloutheō* in the Epistles are 1 Cor. 10:4 and Rev. 6:8; 14:4,8,9,13; 19:14. Of these only Rev. 14:4 relates to the life of discipleship. The 144,000 "follow the Lamb wherever he goes" (Rev. 14:1-5). They belong to him and are described as being in God's presence, the ultimate outcome of their faithful following. (Backmann & Slasby, 1980, 70)
2 Giles, 1979, 68
3 Longenecker, 1996, 72,73
4 Aland, 1978, 74,75
5 Persons who taught or are encouraged to teach include God himself, the Spirit, Paul, Timothy, recognised teachers, elders, the church at Colossae and people at Corinth (Tit. 2:10; 1 Jn. 2:27; 1 Cor. 2:13; 4:17; 14:26; 1 Tim. 4:6,13,16; 5:17; 2 Tim. 1:11; 4:11; 6:2; Rom. 12:7; Col. 3:16).
6 This is similar to the gift of evangelism, where all are expected to share the good news with others, but some are specially gifted to do so to a greater extent.
7 In 1 Corinthians 11:23 Paul uses two technical words of the rabbis. *Paralambanō* (to receive, Hebrew *quibbel*) means to receive a tradition which has been passed on (also in 1 Cor. 15:3; Gal. 1:9,12; 1 Thes. 2:13; 4:1; 2 Thes. 3:6). *Paradidōmi* (to pass on, hand down, Hebrew *masar*) indicates the passing down of tradition (also in 1 Cor. 11:2; 15:3; 2 Pet. 2:21; Jude 3). Together Paul is showing that these traditions may be traced in an unbroken line to Jesus himself. (Rienecker, 1980, 80)
8 Aland, 1978, 194,195
9 See also Mt. 16:18
10 Andersen, 1984, 33
11 Hanson, 1963, 442
12 Aland, 1978, 174,175
13 Arndt & Gingrich, 1957, 491
14 Wilds & Lottich, 1961, 15,90,125,132

15 Jervis, 1996, 145,148
16 Wild, 1985, 133,136,138 (See also Jervis, 1996, 143-162)
17 Is. 59:15-20. Wild, 1985, 136
18 Giles quotes Betz and Schulz who studied the Gospels and Epistles in relation to imitating Christ. They conclude that there is purely a difference in terminology, not essence, between a follower or disciple of Christ and one who imitates him. (Giles, 1979, 69)
19 Not all scholars agree that Philippians 2:5-11 is a call to imitate Christ. Michaelis, Kasemann, Martin and Bauder all hold that Christ's example is far too exalted for any person to dream of emulating. However for those who maintain that the Jesus of history and the Christ of faith are the same person, it is possible for Christians to "strive to emulate the attitude and actions of servanthood that marked" his character. (Hawthorne, 1996, 167-169)
20 Lane, 1996, 219,220
21 Elliott, 1985, 203
22 Michaels, 1996, 267
23 Blomberg, 1976, 10
24 Kurz, 1985, 105
25 These included the household of Stephanus (1 Cor. 16:15-18), Timothy and Epaphroditus (Phil. 2:20-30), churches at Corinth, Thessalonica and in Judea (2 Cor. 9:2,3; 1 Thes. 1:6-10; 2:14) and individuals in Rome (Rom. 16:1-11).
26 Teaching in the early church affirmed the family responsibilities of husbands, wives, parents and children and the necessity of caring for all family members (1 Cor. 7:1-40; Eph. 5:21-6:4; Col. 3:18-21; 1 Tim. 5:4-16). All, whether masters, slaves or free, were encouraged to work for their living as if they were working for Christ (Eph. 6:5-9; Col. 3:22-4:1; 1 Thes. 4:11; 2 Thes. 3:6-13). The sharing of all goods in common which occurred in the newly formed church at Jerusalem was not a continuing pattern in the apostolic period. Believers who had property were encouraged to be generous to the needy, rich in good deeds and willing to share with others (1 Tim. 6:17-19).
27 Junia was an apostle (Rom. 16:7). This does not mean that she was one of the Twelve or had necessarily seen the risen Christ, but was included among the wider group in the primitive church whose apostleship was incontrovertibly linked with the missionary commission (M‚ller, 1975, 134). Phoebe was a woman deacon (Rom. 16:1). Priscilla shared leadership of a house-church with her husband, Aquila (Rom. 16:5). Nympha probably led the church in her home (Col. 4:15). Euodia and Syntyche in Philippi held some form of leadership responsibility. Paul described them as his co-workers having "struggled beside him in the work of the gospel" (Phil. 4;2,3). Chrysostom believed that these two women were the heads of the church in Philippi. (Koperski, 1999, 543)
28 Silas with Paul was flogged, imprisoned and put in the stocks. Priscilla and Aquila risked their lives for Paul. Aristarchus and Epaphras were imprisoned. Aristarchus and Gaius narrowly escaped being lynched. Epaphroditus almost died of illness. Trophimus' ill-health caused him to remain behind in Miletus. Euodia and Syntyche struggled in the work of the gospel. Luke, and possibly Aristarchus, suffered shipwreck.
29 The authorship of the Pastoral Epistles is a matter of some debate. Two main viewpoints are held. (1) The traditional view that Paul was the author, possibly with the assistance of an amanuensis or secretary. (2) The writings are pseudonymous and may or may not contain genuine Pauline fragments. (Lea & Griffin, 1992, 23)
Reasons given for the uncertainty are:
• apparent conflict between the historical references in the Pastorals and Acts.

- differences in style, vocabulary and language between the Pastorals and other Pauline Epistles.
- false teachings alluded to appear very similar to second century Gnostic heresy.
- theological differences from other Pauline writings
- a developed ecclesiology and church organisation beyond that otherwise known in the first century.

All of these are able to be answered reasonably in ways which do not totally rule out Pauline authorship. Donald Guthrie concludes a lengthy examination of all the evidence, "In spite of the acknowledged differences between the Pastorals and Paul's other Epistles, the traditional view that they are authentic writings of the apostle cannot be said to be impossible, and since there are greater problems attached to the alternative theories it is most reasonable to suppose that the early Church was right in accepting them as such." (Guthrie, 1970, 620)

30 The "relationship between Paul and his two young friends in the pastorals is identical to that suggested in 1 Cor 4:17, Phil 2:19-23 and 2 Cor 2:13; 7:6,13." (Lea & Griffin, 1992, 39)

31 Paul refers to him as "my brother", "my partner and co-worker" (2 Cor. 2:13; 8:23), "my loyal child in the faith" (Tit. 1:4).

32 Paul was unable to rest and moved on from Troas because Titus had not joined them (2 Cor. 2:12,13).

33 Paul trusted him to operate "with the same spirit" and "take the same steps" as he would himself (2 Cor. 12:18).

34 Paul referred to Timothy as "my beloved and faithful child in the Lord", "my loyal child in the faith" (1 Cor. 4:17; Phil. 2:22; 1 Tim. 1:2,18).

35 Kurz, 1985, 106,107

36 Older scholars took this to mean a particular lady and her children but by the interchange of singular and plural in the Greek it seems more likely that the writer is collectively referring to the members of a house church. (Marshall, 1978b, 60)

37 It is not clear who this man was and because at that time Gaius was the most common name in the Roman Empire we may not gain too much by trying to identify him. Those mentioned in the New Testament are Gaius of Macedonia (Acts 19:29), Gaius of Derbe (Acts 20:4) and Gaius of Corinth (Rom. 16:23; 1 Cor. 1:14). Tradition associates this Gaius with Derbe. (Stott, 1975, 217)

38 Eusebius comments on Papias of Hierapolis (c.130 AD) who records a tradition that Mark was the interpreter of Peter. (Stevenson, 1970, 52)

39 Judge as cited in Fiorenza, 1983, 169

40 There were eight with him in Macedonia. (Acts 20:4,5)

41 Fiorenza, 1983, 172

42 Erastus and Timothy went to Macedonia (Acts 19:22), Tychicus to Ephesus and Artemas or Tychicus was sent to Titus in Crete. Silas (Silvanus) remained with Timothy in Beroea to proclaim the way of salvation (Acts 17:13-15). Epaphras founded the church at Colossae and always wrestled in prayer for them. Silas and Timothy shared in writing letters to the church at Thessalonica. Priscilla and Aquila explained the Way of God more accurately to Apollos. Epaphroditus carried gifts from the Philippian church to help meet Paul's needs. Others were house church leaders including Philemon at Colossae, Aquila and Priscilla in Ephesus, Rome and possibly Corinth and Gaius probably was at Corinth.

43 Andersen, 1989, 27

44 A number of house-churches existed in Jerusalem (Acts 2:46; 5:42; 12:12), Ephesus (Acts

20:20), Rome (Rom. 16:5,11,14,15), Colossae (Col. 4:9,17, Phm. 1,2), Laodicea (Col. 4:15,16) and Philippi (Phil. 1:1).
45 Banks, 1980, 41
46 Banks, 1980, 40
47 Banks, 1980, 42
48 Chapple, 1984, 206
49 Chapple, 1984, 90
50 Rom. 5:1; 2 Cor. 13:13; Gal. 6:18; Eph. 1:3; 1 Thes. 1:3; 2 Thes. 3:18; 1 Tim. 1:2; 2 Pet. 1:11; Rev. 22:21.
51 2 Cor. 5:16; Phil. 2:7; 1 Jn. 1:1; Rev. 1:5.
52 Rom. 8:34; 14:9; 1 Cor. 2:8; 15:25; Eph. 1:20-23; Phil. 2:9-11; Col. 1:18; 1 Tim. 6:15; Rev. 11:8; 17:14.
53 As previously noted. (Rengstorf, 1967, 417)
54 Apostles did not believe they had authority in their own right. When Paul was guiding the church at Corinth in matters relating to marriage, he clearly distinguished between his words and those of the Lord, although he did not negate the value of his own conclusions which he believed had the endorsement of God's Spirit (1 Cor. 7:10,12,25,40).
55 Rom. 16:17; Gal. 1:6-9; 2:4; Col. 2:8,20-23; 1 Tim. 6:3-5; 2 Tim. 4:3,4; Tit. 1:10-16; Heb. 13:9; Jas. 3:1-2; 2 Pet. 2:1-22; 1 Jn. 4:1-6: 2 Jn. 7-11; Jude 8-16; Rev. 2:14,15,20 etc.
56 Kroeger & Kroeger make a strong case for this heresy at Ephesus involving women acting as oracles of the gods, fertility rites, the practice of magic, ancient myths kept alive by old women and perversions of the Adam and Eve saga. (Kroeger & Kroeger, 1992, 62-76,103)
57 No teacher-learner relationships are apparent in Revelation.
58 Other references to 'one another' in the New Testament are exhortations to love (Jn. 13:34,35; 15:12,17; 1 Pet. 1:22; 1 Jn. 3:11,14,23; 4:12; 2 Jn. 5) and not speak evil or grumble against one another (Jas. 4:11; 5:9) or complain among one another (Jn. 6:43) and to be at peace (Mk. 9:50). Jesus warned that the time would come when many would fall away and betray or hate one another (Mt. 24:10).
59 Prayer was a crucial part of both John (3 Jn. 2) and Paul's relationships with people and the churches. Paul gave thanks and prayed constantly for them (Rom. 1:9). He expected their prayer support to be reciprocal (1 Thes. 5:25; 2 Thes. 3:1). He encouraged prayer for everyone and all situations no matter how trivial, with supplications, intercessions and thanksgivings (1 Tim. 2:1,2,8).
60 "I permit no woman to teach or to have authority over a man; she is to keep silent."
61 Powers, 1975, 57
62 Evans, 1983, 103
63 Anderson as cited in Evans, 1983, 103
64 Kroeger, 1992, 103
65 The leadership of Phoebe, Junia, Priscilla, Nympha, Euodia and Syntyche has already been noted.
66 Tidball, 1986, 114

# PART 4

Chapter 10

Refining the Definition

The concept of 'discipling' as it was understood in the world of the Ancient Near East has been examined and a detailed investigation has been made of its operation in the life of Jesus Christ and his followers as portrayed by the writers of the four Gospels. We have also explored its relevance and practice within the life of the early Christian church by a careful study of the Acts of the Apostles, the Epistles and Revelation.

Before we proceed to assess discipling as an educational strategy within Christian faith communities of the modern era it will be necessary to re-visit our definition of 'teaching' and also to attempt to locate discipling within a family of similar teaching models. Various categories of teaching will be considered. Formal and informal models will be examined. The schooling model, which has proved popular in Christian educational thinking, will be defined. Models of teaching closely related to discipling will be surveyed and their distinguishing characteristics highlighted to enable comparisons to be made and greater understanding of the concept of discipling. Those models to be examined will include parenting and socialisation; learning communities; relationships and collaborative learning; learning webs and networks; apprenticing and mentoring; spiritual direction; and pastoral care, counselling and psychotherapy.

In our search for a suitable contemporary definition of Christian discipling, the *Oxford English Dictionary*, Greek derivations and popular Christian writings will be consulted. The revised working definition which was reached in Chapter Seven will then form the basis for our second and final formulation.

Exploration of teaching

Definition of teaching

Before doing so, we return to the brief definition of teaching proposed in Chapter One, "an attempt by one person (a teacher) to cause another person or persons to learn". The *Oxford English Dictionary* defines 'to teach' as "to show by way of information or instruction" or "to educate, train, school".[1] But educational philosophers have not seen it as quite so simple. They have argued at length whether 'learning' has to take place in order for an action to be classified as 'teaching'. It is not necessary to reproduce that debate here, but some of its elements are helpful. The discussion mainly centres around learning, or the intention that learning should occur.

Scheffler proposed that for an activity to be classified as 'teaching', intention for learning to occur was a sufficient requirement.[2] Hill defined teaching as, "Intervention by one person intended to cause or guide learning by another person."[3] Paul Hirst included both teaching intention and learning intention in his definition: "the activity of a person, A (the teacher), the intention of which is to bring about an activity (learning), by a person, B (the pupil), the intention of which is to achieve some end state (eg. knowing, appreciating) whose object is X (eg. a belief, attitude, skill)".[4]

Kleinig posited the possibility of someone teaching by unintentional example and concluded that teaching is something to which 'responsibility for learning' can be ascribed.[5] He suggested that the task-sense of teaching be dropped altogether and took up Freeman's argument of perficience (something being brought about or achieved through someone's actions). He continues, "Teaching would appear to be almost exclusively a perficiency transaction – unless of course, one wishes to argue that not only is there no teaching without learning but also no learning without teaching."[6] Andersen writes, "It is the impact which is significant rather than the teacher's conscious intention at a particular moment."[7] These all demonstrate that teaching is a difficult concept to define.

Attempts have been made to specify other essential teaching characteristics. Scheffler attempted to exclude 'indoctrination' or 'brainwashing'[8] from being considered as 'teaching', by emphasising the need for the pupil's reasoning ability and understanding to be involved.[9] Hirst and Peters saw it as desirable that teachers indicate or demonstrate the matters to be learnt in such a way that they are intelligible to, and within, the capacities of the learners.[10] These are important issues but they do not constitute necessary conditions for something to be designated as teaching. One may also ask whether teaching is involved in the 'hidden curriculum'[11] with its unplanned or unintended learning.

For our present purposes it is sufficient to note the general concern to stress the importance of intention that learning should take place, the teacher's role in bringing that about and the impact on the learner. We will however return to our original definition of teaching and affirm it as sufficient for our purposes.

Models of teaching

In endeavouring to understand discipling we first must enquire whether it can be located within a family of teaching processes. This is not an easy task. A number of different families or models of teaching have been identified and various teaching methods have been categorized within each model, but because teaching has so many different facets the lines of definition between models may overlap in numerous respects.

Weil, Joyce and Kluwin have proposed four families of teaching methodologies.[12]
- 'Social interaction models' which focus primarily, although not exclusively, on relationships of the individual to society or to others, and include such activities as group investigation and role playing.
- 'Information processing models' which help people respond to stimuli or problems from their environment, analyse data, find solutions and use verbal and non-verbal symbols in the processes. They include concept attainment, inductive thinking and scientific enquiry.
- 'Personal models' involving development of selfhood and the emotional life. They encompass non-directive teaching and awareness training.
- 'Behaviour modification models' which include reinforcement and operant conditioning.

The weakness in trying to use these families to clarify the idea of discipling is that these writers have rooted them all in a schooling system.[13] This immediately causes problems for discipling, since it (a) does not operate under the schooling model and (b) includes dimensions from three of the four categories. Discipling has a social interaction dimension assisting in the development of persons in their relationships with God, others and society. Its information processing dimension encourages development of the mind, knowledge, the ability to think, analyse and problem-solve. And in the area of personal development it seeks to nurture healthy, realistic self-awareness. Thus these models of teaching provide little assistance in clarifying the concept of discipling.

Richards and Hoeldtke cite the anthropologist Fortes' classification of teaching into artificial and real life situations. The first encompasses schooling and formal education while the second includes informal models of education, which operate in a manner similar to the socialisation or parenting models.[14] They see both of these families of teaching models in operation in the Bible. Discipling encompasses elements from both, but has closer associations with informal learning situations. Richards and Hoeldtke make the point that teaching Christianity is much more than right belief. That may be communicated in a formal setting, but there is much else which is better taught informally within and through real life settings.

Thus in attempting to clarify discipling, Fortes' distinctions between the artificial and the real life situations have proved a helpful starting point. Schooling is a formal, institutionalized instrument artificial construct, whereas discipling functions best within the informal interactions of everyday life. It will be helpful therefore first to study the schooling model in order to have a reference point from which to assess other models of teaching which are more closely related to everyday life.

Schooling or formal education

'Schooling' may be viewed in many ways. The *Oxford English Dictionary* defines 'school' as a "place or establishment for instruction".[15] Illich places emphasis on the organisational aspect of 'schooling' as an "age specific, teacher related process requiring full-time attendance at an obligatory curriculum".[16] Walker, Mumford and Steel focus on the people involved as an "organised group of pupils pursuing defined studies at defined levels and receiving instruction from one or more teachers".[17] Hill sees schooling as, "the institutionalisation of learning in a place where professionally trained teachers work with large groups of students in classrooms, structuring their learning through the use of a compulsory, graded curriculum monitored by various kinds of formal assessment".[18]

These definitions serve most aspects of primary and secondary education reasonably well, however some of them do not apply as easily to the formal education supplied by tertiary and adult educational institutions where individual research, tutorials, problem-based learning methods or development of practical skills are commonly recognized practices. But whatever the conditions, schooling and formal education have been artificially constructed and require the presence of a number of organisational structures. These usually find expression in some form of building, entry requirement, prepared curriculum, assessment procedure, teacher qualification and reimbursement for services rendered, and formal recognition for those who achieve a specified level of competence. While every condition may not apply in every situation, the schooling model requires that most of these factors will be present to some degree.

This is not to assert that elements of informal education are never present in schools. In the playground or sports field, at camps, in informal teacher-pupil or pupil-pupil contacts much informal learning occurs. Sometimes it is intentional. On other occasions there is a 'hidden curriculum'. But the predominant emphasis of the schooling model is its institutionalized, formal teaching focus.

Life related, informal education

Educationists such as Paul Goodman have observed that institutionalized learning rather than enriching a child's natural intellectual development, tends to stunt and produce regimented, competitive citizens.[19] In contrast, informal teaching methods which arise naturally from a person's environment, provide the means for satisfying innate curiosity and active participation, thus achieving more effective learning.

Informal education has been defined as, "any organised educational activity outside the established formal system – whether operating separately or as an important feature of some broader activity – that is intended to serve identifiable learning clienteles and learning objectives".[20]

This family of educational models does not require the necessity of withdrawal into a classroom or a structured, controlled environment in order for teaching to take place. For this reason the question may arise as to whether these models are actually teaching at all, or if they would be better classified as learning. In the light of our earlier definition of teaching as an intention or attempt by one person to cause another to learn, we have regarded only those situations in real life where some organisation or intention for learning operates, as models of teaching. These may at times incorporate some aspects of formal education but greater emphasis is given to informal methods. Discipling falls within this family. In this study it will be contrasted with other related models, but first it is necessary to clarify their essential nature.

Socialisation and Parenting

Socialisation and parenting are not always considered as teaching models because individual participants do not always express a teaching intention. However on a broad scale, society and families intend that new members learn.

Socialisation has been defined in various ways over the past century. Ross, writing in 1896, considered socialisation as a teaching model which involved "moulding of an individual's feelings and desires to suit the needs of the group".[21] Brim defines it as "a process of learning through which an individual is prepared with varying degrees of success, to meet the requirements laid down by other members of society for his behaviour in a variety of situations".[22] Socialisation is a special kind of learning activity involving an enormous variety of processes whereby a person acquires their own individual personality and self-identity and absorbs the culture of their society. John Westerhoff combines elements from sociology, psychology and anthropology to describe socialisation as the lifelong formal and informal ways one generation seeks to sustain and transmit its understanding and way of life; seeks to induct its young into and reinforce for its adults a particular set of values and responsible adult roles; and seeks to help persons develop self-identity through participation in the life of a people with their more or less distinctive ways of thinking, feeling and acting.[23]

Although much of its teaching is allied to the hidden curriculum, there is sufficient organisation and intention that learning should occur for it to be considered as a model of teaching performed by an enormous variety of persons, groups or media. It is closely associated with parenting.

The educational role of the family is as old as civilisation. "Families or stable units in which adults are available, able, and willing to assume [responsibilities for the nurturance of children,] are the only viable models human societies have developed as yet"[24] for the early education and socialisation of those born into them. Both Jews and Christians acknowledge the importance of the parenting model of teaching as fundamental to the passage of faith from generation to generation (Deut 4.9, 5.16, 6.1-9, Eph 6.1-4). They use the parent-child relationship to describe the relationship between a believer and his or her God (Hos 11.1, Gal 4.6).

The *Oxford English Dictionary* defines parenting as "to be or act as a parent" or "the single minded unconditional desire to provide a loving caring home".[25]

This is not sufficiently precise for our purposes. Leichter however posits a broad definition for education, which she then applies to parents and family, "the deliberate systematic, and sustained effort to transmit, evoke, or acquire knowledge, values, skills and sensibilities and any learning that results from the effort, direct or indirect, intended or unintended".[26]

Hill believes, "*Parents* are teachers; the learning environments in which they operate are the home and the family outing; and the teaching methods they use are mostly informal."[27] Children learn naturally by watching, asking questions, listening, imitating, repeating, playing, doing, going places, being creative and by their innate curiosity.[28] Parents and the wider family have an important role in nurturing the natural inclination towards learning. They provide a secure, loving environment with appropriate stimulation, and a variety of opportunities for the child to use its senses to explore the world, to be creative, and to gain experiences which will provoke thinking and the use of intellect. They encourage learning by praising, helping, advising and assisting in reflection on successes and failures. Thus many of life's basic understandings, values, attitudes, social skills, behaviours, culture, language and numerous other concepts and skills are learnt and developed.

It is important to note that the present trend towards home-based education cannot always be seen as synonymous with parenting. Where a formal curriculum and organized teaching materials are used, the parents may be little more than formal classroom teacher-substitutes. However the model has advantages over what is normally termed 'schooling' because of its more personalized approach to children as individuals, allowing for the child to proceed at his or her own pace and pursue individual interests. A much greater level of two-way interaction between children and teacher/parent is also possible. It allows for a wider variety of learning relationships apart from those with immediate peers and one teacher, which may result in the development of greater social skills and social maturity. It provides opportunity for the child to be involved in life-related activities associated with parental or community pursuits. And its emphasis on self-directed learning and self-discipline creates more confident independent learners.[29]

Learning Communities

Another model of teaching is the learning community. It may be a small or large group which gathers so that its members may learn together from one another. The teaching process is closely related to the life of the community, although frequently no one person accepts complete responsibility for this. The roles of teacher and learner are often interchangeable.

Community is defined in the *Oxford English Dictionary* as "a body of persons living together and practising more or less community of goods".[30] The Macquarie Dictionary elaborates further, "a group of any size whose members reside in a specific locality, share government and have a cultural and historical heritage".[31] Knapp defines community as "a group of organisms gathered together in close association under common rules."[32] Some degree of common interest amongst its members is implied. A teaching-learning community has the added dimension that it intends to produce learning.

There are many different short and long-term community possibilities which have been utilized for learning over millennia. These range from pre-historic village communities educating their offspring, communities of young men gathered around ancient Greek philosophers, closed communities, religious communities, university residential halls and boarding schools, to organized short-term camping programs for today's youth.

From the early days of the church's history, men and women committed themselves to religious communities for life, and worked towards the benefit of others both within and outside their group. Some concentrated on withdrawal from the evils of society, prayer, contemplation or service, while others had study or teaching and learning as their intention. The latter groups kept the basics of Christian scholarship alive during the Middle Ages. Many produced learning which resulted in changed attitudes, values and behaviours as well as increased knowledge and understandings, although some had the characteristics of closed institutions[33] with their lack of true freedom and beneficial learning.

Not all learning communities exist for lengthy periods of time. Of recent years organized camping has provided temporary communities in which teaching and learning may occur. Slater examines three basic characteristics of organized camping: it takes place outdoors; it involves community; it aims to be educative.[34]

Within the life of an organized camping community many informal teaching-learning interactions arise and opportunity for reflective thinking may be increased. The residential component enables learning of a different nature than is possible in non-residential circumstances. Individuals have opportunities to build relationships through increased time for informal conversations. They learn to focus beyond themselves for the good of the communal group with all its diversity and observation of the attitudes, values and behaviours of others is facilitated. Increased ability to resolve conflict may also result.[35]

Adventure education is an interesting recent model of informal education which often accompanies the camping experience. It fulfils a role similar to initiation ceremonies which were often a model of learning utilized in primitive societies. Adventure education occurs when a person engages in some challenging physical activity, in the natural environment, under the careful supervision of an experienced outdoor educator. It aims to promote learning from risk-taking, without damage or destruction and to achieve an end which cannot be reached in any other way.[36]

These activities provide opportunities for participants to increase in understanding of self, others and the natural world and to reflect on their feelings, experiences and beliefs when pushed to the limits of their endurance and confronted by the element of danger.

Learning through relationships and in collaboration with others

Relationships between persons often result in informal learning. Sometimes a teaching intention is present. Some learning relationships are of a collaborative nature, others may be unequal for a time, as the one with superior knowledge or skills seeks to impart those to another. Hill recognizes that within the community of faith the ultimate outcome of the unequal relationship (between teacher and learner) is that the latter will eventually come to the same degree of understanding as the teacher. "When each recognises the other as essentially an equal, each feels free to learn from the other without feeling put down or inferior, and the roles of teacher and learner see-saw as different needs arise and each explores the gifts and knowledge of the other."[37] He continues, "This situation arises most readily between friends of equal age. Also it is recognised in the New Testament as the most mature level of learning a community of faith can attain in the situation where each is constantly learning from the other."[38]

Collaborative learning frequently results when a group of peers work in cooperation with one another. Friend and Cook have defined 'collaboration' as "a style for direct interaction between at least two coequal parties voluntarily engaged in shared decision making as they work toward a common goal".[39] If we apply this to learning, then collaborative learning involves at least two coequal parties accepting responsibility for, and sharing resources as they work towards achieving some learning goal or outcome for which together they will be accountable. It is considered to be a teaching model when the organisation and intention for learning are expressed in some way. It may operate either informally in real life situations or within a structured teaching environment. Collaborative learning is a major resource in many real life situations including business and industry and professions such as medicine, law, engineering and architecture.[40] Its philosophy may sometimes be associated with the formation of learning communities.[41] Bruffee believes that it is a powerful educative force largely unharnessed by traditional educational methods.

Groups of interested persons who gather to pursue an interest in a voluntary way are widely recognized as places where significant learning occurs. Hill writes, "It is in voluntary settings that passive learning flowers into personal creativity, leadership, and moral responsibility."[42] In Australia there may be as many as 500,000 voluntary organisations involving 4 million people wishing to pursue their own special interests.[43] These include sporting clubs, youth groups, hobby or special interest groups and religious bodies. These groups centre on a shared body of knowledge, beliefs or skills which are conveyed informally through the example of others and personal relationships between members. Not all of these groups are oriented towards learning, and what learning there is may not always be orderly or easily defined.

Learning in relationship with others or in collaboration with peers has provided a powerful force in the educative processes of both young and old throughout the history of the world. It is particularly effective in influencing change and development of attitudes, values, social and practical skills, and behaviours of people of all ages.

Learning Webs and Networking

Ivan Illich observed the inadequacies of the schooling model in both Latin America and the US and proposed an alternative model. He advocated the drastic measure of "deschooling" society and replacing schools with 'learning webs'. These he suggested were things in the environment, models (patterns coming from ideas and practices), and social situations with peers and elders which would arise informally in life situations and had the potential to be used for teaching and learning.[44] He likened the ideal learning environment to a village where every happening influences individual and social life. This model is similar to the processes of socialisation. By building on inherent curiosity and the desire to be active, alert and fluid, he taught that learning takes place in response to life's challenges. He saw the teacher as a facilitator and educator of the self-directed learning opportunities of others.[45] Illich's associate, Reimer, shared his disillusionment with schooling and proposed the establishment of 'networks' consisting of things, people and voluntary educational services to be used informally by learners.[46]

Illich believed that technology should be available to provide an additional resource, although he did not advocate unlimited 'electronic gadgetry'. It is fascinating to see his vision almost thirty years ago of "a vast computer-information storage and retrieval system"[47] as an educational tool fulfilled today in the internet which has become an invaluable learning resource for the more privileged members of the world community.

The critics of Illich are numerous. As a substitute for general schooling, he does not seem to have thought through its full implications. To totally deschool society has serious shortcomings. It may be invaluable for those who are more mature, strongly motivated and enabled by life situations to take advantage of learning opportunities. However not everyone has the maturity, resources, time, motivation or inclination to learn the things which a society expects of its members. If Illich's model was the only one available, very few members of modern societies would learn the advanced knowledge and skills required in our contemporary technological age. The differential between those with knowledge and power and those without would become greater. Numerous uninteresting or distasteful, yet necessary, matters would never be learnt.

However his proposed model of teaching drew attention to the limitless opportunities which exist for motivated individuals to gain knowledge and to learn from others informally.

Apprenticing and Mentoring

A number of different models of learning make use of a combination of formal and informal teaching methods in which some kind of activity or work is performed under the supervision of a person with superior skills or knowledge. This person forms a relationship with the learner with the intention of imparting their skill or knowledge to them. These include athletic training or coaching, apprenticing and mentoring. Our focus is not however on the development of athletic or purely physical skills, so we will confine our comments to apprenticing and mentoring.

An 'apprentice' is defined as, "a learner of a craft; one who is bound by legal agreement to serve an employer in the exercise of some handicraft, art, trade or profession for a certain number of years, with a view to learn its details and duties, in which the employer is reciprocally bound to instruct him".[48]

A distinguishing feature of apprentice-style learning is that it involves a mutual learning agreement with a written legal contract between the apprentice or legal guardian and the employer. This model is used for teaching a younger person the knowledge and skills of a particular craft or trade by a person with recognized competence. Methods include instruction, observation, practice and action-reflection. The action-reflection cycle enables learners to consider possibilities and prepare for them before they actually begin. During and after the process they reflect on their strategies and outcomes, and seek to learn from success and/or failure, before returning to the action once more.

Apprenticing is a model in which the learner receives a growing level of reimbursement for his or her work, as greater levels of skill are acquired, until a recognized qualification as a skilled craftsman is achieved.

Similar to the apprentice model is the concept of mentoring. In Greek mythology Mentor was the name of the Ithacan nobleman whose disguise the goddess Athene assumed. He was put in charge of Odysseus' household while he was away fighting in the Trojan and other wars and he became a wise friend and counsellor to Odysseus' young son, Telemachus. A mentor therefore came to mean an experienced and trusted adviser.[49]

Honore defines mentoring as, "a relationship between a young adult and an older more experienced adult who supports, guides and counsels the young adult as the latter is adapting to the world of work."[50] B. and T. Field describe a mentor as similar to a father figure or teacher, role model, approachable counsellor, trusted adviser, challenger or encourager.[51] It is a one-to-one relationship of an older, more experienced person toward a younger subordinate. Levinson considers that being a 'mentee' or 'mentor' is part of being at particular stages of life. A mentee is often at the 'Settling down' stage (age 30-35) and seeks the confidence, maturity and possible career advancement contributed by an older mentor who is at the 'Maintaining a productive society' stage of life (age 40-70).[52]

In contrast with the apprentice model which usually teaches a craft or technical skill, mentoring is used for more rational or intellectual learning situations, although the division between these two may not be totally clear-cut. Mentoring involves guidance and counsel in matters of vocation and work. The mentor may take some responsibility for mistakes which the recipient makes in the process of learning. He or she may not necessarily be involved in the learner's personal life beyond that which impinges on their working life. Mentoring relationships are commonly used for professional learning in hospitals, factories, schools or business settings and may be informal, voluntary relationships or formally organized and encouraged by an employer.

Of more recent times mentoring has also been used to refer to certain teaching-learning relationships in the faith community. Davis describes Christian mentoring as modelling character by dealing primarily with issues of maturity and integrity.[53] Mallison defines it as, "a dynamic, intentional relationship of trust in which one person enables another to maximise the grace of God in their life and service."[54]

Matthaei includes a teaching component in her description of faith-mentoring as "a nurturing relationship that facilitates growth" and "mediates God's grace for others."[55] She notes that women particularly excel in this and other relational models of teaching. However even when used in the Christian community, this model has an automatic assumption that the relationship formed will be between a superior and their subordinate.

Spiritual Direction

Another model of teaching utilized within Christian communities is 'spiritual direction'. It focuses on issues such as prayer, religious experience and relationship to God and endeavours to help people grow in understanding and living out of his truth.[56] Throughout the history of the church it has been common for older, more experienced men or women, to offer guidance or instruction to others seeking help in these matters.

Barry and Connolly, Roman Catholic fathers with a background in modern psychotherapy, define 'spiritual direction' as, "help given by one Christian to another which enables that person to pay attention to God's personal communication to him or her, to respond to this personally communicating God, to grow in intimacy with this God, and to live out the consequences of the relationship".[57] Max Thurian describes it as "a seeking after the leading of the Holy Spirit in a given psychological and spiritual situation."[58]

The use of the term 'direction' implies an element of command or control.[59] This involves accountability and sometimes direct confrontation. The role of the director may include that of teacher, spiritual father/mother, confessor and guide. Some directors are strongly authoritarian and regimented in nature,[60] while others consider their role to be that of providing an example or clarifying directions. In some religious orders obedience is required.[61]

The monastic movement, various religious orders, colleges, churches and even some modern para-church agencies have at times set up processes to enable the formation of such relationships among clergy, appointed leaders and lay believers. Some say that the relationship between director and recipient is one of essential equality and mutuality before God. Many of the great teachers of the church have stressed its non-directiveness.[62] However the choice of the word 'direction' has given substance to the authoritarian nature of the relationship.

Relationships have generally been one-to-one, but of recent times some spiritual direction has been accomplished in small groups. Women, particularly, seem to have received more help in their spiritual development by meeting in small groups of other women, rather than always meeting one-to-one with a director.[63] Fischer believes group direction should be the normal practice in all churches for everyone except in times of crisis.[64]

Spiritual direction may occur on a once-only basis or regularly for many years or even a lifetime. The recipient may not always be a learner. He or she may simply be reminded of matters already known. The direction process shares much in common with counselling or the helping processes which seek to produce holistic growth and personal development. In reality the director's involvement may deal with only one aspect of a person's life, enabling him or her to seek the mind of God on that matter. Thus the impact of the model may be far less extensive than other teaching models examined.

Because some spiritual direction relationships have been exploitative or unhelpful Kenneth Leech proposes the less authoritative term 'soul friend'.[65] Alan Jones used 'spiritual friend' to accentuate the ordinary nature of the human exchange involved, to allow for the possibility of two-way learning and to encourage the valuing of friendships.[66] However the danger with these interpretations is that in softening the 'direction' process the learning relationship weakens or becomes a spiritual conversation without the elements of accountability, direct confrontation or precision in discernment.[67]

A recent expression of spiritual direction, the Shepherding Movement, has arisen in association with house churches of the charismatic movement.[68] In reaction against a perceived lack of spiritual commitment and community involvement, this has attempted to bring a more holistic approach to many individualistic expressions of the faith. Each person is accountable to a housegroup leader who in turn is responsible to the elders. Important life decisions of members are to be 'covered' or sanctioned by those in authority. This has in some cases led to a spiritual immaturity which discourages personal accountability to God and acceptance of responsibility for finding guidance from study of the Scriptures. As with spiritual direction the danger of manipulation by others may arise.

Pastoral Care, Counselling and Psychotherapy

Pastoral Care, Counselling and Psychotherapy are sometimes regarded as teaching models. Campbell has defined 'pastoral care' as "that aspect of the ministry of the Church which is concerned with the well-being of individuals and of communities".[69]

Following the biblical metaphor of 'the shepherd', the aim of pastoral care is the protection and nurture of the sheep, so that they grow into healthy beings.[70] It provides for the special needs of weaker members, those requiring restoration and ones who have not yet come into the fold. It involves oversight, teaching and discipline. Within a faith community pastoral care is offered by leaders who set an example of humility and model Christ-like qualities in their lives. They are responsible to keep watch over God's people (Heb. 13:17; 1 Pet. 5:2-4) and are concerned with their healthy growth, well being and productive living.

Tidball summarizes Paul's pastoral strategy as encouragement, enabling, exposition, example and exhortation.[71] It does not necessarily have a teaching-learning dimension, although as has been previously noted the gifts of 'pastor' and 'teacher' are closely linked (Eph. 4:11). The person and community which offers pastoral care must be able to show love, understanding and care. Pastoral care involves the development of a relationship but not necessarily a reciprocal or close one.

While pastoral care is concerned for the well being of a person, counselling is the process whereby that person is helped to plan how to make positive changes in their life. Hurding has defined 'counselling' as, "that activity which seeks to help others towards constructive change in any or all aspects of life within a caring relationship that has agreed boundaries".[72] It involves the interchange of ideas or opinions as to future procedures. The counsellor aims to advise, not direct, and there is no obligation that he or she should be involved personally in the process, apart from its planning stage. The counsellor should exhibit care, but the development of a close personal relationship is not necessary or expected. Counselling does not necessarily have a learning dimension, although the counsellor may seek to teach new attitudes or understandings or new ways of behaving.

'Psychotherapy' has been described by Hurding as the term applied when "the aim of 'constructive change' makes more deliberate and consistent use of psychological mechanisms and processes, and where the 'caring relationship' is put on a more professional basis".[73] Instead of being educative in nature, in psychotherapy the constructive change involves the use of psychological means. These may include behavioural as well as cognitive approaches, psychoanalysis or non-directive listening, personalism and transpersonalism.

May proposes the combination of "psychological and spiritual care into a holistic approach to growth or healing"[74], but he warns that this is difficult to achieve because of the danger of its deteriorating into "pastoral-psychological counselling" and losing its spiritual dimension. He contrasts psychotherapy with spiritual direction, but warns that content and intent are different although both lead to growth in spiritual and emotional dimensions of life. Psychotherapy seeks to remedy problems. It considers mental and emotional dimensions with the expectation that through the help of the therapist more efficient living will result and the client will develop qualities considered desirable. Spiritual direction seeks to evaluate sufferings and discomforts in terms of experiences which through God's enabling lead to spiritual growth.

Comparison of these models with 'discipling'

Our description of these informal models of teaching has necessarily been brief, but we now wish to make some comparisons between them and discipling. In a later chapter we will examine modern research into these models in an attempt to establish their educational value. However for the present, similarities and differences will be noted so that the distinguishing characteristics of discipling may be ascertained more readily.

Discipling resembles both socialisation and parenting in that it is a whole way-of-life process. Like socialisation it seeks to bring about development of values, personality and self-identity, as persons grow towards maturity in Christ and take their place as responsible members of the community of faith. Like parenting it is a sustained effort over a significant period of time which brings about learning within a secure, nurturing environment of close, personal relationships. It involves those who at a particular time have greater knowledge and skills, attempting to impart such knowledge and skills to one or more others. Within its intimate circle discipling facilitates learning of basic understandings, attitudes, values, behaviours and skills through informal life situations. It provides numerous opportunities for observation, listening, reflecting, asking questions, imitating, experimenting and practising. However the capacity and level of understanding of the parent/facilitator/teacher limit both parenting and discipling.

The discipling relationship is a voluntary one, while that of parent and child does not usually encompass an element of choice at its inception or for a number of years. The intention of the parenting relationship is much broader than learning alone. It may however be possible for a parenting relationship to develop into a discipling relationship, if both parties make that choice as the child moves towards maturity and acceptance of responsibility for its own life.

Our study of the New Testament has shown that discipling always involved incorporation into a learning community with the teaching process closely allied to the life of the group. Leech believes the discipling of one another in community is a necessary requisite for every intentional Christian community.[75]

Characteristics in learning communities, which Jalongo listed as essential, are also basic requirements for discipling communities.[76] Both usually provide opportunities for members to contribute to the learning of other members. Differences include the fact that discipling is voluntary, whereas not every learning community may involve freedom for its members. A discipling community is oriented away from itself towards others while some learning communities may exist purely for the benefit of their members. An interesting parallel may sometimes exist between adventure education in community, and the outward expression of a discipling relationship, as risks are taken in service towards others. Both may result in discovery learning about self and others through active involvement in dangerous situations.

Learning through relationships and collaborative learning are closely allied with community learning and thus with discipling. The data available does not allow us to say with certainty whether Jesus learned anything in collaboration with his disciples. His position as their Lord was always maintained, but it could well be that he too benefited and learned from being in community with them. We can however be certain that Jesus frequently employed the collaborative learning model among his disciples. He gave ministry responsibilities to be carried out by the long-term partners or among the small groupings of his followers. Collaborative learning and discipling were also clearly demonstrated in the mission teams of the early church as two or more coequal parties accepted responsibility for one another and shared resources as they worked, travelled and learned together.

Learning webs and networks are similar to the networks which operate within the universal Christian discipling community. These permeate every stratum of society and extend worldwide. Learners may access the written word, activities, people and voluntary Christian educational services. Exposure of believers to this extensive community brings a wealth of experience to enrich Christian understandings and learning. Electronic media, the internet, email etc. may provide opportunity for discipling. However, there are dangers that the close, personal relationships required of discipling may be diminished by the use of technology and the impersonal relationships it promotes.

Apprenticing bears many resemblances to discipling because both involve long-term commitment to a close relationship between a learner and one whose knowledge and/or skills are at a particular time considered to be superior. Both involve observation, imitation and growing opportunities to practise certain skills safely. However the apprentice model concentrates mainly on the development of craftsman-type, vocational skills and there is little expectation of wider involvement in other aspects of the learner's life and development. Discipling, while directed towards spiritual development ideally seeks that learning will impact on all aspects of life including attitudes, values, behaviours, skills, rational understandings and intellectual knowledge.

Mentoring shares much in common with discipling. Close, personal relationships are central to both, as are the elements of support, guidance, wise counsel and acceptance of some responsibility for the learner by the one with greater experience. Both models of teaching also share the concept of exemplifying desirable qualities of character, maturity and integrity. However mentoring is not as comprehensive in its commitment to a shared life for an extended period of time as the discipling relationship. Faith-mentoring as outlined by Matthaei is very similar, however it does not necessarily include involvement in a learning community or the outward focus on mission which we have seen to be integral to our concept of discipling.

Spiritual direction has probably been the most frequent practice of the church which closely resembles the way Jesus discipled his followers. Its strength lies in its emphasis on the development of the directee's relationship with God, and his or her accountability toward another person who accepts responsibility for opening up the processes to enable spiritual growth to occur. It also seeks to implant the implications of that relationship in the directee's daily life. While the personal response to God is able to be greatly enriched, the full range of learning, including knowledge, skills and behaviours expected within the faith community may be only incidental by-products. In the history of the use of this model there have been instances of its abuse by authoritarian directors. The benefits received are largely dependent on the capacity of the director.

Spiritual direction contains some element of authority which is lacking in collaborative learning arrangements, although more recent expressions have sought to play down this aspect. Usually the one exercising authority in monastic or religious communities is in turn responsible to a higher authority. Its focus on prayer, religious experience, relationship to God and its intention that growth in understanding should result in a changed life were themes in the teaching of Jesus. It usually involves two individuals, but may operate within a small group. However it is not a reciprocal relationship and in some religious communities spiritual direction is not voluntary. It does not involve the opportunity for all members of the faith community to contribute to others' learning by utilising their spiritual gifts. Nor is it necessarily focused outward on mission to others.

Finally we turn to Pastoral Care, Counselling and Psychotherapy. These models generally centre on the person in need and assist in their adjustment, well being, growth and development. Discipling will involve pastoral care, but all pastoral care is not discipling. Both involve the discipler as an under-shepherd, who nurtures those who follow Christ. Both operate under his authority, not their own. Both share an emphasis on encouragement, enabling, exposition, example and exhortation. But the learning intention, although present, is not predominant in pastoral care. Discipling encompasses a wider range of learnings involving every aspect of the person's life, knowledge, relationship to God, and skills in service for the kingdom of God. Its aim is the attainment of maturity and development of the ability to become a teacher or discipler of others. The protective element of pastoral care may be lacking in discipling, where following Christ could on occasions result in suffering or death! Discipling may also involve a longer period of reciprocal commitment and a closer, more open relationship than pastoral care.

Counselling focuses on problems and seeks to bring about constructive change so that the recipient learns new understandings, beliefs, skills and/or behaviours. These may extend to all aspects of life. The relationship involved in discipling is very different from that expected in counselling or psychotherapy.

Refining the Definition

Indeed a close, personal, reciprocal relationship would be actively discouraged in these fields.

However the boundaries of a counselling relationship are much more restricted than discipling. An all-encompassing commitment of life to the counsellor, like that of disciple to master is not expected, or always considered ethical. The intention of the process is not that the counsellee should ever become counsellor, whereas the disciple it is hoped will eventually become a disciple-maker.

Thus similarities and differences between these models and discipling are emerging and the concept of discipling is being further clarified.

Definition of discipling

Having examined various mainly informal models of teaching with similar characteristics to discipling we are now in a position to revisit our earlier discussion. Our original working definition of discipling proposed in Chapter One[77] and revised in Chapter Seven became,

> *Discipling is an intentional, largely informal, learning activity in which two or a small group of individuals typically in a community holding to the same religious beliefs, make a voluntary commitment to each other to form a close, personal relationship for an extended period of time, to enable the disciples to learn from the other.*

Study of the Acts and Epistles has further enlightened our understanding of discipling and it is now our intention to tighten and expand its definition.

Various attempts at a definition

The *Oxford English Dictionary* classifies the verb 'to disciple' as obsolete in its meaning "to teach, train, educate" and "to subject to discipline; to chastise, correct, punish". Its other meaning "to make a disciple of; to convert to the doctrine of another", is described as rare or archaic. The noun 'disciple' has never been used as an ordinary term for scholar or pupil, but has come into regular usage through its association with the disciples of Jesus Christ and his professed followers. It refers to "one who follows or attends upon another for the purpose of learning from him… one who follows, or is influenced by, the doctrine or example of another".[78]

We therefore deduce that throughout the English speaking world the word 'to disciple' has not been used widely outside of a Christian context. However because of the practice of Jesus it has continued as a recognized method of teaching within the Christian tradition. It involves one person committing him or herself to the teaching of another, 'following' them and submitting to their authority for the purpose of learning from their doctrine or example.

Derivation of 'disciple' from Greek *mathētēs*

In Chapter Two we introduced the Greek word *mathētēs* (disciple) from which the idea of discipling originates. We have noted its general Greek context, its possible associated Hebrew concepts and its many occurrences in the New Testament. We observed the three slightly different meanings of *mathētēs* in Greek literature.

Its primary meaning describes the personal relationship between Jesus and his followers who learnt specific knowledge and conduct under his tutelage and according to his teaching plan. The second meaning of 'disciple' has a stronger emphasis on the authority of the teacher and subservience of the learners and was common in the ancient world. While the Gospels indicate that Jesus possessed the power and authority of God, he did not always choose to exercise it. He adopted the role of servant leader and while expecting their commitment he allowed his followers a greater degree of independence than was usual among disciples. The third meaning denotes an "intellectual link between two persons considerably removed in time whereby one seeks to imitate the other". This is the sense in which the word is used of the early Christians in Acts and the Epistles after Jesus had returned to the Father.

Discipling in popular and scholarly Christian writing

Many popular Christian publications have been written about 'Discipleship' or 'Discipling'. These include, Anton Baumohl's *Making adult disciples*, Stuart Briscoe's *Discipleship for ordinary people*, Leroy Eims' *The lost art of disciple making*, Hanks and Shell's *Discipleship*, Bill Hull's *Jesus Christ disciple maker*, Winkie Pratney's *Doorways to discipleship* and *Handbook for followers of Jesus*, J. Oswald Sanders' *Shoe leather commitment: Guidelines for disciples*, and David Watson's *Discipleship*.[79] Dietrich Bonhoeffer's *The cost of discipleship* explores discipleship in theological terms but does not actually define it.[80]

Most writers assume that their concepts are understood by their readers within the Christian community and immediately launch into describing the life of discipleship or methods of discipling. Only a few attempt to define 'disciple'. "Someone who is learning to do something, or to be something with the help of a teacher."[81] "A learner or pupil who accepts the teaching of Christ, not only in belief but in life-style."[82] "One who is a pupil or an adherent of the doctrines of another."[83]

Some describe 'discipleship'. "Discipleship as Jesus conceived it was not a theoretical task to which men were called to give themselves and all their energies. Their work was not study but practice."[84] It is "…a following, not for study but for service – to help the Master in his mission, to carry out his instructions."[85]

Others describe 'discipling' as "The process by which we encourage another person to be… a follower of Jesus; it means the methods we use to help that person to become mature in Christ and so be in a position where he or she can now disciple someone else."[86]

Hadidian's definition of 'discipling' is helpful. "The process by which a Christian with a life worth emulating commits himself for an extended period of time to a few individuals who have been won to Christ, the purpose being to aid and guide their growth to maturity and equip them to reproduce themselves in a third spiritual generation."[87]

In popular Christian writing 'discipling' seems to be used to describe what happens when a teacher seeks to help a believer move towards Christian maturity. Few writers define it or attempt to differentiate it from other teaching methods.

In our research we have discovered that New Testament scholars have written very little about 'discipleship', apart from references to Jesus' disciples and his teaching of them, or to describe the lifestyle expected of his followers.[88] Even less is written about 'discipling'. Scholars rarely mention its characteristics as a model of teaching. Yet we have seen that the concept underlies many practices in the New Testament, and the present study seeks to profile them as a way of enhancing learning in today's church.

Refining the definition

Within the Biblical section of our research, our study of Acts and the Epistles has reinforced the validity of our revised working definition as being generally appropriate for understanding discipling as it was practiced by both Jesus and the early faith communities. Two additions however need to be made.

Discipling relationships took place within a larger, nurturing community of faith. We have therefore expanded the phrase "...*typically in community...*" to include this idea, "...*who typically function within a larger nurturing community...*".

No one person was always teacher. And those who taught others differed considerably in the length of time they had been believers, the content of their teaching, their particular spiritual gifts, the quality of their lives to be observed, etc. This should be delineated more clearly in our working definition. We have therefore replaced "...*to enable one to learn from the other.*" with "...*in order that those who at a particular time are perceived as having superior knowledge and/or skills will attempt to cause learning to take place in the lives of others who seek their help.*"

There is one concept which seems intrinsic to the nature of Christian discipleship in the Bible and must therefore appear in our definition. Disciples did not undertake learning as an end in itself. From the initial call, discipling implied that learning would make an impact on others. Christian disciples were to be active in serving others and bringing the message of Christ to them. To include this in our definition we must specify that we are now defining '*Christian discipling*'. '*Religious*' is no longer necessary to describe the beliefs and will be omitted. And we add to our definition, *"Christian discipling is intended to result in each becoming an active follower of Jesus and a participant in his mission to the world"*.

We therefore propose as our definition for discipling,

Christian discipling is an intentional, largely informal learning activity. It involves two or a small group of individuals, who typically function within a larger nurturing community and hold to the same beliefs. Each makes a voluntary commitment to the other/s to form close personal relationships for an extended period of time, in order that those who at a particular time are perceived as having superior knowledge and/or skills will attempt to cause learning to take place in the lives of others who seek their help. Christian discipling is intended to result in each becoming an active follower of Jesus and a participant in his mission to the world.

Review

In our search for a definition of the concept of Christian discipling we have done three things. Discipling as it was understood and practised in the ancient world has been briefly surveyed. The Biblical evidence has been scrutinized carefully. This has included an examination of the life of Jesus in calling, relating to, sharing ministry with and teaching his disciples. A synthesis of 'discipling' as Jesus demonstrated it has been made. The discipling model in the early church has been examined and the changes in its operation and function carefully noted.

Finally in this chapter we have looked to educational theory to define teaching itself, proposed two families of methods under which discipling may be categorized, and studied a variety of models of teaching within informal educational practices in order to clarify the essential characteristics of discipling. A definition for the term Christian discipling has been proposed. We are now ready to move on to assess the congruence of discipling as an educational strategy with the objectives of Christian faith communities.

Notes to Chapter 10

1 Simpson, J.A. & Weiner, E.S.C., *The Oxford English Dictionary* (2nd edn) Vol.17 (Oxford: Clarendon, 1989) 688-689. Hereafter *O.E.D.*
2 Scheffler, 1960, 61
3 Hill, 1990, 143
4 Hirst, 1973, 171
5 Kleinig, 1982, 25-6
6 Kleinig, 1982, 29
7 Andersen, 2000
8 For discussion on what constitutes indoctrination and brainwashing see Kleinig, 1982, 54-67
9 Scheffler, 1960, 104

10 Hirst & Peters, 1970, 81
11 The hidden curriculum is defined as "some of the outcomes or by products of schools or non-school settings, particularly those states which are learned yet not openly intended." (Martin, 1976, 137.) Or "Those non-academic but educationally significant consequences of schooling that occur systematically, but are not made explicit at any level of the public rationales for education." (Vallance, 1973, 7)
12 Weil, Joyce & Kluwin, 1978, 3
13 Joyce & Weil, 1972, 2
14 Fortes, M. as cited in Richards & Hoeldtke, 1980, 127-9
15 Simpson & Weiner, 1989, Vol.14, 632,639
16 Illich, 1976, 232
17 Walker, Mumford & Steel, 1973, 100
18 Hill, 1990, 2
19 Goodman as cited in Thomson, 1994, 327
20 Coombs & Ahmed as cited in Smith & Jeffs, 1990, 3
21 Ross as cited in Wentworth, 1980, 17. Brim defines it as "a process of learning through which an individual is prepared with varying degrees of success, to meet the requirements laid down by other members of society for his behaviour in a variety of situations." (Brim as cited in Wentworth, 1980, 37)
22 Brim as cited in Wentworth, 1980, 37
23 Westerhoff as cited in Groome, 1980, 127
24 Gordon, 1995, 53
25 *O.E.D.*, Vol.11, 223
26 Leichter, 1985, 88
27 Hill, 1990, 61
28 "Learning springs naturally in new-born babies and young children." (Hahn, 1994, 74)
29 Waddy, 1997, ch.8
30 *O.E.D.*, Vol.3, 582
31 Delbridge & Bernard, 1988, 185
32 Knapp, 1988, 1
33 To be discussed later in this chapter.
34 Slater, 1984, 43
35 Slater, 1976, 23
36 Miles & Priest, 1990, 1
37 Hill, 1990, 69
38 Hill, 1990, 69
39 Friend & Cook, 1992, 5
40 Bruffee, 1984, 647
41 Bruffee, 1984, 642; Friend & Cook, 1992, 9
42 Hill, 1987, 59
43 Numbers quoted by Margaret Bell, President, Volunteering Australia at seminar conducted by Volunteering WA in Perth 12th November, 1997.
44 Illich, 1971, 12
45 Bowen & Hobson, 1974, ch.9
46 Reimer, 1971, chs.10,11
47 Bowen & Hobson, 1974, 398
48 *O.E.D.*, Vol.1, 583
49 *O.E.D.*, Vol.9, 614

50 Honore, 1994, 1
51 Field & Field, 1994, 65
52 Levinson as cited in Peterson, 1984, 406-7
53 Davis, 1991, 18
54 Mallison, 1998a
55 Matthaei, 1996, 14; Davis, 1991, 14
56 May, 1992, 61
57 Barry & Connolly, 1982, 8
58 Thurian as cited in Leech, 1977, 34
59 Delbridge & Bernard, 1988, 263
60 Thornton, 1963, 11
61 St Francis of Sales wrote, "It is advisable to have only one spiritual father whose authority ought to be preferred to one's own will on every occasion and in every matter." (as cited in Leech, 1977, 75.) Among religious orders or monastic communities some form of spiritual direction may occur, however this is within a wider context of a life of service, prayer or contemplation, so the rules whereby these groups order their lives are not necessarily part of the process of spiritual direction.
62 Leech, 1986, 47
63 Fischer, 1989, 21
64 Fischer, 1989, 22
65 Leech, 1977
66 Jones, 1982, 3-4
67 May, 1992, 10
68 Kingdon, 1995, 786
69 Campbell, 1987, 188
70 That they should produce wool, milk, meat or lambs is implied.
71 Tidball, 1986, 114
72 Hurding, 1995, 81
73 Hurding, 1995, 81
74 May, 1992, 14
75 Leech, C.W., 1989, 33
76 These will be elaborated in a later chapter. We note for the present that they include the presence of trust and respect among members; opportunities to deal with ideas and values which affect direction and priorities even when they might be sources of conflict; acceptance of personal responsibility and commitment to support of one another; freedom to take risks; and acceptance of responsibility for one another and opportunities to learn from others.
77 Discipling is a voluntary, personal relationship between two individuals in community or alone, in which the disciple commits him or herself to learn from the other, by imitation, oral communication and sharing in the life and work of the discipler.
78 *O.E.D.*, Vol.4, 733,734
79 Baumohl, 1984; Briscoe, 1995; Eims, 1978; Hanks & Shell, 1993; Hull, 1984; Pratney, 1975; Pratney, 1977; Sanders, 1990; Watson, 1981.
80 Bonhoeffer, 1959
81 Brow, 1981, 20
82 Sanders, 1990, 8
83 *Dictionary of English Language* as cited in Warr, 1978, 38
84 Manson, 1931, 239

85 Montefiore as cited in Hengel, 1981, 218
86 Watson, 1981, 66
87 Hadidian, 1979, 29
88 'Disciple' is defined as a man who binds himself to a master or teacher in order to acquire his practical or theoretical knowledge. (Muller, 1975, 483-90)

Chapter 11

Congruence with the Christian Faith

Having now developed a stipulation for what will serve as an instance of 'discipling', we need to check the degree to which this construct remains congruent with relevant core values and beliefs of the Christian faith. It has been necessary to limit the scope of this chapter as it could easily expand to encompass the whole of systematic theology. Since the Bible has been our major source in arriving at a definition of Christian discipling, it will be used in association with two of the great credal statements of the church[1] to establish the core values and beliefs which have relevance to our present study.

The nature of God and his relationship with humanity will be examined first. Then the development of that relationship, as described in the Bible, will be traced from creation, to its impairment by disobedience, followed by God's great rescue plan which he began to enact through Abraham and the nation of Israel. We will give attention to the fresh insights gained through Jesus' life, death, resurrection and ascension and his provision for the restoration of the relationship. Note will also be made of the experiences of the early church when it sensed God's presence in the person of his Holy Spirit coming upon its members. Second we will observe the value which is given to each individual as unique in God's sight. Third the importance attached to the community of believers to the life of faith will be established. Some attention will be given to the concept of human freedom, and finally the mission of the church will be defined.

Consideration will be given to making an assessment concerning the 'discipling' model of teaching and whether it is consistent with these beliefs. Some attempt will also be made to evaluate its effectiveness in upholding the values of the Christian faith and inculcating them as part of the teaching process.

Core Beliefs of the Christian Faith

God and humanity in personal relationship

Personal relationship finds its ultimate expression in the triune God – Father, Son and Holy Spirit, three in one, in perfect harmony and relationship yet moving beyond himself to create and sustain the universe. The salvific narrative in the Bible begins with the revelation of God as creator and introduces humankind as his masterpiece, made in his image and likeness (Gn. 1:26-7). The man and the woman related to God in a personal way, received his blessing and heard his communications. However when they disobeyed his command, sin impaired their relationship with God. But God did not completely cast them off. He had a plan for the full restoration of the original relationship (Gn. 3:16-9).

The first part in that drama came when he called the patriarch, Abraham, to leave his country, kindred and father's house and go in faith to the land he would be shown. God promised that through him all nations would be blessed (Gn. 12:1-3). Abraham's descendants were God's treasured possession (Ex. 19:5,6). He loved them and rescued them from slavery in Egypt and formed them into the nation of Israel (Dt. 5:6). He entered into a covenant agreement with them, binding himself to them and in turn requiring their undivided love and loyalty. "You shall love the LORD your God with all your heart, and with all your soul, and with all your might" (Dt. 6:5).

He gave them the law, the land, leaders and kings and when they failed to keep their part in the covenant he spoke through the prophets, warning them of his judgement if they did not return to him. The Old Testament used the shepherd image to describe God's care for his people (Ps. 23; Ezk. 34:11-31). He searched for them, rescued them and brought them to a place of safety and freedom from fear. He provided more than enough for their sustenance, bound up the injured, strengthened the weak and brought justice to all. His relationship with the nation was likened to that of a husband toward his wife (Ho. 2:19), a father to his child (Ho. 11:1) or a mother bird sheltering her young under her wings (Ru. 2:12; Ps. 63:7; 17:8). These intensely personal images expressed the depth of God's love and unreserved commitment to his people.

The second part of the drama of God's relationship with humanity came when Jesus appeared on stage, as God incarnate, the dearly loved Son. He lived, worked, healed and proclaimed the good news of God's kingdom. He cared for his followers like a shepherd with his sheep. He provided for their physical needs but he also demonstrated the full extent of God's love for the world by laying down his life for the salvation of humanity (Jn. 10:1-18). His sacrificial death on the cross made possible the restoration of God's original relationship with all who would respond by placing their faith in him.

In our earlier chapters we have seen that the close personal relationship which Jesus had with his disciples in the Gospels and which continued, albeit in a changed dimension, in the life of the early church, demonstrates something of the relationship which Christians believe that they may share with God. Although Jesus sometimes used the imagery of servant/master to illustrate his teachings, he never addressed his followers as servants. They were his friends (Jn. 15:15) whom he knew and allowed to know him (Jn. 10:14). He looked to them for support (Mk. 3:14; 14:32-41). He loved them, taught, guarded, prayed for and sent them out into the world (Jn. 17:6-19). He was much more than a human master or teacher among his disciples. After his resurrection they worshipped him as Lord and God (Jn. 20:28), and they responded to God in a prayerful relationship much more readily than had previously been the case.

Although Jesus did not refer to his followers as 'servants', most of the writers of the Epistles identified themselves primarily in that way (Rom. 1:1; Jas. 1:1; 2 Pet. 1:1; Jude 1:1; Rev. 1:1). They chose the title to identify with his death, as the suffering servant of Yahweh and in acknowledgment of his lordship in their lives (Is. 52:13-53:12; Phil. 2:6-11).

When Jesus' physical presence was withdrawn, he promised that the Father would send his Holy Spirit to be with them forever (Jn. 14:15-26; 16:7-15). The ministry of the Spirit would be built upon, and the necessary sequel to, that of Jesus.[2] He, also, was 'person' and would continue to teach them and help, encourage, comfort and be an advocate for them (*paraklētos*). He would guide them into truth. The Acts of the Apostles recounts his coming upon Jesus' assembled disciples (Acts 2:1) and his subsequent activities among the Samaritans, Gentiles, disciples at Ephesus and as guide and enabler of the missions of the apostles. The Epistles represent him as God's gift to believers, providing a pledge of their future inheritance as the people of God (Eph. 1:13-4), and giver of gifts for ministry (1 Cor. 12:7-11). "Within persons, and within the church the Spirit is the Spirit of holiness, love, worship and praise, prayer, proclamation…"[3]

Is discipling congruent with these perspectives? In the light of our previous analyses of the Biblical evidence it is clear that discipling by its very nature reinforces the centrality of God as sovereign Lord and Master. He is Father, Son and Holy Spirit, who takes the initiative and calls humanity to a close, personal relationship of learning and following him. Those who respond, express their love for him in worship and prayer. They begin the lifelong task of knowing him personally, learning his will for their lives as revealed through the Scriptures and serving him through the use of their ministry gifts. Christians understand God himself to be the source and supreme example of the values they teach. Disciples learn those values as they experience them expressed toward themselves by God. Thus love (1 Jn. 4:19), forgiveness (Eph. 4:32), holiness (1 Pet. 1:16), comfort (2 Cor. 1:4) and many other qualities are learnt directly from God who gives them to believers when he gives them himself (Gal. 5:22-3).

The value of each individual

Equally integral to the Christian faith is the concept of the distinctive significance of each individual in the sight of God.[4] Every human is created in his image and deemed as "very good" (Gn. 1:27,31), not in the sense of moral worth, but as a being who in a special way reflects the 'image' of God. The value of each individual is evident throughout the Biblical revelation in the significance placed on human life from its very conception (Gn. 9:6; Is. 44:2), in care for the underprivileged, oppressed, weak or dispossessed (Ex. 22:21-27), and in the command to "love your neighbour as yourself" (Lv. 19:18). New Testament teaching proclaims no difference between Jew and Greek, slave or free, male or female (Gal. 3:28). Jesus valued care for the least important as being the same as care for himself (Mt. 25:45), and he would not turn even a little child away (Lk. 18:15-17). God's love shown in Jesus extends to all (2 Cor. 5:14-5), and every person is unique and of worth, yet different from every other being (Rom. 12:6-8; 1 Cor. 12:4-11).

Once again the discipling model is seen to be highly congruent with such perspectives in that it does not discriminate against any person. Every person within a Christian community is considered of equal worth in God's sight and is given gifts whose exercise brings good to all and assists in building up the community of faith. Even the newest member of the community or the oldest and most frail is significant. Discipling takes into consideration the level of understanding and knowledge of God which each individual possesses, his or her pace of learning and preferred style of learning. It embodies a life-centred approach to learning which combines cognitive input, personal experience and practical involvement, and is appropriate for all ages and stages of life.

When special discipling relationships are formed within the community there is no fixed hierarchy of status. Those who teach, only remain in that role while they have some superior knowledge or skills to impart. At other times a previous learner may adopt the role of teacher. Those whose gift is teaching still learn from others. Even "a little child shall lead them" (Is. 11:6).

The community of believers

Among the persons of the Godhead perfect community is expressed. They are in complete agreement of heart, mind, thought and will and it is into this 'community' that believers are welcomed, not as gods but as dearly loved children (Jn. 14:20,23, 1 Jn. 3:1,2). This means that the love shared within the Godhead extends out to his children who then relate in loving community to one another (Jn. 15:12). They become a believing, confessing community which acknowledges the lordship of Christ (Mt. 10:32; Rom. 10:9; 1 Cor. 12:3; Phil. 2:11).

Sherlock comments that the 'image' idea has been assumed to be individual in nature, but that it actually is "a relational and personal reality".[5] Thus while each individual is important, humanity is more than a collection of isolated beings. The relational nature of the triune God leads to those in his 'image' living in relationship as covenant partners with God and each other.[6]

Those who relate to God in and by faith are called out (*ekklēsia*) into an assembly of believers, the body of Christ (Acts 2:44-7; 1 Cor. 12:12), the household and dwelling place of God (Eph. 2:19-22), a family of brothers and sisters (Heb. 3:1), "a chosen race, a royal priesthood, a holy nation, God's own people" (1 Pet. 2:9). These all indicate that the gathering of believers is indispensable to the concept of belief. The church is a worshipping, serving (Mt. 25:40), living and growing community. The New Testament allows for no isolated believers (Heb. 10:24-5). Each member is important, having spiritual gifts to be used for the common good (1 Cor. 12:7) and a contribution to make to the building up (*oikodomeō*) of the body. Love and loyalty in action between members is their aim (Gal. 6:10). All members are servants of Christ together whatever their social status, gender, age or ethnicity.

When we seek to align the concept of discipling with such insights, the congruence is close. In particular, as we saw in the New Testament church in Part Three of this study, discipling is closely allied with the normal life of the community of faith. The process of learning to know God and becoming like him is one which is assisted by others in the faith community. Teaching may come through those who at a particular time have superior knowledge or skills and who seek to impart this to their fellows. It may also come from the community as a whole as it provides worthy models of life and faith or as spiritual gifts are exercised in the supportive, caring community atmosphere or as the community reflects upon its life and ministry. Those with positions of responsibility within the church are representatives of Christ, and by teaching and applying his word derive their authority from him, not themselves.

The focus of discipling is not on the teacher or the community but on Jesus the master-teacher. The process, however, involves a teacher or a teaching-learning community which performs the roles of facilitator, organizer of learning experiences and model. Thus discipling entails: an atmosphere of love and friendship, with openness between teacher and taught; pastoral care for each person's whole being to enable the development of joy and life in all its fullness (Jn. 10:10; 17:13); nurturing, guarding and protecting the learner in a 'safe' but challenging environment; and remembering his or her needs and bringing them to God in prayer.

Christian teaching emphasizes the connection between personal belief and active good works. "Faith by itself, if it has no works, is dead" (Jas. 2:17). By its nature discipling is a dynamic, working relationship. Disciples are involved in the learning process often in active, informal situations. They interact with the teacher or leader, with one another and among those they are serving.

Human freedom

The Christian faith emphasizes that God has given to humanity the freedom to choose between right and wrong. Each person is a responsible moral agent. And although sin entered the world and humanity lost "the rational power to determine [its] course in the direction of the highest good"[7], people remain accountable for their actions. Individuals have the freedom to choose to live under the lordship of Christ, and are free to make choices as to their life of discipleship.

It is therefore highly significant that discipling is a model of teaching which depends upon the voluntary, willing commitment of the learner to the teacher or community and to the learning process, for an extended period of time. As with the disciples of Jesus the freedom exists for the process to be concluded at any time, but with Jesus those who were genuine did not permanently leave. Followers today may choose to enter or leave teacher-learner relationships with others or with particular discipling communities, but in the general course of events their relationship with Christ finds expression somewhere within an enduring community of faith.

It is appropriate here to briefly comment on misuses of discipling as a model of teaching. The role of discipler has on occasions been abused and this has caused some to be wary of its use. Some persons have so imitated the role which Jesus had among his followers that they have initiated their own teachings and endeavoured to exercise their own authority over learners, encouraging unthinking obedience. The Scriptures make it plain that there will be no further revelation from God. All was complete in Jesus (Heb. 1:1,2; Rev. 22:18-9). The authority which Jesus exercised belonged to him because he was divine. No human being can take it from him. Discipling is not about the exercise of personal power. Christian disciplers do not make their own disciples. They point their learners to Jesus as master. Instead of requiring obedience to the discipler, disciples in the Christian community come under the authority of Jesus' words as revealed in the Scriptures. Disciples do not give unthinking obedience to anyone. They are expected to weigh up the words and actions of a discipler or a discipling community (Acts 17:10-11) against the authority of the Scriptures, with the Holy Spirit as guide and enlightener (Jn. 14:26). Each person is responsible for his or her own decisions.

In balance, with individual responsibility is the extra accountability expected of those who have a teaching role. Teachers or discipling communities will be judged severely and their condemnation will be greater if they are responsible for others going astray (Mt. 18:6,7; Rom. 14:21) or if their teaching leads others into wrong belief or sin (1 Tim. 1:6,7; 6:3,4; Tit. 1:11; Jas. 3:1; 2 Pet. 2:1,2).

The mission of the church

The focus of the mission of the church is to make disciples of all nations. This commission from Jesus is recorded in a number of different forms in the Gospels and Acts (Mt. 28:19,20; Lk. 24:46-7; Jn 20:21; Acts 1:8).[8] The message for all time is that "Christ… died for sins once for all, the righteous for the unrighteous, that he might bring us to God" (1 Pet. 3:18). This good news is to be proclaimed to all peoples (Jn. 11:51-2; Acts 26:23; Rom. 1:5; 5:15,18,19; 1 Cor. 1:23-4; Eph. 2:16; Heb. 2:9,10).

Some believed that this mission was fulfilled by the apostles and ceased to be relevant after the passing of their era.[9] But history records that there have been those in every age who went out to other places to make disciples. Some deliberately chose to take the good news to those who had not heard,[10] while others moved to new places for political, social or commercial reasons taking the message with them. From the time of William Carey (1761-1834) it has been a major factor in Protestant missionary endeavour.[11] The making of disciples is to be a continuing process as each generation in turn passes on the message to the next. Paul encouraged Timothy to entrust his message to those who would in turn become its teachers (2 Tim. 2:2). This is not the responsibility of a few, but of all believers.

Congruence of discipling

It may be concluded from the foregoing, then, that the discipling model of teaching in its focus and methods shares a high degree of correspondence with the core values and beliefs of the Christian faith. This will be compared with the schooling model to ascertain which of the two has greater congruence with foundational Christian beliefs and values.

Discipling reinforces the centrality of God as Father, Son and Spirit as supreme. It enables the believer to establish his or her primary relationship in life with him as child, friend and indwelt learner. The relationship it promotes is close, personal and committed to God as Father, Teacher, Example, Guide, Paraclete and Giver of spiritual gifts.

Discipling enables every person to be treated as an individual learner of significance, not a product of mass education. Individual differences can be recognized and addressed in the teaching-learning process. Yet individuals are not isolated. They become part of a community of other believers where they are able to develop open, caring relationships. Their community life is oriented to learning and growth in faith in Christ and, like a family, its members all have a contribution to make to the well being of the whole. There is a pattern of faith expressing itself in works of service, which develops and in turn leads to growth and learning. Opportunities to observe the example of others, remembering past experiences and reflection on present events or activities enable learning to increase. Within the community personal freedom is associated with accountability for one's life and actions and for the lives of one's fellows.

The schooling model has been widely used within the faith community, but there is the danger that it may over-emphasize the need for right belief without touching the attitudes and values behind those beliefs or the behaviours which result from them. Christian beliefs, facts and knowledge are extremely important and the schooling model has been very successful in transmitting these. Preaching and formal teaching in Christian schools, Sunday schools, church-based Christian Education programs and Bible and Theological Colleges have successfully passed down the basic elements of Christian belief to new generations of believers. But formal teaching alone will never communicate the full spectrum of what it means to be a follower of Jesus. That is a completely different way of life.

A personal relationship with God may receive great emphasis in formal teaching, but the relationship itself is more easily 'caught than taught'. People understand what it means by seeing and being with others who have such an experience. Classroom situations are too limited to demonstrate or experience more than a few of the attitudes or behaviours involved in being Christian. It is one thing to teach about the fruit of the Spirit,[12] and another thing for people to be provided with opportunities to develop these in their lives.

Something of the value of each individual is lost in the schooling model because of the groups of learners involved. It is difficult to provide for the range of individual differences which exist in any formal group of learners where set curricula or graded assessments apply. In formal situations the teacher often is the focus of attention, not the learners. Schooling's curriculum-centred approach means subject materials do not arise naturally out of the learning environment and may bear little relevance to the daily lives the learners. Learners may become receptors of information rather than active participants in the process, and frequently spiritual gifts possessed by members of the body and given for the upbuilding of everyone, lie idle or under-utilized while those with teaching responsibilities exhaust themselves trying to meet every demand.

The formality of the schooling model can mitigate against the formation of open, caring relationships and hinder the promotion of community. Development of faith through experiences requiring its exercise is largely absent and opportunities for reflection on such times are divorced from the moment of experience and action.

The processes of schooling and discipling both involve some loss of freedom for learners but those involved in discipling have voluntarily chosen to do so, whereas some of those involved in schooling may be offered no choice in the matter.

Discipling's emphasis on the mission of the church is not reflected strongly in the schooling model. Learners may be formally told to go out in the name of Christ in service to others, but apart from establishing schools or colleges, informal situations are usually required for them to actually implement the commission. Discipling makes that possible.

While Jesus endorsed both the formal and informal teaching models for members of the faith community by his use of them, discipling rather than schooling was the model which he commissioned his followers to use in taking his message to the world. It is a life-centred approach which they could use among future believers no matter what their nationality, gender, age, skills, resources or experience of life.

Conclusions

It becomes evident that true Christian discipling is dependent on a close, personal relationship with God himself as Lord, made possible through the death of Jesus on the cross, into which the learner voluntarily chooses to enter by faith. By his Holy Spirit God enters into the life of the believer, teaches, encourages and gives gifts which are to be used for service and for building up the community of faith.

Discipling gives value to the individual whoever he or she may be. It acknowledges that believers belong to the family of God and enables the community of faith to recognize its role as a teaching-learning body. Discipling encompasses much more than the impartation of 'head knowledge' beliefs, it involves the development of attitudes, values, skills and behaviours which are appropriate for all those who are followers of God.

It allows the development of close, personal relationships. It embodies love, commitment, concern for all, humility and meekness. Every individual within the discipling community is a learner and is able to be used for the building up of others in loving, caring relationships. As God's word is proclaimed and obeyed, as gifts are used, examples are demonstrated, life is experienced, free choices are made and as people are nurtured and encouraged, growth towards maturity in Christ occurs. This is the intention of the gathering and the result of the life of the faith community. "Blessed are those who hunger and thirst for righteousness, for they will be filled" (Mt. 5:6).

Discipling has the authority of Jesus as being the model to be used for taking his message to the world. It is not optional. It is mandatory. As a model of teaching its value cannot be estimated too highly. Its distinctive strength lies in the formation of the discipling communities of faith wherever the gospel is spread. The effectiveness of the discipling community may be judged by the spread of Christianity, in spite of extreme opposition, to almost every nation in the world and by the numbers of those who hold to the faith, which have increased enormously over the last two millennia.[13]

Notes to Chapter 11

1. The Apostles' creed and the Nicene creed (An Australian Prayer Book, 1978, 26 & 118)
2. Morris, 1971, 701
3. Bingham, 1981, 58
4. Sherlock, 1996, 157
5. Sherlock, 1996, 87
6. Sherlock, 1996, 89
7. Berkhof, 1941, 248
8. The longer ending of Mark's gospel, probably attached some time before the mid-second century (Cranfield, 1959, 472) contains the following "Go into all the world and proclaim the good news to the whole creation" (Mk. 16:15).
9. Garrett, 1995, Vol.2, 495
10. These included Patrick to Ireland (432 CE); Columba from Ireland to Scotland (521-97); Augustine to England (597); Celtic monks to Gaul, Germany and Italy (late 6th century); Boniface (680-754) to Germany; English people to Northern Europe (11th century); Dominicans and Franciscans throughout Europe, North Africa, Hungary and Middle and Far East (13th & 14th centuries); Portuguese and Spanish to the Americas (15th &

16th centuries); and Jesuits to almost every corner of the globe (16th century to the present day).
11 Garrett, 1995, Vol.2, 496
12 Love, joy, peace, patience, kindness, generosity, faithfulness, gentleness and self-control (Gal. 5:22-3)
13 32% of the world's population claims to be Christian (i.e. 1,734 million out of 5292 million in 1990 CE) and its growth rate is 2.3%. (Johnstone, 1993, 22-3)

Chapter 12

Congruence with Findings of Present Day Religious and Educational Research

We have so far developed a concept of discipling from biblical precedents and shown, in the previous chapter, that it is highly congruent with the core beliefs of the Christian faith. It may, nevertheless, be found to have no relevance to the life of the modern day church or to be a superseded strategy in terms of contemporary educational theory.

It is therefore necessary to investigate recent research findings into the faith-learning experiences of people in churches today. Towards this end we will briefly overview several surveys into Australian[1] church life and the perceptions of church attenders as to factors contributing to their learning and growth in the faith.

We will also revisit some of the models of teaching examined earlier in our study. By way of establishing a somewhat contrasting benchmark, the schooling model will be examined in greater depth, for despite the observation in the previous chapter, there is more to be said in relation to our present concern. A brief history of its association with the Christian faith will be outlined, its value assessed and the perspective of modern educationists concerning its strengths and weaknesses will be discussed. Some attention will be given to perspectives on schooling held within Christian faith communities.

Research comparing life-related, informal models of teaching with schooling will also be considered. Consideration will then be given to current educational research available for some of these models which share common characteristics with discipling. Alternative strategies and models of teaching put forward by schooling critics will be examined. Modern principles of adult education will be surveyed and their value assessed.

Finally the possibility of congruence between these research findings and the discipling model as we have defined it, will be examined. Conclusions will be drawn as to its value and suitability as an educational strategy for faith development within the present day Christian community.

Research into learning in Australian church life

A number of different studies of Australian church attenders from 1987 to 2000 will enable us to explore people's understanding of factors which contributed to their own spiritual growth. We will then be in a better position to assess the suitability and relevance of the discipling model as an educational strategy within faith communities today.

The Christian Research Association of Australia

In 1987, a combined churches survey on faith and mission[2] asked about influences on persons' faith during the previous year. The level of importance which different church attenders attributed to these varied according to their faith orientation, but some trends emerged. Influences included:

- Involvement in groups (fellowship, Bible study, prayer, service, administration, musical, drama or social justice). Participants appreciated the fellowship, communion with God and growth in understanding the faith or guidance for everyday life.[3]
- The encouragement of family (77%) and friends (46%) was considered to be very important, but if one or the other was lacking, strong support by one was considered sufficient for people's encouragement needs to be met.[4]
- Prayer was considered to be the most important resource of faith for all groups of respondents. 70% prayed daily.[5] But Bible reading, taking theological courses, fasting, confession, retreats or camps and religious literature or media presentations were also considered helpful to some degree depending on the theological orientation of those questioned.[6]
- The local minister or priest was found to have a significant influence on the development of faith. A large majority of the respondents believed a close, personal, friendship with the clergy was desirable.[7]

Religious teaching in denominational or state schools and Sunday Schools was nominated as an important resource for faith development in the past.[8]

The 1991 National Church Life Survey

Research conducted by the 1991 Australian National Church Life Survey[9] and involving 310,000 participants asked three questions concerning respondents' perceived faith development in the previous year. Their responses covered their understanding of the faith, growth in beliefs and relationship to God and changes in their actions or priorities. Findings are briefly summarized below.

UNDERSTANDING THE FAITH

Eighty nine percent of church attenders claimed to have grown in their understanding of the faith in the previous year. Of these 42% acknowledged "some" growth and 47% "much" growth. Those who had grown attributed it to their own congregation (32%), to other congregations or groups (6%) and to their own private study (9%). The more active participants were in the life of their congregation the more likely they were to have grown. Their involvement included reflection and study in small groups, activities through mission/evangelism or service groups and a feeling of belonging to the whole congregation and participating in its worship activities.[10]

BELIEFS AND RELATIONSHIP TO GOD

In the preliminary findings, the 40% who believed they had grown "much stronger" in their beliefs and relationship to God, saw it as a result of their congregation (25%), other groups or churches (5%) and private study (10%) and all saw it directly related to their active involvement and sense of belonging.[11] The 1995 publication of results attributed growth in this area to worship services (54% of attenders, predominantly older people), sharing groups (35%, predominantly middle aged), private prayer (20%), private bible study (17%), friends (13%), natural places (9%) and an assortment of items/events such as books, camps, mission activities, mission groups outside church etc (all registered 5% or less in the overall sample, although it is noteworthy that among teenage respondents 23% nominated camps as significant).[12]

CHANGES IN ACTIONS AND PRIORITIES

The consequences of faith were demonstrated by the 23% who claimed major changes and 46% with some small changes in their actions and priorities over the previous year as a result of their Christian faith. Involvement and belonging affected that also, with the highly involved registering greater changes.[13]

Respondents who felt that they were growing in their faith were more likely to be significantly involved in outward mission activity.[14] The researchers stated that these were not related in a 'cause and effect' manner but claimed that both aspects reinforced each other. In a similar manner the link was clear between growth in faith and participation in congregational life. Thus three dimensions of congregational life and mission appear to be strongly connected – growth in faith, active involvement serving others and a sense of belonging to the community.

Ministers were expected primarily to be educators (52%), and secondarily pastors (50%). Their influence on the spiritual growth of their people was possibly indicated by the importance attached to growth arising from the worship services and from the personal influence of his or her friendship.

The 1996 National Church Life Survey

This survey of 324,000 church attenders[15] did not ask the same questions as the 1991 study. However one inquiry concerned a perceived growth in faith over the previous year. 82% (down by 7 percentage points) answered in the affirmative, and of these 37% (down by 10 percentage points) registered themselves as experiencing "much growth".[16] Those experiencing much growth attributed it to involvement in their own congregation (18%), other groups (13%) or private activities (6%).[17] They believed that growth in faith was strongly related to the numerical growth of their congregation and their active involvement in its prayer and devotional activities. People who were clear about what they believed were more likely to consider that they had grown in faith.[18]

Two thirds of all participants spent time every day/most days/a few times a week in devotional activities and Kaldor concludes, "Those with high levels of private devotional activity are more likely to be growing in their faith."[19]

Comparisons between the two surveys indicate that personal growth arising from church involvement across all age levels declined (down 4%). This seemed related to a decrease in the sense of belonging to the congregation,[20] even though lay participation in worship leading and public sharing increased.[21] Less regular involvement in ministry to the world outside the congregation in evangelistic or outreach activities (6% lower) or congregationally sponsored social care (3% lower)[22] seems a significant contributing factor to this decline.

The 2000 Uniting Church Christian Education Survey

A small national survey of Christian education in the Uniting Church in Australia was conducted in 1999/2000 in a cross-section of congregations. People were asked what factors had contributed to their growth in faith.[23] The highest rankings were given to services of worship (80%+) and relationships with others (friends, family, church members and God's spirit 75%+). Being in nature, clergy and elders and personal Bible study and prayer were also significant, as was being involved and actively serving others or working in church organisations (all registering 50-75%). Involvement in church groups for Bible study was also mentioned (40%+).

Conclusions

From this research it is apparent that people perceive a variety of influences which bring about development of their faith. The majority believe that they learn most from their personal communion with God through worship and prayer within the community of faith and as individuals.

The part played by formal methods of teaching does not feature as prominently as might be imagined. Worship services,[24] Bible study or theological courses and small groups, retreats, camps etc with some segment of formal teaching/learning incorporated into the wider setting are seen to be helpful. But informal learning situations are seen to have greater influence on personal growth.

Informal situations include self-directed activities (prayer, Bible reading, fasting, confession) but the majority involve interactions between individuals and groups. Sometimes one significant person (minister, priest, family member, encouraging friend, or small group leader) takes a degree of responsibility for facilitating the development of the faith of another but this rarely occurs in one-to-one isolated relationships. It is much more likely to occur between those who commit themselves to belonging to a particular congregation and to the formation of meaningful friendships. From these interactions they frequently receive encouragement, fellowship, support, care, concern and guidance in facing the issues of everyday life in a nurturing atmosphere among fellow learners who are able to model the desirable qualities of the faith.

Those who are most expected to grow in their faith not only belong to, but actively participate in the life of their own faith community and in its ministry to the world. Active participation and feelings of belonging seem to be directly related to the level of spiritual development experienced. These people serve in a variety of ways looking outward from themselves to the faith community and beyond, so that they may share their gifts with others and reflect upon and learn from their many experiences of life.

These findings confirm our theory that many of the components included in our concept of discipling have been significant factors in the perceived spiritual development of Australian church attenders. A high degree of correspondence has therefore been found to exist between the discipling model and the findings of Australian church life surveys. In short, the usefulness of embracing a more explicit discipling policy is therefore reinforced by such considerations.

The schooling model

Personal reflections

For a number of years I facilitated a course with young adult full-time students, within a Christian educational institution. The course was designed to deal with questions and matters of concern arising out of their other studies or from their experiences of daily life. It also aimed to encourage the development of Christian behaviours, attitudes and values. After a number of years I knew roughly the kind of territory we would cover during the course, but made no specific weekly plans as to what matters would form the basis of our discussions. There was no required assessment, but full participation was expected. Close personal learning relationships formed within the free, informal atmosphere of the group and many of these have continued to the present day.

Then came a year when the emphasis of the institution changed and greater import was attached to the gaining of academic credentials. Course outlines were produced and specified weekly lecture topics were set. The course became accountable to an external governing body with a curriculum specifying what was to be learnt. Assessments were set and an exam was given at the conclusion of the semester.

I received the message that other academic staff considered things were definitely 'better'… but I always wondered if that were so. Were the basic questions of the students being addressed? Was integration into a holistic learning experience occurring? Which was the more effective learning, to allow these young adults to decide matters for discussion, which were of immediate relevance to their lives and thinking, or to follow a curriculum set by unknown persons thousands of kilometres away?

Now I realize that the schooling model took over from what had been a much more informal model of teaching and learning. Whilst being appropriate in some settings, it did not appear to me to be suitable for this kind of learning. However its advantage was that it was much easier to control, to assess and to expect accountability. But was it effective in achieving the goals I had for the students' lives?

History of the schooling model within Christian communities

The schooling model of teaching and learning has been a prominent one in faith communities since the first Christian schools were established in the fourth century C.E.[25] Throughout the Middle Ages in Europe learning was kept alive in monasteries and cathedral schools,[26] and in the first universities established in the late twelfth century C.E.[27] Formal teaching methods (e.g. lectures and discussions) were used, but they were supplemented by other methods. Great 'school men' flourished from the eleventh to fourteenth centuries,[28] however schooling was only available for the elite. The vast majority of members of the community of faith were largely untaught, ignorant and superstitious.

The Protestant Reformation brought a new emphasis on learning and with the development of the printing press and the translation of the Bible into the vernacular of the common people throughout Europe, schooling gradually became available to a wider group. In the mid-sixteenth century the Jesuit emphasis on education led to the establishment of hundreds of schools, colleges and universities across the world.[29] The eighteenth century Protestant missionary movement founded schools and seminaries wherever the gospel was taken and in England the Society for Promoting Christian Knowledge began its move "to promote and encourage the erection of charity schools in all parts of England and Wales".[30]

Although originally begun for the education of the working classes, the Sunday School movement for much of the past two centuries has been seen by Protestants as making an important contribution to the Christian Education of children and in some quarters, adults.[31] The schooling model of teaching with formal curricula, graded lessons, classes and teachers, has been seen as closely associated with fulfilling the educational aims of the Christian community, both Protestant and Catholic. It has featured as the most prominent model in the fields of Christian Education, Religious Instruction and Theological Education. Alternatives such as the "kids' club" or "prayer and share group" have sometimes been dismissed as lacking in educational value, although possessing relational or spiritual worth.

This emphasis is rather surprising, considering the fact that there is nothing in the Bible about schools or schooling, even though as we established earlier, it was a familiar concept in the ancient world and within first century Jewish,

Greek and Roman societies. In the first century CE most Jewish boys obtained an elementary education at the synagogue school, 'the house of the book'. The Romans had a custom of assigning a personal slave-attendant (*paidagōgos*) to escort the child to school, to discipline and teach him good manners and test his memory by making him recite the lessons. Paul alludes to this practice twice (Gal. 3:24-5; 1 Cor. 4:15), but the context tells us nothing more about schools or schooling. These slaves were not teachers. For the Jews, higher education such as Paul received, took place under the direction of rabbis in 'the house of study'.[32] The only possible reference to a school in the New Testament is in Ephesus when for two years Paul argued daily in the *scholē* (school) of Tyrannus. A more accurate translation of this word is 'lecture hall'. Nothing may be inferred from this, other than this was the building which Paul used in an *ad hoc* manner to dialogue with visitors from all over Asia. Disciples were present, but they do not appear to be the focus of his apparently evangelistic discussion/arguments concerning "the word of the Lord" (Acts 19:9,10).

Jesus sometimes sat as a rabbi and used more structured, formal teaching practices with the crowds and his disciples, but he never founded a school. Neither is there any hint in the New Testament that any of the apostles or their followers ever contemplated the schooling model as a means of teaching the elements of the faith. Edwin Judge argues that Paul deliberately shunned any attempts to be treated by his churches or converts in the manner appropriate for a tertiary teacher of his time.[33]

Until the split between Jews and Christians was irreconcilable, Jewish sons continued to be sent to the synagogue school to learn to write and read the Hebrew Scriptures. Sons of wealthy Hellenistic Christian families attended schools or received their elementary education privately. However there is no evidence that this model was ever adopted by the faith community during the New Testament period. None of the Epistles recognized the teaching practices of the churches as a type of schooling.

Thus the popularity of the schooling model within the faith community seems to be more a matter of later tradition than being inherent in the faith itself.

The value of the model

Very few today would deny that the schooling model has its value. Even the most vocal of its critics acknowledge its benefits, even if it is only in their own lives. Most people would never achieve literacy or numeracy skills without it. Its graded curriculum allows for a wide variety of teaching content to be presented in sequential order. Much of this content may never arise in informal settings. Formal schooling fosters the development of critical thinking and enables learners to rise above the restrictions of their own environment and to draw on knowledge from a wide variety of sources. Barrow writes, "What has been consistently maintained by educators in favour of schooling is that there are some abstract bodies of knowledge that have a value and can be (most) effectively taught in schools."[34]

Hill maintains that universal schooling has improved the lot of the masses, enabled people to understand the modern world, developed some level of knowledge and skills in most children, reduced ethnic misunderstandings in multicultural communities, provided minimum levels of competence to provide access to the work force, widened options for leisure, empowered people to exercise their political freedom more discerningly and enabled the development of critical faculties to protect members of the society against the wiles of new technology.[35]

Within the Christian faith community a formal schooling approach has been used in Sunday schools or church schools, Bible or theological colleges and universities to transmit the Christian system of beliefs and practices. The stories of the faith have been told, the critical faculties of learners have been developed. Ministers and church leaders have received a large proportion of their training and qualifications for Christian ministry under the schooling model. Its value is undeniable.

Criticisms of the model

In more recent times, however, the effectiveness of the schooling model as the major model for the transmission of learning has been questioned by both secular and Christian educationists. There is a widespread recognition that there is a crisis in schools.[36]

In the 1960s and 1970s John Holt, Ivan Illich and Everett Reimer stirred up an animated debate about the usefulness of the schooling model when they observed its high percentage of failures.[37] Holt was particularly provocative, describing schools as places where students follow "meaningless procedures to obtain meaningless answers to meaningless questions".[38] Reimer considered that schools actually stifle curiosity as a motivation for learning and substitute lifeless teaching of what some people think others need to know.[39] These writers believed schools were destructive of community values and self-reliance and an instrument for reinforcing social control of the ruling class over the poorer classes.

ILLICH

Illich recognized that most learning does not take place in schools. He did not however, give any credit for what schools do achieve but strongly advocated their abolition. He dismissed their distinctives of compulsory attendance, competition and sequential teaching as being of little educational value. He maintained that schools deaden the innate desire to learn,[40] turn knowledge into a commodity and act as instruments of social control because of the operation of the "hidden curriculum".[41] To Illich, schools were particularly inefficient in instruction[42] because they prevented the formation of voluntary, close, personal, learning relationships, which he considered to be one of the chief means of education.[43]

These views have strongly influenced much recent educational thought. In response, schools have expanded the variety of formal teaching methods employed and increased in awareness of the importance of informal methods.

In this study of the discipling model it is nowhere suggested that formal learning be abandoned, however its educational limitations must be recognized. Illich's strong support for informal models of education we believe has direct relevance for the community of faith.

General research findings of the 1970s

In the 1970s Averch and others critically reviewed thousands of educational research findings about schooling. They formed the dismal conclusion that "research has not discovered any educational practice (or set of practices) that offers a high probability of success over time and place".[44] However they acknowledged that their problem was that, apart from some isolated examples, no research existed of models other than schooling and its outcomes were measured almost exclusively in the cognitive domain.[45] They believed a "vastly different form of education" was called for, but had no real solutions as to what form that might take.[46] They recognized the influence of a child's environment and experiences outside school, and acknowledged how ineffectual schooling was in affecting attitudes already formed.[47] They found "considerable evidence that non-school factors may well be more important determinants of educational outcomes than are school factors".[48]

A ground swell of discontent continued throughout the 1970s. Barrow claimed that "according to some research children are consciously in attendance for only ten minutes a day at school".[49] Douglas Holly asserted that for many pupils, except some middle class members of the dominant culture, schooling is "profoundly alienating".[50] Bereiter believed the effects of schooling have been greatly exaggerated. "Schools do not, and cannot, successfully educate – that is, influence how children turn out in any important way. The most they can do successfully is to provide child care and training."[51] He argues that any other content apart from literacy, numeracy and basic skill training is ethically untenable, because it is an invasion of personality, unless it has been voluntarily chosen as a matter for study. Richmond saw the value of the personal teacher-learner relationship but believed that it operates best when not confined by schooling.[52] Educationists began to suggest possible alternative models, however there was no widespread abandonment of the schooling model as a result of the turmoil of the debate.

Subsequent attitudes to schooling

In the 1980s it was widely recognized that there was a crisis facing public education in the United States. Aronowitz and Giroux wrote of a "failure to prepare students adequately for the ever changing demands of a sophisticated technology… [and] failure to prepare students to think critically and creatively.".[53] "The legitimacy of schools as educational institutions was challenged by low attendance and plummeting test scores."[54]

Although many innovations have come into the schooling model of recent years, dissatisfaction with it is still being expressed. In Louisiana a ten year study of school effectiveness led to the conclusion that only 25% of the variations in individual achievements could be attributable to schooling (12% to teachers and experimental factors within classes, 13% to differences between schools). The remaining 75% was directly linked to student characteristics.[55]

In 1987 Resnick wrote, "…there is growing evidence, then, that not only may schooling not contribute in a direct and obvious way to performance outside school, but also that knowledge acquired outside school is not always used to support in-school learning. Schooling is coming to look increasingly isolated from the rest of what we do…".[56]

In Australia S.L. Smith comments, "Schooling has been criticised throughout the century for failing to teach the basics… Today this schooling is inadequate and obsolete. Schools do not offer enough options to allow the diversity of talent among our young people to be nurtured, nor do they provide the conditions necessary for the development of creative, innovative, analytical people."[57] The Youth Affairs Council of WA referred to 'action poverty' which schooling often implies for the young because they are "shielded from responsibility… held in dependent status… kept away from productive work".[58]

Today schools are expected to fulfil a much wider role in the education of society than has previously been the case. Many look to schools for cures for all of society's ills. They fail to recognize that the impact of schools on the attitudes and values of society as a whole can only be minimal. Family and social environment are much more influential in establishing these.[59] In educating for the development of relationships, schools reinforce predetermined roles between teachers and learners, and thus disempower students in their acceptance of responsibility for some relationships.[60]

Schooling was not regarded as the prime agency of education before mass schooling was inaugurated. "One effect of this [being regarded as the prime educational agent] has been to denigrate other agencies which formerly provided important learning experiences, such as the family, the master-apprentice relationship, discipling, private tutoring, voluntary interest and service groups and travel."[61] For most, the wheel has turned full circle and these other agencies are perceived again as being essential in the nurturance and development of all children in society.

In an impassioned call to a recent USA conference on *School-Community Connections*[62] Gordon recognized that, "The problems of education and development for the low-status people of our nation have reached crisis proportions, so much so that the stability of the social order is now threatened."[63] He perceives a national lessening of commitment to the nurturance of all children in a time when the nature of the family and the nature of childhood is changing.[64]

He pleaded for a society in which children receive nurturance, not only from schools, but also from families and other institutions of child development and nurturance.[65]

WITHIN THE CHRISTIAN FAITH COMMUNITY

Within faith communities the schooling model has often been equated with Christian education. The very structure of many church buildings supports this emphasis, with provision made for one person to speak from the front to large numbers of people, and with small classroom areas for the Sunday School. In church and Christian schools, theological and Bible colleges, Sunday schools, Bible schools and pulpit ministry, formal teaching methods are the predominant ones used. It may be acknowledged that other models of teaching are also valuable, but little attention has been given to encouraging or understanding their use.

In the 1970s Hill asked, "Is it time we deschooled Christianity?" "The school has proved to be effective in teaching facts… but it has not proved able to change significantly personal values and commitments."[66] "Formal education, which is needed to help all children to come to terms with the contemporary social realities, must be complemented by nurturing groups like homes, clubs and church fellowships."[67] He comments that, if church or Christian schools are seen as means for educating in the faith "there is evidence that the Catholic parochial school has been more effective than most in reinforcing continued church allegiance."[68] However he continues, "There is research evidence from Australia as well as from other countries that the church school may inoculate many students against truly personal faith by wrongly equating it with conformity to the rules of a Christian school."[69] "Yet great energy and vast resources have been invested in church schools and, in the last two centuries, Sunday Schools."[70]

In Australia, society's emphasis on credentials and the schooling model has permeated the Christian community. In 1991 the percentage of the country's population who had a university degree was 6%, however 17% of the church-attending population were in this category.[71] These statistics increased by 1996 when 10% of the population and 19% of church attenders had university qualifications.[72]

It appears that the lower number of church attenders who rely on public housing (Population average is 7%, church attenders are 4%) demonstrates the greater proportion of middle or upper class, educated people within the ranks of attenders.[73] The attraction of the schooling model may actually tend to exclude the working classes from joining or participating in Australian faith communities.

CONCLUSIONS

Thus research has shown that the schooling model of education has enjoyed great popularity over the centuries, but its achievements have been somewhat limited. Hill summarizes the situation, "We know from abundant research in the field that schools can transmit useful ideas and information; they can foster critical thinking, physical skills and social awareness; they can acquaint students with the modern map of knowledge; and they can develop individual strengths and skills in the areas of thinking, feeling and self-expression."[74]

However its disadvantages are plain to see. Its compulsion has been shown to stifle natural curiosity, imposing on groups of learners the priorities for learning decided by others. Schooling does little to develop responsibility in relationships. Desirable attitudes and values are influenced more by the hidden curriculum than by intentional teaching. Schooling creates competition and social control. It often reinforces middle or upper class values, but for the working or lower classes it tends to be an alienating experience. Schooling works against the formation of close, personal learning relationships in informal settings when learners take responsibility for pursuing their own experiences and interests and learn by seeking to satisfy their own curiosity.

Christian faith communities seek to encourage the nurture of persons as 'whole' beings. They are not just concerned with detached, intellectualized, spiritual development but seek to enable their members to take their place as mature believers in an amazingly complex modern society. This endeavour requires a variety of teaching models, including schooling, but also drawing on a wide range of informal models among which discipling takes an important place.

Alternatives to the schooling model

In order to define discipling more clearly, we have previously examined a number of life-related, informal models of education with characteristics in common with discipling. These included socialisation and parenting, learning communities, collaborative learning, learning webs and networks, apprenticing and mentoring, pastoral care, counselling and psychotherapy. It is now our intention to

- compare life-related models of teaching with the schooling model.
- examine alternatives put forward by critics of the schooling model and some of the essential principles in the theory of adult education.
- briefly examine the educational research on some of the models previously mentioned, to discover what value may be placed on the learning processes which they share in common with discipling.

Life-related teaching models compared with the schooling model

The value of life-related teaching and learning is recognized by many educationists. Home and family, friends, the media, the internet, travel, hobbies, work and leisure all provide informal educational experiences. They provoke a strong motivation to learn because their relevance is immediately obvious.[75] In comparison, the schooling model is much less effective in both short and long-term learning.[76] Goodman recommended, "Structure all of society and the whole environment as educative, with the schools playing the much more particular and traditional role of giving intensive training when it is needed and sought, or of being havens for those scholarly by definition."[77]

Coleman, responding to the problem of the passive role assumed by many adolescents in formal education advised, "Put the young where everyone else is and where the action is, 'inside the economic institutions where the productive activities of society take place'".[78] Van Onna writes, "[Some] competencies, however general they may be, can only to a limited extent be taught in an explicitly didactic manner and in simulated learning environments… The ability to think in terms of complex interrelationships is not fully acquired until practised in real-life situations."[79]

However the mere presence of 'real-life' or 'work' offers no guarantee that learning will occur and may even result in less learning than the schooling model. Bauer and Herz warn, "It cannot be taken for granted that instructors… will be sufficiently able to meet the challenges implied, that is, to understand work situations as learning situations and to make them accessible to the individual so that he or she may profit from it."[80] At a recent conference of Australian educators George Walden was quoted, "The idea that every child can advance at his own pace by informal, non competitive techniques that favour spontaneity over effort is a beautiful dream, which lodged in impressionable minds and given scientific status becomes unconscious dogma. In reality it has led to overstressed teachers, low aspirations for the gifted and ungifted alike, bored and disaffected pupils and an enormous waste of time and money."[81]

Informal models of teaching, as with formal models, could be disastrous if used by the unskilled, but if those employing them are proficient, maintain a focus on intentionality and pursue identifiable educational goals, the gains will be considerable.

Thus while informal education is considered very effective it is important that learners have access to those whose intention it is to teach and who possess the ability to use informal situations to demonstrate, guide and provide opportunities for action and reflection.

Some proposed alternatives to schooling

ILLICH'S LEARNING WEBS

Illich, as we have seen, was one of the major advocates of the abandonment of the schooling model. While Illich has many critics who see his view of humanity as far too idealistic, he has had significant influence on educational thinking. He proposed replacing the schooling model with a system of totally informal education in a 'village community' type setting in which all of society was transformed "into one huge classroom".[82] He believed that individual and social life could coexist in such a way that natural curiosity and concern for the environment would result in learning. His methods incorporated aspects of a number of different types of learning: community, collaborative, experiential, modelling, apprenticeship and life-related. The basic structure would be that of "learning webs" which would operate around four basic resources, "things, models, peers and elders".[83]

He placed great importance on modelling of skills, values, attitudes and behaviours and held that frequently one good demonstration was all that was necessary in order for learning to occur.[84] His concept of 'peer matching' recognized the value of gaining understanding by talking or arguing in a voluntary setting with fellow learners. Yet he also saw the necessity of drawing on the resources of 'elders' who would freely provide leadership, guidance, assistance, confrontation or criticism for those seeking to learn from their greater knowledge or skills.

Illich also recognized the value of involvement in the learning process and the apprenticeship model of learning.[85] He believed that a learner "needs to see, to touch, to tinker with, to grasp whatever there is in a meaningful setting".[86] He saw education as a reciprocal interaction between members of the village community.

A good educational system should have three purposes: it should provide all who want to learn with access to available resources at any time in their lives; empower all who want to share what they know to find those who want to learn it from them; and finally, furnish all who want to present an issue to the public with the opportunity to make their challenge known.[87]

FREIRE'S INVESTIGATORS IN DIALOGUE WITH OTHERS

The Brazilian educator, Paulo Freire, wrote against the backdrop of an awakening of the disinherited masses in Latin America in the 1960s. He believed education is the result of communication and dialogue.[88] This happens, not in traditional hierarchical teacher-learner relationships, but when persons in loving, trusting, horizontal relationships with others critically search for learning and both become responsible for a process in which all seek to grow.[89] Students then become "critical co-investigators in dialogue with the teacher".[90]

Freire believed in the distinctive human characteristic of being able to reflect on one's self, one's actions and experiences. He held that learning occurs through this continual, simultaneous action and reflection (shared praxis) with others or in a community.[91] By encouraging illiterate, oppressed peasants to think critically about their lives in a dialogical encounter with others,[92] he was able to develop their self-awareness, dignity and hope for the eventual transformation of their world. This process was a prerequisite for their involvement in their own liberation. It was the aim of their education. He did not believe that a paternalistic group could achieve this for them or it would lead to one oppression being substituted for another.

He advocated the gradual withdrawal of teachers from their role as the directive learning force, thus enabling students to exercise their critical initiative and organize their own learning experiences and agendas.[93] While teachers would retain their authority they would do so in a non-authoritarian manner, maintaining their differences but seeking to develop the students' freedom of choice. "Through dialogue, reflecting together on what we know and don't know, we can then act critically to transform reality."[94]

Dewey, and Knowles' principles of adult education

The philosopher, John Dewey, has strongly influenced theories of informal education in the present age and provided the foundation for the development of adult education as a separate field to pedagogy (education of the young). His system of ideas is based on two key concepts: first, that "all genuine education comes about through experience"[95] and the task of the educator is to select experiences which will result in present and future learning; second, that arrangements for learning should be democratic and take into consideration the purposes of both teacher and learner.[96] The skill of the educator is in knowing, "…how to utilise the surroundings, physical and social, that exist so as to extract from them all that they have to contribute to building up experiences that are worth while".[97]

They also must provide opportunity for experiences to be interpreted in interaction with others so learning results. Dewey continues,

> Education is essentially a social process… The teacher loses the position of external boss or dictator but takes on that of leader of group activities… intelligently aware of the capacities, needs, and past experiences of those under instruction, and [allowing for the development of a plan for learning] contributed and organised into a whole by the members of the group… [as] a cooperative enterprise, not a dictation.[98]

Malcolm Knowles took Dewey's theories seriously and incorporated them into his thinking concerning the education of adults. He believed that the teaching of adults was in some ways different to that of children and therefore coined the word 'andragogy' (education of adults). He postulated that

- Adults are motivated and ready to learn as they become aware of particular needs and interests that learning will satisfy. Thus awareness may be stimulated by exposure to better models or encouragement to higher levels of aspiration and self-diagnostic procedures.
- Because the orientation of adults is toward life-centred activities they want to actively participate in learning and implement their learning immediately. Thus learning may be organized around life situations, not subjects.
- Adults see themselves as the sum of their experiences, so the richest resource for learning is analysis of experience.
- Adults have accepted responsibility for their own lives, so their learning needs to be under their control with a sense of progress towards their goals, as they seek to discover from and with others what they want to know.

- Because individual differences increase with age, educators of adults should provide for differences in style, time, place and pace of learning.[99]

Knowles advocates a learning environment for adults different from the schooling model, in which the teacher-learner relationship is characterized by a caring environment, mutual trust, respect and helpfulness and in which there is freedom of expression, acceptance of differences and openness.[100] Educators of adults must be able to assist in diagnosing needs for learning, planning, motivating, selecting effective methodology, providing resources and evaluating.[101] He promotes the use of discovery learning in "a climate which encourages experimentation (hypothesis-testing) and is tolerant of mistakes provided something is learned from them".[102]

The qualities of a helpful adult learning environment may be summed up by collaboration (not competitiveness), encouragement of group loyalties, supportive interpersonal relations and interactive participation.[103]

Some educationists believe that adults learn automatically and question the value of any interference in the process. "Adults cannot help but acquire new skills and knowledge as they proceed through life."[104] However with the rapid changes in our modern world, lifelong education is now more of a necessity than a luxury. Because "learning which occurs without the continued supervision of a professional adult educator is often chaotic, serendipitous and ineffective",[105] many adults voluntarily seek for support of another person or persons to make sense of the experiences they are encountering and to learn within them.

These principles of adult education are helpful for our study of discipling, however discipling is not a method for adults alone even though it incorporates many of the same principles. Children have always been a significant part of discipling communities and while being especially under the nurture of their parents or families, their role as both contributors to, and receivers of discipling was taught by Jesus and has been widely recognized since. Discipling also differs from andragogy in requiring commitment to close, loving relationships whereas adult education requires care, trust, respect and tolerance without the necessity of long term relational warmth and love.

Research on alternative models of education

PARENTS OR FAMILIES AS EDUCATORS

In contemporary Western society there are a wide variety of patterns of family life. These include extended families, nuclear families, single-parent families, skip-generation families[106] and blended families. Leichter speaks of a complex social unit "with multiple and parallel activities going on much of the time".[107] But whatever its structure the household unit is highly influential in the development of children and indeed all family members. Anecdotal evidence would support the premise that learning within families or household units is mutual, as adult members learn and grow to maturity from their interactions with children and young people. A 1981 OECD inquiry into *The Educational Role of the Family* found that the family is "the most crucial agency of education".[108]

Nurture of children within the family is usually regarded as an aspect of child development, however frequently it is much more intentional than the use of the term 'development' would imply. The anthropologist, Margaret Mead "perceived all children in all cultures as learners who acquire universal skills like walking, eating, talking and who learn particular and unique skills provided that they have the opportunities to do so."[109] The role of the family is to provide the circumstances in which this learning can take place. "Parents in fact have been discovered as critical to the education and development of their children."[110] They "have a hitherto underestimated contribution to make to their children's development".[111] This includes "the informal, incidental process of learning… gradual skill acquisition, and the evolving of techniques for social and emotional survival".[112]

The family is also involved "in reappraising, questioning, consolidating and embellishing knowledge acquired through other institutions".[113] Hill believes, "The genius of the family is the casual interaction which occurs, the acceptance of the child-self not for what [he] achieves but for what and who [he] is, and the free dialogue of persons."[114]

A growing body of research today shows the value of parental involvement in children's learning both within and outside the school.[115] This presupposes that it is always beneficial for the education of a child to have parental input. Not all families will exert what society considers to be a positive influence on children. This calls for parental education. Some believe that "the educational role of parents within the family is… so crucial that school based formal learning cannot effectively proceed unless parents are aided and supported to realise and maximize their own educative role."[116]

Writing from a Christian perspective, Goodliff believes that in our postmodern society "'Family' is too fragile an institution to bear the burden of responsibility placed upon it". Citing family breakdown and rapid changes in society he postulates that, "The church, not the family, is the institution that primarily conveys God's grace and is the community to which we owe our prime allegiance."[117] His belief strongly supports our contention that the household of faith, the discipling community, is ideally suited to the task of nurturing the spiritual development of its members no matter what the nature of their home or family environment. As the faith community with its multiplicity of gifts carries out the mission of Christ to the world it can provide an effective environment in which children and adults are nurtured to grow and develop to the full extent of their potential.

Learning through relationships

Many writers including the Jewish Philosopher, Martin Buber have emphasized the importance of relationships to learning. He believed that humans have an instinct for communion,[118] and that all real living is 'meeting' and relationships.[119] He taught that successful learning involves direct communication and mutual dialogue between teacher and learner.[120] Relationships for him were of two kinds, either "I-It", in which persons are treated as objects, or "I-Thou" in which persons are considered as significant beings of worth.[121] Writing in the non-inclusive idiom of his era, he said,

> It is only when a man is truly able to confront another with openness, directness, and honesty; when he is able to trust and assume responsibility for another; when he meets another's Thou; only then does a man experience genuine humanity. Anything else would leave a man in the world of the It, and although he might find comfort and security, he would never truly know what it is to be a man, to be human.[122]

Barnes concurs with Buber in the value he attributes to relationships, "A being exists as a person only in so far as he is related to other persons... Personality is other-centred".[123]

For Buber, character is moulded and education takes place only through I-Thou relationships of mutual respect. He expected teachers to take responsibility for the establishment of close, honest and open relationships. They also should demonstrate naturally and spontaneously in their own lives the qualities of character to be instilled. He believed that learners would best be nurtured in a teaching environment selected by the teacher,[124] involving mutuality and reciprocity between persons. Their relationship is probably best described as friendship.[125]

Buber conceived of these relationships taking place within community where people relate to one another on a personal, not purely functional level. He described the characteristics of the resultant dialogue:
- engages the whole of one's 'being' and of the other's 'being';
- requires that one be truly present to the other;
- is marked by genuine openness;
- is characterized by *agapaic* love;
- has a profound sense of responsibility for and loyalty to the other.[126]

Hill believes Buber's portrait of this type of teaching relationship "has not been bettered".[127] Noddings suggests that the outcome of this relationship will be the teacher's response of care or protection of the welfare of the learners,[128] seeing things from their perspective. She believes that when learners perceive an attitude of caring in teachers they "grow" and "glow".[129] Gilligan notes that women's personal growth to maturity is developed in a "context of attachment and affiliation with others." They particularly seem to respond to relationships of care.[130]

It is widely endorsed that the teacher-learner relationship is the most important factor in achieving educational goals, whatever the subject matter involved, and that people are only truly human when they are in relationship with others.

APPRENTICING AND MENTORING

In an earlier chapter we introduced apprenticing and mentoring as models of teaching. The value of apprenticing has been recognized over much of the history of civilisation. In recent years there has been a resurgence in its popularity. Collins, Brown and Newman acknowledge the effectiveness of "apprentice-like" methods for a variety of cognitive and social skills much wider than those usually associated with apprenticing and craftsmanship.[131]

A notable recent example of its worth is the German education system which uses the apprenticeship model to train the majority of those who do not proceed to university education. Two-thirds of their post-secondary young people are involved. The model has been highly successful, with 90% fulfilling the requirements to gain their credentials giving them the necessary skills for their chosen occupations.[132] It utilizes practical on-the-job experience in businesses and firms, and formal theoretical instruction in vocational schools. This has proved so effective that it has attracted attention around the world, with groups from other countries travelling to Germany to study its processes, and seek advice in developing similar systems.

The value of experience in learning, which is fundamental to the apprentice model is strongly supported. "Experiential learning has always been and will continue to be a major, if not the major, way in which most of us attempt to make sense of our universe."[133] And the learning of skills through imitation of those with more experience is recognized as being especially appropriate for tasks that have little cognitive structure, such as attitudes, beliefs or performance skills.[134]

The success of mentoring has been documented for centuries.[135] Cohen quotes a number of recent studies to show it has achieved a significant status in educational, business and government circles and has a powerful influence in promoting retention and enrichment of learning. He adds, "The importance of mentoring relationships as a factor in personal maturation and successful adult adjustment to numerous life roles is… a general theme of the adult development and counselling literature."[136]

Since 1975 there have been numerous experiments throughout the world involving tertiary students tutoring and mentoring in local schools.[137] These have generally resulted in significant learning benefits for the tutees. Outcomes for tutors were more within the social/affective domain than in cognitive and/or transferable skills.[138] Research into both formal and informal mentoring relationships with adult students has shown much value for learning which is derived from such relationships, however even greater benefits have been found to result from peer relationships.[139]

Apprenticing and mentoring are widely recognized as very effective models of teaching and learning in the present day. Research only confirms what has been accepted for centuries.

Learning communities or groups of learners

Another family of teaching models centres on small groups or communities of learners with or without a specified teacher. These include short or long term learning communities (religious communities, college residential halls, camping), total institutions, collaborative learning arrangements, small groups and the value of hospitality. Research findings concerning the educational benefits of some of these will be examined.

Qualities for effective learning in communities

Jalongo has listed five necessary characteristics of a community in order for effective learning to take place.[140]
- It must develop mutual trust and respect among all members. In order for this to occur the community must walk the fine line between respecting and supporting the learning efforts of the less knowledgeable or competent, and meeting the needs for significance and power of the stronger members.
- The community must provide opportunities to deal with ideas and values which affect direction and priorities even when they might be sources of conflict.
- Members of the group must accept responsibility for their own actions, successes and failures, but remain committed to the support of one another in the learning situations of which they are a part.
- There must be freedom to take risks in order to be creative and innovative, without making changes for change's sake.
- Members must be willing to share responsibility for one another and allow opportunities for learning from others' experiences as well as through interaction with colleagues.

Not all communities or individuals, possess these qualities but where they are nurtured the possibility exists for the formation of a community where significant, desirable learning may take place.

Long-term communities – residential colleges

Residential colleges, which are the oldest learning institutions in Western higher education, have been shown to have a powerful developmental effect. They do make use of the schooling model but the community itself is also a powerful educative force. Pascarella, Terenzini and Blimling synthesized 2,600 studies on the impact of college on students in the US. They found that study habits, academic performance and intellectual achievements were not changed, but some general cognitive growth (e.g. critical thinking) appeared attributable to participation in a residential community.[141] Learning in other domains was considerable. In comparison with students living at home, residential students were more likely to persist until graduation and to make "significantly greater positive gains in such areas of psychosocial development as autonomy and inner-directedness, intellectual orientation, and self-concept" and to demonstrate "significantly greater increases in aesthetic, cultural, and intellectual values."[142]

They also found these students achieved "higher cultural and aesthetic interests… positive effects on self-reliance, self-understanding, interpersonal skills and personal discipline".[143] Even after allowance was made for the fact that students who chose to live in residence would be predisposed to benefit from the experience, the difference in outcomes was noticeable. They discovered that if students were assigned shared living arrangements on the basis of a particular trait, the experience tended to create a culture which rewarded that value or behaviour.[144] Thus those students assigned together because of academic ability, performed better than if they were with mixed ability groups, but their experience of diversity and a well-rounded education was limited, and so other students were deprived of the benefits of their role modelling.[145]

Welty discovered that students in residential halls gained a variety of alternative learning opportunities because student-faculty contact and feedback were improved and there was more time given to tasks and cooperation between students.[146] Schroeder cites studies, which found that student involvement increased in residential halls, and benefit from educational experiences grew as a result.[147] Increased faculty contact with students has been shown to lead to improved teaching skills.[148] Creamer cites evidence that fewer students drop out from smaller cohesive residential groups because of their social environment, than large impersonal high-rise accommodation.[149]

Living in a residential community generally leads to conflict situations. Research has found that resolution of conflict often results in greater learning.[150] Rather than seeking to suppress it a wise educator will use the potential for increased growth and learning among community members when conflict situations arise. "Controversy, compared with concurrence seeking and individualistic study, promotes higher achievement and retention, greater search for information, and more cognitive rehearsal, accurate understanding of the two perspectives, continuing motivation, and positive attitudes toward controversy and classmates."[151]

However not all learning in residential halls may be considered by educators as desirable. Feldman and Newcomb list negative impacts of residential halls as encouragement of superficiality in interpersonal relationships and the blunting of social perceptions; fostering attitudes of social superiority, snobbishness, and prejudice toward a variety of 'out-groups'; demands for excessive group participation and conformity; discouragement of openness to novelty and change-inducing experiences; promotion of aggressive and regressive behaviour (including the acting out of primitive aggressive and sexual impulses); encouragement of simplistic concepts of masculinity and femininity; and creation of an atmosphere favourable to heavy, even excessive drinking."[152]

Taking this negative impact into consideration there still remains an increasing body of research favourable to them. Thus residential colleges are experiencing a renaissance in the US,[153] because of the improved learning in many different areas and because they "embody a commitment to academics by providing an educational environment that values students and their holistic development."[154]

Long-term communities – total institutions

Long term, 'closed', total institutions such as mental hospitals, prisons, concentration camps, armies, monasteries and old-style boarding schools,[155] produce changes in attitudes and belief systems and a certain kind of learned behaviour. They operate by confining inmates to one place, under the same authority for all activities of their day and night, without freedom to leave or to engage in unrestricted social interaction with outsiders. Learning occurs as inmates are in the immediate company of many others treated similarly and under the supervision of a small staff charged with fulfilling the official aims of the institution.[156] The life of the institution itself is the teaching medium and frequently the curriculum is hidden.

Many of the characteristics for promotion of desirable learning are lacking in these communities and not all learning is helpful. Those with a teaching intention depend more on a conditioning process involving rewards and punishments, than a true communal life with constructive teacher-learner relationships. The greater or lesser level of adaptation of persons towards their situation depends on their previous home world experiences or their adherence to strong religious or political beliefs.[157] The ethical validity of such a model of teaching is a matter of concern because it depends on compulsion and many of its outcomes are detrimental to the holistic development of participants.[158]

Short-term communities – camping and adventure education

Educational camping is an informal model of teaching which provides opportunities for learning in a short-term community. Adventure education, which is often associated with camping, has been shown to increase understanding of self and relationships with others and the world of nature.[159] The need to change is highlighted and any personal decisions to make changes are supported.[160] Those with special needs have been particularly shown to make positive changes in self-esteem and self-confidence.[161] It fosters communication, cooperation, trust, conflict resolution and problem solving and provides opportunity for holistic development by raising some of the fundamental questions of life. When given the opportunity to constructively reflect on the experience, greater understanding of one's own belief system is achieved and/or a significant contribution to moral and religious education may result.[162]

Hospitality

Hospitality is considered here as a very short-term community. Although it has a much more limited learning impact than other forms of community it has

sufficient value to be included here. Nouwen believes it can create a helpful learning environment,
> "Hospitality… means primarily the creation of a free space where the stranger can enter and become a friend instead of an enemy. Hospitality is not to change people, but to offer them space where change can take place. It is not to bring men and women over to our side, but to offer freedom not disturbed by dividing lines. It is not to lead our neighbour into a corner where there are no alternatives left, but to open a wide spectrum of options for choice and commitment."[163]

COLLABORATIVE AND SMALL GROUP LEARNING, AND THE VOLUNTARY GROUP

Collaborative and group investigation approaches complement each other to achieve a wide range of educational objectives in both cognitive and social domains.[164] Intensive research over the past twenty years has shown that collaborative or cooperative learning is an extremely powerful model of teaching and learning. Hull believes that "the best learning especially in the case of adults is almost always in groups".[165] Learners achieve more when they receive help from their peers, and those offering help learn both from the receivers and from the process itself.[166] "Research on cooperative learning is overwhelmingly positive… The more complex the outcomes (higher order processing of information, problem solving, social skills and attitudes), the greater are the effects."[167]

Writing concerning a discipling program in an American church, Olsen commented that its designers were "caught off guard by the tremendous spiritual power of the group experience."[168]

Hawryluk and Smallwood summarized a number of studies which found that cooperative group learning activities in schools "…resulted in more cooperative and altruistic attitudes toward peers, increased helping behaviour among classmates, increased feelings of being liked and supported by peers, more frequent cross-racial friendship choices, and increased acceptance of mainstreamed handicapped students by non-handicapped peers".[169]

The value of cooperative learning has been summarized by Bellanca:[170]
- Students who learn co-operatively perform better academically than students who learn in individualistic or competitive models;
- Because of the quantity of 'cognitive rehearsal', all students of all abilities in co-operative learning teams enhance their short and long-term memory as well as their critical thinking skills;
- Co-operative experiences promote positive self-acceptance resulting in students improving their learning, self-esteem, liking for school and the motivation to participate;
- Because co-operative learning leads to positive interaction among students, intrinsic learning, motivation and emotional involvement in learning are developed to a high degree;

- Co-operative learning nurtures peer relationships and structures positive interaction, resulting in students developing stronger scholastic aspirations, more pro-social behaviour and more positive peer relationships.

Wlodkowski and Knowles endorse many of the qualities for effective learning which were listed above under communities. They add the following characteristics as necessary for effective learning to take place in groups.[171]

- A people-centred learning environment which is accepting, caring and warm and provides all members with a strong sense of belonging.
- People who are open to both listening to one another and sharing information, ideas, thoughts, feelings and reactions to the issues being addressed.
- A collaborative atmosphere in which cooperation, not competitiveness prevails.
- Group goals which are clear, valued and accepted by the members .
- The perception that changed behaviour is necessary, desirable and able to be practised without danger of censure.

Many groups in which learning takes place are voluntary in nature. Voluntary youth organisations are widely recognized as providing education for adult life unable to be replicated in the compulsory, hierarchical structure of the school. Research conducted by the Australian Senate Standing Committee on Employment, Education and Training into the value of these groups concluded that, "the most effective way of enabling young people to learn about the rights and responsibilities of adult life, including citizenship is by experiencing how decision making works, not just being told about it".[172]

Voluntary groups share prominently with the home, and to a lesser extent the school, in the formation of values.[173] Those groups which have a teaching intention find motivation to learn is high.[174] Because the interests and goals have been freely chosen, members are receptive to the values and life-style embodied in the group.[175]

SUMMARY

We have found that a considerable body of educational research has affirmed the value of life-related, informal models of learning. "An impressive body of anecdotal evidence" also exists.[176] Thus through parenting and education within the household, close personal teacher-learner relationships, apprenticing, mentoring, short and long-term communities, adventure education and collaborative and small group learning, opportunities abound for teaching and learning. Involvement in informal learning relationships and processes increases the number and level of educational outcomes. Teachers and fellow learners are able to function as instructors and role models. Quality of teaching improves where teachers are able to relate as part of a community. Academic results achieved by these models are about the same or maybe not as productive as the schooling model, but the holistic development of the learners in a wide variety of aspects of their lives is noticeably enhanced.

Each of these models with its valuable contribution to the educational process shares characteristics in common with the discipling model. Some of them were identified in Chapter Ten when we were tightening our definition of discipling, and comparisons made at that point are germane to the present chapter, except that here we have been addressing the question of support in the literature of educational research into such patterns.

In summary, we have discovered that there are a number of alternative models of teaching to the schooling model. They do not abandon the teacher-student relationship, but allow it to operate in an informal way, giving the learner a greater degree of responsibility for what is to be learnt and making use of real-life or hands-on situations and experiences which enable growth and development.

Conclusions

In previous chapters it has been established that the discipling model of teaching is ideally suited to transmitting the elements of the Christian faith. These include its understandings of the infinite God, Christ-like behaviours and beliefs, attitudes and values expected of his followers and the skills for serving him among others in this world. In this chapter we have sought to discover if the discipling model is of value as an educational methodology in the present day.

The Australian Church Life surveys strongly affirm that modern day church attenders learn and grow in their faith primarily as they commit themselves to relate in prayer and worship to God himself, as individuals and as members of a faith community. Close, caring relationships with other members of the community whether they are family, friends, fellow group members or community leaders have also brought significant development to people's faith experience. And living out that experience in active service further reinforced their learning. Formal models of teaching had some influence on growth, but did not play a major role. These characteristics of teaching/learning scenarios within the church closely parallel the components of the discipling model of teaching as we have defined it. Thus research findings into church life demand that attention be given to the discipling model. This is because it incorporates the majority of factors identified by church attenders as being most conducive to growth in relationship with God and understanding the faith, and most influential in promoting changes in attitudes, values and behaviours.

In our survey of relevant contemporary educational critique we have seen that the strength of a formal, schooling model of education is in conveying knowledge, beliefs, ideas and information. It cannot be used as an all-inclusive model to convey the whole spectrum of learnings required of members of the Christian community of faith. Modern educational research endorses the effectiveness of the wide variety of informal models of education which we have discussed, in communicating attitudes, values, beliefs, skills and behaviours.

These models are not limited by age, culture, class, gender, intellectual ability, previous experience, or material wealth. They start with the learners' lives and experience and are under their control. And through close relationships formed with others, teaching occurs in response to the actions and/or reflections of the learners.

Thus our exploration of these present day research findings has established that a high degree of congruence exists between informal, life-related models of teaching and the teaching methods which we have seen to be closely associated with the discipling model. We therefore conclude that the discipling model is an effective educational strategy particularly relevant to the community of faith in our contemporary world. The results of our study lead us to believe that it is an educational practice to be strongly recommended as worthy of greater attention in the Christian community, and of considerable significance to the church of the present day.

We are now ready to move into our concluding area of research in this study of the discipling model. In the next chapter an examination will be made of current theories and practices within the Christian church in different places in the world, to test whether the discipling model as we have defined it, is supported by others in the fields of Christian education, small groups and cell churches, and theological education.

Notes to Chapter 12

1 This is offered as one example of church life in a contemporary Western culture.
2 Results are published by the Christian Research Association in Blombery & Hughes, 1987 and Hughes & Blombery, 1990.
3 Hughes & Blombery, 1990, 47-50
4 Hughes & Blombery, 1990, 50-54; Blombery & Hughes, 1987, 46. Percentages indicate the number of respondents who made the statement against the total number who were surveyed.
5 Blombery & Hughes, 1987, 49
6 Hughes & Blombery, 1990, 54-6
7 Hughes & Blombery, 1990, 56-9
8 52% of respondents rated their school religious education (whether in state or denominational schools) as very important and 32% of some importance. 48% of the sample had spent some time in a denominational school. 72% of Protestants listed Sunday School as important. (Blombery & Hughes, 1987, 44)
9 This involved all major denominations.
10 Kaldor, 1992, 79; Kaldor & Powell, 1995, 84
11 Kaldor, 1992, 80
12 More than one response was permitted, so these percentages are more than 100%. (Kaldor & Powell, 1995, 84)
13 Kaldor, 1992, 80; Kaldor & Powell, 1995, 76-7
14 Kaldor, 1992, 81
15 Results were published in Kaldor et al., 1999a and 1999b
16 Kaldor, 1999b, 131

17 Kaldor, 1999b, 78-9
18 Kaldor et al., 1999a, 82
19 Kaldor, 1999b, 80
20 Kaldor, 1999b, 131
21 Up by 4% and 5% respectively. (Kaldor, 1999b, 133)
22 Kaldor, 1999b, 132
23 Hughes & Bond, 2000, 6-7
24 No attempt has been made to comment on style of worship.
25 Judge, 1966, 34
26 Smith, 1976, 228, 239
27 Latourette, 1954, 496-7
28 Latourette, 1954, 495-519
29 Donnelly, 1977, 413
30 Cowie, 1977, 473
31 Latourette, 1954, 1186-7; Collinson, 1987, 5
32 Paul received his rabbinic education from the leading Pharisee Gamaliel. Sitting at the feet of the teacher was the posture of a student (Acts 22:3; 5:34).
33 Judge, 1983, 11-12
34 Barrow, 1978, 141
35 Hill, 1997, 201
36 Richmond, 1975, 25
37 Illich, 1973; Reimer, 1971; Holt, 1974, 39-43
38 Holt as cited in Hurn, 1978, 5
39 Reimer, 1971, 89
40 Illich, 1973, 403
41 The social and psychological factors which pressurize the child to conform, make up what Illich calls the "hidden curriculum". (Illich as cited in Bowen & Hobson, 1974, 396)
42 Illich, 1973, 24
43 Illich as cited in Bowen & Hobson, 434
44 Averch, 1972, xi
45 Averch, 1972, 153
46 Averch, 1972, xii
47 Averch, 1972, 159
48 Averch, 1972, 158
49 Barrow, 1978, 98
50 Douglas Holly as cited in Richmond, 1975, 40
51 Bereiter as cited in Richmond, 1975, 73
52 Richmond, 1975, 6
53 Aronowitz & Giroux, 1985, 23
54 Aronowitz & Giroux, 1985, 57
55 Teddie & Stringfield, 1993, 25
56 She appears however, to be equally unenthusiastic about informal education suggesting that much of what is learnt in experiential programs has little transferability to other settings. (Resnich as cited in Kraft, 1990, 181)
57 Smith, 1991, 88
58 Youth Affairs Council of Western Australia as cited in Parliament of the Commonwealth of Australia, 1989, 64
59 Hill, 1997, 203

60 Hill, 1990, 47
61 Hill, 1997, 198
62 Rigsby, Reynolds & Wang, 1995, xiii
63 Gordon, 1995, 46
64 "Today, those choosing to have children do not make that choice in order to enhance future family or personal security." Children are no longer regarded as family assets, but as liabilities. Society no longer values children. But they are the citizens of the future. Resources for their nurturance must be adequate. Stable social units in which to develop children are absolutely necessary for their very survival and for the well being of the nation's future. (Gordon, 1995, 49,54,57)
65 Gordon, 1995, 45-57
66 Hill, 1978, 13
67 Hill, 1978, 15
68 Hill, 1978, 16
69 Hill, 1978, 19
70 Hill, 1997, 198
71 Kaldor, 1992, 26
72 Kaldor, 1999b, 19
73 Kaldor, 1992, 26
74 Hill, 1990, 22
75 Simons, 1992, 167
76 Richmond, 1975, 6
77 Goodman as cited in Barrow, 1978, 100
78 Coleman cited in Richmond, 1975, 5
79 Van Onna, 1992, 129
80 Bauer & Herz as cited in Van Onna, 1992, 131
81 Walden as quoted by Woodhead, 1999, 8
82 Illich as cited in Bowen and Hobson, 1974, 403
83 Illich, 1973, 81
84 Illich, 1973, 90
85 Illich as cited in Bowen & Hobson, 1974, 403
86 Illich as cited in Bowen & Hobson, 1974, 410
87 Illich, 1973, 78
88 Freire, 1973, 137
89 Freire, 1972, 53
90 Freire, 1972, 54
91 Freire, 1973, 133
92 Freire, 1972, 12
93 Shor & Freire, 1987, 90
94 Shor & Freire, 1987, 99
95 Dewey, 1938, 13
96 Dewey as cited in Knowles, 1984, 86
97 Dewey, 1938, 35
98 Dewey, 1938, 61-66
99 Knowles, 1984, 31
100 Knowles, 1984, 83
101 Knowles, 1980, 26
102 Knowles, 1984, 120

103 Knowles. 1984, 120
104 Brookfield, 1983, 1
105 Brookfield, 1983, 2
106 Berger, 1995, 81
107 Leichter, 1985, 87
108 Wolfendale, 1983, 167
109 Mead as cited in Wolfendale, 1983, 153
110 Grotberg as cited in Wolfendale, 1983, 151
111 Wolfendale, 1983, 154
112 Wolfendale, 1983, 11
113 Leichter, 1985, 86
114 Hill, 1966, 408
115 Davies, 1995, 269
116 Wolfendale, 1983, 157
117 Goodliff, 1995, 62-3
118 Buber, 1961, 114
119 Panko, 1976, 28
120 Buber, 1961, 125
121 Buber, 1937
122 Buber as cited in Panko, 1976, 119
123 Barnes, 1966, 21
124 Buber, 1961, 132, 134
125 Buber as cited in Noddings, 1984, 66
126 Buber as cited in Groome, 1991, 107
127 "Buber's portrait of the teacher who nurtures with love and pain the developing self within each child, yet keeps sufficient subjective distance so as not to overwhelm [him], has not been bettered, though it could have been expanded to accommodate group relationships." (Hill, 1966, 406)
128 Noddings, 1984, 9
129 Noddings, 1984, 66
130 Gilligan, 1982, 169-70
131 Collins, Brown & Newman, 1989, 453
132 Glover, 1996, 84
133 McLuhan as cited in Kraft, 1990, 175
134 Gage as cited in Knowles, 1984, 94
135 Cohen, 1995, 1
136 Cohen, 1995, 4
137 Goodlad, 1995, 6-7
138 Topping & Hill, 1995, 13-31
139 Clulow, 1995, 97, 101-2
140 Jalongo, 1991, 38-40
141 Pascarella, Terenzini & Blimling, 1994, 40
142 Pascarella, Terenzini & Blimling, 1994, 39
143 Pascarella & Terenzini as cited in Smith, 1994, 250
144 Moos reports that students high in religious concern create residential group living environments high in traditional social orientation which helps them to maintain or consolidate their initial religious values. (Moos, 1979, 101)
145 Pascarella, Terenzini & Blimling, 1994, 41

146 Welty, 1994, 79, 80
147 Astin as cited in Schroeder, 1994, 167
148 Smith, 1994, 247-8
149 Creamer, 1990, 133
150 "I draw on the work of Piaget (1968) in identifying conflict as the harbinger of growth and also on the work of Erikson (1964) who, in charting development through crisis, demonstrates how a heightened vulnerability signals the emergence of a potential strength, creating a dangerous opportunity for growth, 'a turning point for better or worse'."(Gilligan, 1982, 108)
151 Smith, Johnson & Johnson, 1981, 651
152 Feldman & Newcomb, 1969, 215
153 Smith, 1994, 241
154 Smith, 1994, 263
155 Goffman, 1961, 4
156 Goffman, 1961, 6
157 Goffman, 1961, 66
158 Goffman, 1961, 61-4
159 Shackles, 1991, 70-2
160 Priest, 1990, 114
161 eg. Mental patients, academic underachievers and delinquents (Iida, 1975, 234)
162 Shackles, 1991, 7; Hunt, 1990, 127
163 Nouwen as cited in Foster, 1994, 67
164 Sharan, 1980, 267
165 Hull, 1991, 17
166 Bruffee, 1984, 638
167 Joyce & Weil as cited in Hough & Paine, 1997, 143
168 Olsen, 1994, 127
169 Hawryluk & Smallwood, 1988, 376
170 Bellanca et al. as cited in Hough & Paine, 1997, 143
171 Wlodkowski, 1990, 192; Knowles, 1984, 101
172 Parliament of the Commonwealth of Australia, 1989, 64
173 Hill, 1990, 80
174 Attitudes towards coaching in sports well illustrate this high motivation.
175 Hill, 1997, 207
176 Hill, 1987, 60

Chapter 13

Congruence of Discipling with Educational Theories in Today's Church

Having examined present day educational research into models of teaching which have elements in common with the discipling model, we now turn to examine three fields of research within the life of the church today. It has been necessary to limit our study to the fields of Christian Education, the Small Group Movement and Theological Education and within these fields the investigation has been further limited to the writings of a select few influential persons. By this method we hope to provide insights into current thinking, assess the congruence between discipling and these present day studies, and make some recommendations for future directions in Christian education in the light of the discipling model.

First, the Christian education theories of John Westerhoff, Lawrence Richards and Thomas Groome will be discussed. Second, the small group movement and writings of John Mallison will be examined and compared with cell church theory and the writings of Ralph Neighbour. Third, the writings of Robert W. Ferris and Robert Banks on the future of theological education will be considered.

Christian education

Many writers provide invaluable assistance in understanding the theory and practice of Christian education. They even seek to define it as a field, but their mindset is often focussed on a schooling model. Westerhoff, Richards and Groome have been selected for investigation because of their strong influence on the development of the whole field of Christian education. Each represents a different theological perspective (liberal and evangelical Protestants and Roman Catholic). All share the common belief that Christian education is a whole process of transmitting the faith with its values, beliefs and behaviours. From this broad perspective they step beyond the schooling model to consider a wide range of formal and informal teaching/learning experiences. The largely informal nature of discipling means that their writings provide a useful resource for implementing the model. Thus we shall test their theories to discover whether they accommodate the values of the discipling model as a means of transmitting the faith and enabling believers to grow in spiritual maturity.

The need for change

Westerhoff and Richards addressed the issue of Christian education in the USA, against the backdrop of the boom-times of the 1940s and 50s when church-related educational institutions and production of curriculum resources were at the peak of their demand. During the 60s and 70s the schooling model became the basis for many "imaginative, important, and relevant contributions to Christian education".[1] But as society changed and the educational role of the community, family, church, religious periodicals and other institutions began to crumble, more and more was being required of schools and the schooling model. Under these strains its effectiveness came into question as a replacement for the religious education previously provided through a number of different sources. This was at the same time as Illich and his contemporaries were questioning the schooling model in general education.

Westerhoff observed, "You can teach about religion, but you cannot teach people faith."[2] He realized that there was more required in the transmission of the faith than what could be conveyed through the schooling model alone. Use of other educational strategies was imperative. "Until we can imagine an alternative to our present schooling-instructional paradigm, our efforts at Christian education will be inadequate and increasingly ineffective."[3]

John Westerhoff

Noting the effectiveness of the socialisation process in transmitting the culture of a society to its members (attitudes, values, skills and behaviours) Westerhoff recommended something similar for Christian education. He described it as 'religious socialisation', "a process consisting in lifelong formal and informal mechanisms, through which persons sustain and transmit their faith (worldview, value system) and life-style".[4]

He saw Christianity as having "one pervasive, dominant loyalty to the church as a natural community".[5] Participation in the life of that community he considered was essential for acquiring, sustaining and communicating the faith. The life-style of the community reinforced its teachings and focused its attention away from itself to the needs of those around.[6] He could conceive of no religion without affiliation with its religious community[7] and advocated full participation in "its rites, rituals, myths, symbols, expressions of belief, attitudes and values, organisational patterns and activities".[8]

He stressed continuity and permanence and believed that small, closely relating supportive communities encouraged the identification and formation of desirable beliefs, values, attitudes and behaviours and thus were more effective than a large, impersonal groups of people.[9] Westerhoff drew attention to unintentional learning, the 'hidden curriculum', which he showed frequently cancelled out the intentional curriculum.[10]

He saw the task of religious educators as forming and sustaining the life of small groups in order to nurture an intimacy of life with God and to effect changes in the lives of their members. He believed the creation of meaningful rites and rituals would convey the meaning of the faith by providing opportunities for learners to experience and reflect upon the faith and express it in personal and social action.[11]

Westerhoff later rejected the idea of a teacher thinking that he or she could or should control the spiritual learning of another person.[12] Consequently he urged all members of the faith community to be in a continual, dynamic, cooperative, learning relationship with others across the generations,[13] and with God.[14] This he labelled as 'faith-enculturation'. He believed that the most effective communities would be those which were united in their basic beliefs, and although small[15] had people of different ages, spiritual gifts and ethnicity involved.[16] He encouraged experimentation, questioning and knowing, understanding, owning and living out the Christian faith. He advocated shared experience, story telling, celebration, action and reflection between and among equal 'faithing' selves.[17]

He outlined four stages or styles through which he believed faith develops:[18]

- Experienced faith, which sees faith demonstrated and responds by seeking to "explore and test, observe and copy, imagine and create, experience and react".
- Affiliative faith, in which a sense of belonging to the community develops as persons begin to contribute to its activities.
- Searching faith, in which persons doubt, experiment and explore alternatives until they commit themselves to their convictions.
- Owned faith, in which persons stand up for their convictions and commit themselves to personal and social action.

In his later writings Westerhoff rejects the terminology 'faith-enculturation', in favour of 'catechesis', "to indicate all intentional learning within a community of Christian faith and life."[19] He seeks to relate intentional educational activities to real life situations and stresses the necessity of being open to new experiences and willing to move away from the home environment into shared community. He emphasizes *praxis* (participation and contemplation; action and critical reflection) as the only means of gradually assimilating new understandings in the faith and publicly committing oneself to actions consistent with them.[20] He believes persons need instruction in knowledge and abilities useful for responsible personal communal life in church and society.[21]

David Heywood criticizes Westerhoff for making no attempt to locate the Christian community within its own contemporary pluralistic culture. He believes that his insistence on stability and continuity is unrealistic considering the transience implicit in modern society.[22] Westerhoff conceives of people primarily as members whose identity and growth can only be understood in terms of one community. But Heywood points out that people in Western society may at any time belong to a number of diverse communities (family, work, ethnic community, sports clubs and the neighbourhood).[23] He believes Westerhoff undervalues teacher-pupil relationships by his emphasis on 'fellow pilgrims', and gives no clear direction as to how his theory becomes coherent educational practice.[24]

Heywood calls instead for a 'kingdom' model of religious socialisation, not as a sub-culture, but with Christians being members of an outward looking learning group, acting as 'leaven' in the wider society, bringing good from their shared perspectives and common understandings.[25]

Lawrence Richards

Much of the educational thinking of Lawrence Richards is similar to that of Westerhoff, even though his religious tradition and theological understandings are very different. Richards defines Christian education as, "the process of guiding the community of faith toward shared experience of revealed reality".[26] Both men place Christian education firmly within the life of the faith community's formal and informal educational experiences. Richards designates these as 'discipling', whereas Westerhoff does not use the term. Its use is so rare that even Cully and Cully in their comprehensive *Encyclopedia of Religious Education* have no entry for 'Discipling'[27]. Richards strongly emphasizes the theological foundations of discipling as well as its implementation in a variety of situations.

Richards' foundational principles of Christian education have remained much the same over the years, although he has adapted and expanded them and emphases have changed. His understanding of discipling however, has recently changed considerably.[28]

In his early writing, *Creative Bible Teaching*, he dealt primarily with formal models of teaching.[29] However Richards recognized the weaknesses of the schooling model with its distorted emphasis on cognitive learning. "It seems that when we adopted from our culture the formal school approach to nurture, we in fact set up the conditions under which discipling and growth in likeness are least likely to take place!"[30]

He saw the Christian faith, not as overt actions, but as a whole way of life communicated best by the home or the Christian community in its total life, "an effective learning group where members help members and where morale is high".[31] Truth should not just be verbalized, but "all aspects of personality: abilities, knowledge, motivation, conscience, feelings"[32] should be learned through a 'socialisation-type' process and multiple models of faith.[33] Leaders should not only teach, but also demonstrate the qualities of life they are seeking to instill in those they relate to closely.[34] And by exercising their God-given gifts all are able to share in nurturing one another both formally and informally.[35] He quoted Bradford, "Until the thoughts, feelings, and behaviours needing change are brought to the surface for the individual and made public to those helping him (or her)... there is little likelihood of learning or change."[36]

Richards stipulated seven conditions necessary for the development of worthwhile learning relationships. These were: frequent long-term contact;

warm loving relationships; exposure to the inner states of model(s); opportunity to observe one another in a variety of life settings and situations; consistency and clarity exhibited in behaviours, values etc.; a correspondence between the behaviour of the model(s) and beliefs (ideal standards) of the community; and explanation of the life-style of model(s) and instruction accompanying shared experiences.[37]

In more recent writings Richards has considerably changed his thinking concerning discipling. In our study of Discipling in the Acts of the Apostles we noted his demand that discipling be totally abandoned because it leads to "theological and personal corruption" of leaders. He believes discipling is a leadership responsibility associated with the task of shaping the Christian faith community. This he now believes is better achieved by nurturing relationships and servant leadership, not adopting a role similar to that of Jesus with his disciples.[38]

Our criticisms of Richards' recent discipling theories have already been expressed. He advocated abandoning discipling as a rabbinic method of no relevance to Christianity beyond the time of Christ. But we noted that he did not attempt to explain why Jesus issued the commission to make disciples of all nations. Nor did he make any effort to explain why the early church used the word to describe believers if they did not still consider themselves as disciples, albeit in changed circumstances once Jesus was no longer physically present.

Others have also criticized him. Peter Smith believes Richards' theory neglects formal learning processes, even though the content of his writings shows that this is not his intention.[39] He fails to offer practical suggestions as to how his informal teaching theories might be implemented. In the 'probe' section of each chapter he includes more formal teaching processes than would be expected, considering his emphasis on the informal.[40] Smith also questions Richards' lack of emphasis on practical ways of relying on the supernatural power of God, through preaching, prayer and worship.[41]

Thomas Groome

Thomas Groome writes from a strong Catholic tradition,[42] but his ideas come out of the same Christian education scenario which produced the writings of Westerhoff and Richards. Groome criticizes Westerhoff's idea of "intentional religious socialisation" because he believes that it does little more than maintain the *status quo*. As an alternative, he proposes "an intentional activity of continually measuring our present in the light of God's Word and in the light of the Vision of God's Kingdom in whose building we are called to be co-creators".[43]

He writes that Christian religious education is not a matter of 'knowledge' but should "engage the whole 'being' of people, their heads, hearts, and lifestyles, and is to inform, form, and transform their identity and agency in the world".[44]

He recognizes the importance of close relationships within the Christian community of faith so that all other relationships might be influenced.[45] Instead of traditional teacher-learner relationships he promotes the idea of a community of equal fellow-learners ("like-minded disciples"[46]), participating in dialogue with one another. These relationships must be personal rather than functional and lead to meaningful dialogue. His thinking builds on Buber's 'I-Thou' model which was discussed in our previous chapter.

For Groome the ultimate aim of Christian religious education is twofold: to enable persons as communal beings to reach for that "eternal union with the relational God" from whom their being is derived; and to invite all people to fully participate in using their gifts as disciples of Jesus, so that the community of the church will be an effective symbol of God's reign, in teaching, worship, witness and service.[47]

Following the philosophy of Paulo Freire, Groome believes that education is not a passive exercise. It involves participation in acts of faith, hope and love between persons in relationship with one another. These occur within a teaching-learning community[48] when simultaneous action and reflection (shared *praxis*) results in their dialogue with one another. Socialisation processes operating within a faith community, he believes, will result in acceptance of conventional standards of faith and moral development but will fail to promote "the ongoing conversion of participants, the reformation of the church, and the transformation of society".[49] It is only as members critically reflect on the beliefs of previous generations, that they are able to make them truly their own.[50]

Thus critical reflection and dialogue is vital for growth in understanding of one's self, others and God. Memory (past), reason (present) and imagination (future) are necessary for significant learning.[51] Past Christian traditions, stories, visions and communal narratives (both good and bad), are important in this process. Present sociocultural context ('place') and how it shapes and is to be reshaped by persons' 'being' must be considered. And creative imagining about the future must occur, so that possible consequences may be assessed and appropriate actions taken.

Groome believes every function of the ministry of the church provides a scenario in which people are educated in faith.[52] Christian educators as 'leading-learners'[53] facilitate learning by using the community and its events to enable reflection and partnership learning.[54] Their role is "to promote an understanding of persons as 'agent-subjects-in-relationship' who reflect the image of God by whose self-communication they have their very 'being,' and our pedagogy should help to realise this understanding by educating people to be free and responsible historical agents of their own becoming 'fully alive' to the glory of God".[55]

He outlines five movements which are involved in the process of action and reflection (shared *praxis*).[56] They are:
- Naming present action (emphasis is on 'what is')

- Critical reflection by participants on what was expressed as 'present action' in movement 1 (Why do we do what we do? deep seated attitudes, interests, beliefs)
- Making accessible expressions of Christian Story and Vision as appropriate to the generative theme or symbol of the learning event (What we should be doing and hoping for)
- Dialectical hermeneutic between the inspirational story and participants' stories [1 & 2] with Christian story/vision [3]
- Decision/response for future action, lived Christian faith.

Groome, too has his critics. He begins by seeking to provide a basis for Christian religious education chiefly within a schooling setting, so some of his conclusions concerning a community of faith seem inappropriate to a scenario in which not all hold Christian beliefs. However the educational principles which he proposes do have relevance to the Christian faith community and in his second book, *Sharing Faith* he broadens his theory of 'shared *praxis*' to include the wider ministry of the church.[57]

Lovat comments that Groome does not appear to leave sufficient room for genuine critical appraisal of the inspirational story.[58] His fundamental premise that God's Word and the vision of His kingdom are to be found within the Christian story is never questioned. This means that his own faith stance does not fit into the framework of critical dialogue which he advocates.

Vic Lehman, critiques Groome from an evangelical perspective.[59] He questions some elements of Groome's theological belief and his language, but he strongly affirms his educational principles. He values the significant place given to learners as well as teachers, believing that each individual has something to contribute to the whole. This lessens divisions between clergy and laity and elevates the relevance of church education. He validates the dialogical method because it enables the learner to integrate new learning with what is previously known. And he sees benefit in the treatment of Scripture as alive, relevant and dynamic in its relation to the life situations of its readers, although he would not agree that Scripture is just one among many other life experiences to be shared.[60]

Lehman encourages evangelicals to learn from Groome's model and to be involved in active critical dialogue with society so that the Christian may be salt and light within society. He affirms the holistic learning involving growth in "knowing, being and doing". And he sees the influence of the Christian story coming to the Christian community in a myriad of different forms.[61]

While acknowledging that Groome does not share his concerns, Lehman questions the number and ability of participants who are able to engage in the dialectical method at any one time, and its effectiveness in transmitting content.[62]

Congruence of theories of Westerhoff, Richards & Groome with discipling

Having briefly outlined the main educational theories of Westerhoff, Richards and Groome, insofar as they bear on the focus of the present study, a brief comparison will be made with various elements in our definition of discipling: formal teaching; smaller groups within a larger nurturing community; close personal relationships; a teaching intention by those perceived as being able; and emphasis on the mission of the church.

VALUE OF FORMAL TEACHING

Discipling, while being a largely informal model of teaching, acknowledges the importance of formal teaching methods particularly in the transmission of knowledge and beliefs associated with the faith.

Westerhoff concurs. He recognizes the value of the schooling model as having made "a great number of imaginative, important, and relevant contributions to Christian education"[63]. Thus adults, young people and children have been instructed in the knowledge of the faith and acquired the skills necessary for participating in Christian community life.[64]

Richards condemns formal methods as least likely to lead to growth although he allows that they are effective in conveying knowledge. He promotes informal methods which pass on ideas, beliefs and feelings.[65] However the 'probe' sections which reinforce his teachings in his books often suggest formal procedures for his readers. Is his teaching inconsistent? Smith implies that Richards actually resigned and left "the formal teaching situation at Wheaton, showing consistency with the priorities he advocates."[66] This supports the notion that Richards considers informal models of teaching as being of much greater worth to the Christian community than formal models.

Groome's 'shared *praxis*' has the capacity for use in both formal and informal situations. It is however easier for teacher and learner/s in a partnership to use it informally in dialogue about 'natural' (life-oriented) situations.[67] While giving prominence to the informal, he considers the formal presentation of ideas, beliefs and events which form part of the Christian Story as appropriate.[68]

All three writers uphold the place of formal instruction as beneficial for conveying Christian beliefs and ideas, even though their greater emphasis, like that of discipling, is on informal teaching methods.

SMALLER GROUPS WITHIN A LARGER NURTURING COMMUNITY

Discipling involves two or a small group of individuals who function within a larger nurturing community.

Westerhoff considers the collaborative community as the essential medium for conversion, nurture and passing on the faith – through its rites of worship, its physical environment, celebrations associated with the church calendar, its understanding of ministry, its discipline and behaviours, social interaction, role models and verbal and non-verbal language.[69] He strongly emphasizes the fellow pilgrim/learner life of the community.[70] Religious education focuses "on the formation and continuing life of small groups that can and will become communities of changed persons with a common shared faith".[71] He believes that, "education grounded in the Christian faith cannot be a vehicle for control; it must encourage an equal sharing of life in community, a cooperative opportunity for reflection on the meaning and significance of life".[72]

Richards claims discipling involves shaping a truth-centred community in which persons are involved and 'socialized' into Christlikeness.[73] He conceives of these relationships as occurring one-to-one or preferably in small groups within a larger faith community.[74] He sees the church as a living, growing organism whose educative processes bring about progressive transformation of the personality and character.[75] He believes that the strong emotional ties formed within the community will lead to persons 'identifying' with others, imitating them, and actually experiencing their successes and failures as if they are their own.[76] He endorses the 'upbuilding' concept of the Epistles and advocates a transparent openness of persons to others so that collaborative learning is facilitated.[77] "Each person perceives the other as like him, and… each freely shares in the give and take of self-revelation and mutual ministry."[78]

Groome's teacher-learner relationship in a nurturing community where collaborative learning takes place also endorses our discipling concept although he does not use the term. "Christian religious educators are to teach persons as communal beings who are to grow in right and loving relationship with God, self, others and creation."[79]

Thus these three educationists consider the collaborative nature of the learning process within the faith community to be indispensable. Learning and growth occurs as small groups of 'fellow pilgrims' move through a variety of life experiences and reflect together, openly sharing and identifying with the joys and sorrows of one another.

CLOSE PERSONAL RELATIONSHIPS

Associated with its emphasis on community, the discipling model encourages commitment to close personal relationships for an extended period of time. This, too, is implicit in the writings of these three, although Westerhoff and Richards do not strongly emphasize it.

Westerhoff calls people to give the time to committing themselves (lives and resources) to small, close-knit cohesive communities of faith in which meaningful two-way-interactions between persons are possible. He recognizes that as faith is seen in operation, and experienced within the events of people's lives,[80] then reflection and learning are possible.

Richards sees strong emotional ties and loving relationships as important for nurture and growth of individuals and the Christian community as a whole. He believes that modelling is the most effective way of bringing about changes in the lives of others.[81] He quotes research from Kohlberg and the behavioural sciences showing that modelling is more effective when the relationship is close, warm, loving and open.[82]

Groome's relationship between teacher and learner is an important factor in his theory. His use of Buber's I-Thou concept shows the personal nature of their interaction and dialogue.[83] He acknowledges that there is an element of authority associated with the teaching role, but he sees the teacher as a brother or sister pilgrim with their students.[84] The teaching-learning event, he proposes, is always shared, a "mutual partnership, active participation, and dialogue with oneself, with others, with God, and with the Story/vision of Christian faith".[85]

However while all three acknowledge the importance of quality, personal relationships between teacher and learner, and would heartily endorse the principle of loving others as we love ourselves, their educational theories seem to stop short of the committed family-type relationships of transparent openness and love which are envisaged in New Testament teaching on discipling.

A TEACHING INTENTION BY THOSE PERCEIVED AS BEING ABLE

Discipling is an intentional activity in which those who at a particular time are perceived as having superior knowledge and/or skills will attempt to cause learning to take place in the lives of others who seek their help.

Westerhoff questions whether it is possible or right to make judgements concerning the life and faith of others and thus whether one person should attempt to cause another to learn. He recognizes that Christian education can only provide opportunities and that ultimately each person is responsible for his or her own growth in the faith.[86] He does not advocate a superior 'teacher' attitude, but that mutual respect and willingness to learn from others should undergird all relationships.[87]

Richards understands that there will be teachers (pastors, lay leaders, parents, Sunday school teachers etc.) who attempt to cause learning to take place in others' lives. He asserts that while everyone should aspire to be consistent in what they say and do,[88] only those who succeed in displaying the qualities they wish to teach should actually be teachers.[89] He does recognize that growing maturity will naturally express itself by persons teaching and seeking to reproduce God's life in others, an expectation not required of 'babes'.[90] He also acknowledges that important faith decisions are not something that one can be nurtured into. Learners must cooperate in the enterprise.

Groome deals mostly with religious education which has its main *locus operandi* in compulsory schooling and therefore the role of teachers is much more closely circumscribed. In *Sharing Faith* he does however extend his theory to include the whole 'being' of the Church in the world as faith education and thus 'ministers', regardless of their specific function, have an educative role.[91] He considers them 'leading-learners', facilitating the learning of others but always participating in every event as co-learners.[92]

EMPHASIS ON THE MISSION OF THE CHURCH

In Christian discipling it is intended that both teachers and learners will not only follow Jesus but also become active participants in his mission to the world.

Westerhoff believes that faith communities must be oriented towards others outside the gospel, particularly in helping alleviate suffering and oppression of the poor, hurt and needy.[93] Their responsibility of passing on the faith is mainly seen as referring to the needs of younger generations within the community itself.

Richards sees the mission of individuals and the church almost exclusively in terms of bringing the gospel to others and teaching them.[94] His teaching concerning the exercise of spiritual gifts seems to be confined within the Christian community with scarcely a hint that believers may have wider responsibilities to those outside their community, except as witnesses to them.[95]

Groome holds that all Christian ministry carries on the mission of Jesus to the world. He sees this as preaching the healing and prophetic word of God to all; tending with love and justice to human suffering and alienation; calling people into a community of people in a free and right relationship with God, self, others and creation; and living as if God rules in their lives.[96]

Each of these writers recognizes the mission of the church to those outside as important, but because they are dealing with Christian education and not social action or evangelism, they do not make it the main emphasis of their writing. Westerhoff and Richards appear to be at opposite ends of the 'social gospel/evangelism' spectrum. Groome adopts a more middle of the road approach. Christian discipling, as we have defined it, has a stronger orientation towards both social action and evangelism than is generally accepted by these and other Christian educationists. It is the very activity of sharing in the mission of Jesus to the world, which becomes a crucial part of the educational process of the discipling model. In this regard discipling appears to be unique.

CONCLUSION

We have found a high degree of congruence between the theories of these educationists and the discipling model in most of the aspects which have been considered whilst at the same time the model provides a means of detecting areas of deficiency in them. Thus, in some respects the concept of discipling emphasizes some things more strongly than these educationists, but the elements we have identified in it are present in all their theories. Discipling is a broader process than Westerhoff's community with its intentional and hidden curricula aimed at faith development; Richards' identification and modelling aimed at Christlikeness; and Groome's fellow learners, reflecting together on experiences in the light of the Christian story and vision. The greatest divergence, however, appears in their attitudes to the mission of the church. As far as can be ascertained from the writings considered, none of them regards the fulfilling of the mission of the church as being foundational to the Christian educational process.

The small group movement

Introduction

The terms 'small group', 'cell group', 'house church' or 'cell church' cover a number of different expressions of church life today. Many of these are committed to long-term, close, personal relationships within the group so that they might learn together and disciple one another. Two of these will be examined, the church with small (cell) groups and the cell (house) church. Similarities and differences will be noted and we will seek to discover what congruence they have with the discipling model as we have defined it.

While there are many worthwhile writings on ministry through small groups and small group theory[97] I have chosen to examine those of John Mallison. He has had a significant influence for almost fifty years in Australia and beyond, as writer, Christian educator, mentor and founder of the Australian Small Group Network. Ralph Neighbour has written extensively on discipleship and the cell church and although he is no longer with Faith Community Baptist Church in Singapore, his contribution to the theory and practice of the cell church movement as represented by that church will be discussed.

Snyder makes the point that throughout church history the use of small groups seems to have been a common factor in significant movements of the Holy Spirit.[98] Since the 1960s and 1970s many churches have introduced small groups as a part of their life and ministry and enjoyed resultant growth. Richards describes small groups as "eight or twelve believers gathered to minister to each other, to grow in their sensed love and unity, and to encourage one another to full commitment to Christ".[99]

Wagner introduced small groups as an integral part of the whole of a church's ministry. He advocated a three tiered structure of church life.[100]

- Celebration, in which the whole church gathers as a large group for a special kind of worship. There is no necessity for people to know one another at this level.
- Congregation, in which personal fellowship and relationships occur. Each congregation has its own pastor and accepts responsibility for its own government and decisions. It is expected that everyone will know each other.[101]
- Cell or small groups, in which deeper sharing, pastoral care and nurturing interpersonal relationships are formed.

House or cell churches are different from these. They exist as entities in themselves. There is no larger body of which they are a part. They operate autonomously and are responsible for their own decisions and government. Within their life all the spiritual gifts operate,[102] and all the activities of the church take place. However it is interesting to note that many cell churches choose to gather periodically with similar groups for worship, evangelism or teaching.

Mallison and the church with small groups

In Australia, John Mallison has been a key leader, involved in training seminars and writing about small groups for many years. He is more a practitioner than a theoretician but his writings are helpful for this study. The church with small (cell) groups consists of people who are usually associated with that church, who meet together in groups for varying lengths of time for a specific purpose. They are not the church, nor do they have responsibility for the diverse functions performed by a church.

Taking up many of Richards' ideas[103] Mallison recognizes that changes in beliefs, ideas, attitudes, values and behaviours are socially anchored. They are most effectively achieved within a faith community whose members are committed to a climate of loving, nurturing relationships. He teaches that God calls his people to a community in which all members have responsibilities for ministry. These he believes are best fulfilled in small groups, meeting regularly to honour God and to study, discuss and put his Word into practice.[104] He advocates groups resembling the household churches of the New Testament era, which were "centres of worship and hospitality, of Christian teaching and missionary proclamation."[105] They include all generations and all members of the household.

The church with small groups provides increased opportunity for development of lay leadership gifts. Groups contribute to the nurture, teaching and pastoral care of their members and cater for individual differences within a heterogeneous community of faith. Thus the ministry of the church is expanded and spiritual development promoted.

Mallison calls for 'facilitator-enabler' leaders who are open to self-disclosure and have good communication skills.[106] He believes that action-reflection learning is particularly effective in small groups.[107]

The writings of Mallison will be compared with the various elements we have identified in our definition of discipling, so that we might ascertain the degree of congruence between the discipling model and small groups as they operate within the life of a church.

As with discipling, Mallison recognizes the need for some formal teaching within the informality of small group meetings. His writings provide a large number of creative ideas for groups studying the Bible together.[108] Some of these are quite formal requiring the leader/facilitator to adopt the role of teacher, planning aims, study materials and procedures and well as the group sessions.[109] He believes however that "learning is not restricted to formal teaching situations. On the contrary, the greater part of learning probably occurs informally, through experience in all kinds of life situations."[110] These informal teaching opportunities may arise from observation of the examples of others in the group,[111] or even when no learning intention has been stated.[112]

In the discipling model, small learning groups function within a larger nurturing community. Mallison's writing does not see groups as isolated entities. They are always an expression of the life of a larger church community. Their more intimate environment enriches that community by providing opportunities for pastoral care and exercise of spiritual gifts which are not able to be achieved in the larger group. He believes voluntary commitment to a small group should be the aim of all members of the faith community, but is aware that this may never be fully achieved. Within groups he encourages collaborative learning with every member taking responsibility as "a stimulator of the faith of the others, as well as a learner."[113] He believes "every true follower of Christ has at least one spiritual gift" to be used for the upbuilding of others,[114] and so his focus is on persons making themselves accessible and available to God and to fellow group members.

Development of long-term close, personal relationships is fundamental for discipling. So, too, Mallison appreciates that people need a sense of love from others[115] and commitment to relationship. He suggests that groups make a covenant with each other, so that the level of commitment expected of members is freely negotiated at the outset and all understand the expectations of one another.[116] His writing on mentoring acknowledges the importance of relationships (friendships) with opportunities for mutual love and care.[117]

The learning intention of a discipling relationship is obvious. Learning is not always implicit in the small group process. Many join groups for other reasons. However Mallison believes that learning is vitally important for the church and groups should encourage this formally or informally.

Discipling recognizes the need to carry on the mission of Jesus and to make disciples of all nations. This is implicit in Mallison's writings. He is convinced that small groups which meet for fellowship and Bible study are the best means "to provide the conditions and circumstances in which God may awaken people or reawaken them."[118] The prime purpose of all Christian community he considers is "to honour our Lord and God".[119] Thus his emphasis is on relating to God as Lord and bringing others to him. That purpose begins to be fulfilled when small groups meet in everyday life situations where all are treated with integrity, met at their point of need of understanding, befriended in long-term relationships and have opportunity to contribute to the spiritual needs of others.[120] Then people will be prepared for mission in "our alienated, hurting world".[121] He encourages reflection and social action on a local and global scale.

While we have discovered a high level of congruence between discipling and Mallison's small group theory, he does not. He refers to discipling as one aspect of a mentoring relationship.[122] He believes it is an important teaching model within the faith community. But he uses the concept in its more popular sense, to describe a one-to-one relationship established for a short time in order to help a new believer become established in the faith. Aspects of the mentoring relationship which he promotes are closer to what we have defined as the discipling model. But the full range of formal and informal teaching processes which we see as encompassed by discipling is much broader than anything he attributes to mentoring.

We have seen that small (cell) groups as Mallison envisages them, have a considerable degree of congruence with our definition of the discipling model. We may therefore confidently assert that these groups provide an ideal situation in which the discipling model is able to operate and provide a rich resource for the discipling ministry of the faith community. However because these groups are not fundamental to the life of most churches, only a percentage of the church's people are able to receive the benefits.

Neighbour and the cell church

The cell church shares much in common with a church which has small groups as part of its life, but it has major differences in its structure and methods of operation. A 'cell church' or 'house church' is a small group of people,[123] which exists as an entity in its own right. Ralph Neighbour refers to them as 'basic Christian communities'.[124] In many cases there is no external human authority to which each church considers itself accountable. The life of the cell church involves all the basic functions of a church – exercise of spiritual gifts, worship, the Lord's supper, teaching, pastoral care, evangelism, discipling and service to the wider community.[125] Although it has a recognized leader there are no clergy.[126] It meets in homes and thus buildings are not important.

Cell churches usually maintain links with a geographically dispersed network of such groups. Like many cells coming together to form an organism, they often choose to meet together at intervals in groups characterized by Wagner's two upper tiers already referred to, congregation and celebration groups.

The cell church recognizes that it is impossible for many people in the contemporary world to leave home and family to join a learning community for extended periods of time. It is however possible for them to be part of a small community of persons who commit themselves to each other on a weekly basis for an extended period of time. They are able to share their time, their lives and their spiritual gifts with a closely-knit group, which results in spiritual growth and learning for all members however long they have been in the faith. By accepting responsibility for the nurture of one other and being accountable in turn to one another it is assured that everyone receives personal nurture and is encouraged in his or her own life and spiritual development. Small, intimate groups are designed, in theory, to enable all participants (children, adults, believers and unbelievers) to feel a sense of acceptance and belonging, and to participate freely in the life of the cell.

The focus of the group is to be on relationships and as a loving, caring community is developed, it is expected that evangelism will happen naturally,[127] pastoral needs will be met and members equipped to serve and build one another up by the use of their spiritual gifts. Apart from more formal weekly meetings, it is anticipated that members will contact one another informally at other times, thus allowing for modelling and sharing the life of faith in an everyday context of life experiences. This is expected to occur because their commitment is to the cell, not to a larger church with its associated structures and numerous meetings. This is seen as an advantage of cell churches over traditional churches, however if Faith Community Baptist Church, Singapore, where Neighbour was involved for some years, is typical of cell churches there do not seem to be any fewer meetings. There may be more.[128]

The unrealistic expectations of single pastors in traditional churches is replaced by the expectation that all participants will use the increased opportunities to exercise their spiritual gifts for building up one another. Pastoral care is much more manageable and achievable when provided by fellow cell members. The emphasis is on the exercise of ministry, not on listening or passive 'education'. Cell churches are designed to provide opportunities for leaders to shepherd and apprentice others before freeing them to repeat the process in a newly formed group.

While cell churches may have a number of advantages over small groups in a larger church,[129] it is difficult to see the logic in Neighbour's claim that small groups "are always tacked onto the existing structures. Thus they are ineffective and poorly managed,"[130] or to agree whole-heartedly with his statement that, "cell churches are the only way that true community can be experienced by all Christians".[131]

Evangelistic efforts of traditional churches can often emphasize the invitation to 'come', whereas the cell church is among people in their home, family and community, and evangelism may occur more easily in a non-threatening environment where relationships have already been established.

Although more recent times have seen changes, the organisation of Faith Community Baptist Church (FCBC) in Singapore, during the 1990s, provides a well documented example of cell churches in operation. Cells were regarded as the basic groups, not the church.[132] Drawing heavily on the theories of Ralph Neighbour, their practice was such that the cells did not stand in isolation.[133] Actually the structures which developed were quite authoritarian in nature with strong directives coming from the organising leadership. Five cell churches came together to form larger groups known as 'zones'. Five zones formed a 'congregation' which met weekly. Its ministry was strongly people oriented and provided opportunities for formal teaching and prophetic statements to be delivered and special training or encouragement to be given. Five congregations joined together every few months for a 'celebration' event[134] where provision was made for different experiences of praise and worship, opportunities for equipping those with special gifts, evangelistic activities, community projects and specialized Christian action in society at large.[135] While FCBC welcomed and expected that everyone would be part of a cell church, it is not clear how this would be handled in places other than Singapore's highly structured society, where people may wish to belong at congregational level only. The FCBC model theoretically allowed for no members at the congregation or celebration level whose first commitment was not to a cell church.

Outreach and evangelism were expected to be crucial emphases in the life of each cell. Every member was regarded as a minister and all were considered to be responsible for 'making disciples'. The groups were expected to grow and divide every 22+ weeks or whenever their numbers exceeded fifteen. Groups with static growth were closed after a period of time. It was expected that arising out of the life of the group, unbelievers would come to faith. Special 20 week 'share groups' led by a small group of more mature believers particularly sought to share the faith with hard core unbelievers.[136] Cell churches supposedly allowed more time to develop close relationships, however the practice at FCBC of new people continually joining the cell and groups dividing every 22+ weeks causes us to question if such was the case. It seems insufficient time to develop meaningful relationships, and once a level of intimacy was established within a group, it would be diminished each time a new member joined and the dynamics changed.

At FCBC cell members were encouraged to act as 'shepherds', loving and caring for others and seeking to facilitate their spiritual growth by exercising their spiritual gifts and sharing their lives with transparency. They were revealers rather than teachers. The 'each one, equip one' theory was widely encouraged, so people were expected to be responsible for someone younger in the faith, and accountable to another for their own spiritual growth.

There were various levels of servant leadership and accountability within the church. All leaders were responsible for equipping, guidance and nurture of those under them. Leadership at all levels was considered important, but the most significant leadership was within the cell. Cell leaders were trained by a system of internships in which at the outset the leader selected someone to be trained to lead the new group when growth caused them to divide. The intern relationship was one of observation/modelling, explanation, action-reflection, supported freedom to do the task, repetition of the process for another and final equality.[137]

We must ask if there is a congruence between cell church practice as outlined by Neighbour and implemented at FCBC and the distinctive elements we have found to be essential for the discipling model? The discipling model frequently uses formal teaching to supplement the largely informal nature of its teaching methods. In the cell church, the emphasis is on relationships, not formal teaching.[138] The schooling model is generally seen as unimportant. Neighbour states that, "with few exceptions the equipping ministry of a Shepherd group (cell group) church should not utilise classrooms".[139] Cell meetings have a teaching component which starts with the needs of the group and then proceeds to study relevant Scriptures. The weekly congregational meetings and celebration activities have teaching as one part of their activities. The formal teaching component of the discipling model is able to bring a greater breadth to the content presented than may be the case in the cell church, which has a strong 'people-centred' approach. Cell churches may lack careful planning to ensure that many

Christian beliefs, understandings and practices are not neglected, while other matters may be continually repeated.

Discipling relationships function within a larger nurturing community. This provides a level of accountability for the actions, beliefs and practices of those within such relationships. The independence and lack of formally qualified leaders may leave the cell church in danger of wandering from the truth. The leadership and accountability structures built up at FCBC Singapore guarded against that eventuality. The focus on active ministry and learning by experience is valuable, provided there are associated teaching opportunities arising from intelligent reflection, otherwise emotionalism may become the major criterion for making judgements.[140]

The development of close, personal relationships and a sense of belonging is central to the effectiveness of both the cell church and the discipling model. The cell church builds on the universal human need to be loved and accepted by a community of people and seeks to develop each cell as a small community.[141] Cell church members, in theory, have time and energy freed up so they can give relationships their undivided attention. The discipling model involves commitment to a learning relationship which may then be part of a group or community. In the cell church, commitment is more to the group within which learning relationships form.

Discipling involves those who are perceived as having superior knowledge or skills attempting to cause learning to take place in the lives of others committed to the relationship. In cell churches learning is a by-product of their coming together. The members frequently see each other informally during the week across a range of life situations. It may not be stated that the primary intention of these encounters is that learning should occur, but whatever the reason (evangelism, pastoral care or development of a healthy spiritual life), their open sharing with one another, prayer, modelling the life of faith, and exercise of spiritual gifts should result in faith being built up. More mature believers have greater responsibility for the teaching of others and should be aware of the influence of their values, attitudes and beliefs on the spiritual development of others. If their modelling of Christian principles is unhelpful, then the hidden curriculum will still produce learning, but it may not be appropriate for followers of Christ. "The closer people come to one another in love and understanding, the clearer all personal faults are seen. In this way edification becomes a mutual ministry."[142] Neighbour continues, "Edification is unique for all persons. It will be based on where they have been and where they are."[143]

As in discipling, within cell churches there is a strong emphasis on the mission of making disciples. Each person is expected to be a disciple-maker,[144] by openly revealing God's life in them to friends, family and others, rather than 'preaching at' them. Cell churches are such that unbelievers are welcome and the open, home environment is able to provide a non-threatening community. Numbers are small enough for unbelievers not to feel overwhelmed and to be able to relate to others easily. As people are coming to faith, the cell provides them with a loving, nurturing community to encourage their growth. However the small numbers may cause the group to stagnate and become focussed on itself and lose the vision for outreach. At FCBC 'sharegroups' and special evangelistic activities organized at 'congregation' or 'celebration' level sought to bring outsiders to faith. Special interest groups[145] with participants coming from a number of different cells enable service to the wider local community and beyond.

Thus we have found much common theory and practice between cell churches and the discipling model. Many of those differences enunciated appear to be more in emphasis than in basic philosophical understanding. Informal learning processes which achieve best results in changing attitudes, values and beliefs predominate for both discipling and the cell church. Both involve active learning through use of the learner's spiritual gifts and being with others who are using their spiritual gifts for the good of all. Our brief reference to the experiences of Faith Community Baptist Church in Singapore provides a valuable example of one pattern (albeit with inadequacies), for establishing something of the discipling model in the modern day.

Theological education

Having tested the theories of some leading thinkers in Christian Education and the theory of Small Groups, in relation to our concept of discipleship we now turn to Theological Education. As has been noted, in other educational fields there has been a general dissatisfaction with the schooling model and teaching processes employed within theological education.[146] The 1980s also saw considerable discussion as to what was theological about theological education.[147] General debate and overall discontent has resulted in questioning of the teaching methods used and the outcomes in the lives and ministry of theological graduates. These problems have been addressed in various ways including the implementation of informal models of teaching in Spiritual Formation, Supervised Field Education and Clinical Pastoral Education.

Many would not consider that the discipling model of teaching used by Jesus has any relevance at this level of tertiary education today. Joe Bayly has commented cynically that the only similarity between modern theological training and Jesus' training of the Twelve is that both take three years.[148]

In 1983 the International Council for Accrediting Agencies produced a *Manifesto on the Renewal of Evangelical Theological Education*.[149] Based on this document Robert Ferris surveyed a number of institutions worldwide and in 1990 wrote *Renewal in Theological Education: Strategies for Change*. More recently Robert Banks has proposed another perspective in his *Reenvisioning Theological Education: Exploring a Missional Alternative to Current Models*.[150] These publications provide useful sources for an analysis of the discipling model for training of leaders within the faith community, and bases for further recommendations concerning the discipling model and its usefulness in theological education today.

Current thinking, the need for change

Theological education is not the same as Christian education. Christian education involves all church members.[151] Theological education is concerned with nurturing those who nurture the church.[152] In the past it was mainly directed towards preparation of men and women "for ordained ministry, for vocations such as religious education and for other work done under religious auspices".[153]

In more recent times it has included an increasing number of lay leaders,[154] and the demands placed upon theological education have changed. In the late sixties three strands were considered to be necessary:
- the pursuit of truth in open inquiry,
- the apprehension of the meaning of the Gospel as experienced in the confessing community, and
- vocational training for leadership roles.[155]

Thirty years later Banks lists aims of theological education which reflect greater involvement of laity in church leadership:
- Preparing lay leaders to help in the educational ministry of the church
- Preparing ministers of the "Word and Sacraments" to equip the whole people of God, develop leaders for mission, and help the church articulate its faith;
- Producing teachers of ministers and "doctors" of the faith.[156]

Various inadequacies in fulfilling the goals of theological education have been widely recognized. Many consider that traditional methods have failed.[157] Theological educators express desire for change[158] but can be slow to respond to new ideas.

The 1983 *Manifesto on the Renewal of Evangelical Theological Education* affirmed twelve values to be pursued in the search for excellence in theological education. These were: cultural appropriateness, attentiveness to the Christian community being served, flexible strategising, theological grounding, outcomes assessment, spiritual formation in nurturing educational communities, holistic curricularising of spiritual, practical and academic aims, orientation to servant leadership, creativity in teaching, a Christian world view, a lifelong developmental focus and a cooperative spirit.[159]

Ferris – renewal of theological education

Robert Ferris used the *Manifesto* to launch his ideas on *Renewal in Theological Education*.[160] He began by summarising the various fruitless efforts of different bodies in evaluating theological education as an academic enterprise and in its leadership development potential.[161] Then he described a number of new directions in theological education being undertaken by eight colleges in different parts of the world.[162] He concluded by identifying the common factors which he observed in each of the institutions studied. These included: a strong missions emphasis; attention to the training needs of the related churches; a conscious effort given to spiritual formation and ministry skills development; faculty making themselves vulnerable to students through individual and small group mentoring and through involvement with students in ministry; and awareness of principles of adult education.[163]

In further writing Ferris differentiates between theological schooling and theological education.[164] The schooling model, he believes, is good for developing research scholars and dealing with abstract concepts, but has serious limitations for ministry education, even though it allows efficient access to teachers and resources.[165] "By orienting toward the secular research university, seminaries as schools contribute to surfeiting of biblical and theological scholarship, and thus heighten dissatisfaction with theological education on the part of students and church leaders."[166]

He believes education for ministry and development of ministry gifts and skills is best achieved in the context of ministry especially where servant leadership is modelled.[167] He acknowledges the value of informal learning situations in shaping attitudes and values and developing spiritual maturity.[168] He strongly advocates the learning contract as recommended by Malcolm Knowles.[169]

Ferris emphasizes the value, significance and freedom of each person and warns educators against manipulating students toward pre-determined ends, instead of allowing teachers and learners to work collaboratively.[170] He recognizes that learning is a social process and acknowledges the importance of a community experience where opportunity for development of individual gifts is provided, people are equipped for shared leadership and skills are fostered for developing the faith of others.[171] In learning communities formal teaching is enhanced by faculty investing their time in non-authoritarian brother/sister relationships.[172]

He recommends offering a wide variety of electives and increasing church-based and community-based ministries in which learning goals are negotiated between the parties involved and ample opportunities for suitable guidance and reflection are provided.[173] "Helping students apply learning in ministry is our first challenge; helping them reflect critically and biblically on that experience so as to learn from it is our second."[174] He is not against scholarship but maintains that academic recognition should only apply where adequate supervision is present.[175]

Ferris and the *Manifesto* have provided a number of new insights into theological education, however the programs of the various colleges which he describes are offered without analysis or criticism and the reader has no way of knowing whether they are actually better or worse than what is presently offered in other places. He has been criticized because he refers to 'ministry education' rather than pure 'theological education'.[176] However the need for vocational training for leadership roles as a necessary part of theological education has been widely recognized.[177] Few would deny the importance of relating the study of theology to the contemporary world.[178]

Another perceived weakness is that Ferris seems more concerned with the human dimensions to learning rather than prayer, worship and promotion of the spiritual life and relationship with God. He does however mention the need for spiritual formation. This is seen as of paramount importance by some. Kelsey believes, "The overarching end or goal of theological schooling is to understand God; and to 'understand' is to come to have certain conceptual capacities, *habitus*, that is, dispositions and competencies to *act*, that enable us to apprehend God and refer all things including ourselves to God.[179]

Ferris also does not take into account that the theological educational process is not the only activity which is happening in the student's life. The wider community to which the student belongs, the media, part-time employment, family responsibilities, friends and other organisations all impinge on the student's life. Few these days opt for a monastic existence and thus theological educators must seek to use what limited opportunities present themselves rather than setting unachievable goals.

The *Christian Education Journal* carries a lengthy debate between Ferris and David Wright in which Wright accuses Ferris of dealing only with matters internal to colleges or seminaries, while neglecting the wider context of post-modernism and secular scientific humanism within society. Wright considers that post-modernism has precipitated a crisis within theological education[180] and advocates a radical redefinition of "the nature and role of religion, theologians and ministers".[181]

Ferris believes that truth is revealed and does not need redefinition. It is not to be abandoned, compromised or reduced to a ghetto mentality, but proclaimed with a prophetic voice.[182] He argues that theological education can only be renewed, as church leaders are equipped to translate their faith into Christian living and to articulate Biblical truth boldly to their neighbours. He believes that the crisis in theological education is due to weaknesses in education and leadership which are both able to be addressed by the seminary. He sees relationships as fundamental to the new kind of learning and the role of faculty as role models in all of life as a crucial factor.

Wright seems more concerned about diagnosing the problem than suggesting remedies but in his concluding remarks he does make some suggestions for the future.[183] These Ferris supports, including his emphasis on Christocentric, redemptive communities and the re-examination of the theological education task. Ultimately Ferris does not argue for an appreciation of the secular context but a Biblical understanding of the church, its leadership and of its leadership formation.[184]

Banks – A missional alternative to current models

Robert Banks writes out of a long history of involvement in both theological and lay education and seeks to put forward his vision for theological education in the future. He begins with a comprehensive account of the key positions in recent debate concerning theological education. These are the classical, vocational, dialectical and confessional models.[185] He challenges some of its assumptions and identifies some limiting factors which prevent "a proper reenvisioning of theological education".[186] In seeking for a more satisfactory model he examines Biblical models of formation for ministry, but carefully scrutinizes his methods and findings to avoid using inadequate hermeneutical principles or becoming anachronistic. The common elements he draws out of the biblical materials include: pursuing a close, personal association with a key figure in collaborative service; withdrawing from normal relationships or surroundings; commitment to being part of a community of active, serving learners; and learning in diverse settings through observation, imitation, informal discussion, action-reflection, and direct instruction.[187] This leads to his "missional" model.

This is not just a mission-oriented or missiological education, but a model of education which "places the main emphasis on theological *mission*, on hands-on *partnership* in ministry based on interpreting the tradition and reflecting on practice with a strong spiritual and communal dimension".[188]

He sees this model as enabling holistic development, by focusing on acquiring cognitive, spiritual-moral and practical obedience and "undertaken with a view to what God is doing in the world, considered from a global perspective".[189]

Banks does not ignore the importance of "learning the tradition – biblical, historical, theological",[190] but he also emphasizes a life-related, practical ministry approach to all theological learning. Thus he advocates collaborative learning and field-based education using Groome's action-reflection cycle and involving observant participation and reflective action. He sees use of Scripture in the reflective process as being essential, because it provides a foundation for the learner's "conversation with life"[191] as she or he is involved in daily service of the kingdom.

Banks, a teacher himself, believes that "effectiveness as teachers flows ultimately from who we are and how we relate as much as what we do".[192] He stresses that openness in relationships, and sharing of life as well as beliefs, brings life-giving changes to others.[193] He sees it as imperative that theological faculty are able to integrate intellectual understandings of the faith with wider social and cultural issues so that both individually, and among themselves communally, they are able to express their beliefs in their lives and interactions.

He suggests that "the prime need in church and world today is for community builders" and acknowledges that theological education usually takes place in a learning community which is also a community of faith.[194] He therefore sees the role played by small groups in building community as particularly important.[195] Banks also values learning opportunities between faculty and students in "largely informal missional activities".[196]

Congruence of theories of Ferris and Banks with discipling

In many respects the writings of both Ferris and Banks are very similar to the discipling model as we have defined it, however some lack of congruity is present. While maintaining its largely informal component the discipling model does not dispense with formal teaching processes. Ferris and Banks both clearly recognize the value of informal teaching while continuing to uphold the schooling/seminary model as suitable for the transmission of the knowledge and beliefs of the Christian faith. In his illustrations Banks concentrates mainly on the schooling model, but does allow for the value of extension centres, continuing education, distance learning, one-to-one or small group academic mentoring and "the role of conversation".[197]

They both acknowledge that the theological institution enables the achievement of what we have already considered to be a necessary strand to theological education, "the pursuit of truth in open enquiry". The schooling model has produced excellent research scholars and people capable of thinking about and arguing for the faith, but it is not effective for the full range of learnings required within a theological education.

Membership of a learning community is a significant part of the discipling model. This same emphasis on the social process of learning is found in Ferris and Banks, both of whom stress that membership of a learning community provides an effective learning environment, especially for those who are being educated to serve in the wider Christian community. As Mackie also comments, "If the minister is to serve as the focus of a Christian community, he (or she) must know what Christian community can mean, and must learn to use the resources of Scripture, prayer and liturgy within such a community."[198]

Collaborative learning may also take place within a community. Ferris recognizes the value of collaborative learning as a sound adult educational practice and the benefit to be gained by adults from sharing their knowledge and experience with one another. Thus the roles of teacher and learner may be interchangeable. While Banks would probably acknowledge this as happening on occasions, he does not emphasize the interchangeable role of teacher and learner. Both however, acknowledge the value of team members working collaboratively in ministry situations and believe that the skills developed are those essential for spiritual and pastoral leadership.

The emphasis on formation of close, personal relationships in discipling is important for both writers. They stress the importance of faculty opening themselves not only to convey academic information but mentoring-type relationships in living, working partnerships with individuals or small groups. If faculty have only scholarship to offer students then their example is unbalanced. This may put them in a vulnerable position, but by open and honest relationships they should be able to model living faith and promote both general and spiritual maturity among students. The spiritual formation of students occurs when worthy attitudes, values and beliefs are demonstrated and reflected upon. Close relationships help to nurture the development of spiritual gifts and provide opportunities for their exercise.

Discipling is a voluntary learning agreement in which the choice of teacher, and to some extent subject matter, lies in the learner's control. Ferris recommends that the element of choice be utilized by the provision of a wide variety of electives and opportunity for negotiation of individual learning goals and contracts. Students may thus pursue the interests, understandings and skills required for them to exercise their particular spiritual gifts.

As in the discipling model, Ferris and Banks see the local and worldwide mission of the church as integrally involved within the processes of theological education. They advocate development of ministry gifts and skills within the context of service. This is not just role-playing or situations detached from life but the reality of life itself as the learning environment for ministry. Banks sees the college itself as an expression of 'real life' and its daily interactions as providing rich learning opportunities. Ferris promotes theological education that seeks to meet the training needs of the churches and groups within which students minister. Banks concurs. Ministry must be relevant to the wider world and general thinking of the society in which it is exercised. Banks sees in-service ministry activities as of primary importance and stresses a strong interconnection between seminary and church, study and practice. He believes theological education "should concentrate…on developing habits of self-reflection on spiritual formation, faith, leadership quality and practice".[199]

Differences do exist between discipling and Ferris' theories in the area of leadership development. We have already noted that vocational training for leadership roles is an important strand in theological education, but it is not necessarily so for discipling. Not all disciples will function for the majority of their time as leaders, although servant-leadership skills are required for the disciple's task of making disciples. Discipling is a model of teaching suitable for all members of the faith community, who possess any of the many spiritual gifts within the body of Christ, not just those who lead or nurture other leaders. Banks adopts a position closer to that of discipling because he believes that theological education ought to encompass the broader people of God, not just an elite cadre.

Conclusions

The recommendations for the improvement of theological education that have been made by the Ferris, the *Manifesto* and Banks are similar to the approaches that we have found to be useful in the discipling model of teaching. They agree that there is an important place for formal education in firmly grounding leaders of the faith community in Christian knowledge and beliefs and enabling them to pursue truth with an open mind. But they concede that formal education is insufficient and that informal models of teaching and learning are essential. These include: being part of a collaborative learning community; forming close, personal relationships with fellow learners and teachers where qualities of openness and vulnerability are present; freedom for individuals to make choices about their learning goals; ministry skills development under supervision in church based or community based ministries.

They also recognize that theological students belong to families, churches and a wider community within a particular society. Some pursue studies part-time. Withdrawal into an exclusive learning community is rarely possible today, nor is it desirable. Theological education therefore must assist them in integrating these responsibilities into a holistic response to life, while also being aware of the worldwide dimension to the mission of the church.

As the discipling model emphasizes the believer's close, personal relationship with the Lord, so in theological education it is recognized that keeping the Christocentric dimension to the faith is extremely important. There is a danger that the Godward dimension may be lost in the maze of 'religious' studies.

Summary of findings

Thus the examination of the writings of Westerhoff, Richards, Groome, Mallison, Neighbour, Ferris and Banks have confirmed that the discipling model, as we have defined it, is highly congruent with much contemporary Christian educational thought. The findings of our present research have given considerable support to the view that the discipling model be revived as a worthy model of teaching in the Christian community. Our main findings and associated recommendations may be summarized as:

- The commission of Jesus to his own disciples to go and disciple others was intended to provide a pattern of teaching for his people for all time and as such is to be taken seriously by the Christian church in the present age.
- The inadequacies of the schooling model must be recognized and its limitations accepted before the need for alternative strategies of teaching will be able to be explored or utilized. Teachers and leaders are the most likely to have been successful products of the schooling model. Until they are convinced of its weaknesses and ready to consider other models and adopt different styles of teaching the present strategies will continue to prove ineffective in many respects.
- Greater emphasis should be given to the discipling model of teaching as a model of proven theological and educational value in conveying not just the knowledge and beliefs of the Christian faith but the whole range of attitudes, values and behaviours which constitute Christlikeness. The model is also useful in transmitting the skills required of those involved in continuing the mission of Jesus to the world.
- Key leaders and teachers within the wider Christian community will usually need to be re-educated (not through the schooling model alone!) so that they are able to model discipling relationships with others.

This will involve education for: maintenance of community skills, conflict resolution, relational skills, collaboration, servant leadership, transparency, commitment to God and others, promoting intentional learning situations, facilitating learning, helping others identify and use their spiritual gifts.

And education away from: competition, personal success, formal award structures, privacy, power politics, reliance on structures.

- The variety of methods which the discipling model utilizes needs to be granted validity, explored, promoted, demonstrated and resourced so that greater skills in their implementation are developed within the Christian faith community.

These will include: modelling, short and long term community, hospitality, conversation, small groups, collaborative learning, mission involving action and reflection, adventure education, mentoring.

Notes to Chapter 13

1. Westerhoff, 1976, 7
2. Westerhoff, 1976, 22
3. Westerhoff, 1976, 24
4. Westerhoff, 1974, 41
5. Heywood, 1988, 69
6. Westerhoff & Neville, 1974, 156
7. "Religion requires a religious community and to live in a religious world requires affiliation with that community." (Berger & Luckmann as cited in Westerhoff & Neville, 1974, 46)
8. Westerhoff & Neville, 1974, 43
9. Westerhoff & Neville, 1974, 149
10. These include such matters as worship, mission, the place of children and what it means to be Christian. In the life of the faith community non-verbal messages are given concerning how these are to be viewed. These implicit ideas are much more powerful than any verbal teachings on these matters.
11. Westerhoff & Neville, 1974, 83,130,151
12. Westerhoff, 1976, 79
13. Each generation brings its distinctive perspective from the past, or for the present or into the future. (Westerhoff, 1976, 53,20)
14. Westerhoff, 1976, 36
15. He considered 300 persons to be the maximum. (Westerhoff as cited in Heywood, 1988, 66)
16. Westerhoff, 1976, 52; Westerhoff as cited in Heywood, 1988, 66
17. Westerhoff, 1976, 34, 88
18. Westerhoff, 1976, 92-9
19. Westerhoff, 1987, 580-81
20. Westerhoff, 1979, 61-2
21. Westerhoff, 1992, 266-7
22. Heywood, 1988, 65, 70

23 Heywood, 1988, 66, 70
24 Heywood, 1988, 65, 68
25 Heywood, 1988, 70
26 Smith, P.J., 1984, 5-14
27 Cully & Cully, 1990
28 See earlier discussion in Chapter 8 (Richards, 1992, 3-11)
29 Downs, 1983, 52
30 Richards, 1975, 114
31 Richards, 1975, 107
32 Baldwin as cited in Richards, 1975, 82
33 Richards, 1975, 77
34 Richards, 1975, 144
35 Richards, 1975, 81-84
36 Bradford as cited in Richards, 1975, 107
37 Richards, 1975, 84, 85
38 Richards, 1992, 9-10
39 Smith, P.J., 1984, 5-14
40 Smith, P.J., 1984, 5, 10
41 Smith, P.J., 1984, 11, 12
42 He has been described as contributing, "one of the most comprehensive weldings of religious education to contemporary educational thinking ever made available in the English speaking world". (Lovat, 1988, 32)
43 Groome as cited in Lehman, 1992, 9
44 Groome, 1991, 2
45 Groome, 1980, 188
46 Groome, 1991, 19
47 Groome, 1991, 430, 444
48 Groome, 1991, 143-4
49 Groome, 1991, 101
50 Groome, 1991, 19
51 Groome, 1991, 104
52 Groome, 1991, 296
53 Groome, 1991, 449
54 Groome, 1991, 104-6
55 Groome, 1991, 429
56 Groome, 1991, chs.6-10
57 This includes liturgical planning and preaching, justice and social concern ministry and pastoral counselling. (Groome, 1991, chs.11-13)
58 Lovat, 1988, 34
59 Lehman, 1992, 7-17
60 Lehman believes that Scripture, interpreted with integrity, must have a major voice in the dialogue of shared praxis. (Lehman, 1992, 13)
61 Groome states that these include Scriptures, traditions, liturgies, creeds, dogmas, doctrines, theologies, sacraments, rituals, symbols, myths, gestures, religious language patterns, spiritualities, values, laws, expected life-styles, songs, music, dance, drama, art, artefacts, architecture, memories of holy people, sanctification of time, celebrations of holy times, appreciation of holy places, community structures and forms of governance. (Groome, 1991, 139)

62 Lehman, 1992, 11
63 Westerhoff, 1976, 7; Westerhoff & Neville, 1974, 120
64 These included content of Scripture, history and tradition. (Westerhoff, 1987, 581)
65 Richards, 1975, 315
66 (Smith, P.J., 1984, 11) Richards left Wheaton to concentrate on developing alternative strategies for Christian education of children within local congregations (Richards, 1975, 206). He subsequently engaged in a full-time writing ministry. (Richards, 1992, 3)
67 Groome, 1991, 148-150
68 Groome, 1991, ch.8
69 Westerhoff, 1992, 272-3
70 Westerhoff as cited in Heywood, 1988, 68
71 Westerhoff & Neville, 1974, 151
72 Westerhoff, 1976, 20
73 "Christ likeness is learnt through seeing that lived in others with whom one identifies". (Richards, 1975, 84. See also 77)
74 Richards, 1975, 252-3
75 Llovio, 1984, 16.
76 DeNike & Tiber as cited in Richards, 1975, 83
77 Richards & Hoeldtke, 1980, 45, 151
78 Richards & Hoeldtke, 1980, 133
79 Groome, 1991, 430
80 C. Ellis Nelson as cited in Westerhoff, 1976, 51
81 Richards as cited in Llovio, 1984, 17 and Downs, 1983, 53
82 Richards, 1975, 84
83 Groome, 1980, 188
84 Groome, 1980, 137
85 Groome, 1991, 142
86 Westerhoff, 1987, 590
87 Westerhoff, 1976, 88
88 Richards, 1975, 31
89 Richards, 1975, ch.8
90 Richards, 1975, 122
91 Groome, 1991, 296-7
92 Groome, 1991, 449-50
93 Westerhoff & Neville, 1974, 156
94 Richards, 1975, ch.5
95 Richards, 1970, chs.19,20; He mentions that believers impact on the world in terms of justice, but gives no further explanation. (Richards, 1975, 117)
96 Groome, 1991, 299-300
97 Wuthnow, R. (ed.), *I came away stronger: How small groups are shaping American religion* (Grand Rapids: Eerdmans, 1994); Cho, P.Y., *Successful home cell groups* (Plainfield: Logos International, 1981); Richards, L.O., *Sixty-nine ways to start a study group and keep it growing* (Grand Rapids: Zondervan, 1973); Johnson, D.W. & Johnson, F.P., *Joining together: Group theory and group skills*, 2nd edn., (Englewood Cliffs: Prentice Hall, 1982); Tindale, R.S. et al. (eds.), *Theory and research on small groups* (New York: Plenum, 1998)
98 Snyder, 1975, 139
99 Richards as cited in Wagner, 1976, 108

100 In smaller churches two or three of these tiers might coincide, but for growth to occur Wagner believed each of these elements should be present. (Wagner, 1976, 97)
101 Thus numbers are limited to about 250 persons as a maximum
102 These include leadership, evangelism, worship, teaching and pastoral care
103 Mallison, 1978, 8, 9, 18, 75
104 Mallison, 1978, 11
105 Mallison, 1978, 23
106 Mallison, 1978, 130, 137-141
107 Mallison, 1989, 89
108 Mallison, 1996, ch.12
109 Mallison, 1996, ch.10
110 Mallison, 1989, 89
111 Mallison, 1989, 37
112 These groups include: task, friendship, interest, personal development, support, fellowship (koinonia), evangelism, prayer and mission groups. (Mallison, 1996, ch.2)
113 Mallison, 1989, 10
114 Mallison, 1989, 10
115 Mallison, 1989, 55
116 Mallison, 1989, 27-30
117 Mallison, 1998b, 1-2
118 Mallison, 1989, 73
119 Mallison, 1989, 7
120 Athol Gill as cited by Mallison, 1989, 73
121 Mallison, 1989, 10-11
122 Mallison, 1998b, 1-2
123 The ideal number in a 'cell church' is considered to be between 7 and 15 persons. Writing concerning 'house churches' Robert Banks does not specify numbers but suggests it be small enough to establish genuine, open, sharing relationships between everyone. (Banks, 1986b, 98)
124 Neighbour, 1990, 94
125 Neighbour, 1990, 26
126 Many leaders of cell churches have had no pastoral or theological education.
127 Some suggest these cell churches grow and divide every 4 to 24 months. (George, 1992, 101)
128 Their expectations include weekly attendance at cell church for at least 2 hours and congregational meetings, informal meetings with cell church members during the week, a meeting with someone younger in the faith to encourage them and a meeting with one's own encourager. For more mature believers there is also involvement with unbelievers in a 'share group' weekly and then for everyone there is the celebration experience every few months.
129 He describes a traditional church as a 'program based design' church.
130 Neighbour, 1990, 77
131 Neighbour, 1990, 112
132 The test of which entity is the basic one is to stop the other meeting and see whether the remaining body continues to function. When cell churches are in operation the congregation or celebration may cease to function without requiring the demise of the cell.
133 Neighbour, 1990
134 This follows Wagner's three tiered structure. The 'congregations' consist of approxi-

mately 200 persons and the 'celebration' group is over 1,000.
135 Neighbour, 1990, 204
136 Neighbour, 1990, 214
137 Neighbour, 1990, 218
138 Although the relationships have a stronger emphasis on spiritual needs and do not exist to satisfy emotional needs alone.
139 Neighbour, 1990, 361
140 Finnell, 1995, 29
141 Neighbour, 1990, 26
142 Neighbour, 1990, 178
143 Neighbour, 1990, 219
144 Neighbour, 1990, 221
145 Groups there include building remarriage, grief recovery, mothers of excellence, new hope seniors, overcoming sorrow, total healing, separation survival, divorce recovery, cooking for diabetics, weekend getaways. (Neighbour, 1990, ch.15)
146 World Council of Churches, 1980, 3; Farley, 1983, 3-23; Kinsler & Emery, 1991, 3-4; Wright, 1995a, 87
147 Kelsey, 1993
148 Richards, 1975, 163
149 International Council of Accrediting Agencies for evangelical theological education, 'Manifesto on the renewal of evangelical theological education' in Ferris, 1990a, 136-143
150 Banks, 1999
151 Ferris, 1995b, 250
152 Ferris, 1995b, 251
153 Cully & Cully, 1990, 647
154 Leadership may be broadly interpreted to include pastoral ministry, academic scholarship or responsibility for a group of people fulfilling particular spiritual roles within the life of the faith community.
155 These were outlined in the Northwood Consultation on Theological Education, a World Council of Churches study. (Mackie, 1969, 71)
156 Banks, 1999, 132
157 Richards and Martin believe much seminary training is "little more than a gathering of intellectual data about the faith." (Richards & Martin, 1981, 242)
158 Ferris, 1990a, 32, 38, 39, 41
159 International Council of Accrediting Agencies for evangelical theological education, 'Manifesto on the renewal of evangelical theological education' in Ferris, 1990a, 136-143
160 Ferris, 1990a
161 Ferris, 1990a, 19
162 These came from his survey of 242 International Council of Accrediting Agencies (ICAA) colleges worldwide.
163 Ferris, 1990b, 74-5
164 Ferris, 1993a, 5
165 Ferris, 1993b, 6
166 Ferris, 1993a, 6
167 Ferris, 1995b, 258
168 Ferris, 1993b, 7-8
169 Knowles as cited in Ferris, 1995b, 256
170 Ferris, 1993b, 3-5

171 Ferris, 1993b, 3, 9
172 Ferris, 1993b, 6; Ferris, 1993c, 9
173 Ferris, 1990a, 131-135
174 Ferris, 1993c, 7
175 Ferris, 1993c, 3, 4
176 Dyrness, 1993, 42
177 Mackie, 1969, 70, 73
178 Bridston as cited in Mackie, 1969, 104
179 Kelsey, 1992, 228
180 Wright, 1995a, 87-98; Wright, 1995b, 105-7
181 Wright, 1995a, 89
182 Ferris, 1995c, 99-104
183 Wright, 1995b, 105-7
184 Ferris, 1995d, 108-10
185 Classical emphasizes theological formation in which a person's moral and spiritual character is shaped and acquiring cognitive wisdom is important. Vocational emphasizes theological interpretation, development of skills in relating Christian tradition to contemporary issues and shapes definition and practice of ministry. Dialectical seeks to find an overarching vision or practice focussing on God, but affecting personal, vocational and societal life. Confessional concentrates on theological information or understanding which shapes Christian beliefs and provides direction for personal growth and practice of ministry (Banks, 1999, 143)
186 Banks, 1999, 12
187 Banks, 1999, 92
188 Banks, 1999, 144
189 Banks, 1999, 142
190 Banks, 1999, 157
191 Banks, 1999, 161
192 Banks, 1999, 170
193 Banks, 1999, 172
194 Banks, 1999, 204
195 Banks, 1999, 206
196 Banks, 1999, 254
197 Banks, 1999, 126, 138, 180
198 Mackie, 1969, 125
199 Banks, 1999, 159

Chapter 14

Conclusions

The initial research question

Initially a dissonance was identified between New Testament practice, particularly in regard to Jesus' commission to "disciple" all nations, and current educational practice in churches. The predominance of the schooling model in more recent times seemed to have produced limited results in communicating Christianity as a whole way of life for many people. And while the concept of discipling offered a possible alternative approach, its theological and educational foundations appeared to have been neglected. Little attention has been given by the church as a whole, or by its educational institutions to equipping people as 'disciple-makers'.

The aim of this study was, then, to arrive at a coherent understanding of the discipling model through a four-part investigation which considered, redefined and tested the concept. Part One introduced the research, proposed a working definition and briefly outlined the background to discipling before the time of Jesus. Part Two was a close study of the discipling relationships and activities of Jesus as portrayed in the texts of the four Gospels. The working definition was revisited in the light of these findings. Part Three sought to discover how the discipling model was reinterpreted by the early church in the period of the Acts and Epistles and further refined the definition. Part Four tested the definition for congruence with the core values and beliefs of the Christian faith, and present day research into various teaching models and methods, and was used to evaluate educational thinking of the church in the Western world today.

Given that Jesus of Nazareth is regarded by many as one of the greatest teachers who has ever lived on this earth, and that he was the originator of the Christian faith and issued the command to make disciples, it may be safely assumed that there is validity in considering the methods of discipling which he implemented as worthy of consideration for those carrying out his mission in today's world. This study has endeavoured, therefore, to closely examine the characteristics and activities of the discipling relationships which Jesus formed with his disciples. It was necessary in some instances to differentiate between the term and the concept of discipling so that its essential qualities and conditions were the determining factor in deciding which relationships truly embodied the discipling concept, rather than literal occurrences of the word alone.

Our study was then extended into the practices of the New Testament church. In doing so we noted that there were differences between the practice of Jesus in the Gospels and that of the early church. The discipling roles which Jesus had previously held were divided. He retained his Lordship and authority and maintained a close, loving relationship with his followers, albeit in a different dimension. His Holy Spirit continued as teacher and enlightener. His words of teaching and the implications of his life and death as recorded by apostolic writers became definitive. His body, the church, became the discipling community where teaching and learning was a mutual exchange. And his people whether leaders, teachers, evangelists or all members of the faith community who exercised their spiritual gifts, became disciple-makers.

All this presupposed that it is useful to look back in this way. In order to ascertain if this was so, the discipling model was then examined in the light of the core Christian beliefs held by the faithful down through the ages. An investigation was also made into contemporary educational research to determine whether the key elements found to distinguish discipling from other models of teaching were upheld as being of value in the teaching process. Finally some of the theories and practices of the present day church were surveyed to determine their congruence with the discipling model. Recommendations for its implementation were presented.

Findings and definition

Our principal findings were gleaned from the Greek background to the word 'disciple' (*mathētēs*), the activities of Jesus and the practices of the early church. These were then tested against other models of education so that in the discovery of similarities and differences the concept of discipling might be clarified and refined. It was discovered that the discipling model of teaching has six components.

Relational

An essential component within Christian discipling is a close loving relationship with God as Father, Son and Holy Spirit. Ultimately he is the Lord, the master discipler. The second constituent element of relationship in discipling is that between the person (or persons) teaching and the learner (or learners). Discipling requires that this relationship be voluntary, committed to the long term and of a close, loving nature.

Intentional

Discipling is not pure friendship. The purpose of the relationship is that teaching will take place and that learning will occur. It requires a commitment to that purpose from all parties involved.

Mainly Informal

Although it is agreed that some formal teaching is frequently necessary, the main teaching methods employed will be informal (life-related), not necessarily requiring buildings, institutions, professionally trained teachers, classes, compulsory graded curricula or formal assessment.

Typically communal

The regular, committed, gathering together of individuals and small groups of learners into a larger, nurturing community of 'like-believing' people is of great importance. Differences in gender, age, ethnicity, social background and educational achievement, rather than causing division, are intended to enrich the learning dimension of all members of the community.

Reciprocal

No one person is always teacher or always learner. Although some may have a gift of teaching (*didaskō*-teaching) which they frequently use, or superior knowledge or skills which they seek to impart at a particular time, all members of the community have a responsibility for enriching and contributing to the upbuilding (*oikodomeō*-teaching) of others. This is achieved in part by the exercise of their own spiritual gifts and the example of their faithful, Christlike living. Learning thus becomes a mutual, collaborative affair.

Centrifugal in focus

In the discipling model the actual learning process itself involves participants going out from the community to be involved in service and mission to the world. It does not focus on personal growth for its own achievement but in looking outward and serving others finds personal growth as a by-product. This entails cycles of action and reflection, as the matters which have been learned are observed, implemented, tested and reflected upon under the light of life's reality and in association with a supportive, nurturing environment.

In sum, the refinement of these criteria ultimately gave rise to the following stipulative definition.

> Christian discipling is an intentional, largely informal learning activity. It involves two or a small group of individuals who typically function within a larger nurturing community and hold to the same religious beliefs. Each makes a voluntary commitment to the other/s to form close, personal relationships for an extended period of time in order that those who at a particular time are perceived as having superior knowledge and/or skills will attempt to cause learning to take place in the lives of those others who seek their help. Christian discipling is intend-

ed to result in each becoming an active follower of Jesus and a participant in his mission to the world.

Congruence with core values and beliefs of Christian faith community and with contemporary educational theory and practice

Having reached a definition of the discipling model, it was then tested by three different criteria and comparisons were made with the schooling model. The criteria were:

Congruence with the core values and beliefs of the Christian faith

Discipling was found to have a high level of congruence with Christianity, placing relationship with God at the centre and each individual as significant before him. The church was affirmed as the community of believers, the body of Christ, and the medium through which his ministry continues. That ministry includes proclaiming the kingdom, nurturing the faithful and equipping them to participate in his mission to the world.

Congruence with the findings of present day religious and educational research

The factors which a large number of church goers identified as contributing to their own spiritual growth reinforced the belief that communion with God, a sense of belonging to the faith community and participating in its mission, close relationships and small groups were of key importance. These findings strongly support the effectiveness of what we have recognized as components of the discipling model of teaching in contrast with the schooling model.

Contemporary educational research also validated our support for the discipling model. Principles of adult education and more life-related methods and models of teaching were found to address some of the recognized inadequacies of the schooling model. No one method or model was seen as warranting the exclusion of all others. The worth of the discipling model is in the number of different elements of both formal and informal education which can be incorporated into it and the freedom of choice allowed to its teachers and learners.

Congruence with educational theories in today's church.

The Christian Education theories which we explored strongly endorsed the benefits of informal teaching models and were found to reflect in varying degrees all the constituent components of discipling. Small group and cell church theory and practice reinforced the discipling model to some extent, although the need for some use of more formal approaches was not totally supported. The calls for renewal or re-envisioning of theological education expressed the same dissatisfaction with the schooling model as we noted in all other fields of education, and the thrust to utilize more informal methods in ministerial education confirmed the validity of the discipling model in this cause.

A high degree of congruence was found between the discipling model and all the fields of research which were explored. Our investigation has found considerable support for the discipling model as a valuable educational strategy for use in the Christian community of faith. This support has been substantial enough for us to recommend with some vigour that this model be revived in the educational practice of the Christian community of faith. And given this status we strongly recommend that it be given more emphasis and consideration by those involved in the promotion of education within faith communities. We believe that the implications of this study for church life and practice could be quite substantial, especially in the current climate of criticism of the schooling model.

Main conclusions

In our penultimate chapter an attempt was made to suggest how these discoveries might be worked out in the life of a modern faith community. To reiterate the main conclusions:

- The commission of Jesus to his own disciples to go and disciple others was intended to provide a pattern of teaching for his people for all time and as such is to be taken seriously by the Christian church in the present age.
- The inadequacies of the schooling model must be recognized and its limitations accepted before the need for alternative strategies of teaching will be able to be explored or utilized.
- Greater emphasis should be given to the discipling model of teaching as a model of proven theological and educational value in conveying the whole range of knowledge, beliefs, attitudes, values and behaviours which constitute the Christian life. The model is also useful in transmitting the skills required of those involved in continuing the mission of Jesus to the world.
- Key leaders and teachers within the wider Christian community may initially need assistance so that they are able to implement the discipling model of teaching and learn to intentionally demonstrate it in their relationships with others.
- The variety of methods which the discipling model utilizes needs to be granted validity, explored, promoted, demonstrated and resourced so that greater skills in their implementation are developed within the Christian faith community.

Recommendations for future research

Inevitably in answering questions such as this, more questions are raised than are answered. Those which may be pursued in future research include:

- Understanding more of the Godward dimension to discipling and how the faith community might be able to enhance learning through responses to what may be perceived as communion with God and his direct working in a person's life.
- Studying the discipling model of teaching under its various guises as it has been implemented throughout the history of the Christian church or in cultures other than Western European.
- Exploring how the discipling concept is utilized within the practices of other world religions. (A two way sharing of experiences may be helpful in expanding the educational practices and understandings of all parties involved.)
- Providing educational practitioners with ideas and resources for a variety of teaching intentions and strategies within life related, informal situations without actually recommending a syllabus or curriculum approach which properly belongs to the schooling model.
- Applying the basic elements of the discipling model to the learning needs of the children who are part of the faith community and developing strategies appropriate for different ages or intergenerational groupings.
- Finding ways and means of assessing the value of, and learning through, the discipling model as it is applied within the faith community.

Recommendations for future church practice

Before concluding this study it is important to clarify how, in general, the discipling model may be applied in modern church life. The following general guidelines may be adduced:

Helping believers begin and maintain a close, relationship with God

Central to the whole process of discipling is ensuring that people have a personal relationship with God. He calls them to himself through Jesus. He is the Lord and those who hear his call express their response through prayer, worship and obedience to his word.

Suggestions for further thought: Silent retreats, meditation on the word of God, quietness in God's presence, prayer and Bible reading, time out for reflection, retreat, worship experiences from different Christian traditions.

Helping believers as members of a faith community

All believers are God's family and are called together as a nurturing, discipling community in which all members are engaged in cooperative, lifelong learning. This involves both formal and informal situations. Opportunities for formal learning should not be discounted but should go hand in hand with other informal strategies which we have found to be intrinsic to the discipling model.

Public acceptance into the discipling community is usually expressed by baptism or some other welcome or acknowledgment, which among other things, helps develop a sense of belonging. Maintenance of community life in ways additional to worship gives increased opportunity for members of the community to function as a corporate whole, promoting learning through a variety of expressions of community life in a socialisation-type process.

All are to be welcomed into this heterogeneous community irrespective of age, gender, ethnicity, social class, achievements or abilities. Diversity in backgrounds, gifts, abilities and experiences brings a breadth and richness to learning relationships. Thus individual differences and learning needs are met. All are gifted by God's Spirit to make a unique contribution to the *oikodomeō*-teaching of the whole. If the group is too large to enable all members to contribute in a meaningful way then provision must be made for smaller groups where this may be achieved.

Leadership within the community should be of a servant nature, equipping and facilitating others in the use and development of their gifts. Skills for the preservation of community life, resolution of conflict, helping people grow and work together to achieve goals are essential.

The intention to cause learning to take place should undergird many of the activities of the faith community. Leaders and more mature believers must be alert to see the potential of informal situations, being ready with the right comments when situations provoking interest arise. They may initially need guidance in achieving this aspect of their leadership.

An inward looking faith community concerned only with its own growth or teaching will not be as effective in promoting learning as one which seeks to fulfil Jesus' commission to participate in his mission to the world. There is something in the outward orientation which brings to those involved greater opportunity and motivation to change. Reflection on such activities with persons having more experience will further enhance development.

Suggestions for further thought: Short-term mission trips; group involvement in service or evangelism efforts outside the church's environment; camps/travel/holidays together; adventure education/risk taking; communal living; assisting people in identifying their spiritual gifts or equipping them for more effective use; assisting leaders in developing their skills in devising intentional learning situations; rethinking the potential that resided in some of the more 'peripheral' activities of churches in past times, e.g. picnics, working bees, concerts, fêtes.

Helping believers relate closely and personally with one another

Individual relationships of a deeply loving, open quality are essential for discipling to take place between individuals. The sharing of lives, and one's vulnerability, in transparent, close encounters with one another through a wide variety of life's experiences enables modelling of Christlike behaviours.

The educational prominence of the home and hospitality is crucial in developing close relationships.

The essentially egalitarian nature of relationships between fellow believers allows collaborative learning to flourish.

Suggestions for further thought: Many, including Christian leaders, need help in developing relational skills. Western society encourages privacy and reserve. People are reluctant to risk transparency and openness. They may need help from Christians in other cultures. Wisdom is needed in knowing how much openness is appropriate. More use could be made of sharing of car travel, meals, accommodation, communication through technological advances, leisure activities, employment, child-minding etc.

Suggestions for Theological education

Theological education should be recognized as having two functions with limited overlap: (a) equipping scholars for theological reflection, research, teaching or writing; (b) equipping people for lay and ordained ministry, leadership and nurture. The schooling model should be used primarily for equipping scholars and informal models of teaching should receive greater prominence in the task of equipping for ministry.

A concerted effort be made to provide a variety of teaching models, including discipling, within theological programs. Teaching methods and assessments allowing for more cooperative activities, collaborative learning, and personal and peer group action-reflection in subjects additional to Supervised Field Education should be promoted.

Faculty and learners should be encouraged to develop close, personal learning relationships with one another in a variety of community activities, so that patterns are set for the development and modelling of discipling relationships with others in future ministry settings.

The power of the hidden curriculum should be recognized in the attitudes and values which are transmitted, while faculty and staff seek to model Christlikeness in their lives and in the structures and processes of the institution.

A personal concluding comment

I return now at the end of this research to the original relationships I had with two of my students in which they expressed appreciation for my input into their lives and learning. Both had been present in classes where I was lecturing, but in both cases there was a much wider dimension to our relationship.

They had both freely chosen to come to the college at which I was then a lecturer, and both had elected to study the particular subjects for which I was responsible. Both had entered wholeheartedly into the life of the college community and in their final years each had been elected to the position of president of the student body.

They were committed for the duration of their courses and lived for a time on the college campus.

But my relationship with both of them was much closer than that. Although they were a few years younger than I was, they became my firm friends. They had been guests in my home: the first came for meals with his wife on several occasions; the second accepted my hospitality to stay for longer periods. Both reciprocated by inviting me to their homes. We talked together, introduced other members of our families to each other, shared problems, encouraged and prayed for one another. My nurture of their growth was reciprocated by their supportive input into my life.

Along with their academic studies I was conscious of providing them with an example of Christian qualities of character and leadership, even though my example was far from perfect. As they assumed leadership responsibilities within the college community I sought to support them. I tried to listen and help them reflect on the problems arising, encouraging them to develop strategies for carrying out their tasks. And as they moved out into Christian ministry and accepted greater leadership responsibilities I continued to pray for and encourage them as time and distance permitted.

Without being aware of it there were many elements of discipling in our relationships. So it turns out that much which has been presented here perhaps does no more, in one sense, than renew and refine the theological and educational foundations for what had already been happening down through the ages of the Christian church. Perhaps it is only that the schooling model has over the centuries progressively obscured some of these key elements. Hopefully the contribution of the present research will be to enable leaders and members of the Christian community of faith to be more alert to seize the discipling opportunities which arise in every part of their lives.

Bibliography

Aland, K., *Vollstandige konkordanz zum Griechischen Neuen Testament* (Berlin: Walter de Gruyter, 1978).
Albright, W.F. and C.S. Mann, *Matthew* (Anchor Bible; New York: Doubleday, 1971).
Andersen, W.E., 'A Biblical View of Education', *Journal of Christian Education*, Papers 77, (1983): 15-30.
– 'From Gospel into Education: Exploring a Translation', Part 1, *Journal of Christian Education*, Papers 79, (1984): 26-37.
– 'The Outcomes of Community Building', *Journal of Christian Education*, Papers 95, (1989): 23-31.
– Private correspondence, (8 January 2000).
Anderson, G.B., *The Theology of the Christian Mission* (London: McGraw-Hill, 1961).
Arndt, W.F. and F.W. Gingrich, *A Greek-English Lexicon of the New Testament and other early Christian Literature* (Chicago: University of Chicago Press, 1957).
Aronowitz, S. and H.A. Giroux, *Education under Siege: The Conservative, Liberal and Radical Debate over Schooling* (London: Routledge & Kegan Paul, 1985).
Arias, M., 'Church in the World: Rethinking the Great Commission', *Theology Today*, 47, 4 (1991): 410-18.
Astley, J., 'The Role of Worship in Christian Learning', *Religious Education*, 79, 2 (1984): 243-51.
– (ed.), *How Faith Grows: Faith Development and Christian Education* (London: National Society/Church House, 1991).
– *The Philosophy of Christian Religious Education* (Birmingham, Alabama: Religious Education, 1994).
Astley, J. and D. Day (eds.), *The Contours of Christian Education* (Great Wakering: McCrimmons, 1992).
Astley, J. and L.J. Francis (eds.), *Christian Perspectives on Faith Developments: A Reader* (Grand Rapids: Eerdmans, 1992).
– (eds.), *Christian Theology and Religious Education* (London: SPCK, 1996).
Astley, J., L.J. Francis and C. Crowder (eds.), *Theological Perspectives on Christian Formation: A Reader on Theology and Christian Education* (Grand Rapids: Eerdmans, 1996).
Atkinson, D. and D. Field (eds.), *New Dictionary of Christian Ethics and Pastoral Theology* (Leicester: Inter-Varsity Press, 1995).
Au, W., 'Holistic Catechesis: Keeping our Balance in the 1990s', *Religious Education*, 86, 3 (1991): 347-60.
Aune, D.E., 'Following the Lamb: Discipleship in the Apocalypse' in R. Longenecker (ed.), *Patterns of Discipleship in the New Testament* (Grand Rapids: Eerdmans, 1996): 269-84.
Averch, H. et al., *How Effective is Schooling? A Critical Review and Synthesis of Research Findings* (Santa Monica: Rand, 1972).
Backmann, H. and W. Slasby, *Computer konkordanz zum Novum Testamentum Graece* (Berlin: Walter de Gruyter, 1980).
Bailey, K., *Poet and Peasant and Through Peasant Eyes: A Literary and Cultural Approach to the Parables of Luke* (Grand Rapids: Eerdmans, 1976).
Banks, R., *Paul's Idea of Community: The Early House Churches in their Historical Setting* (Grand Rapids: Eerdmans, 1980).
– *Going to Church in the First Century* (Chipping North, NSW: Hexagon, 1980).

- *The Home Church: Regrouping the People of God for Community and Mission* (Sutherland, NSW: Albatross, 1986).
- 'Home churches and Spirituality', *Interchange*, 40 (1986): 13-25.
- *Re-Envisioning Theological Education: Exploring a Missional Alternative to Current Models* (Grand Rapids: Eerdmans, 1999).

Barnes, K., *The Involved Man: Action and Reflection in the Life of a Teacher* (London: National Children's home, 1966).

Barrow, R., *Radical Education: A Critique of Freeschooling and Deschooling* (London: Martin Robertson, 1978).

Barry, W.A. and W.J. Connolly, *The Practice of Spiritual Direction* (New York: Seabury, 1982).

Barth, G., 'Matthew's Understanding of the Law' in G. Bornkamm, G. Barth, and H. Held, *Tradition and Interpretation in Matthew* (London: SCM Press, 1963): 58-164.

Baumohl, A., *Making Adult Disciples: Learning and Teaching in the Local Church* (Sydney: ANZEA, 1984).

Beasley-Murray, G.R., *John* (WBC, Vol.36; Waco: Word, 1987).

Beckenham, W., *Introductory Cell Church Seminar: A Call for a Second Reformation* (Unpublished booklet produced for 7th International Conference on Cell Group Churches, Australia, 1998).

Belleville, L.L., '"Imitate me, just as I imitate Christ": Discipleship in the Corinthian Correspondence' in R. Longenecker (ed.), *Patterns of Discipleship in the New Testament* (Grand Rapids: Eerdmans, 1996): 120-42.

Bennett, J.C., 'Book Review of Renewal in Theological Education: Strategies for Change by R.W. Ferris', *Missiology*, 20, 1 (1992): 92-3.

Berger, E.H., *Parents as Partners in Education: Families and Schools Working Together* (Englewood Cliffs, New Jersey: Prentice Hall, 1995).

Berkhof, L., *Systematic Theology* (London: Banner of Truth, 1941).

Best, E., 'The Role of the Disciples in Mark', *New Testament Studies*, 23 (1977): 377-401.
- 'Peter in the Gospel according to Mark', *Catholic Biblical Quarterly*, 40, 4 (1978): 547-58.
- *Mark: The Gospel as Story* (Edinburgh: T. & T. Clark, 1983).
- *Disciples and Discipleship* (Edinburgh: T. & T. Clark, 1986).

Beyer, H.W., '*Diakoneō*' in G. Kittel (ed.), *Theological Dictionary of the New Testament*, Vol. 2 (Grand Rapids: Eerdmans, 1964): 81-7.

Bingham, G., *The Things we Firmly Believe* (Adelaide: New Creation, 1981).

Blauw, J., *The Missionary Nature of the Church: A Survey of the Biblical Theology of Mission* (London: Lutterworth, 1962).

Blomberg, D.G., 'Apologetic Education: Francis Schaeffer and L'Abri', *Journal of Christian Education*, Papers 54, (1976): 5-20.

Blombery, 'T. and P. Hughes, *Combined Churches' Survey for Faith and Mission, Preliminary report* (Melbourne: Christian Research Association, 1987).
- *Faith Alive: An Australian Picture* (Melbourne: Christian Research Association, 1993).

Bolt, P., 'What fruit does the vine bear? Some pastoral implications of John 15.1-8', *The Reformed Theological Review*, 51, 1 (1992): 11-19.

Bonhoeffer, D., *The Cost of Discipleship* (London: SCM Press, 1959).

Bornkamm, G., *Jesus of Nazareth* (London: Hodder & Stoughton, 1960; German orig., 1956).

Bornkamm, G., G. Barth and H. Held, *Tradition and Interpretation in Matthew* (London: SCM Press, 1963).

Bowen, J. and P. Hobson, *Theories of Education: Studies of Significant Innovation in Western Educational Thought* (Brisbane: John Wiley, 1974).

Bramer, P., 'Book Review of Renewal in Theological Education: Strategies for Change by R.W.Ferris', *Christian Education Journal*, 13, Aut (1992): 129-30.
Briscoe, S., *Discipleship for Ordinary People* (Wheaton: Harold Shaw, 1995).
Brookfield, S.D., *Understanding and Facilitating Adult Learning: A Comprehensive Analysis of Principles and Effective Practices* (San Francisco: Jossey-Bass, 1986).
– *Developing Critical Thinkers: Challenging Adults to Explore Alternative Ways of Thinking and Acting* (San Francisco: Jossey-Bass, 1988).
– (ed.) *Training Educators of Adults: The Theory and Practice of Graduate Adult Education* (London: Routledge, 1988).
Brow, R., *Go Make Learners: A New Model for Discipleship in the Church* (Wheaton: Harold Shaw, 1981).
Brown, C., 'Prophet' in C. Brown (ed.), *New International Dictionary of New Testament Theology*, Vol.3 (Exeter: Paternoster, 1978).
Brown, R.E., *The Gospel According to John* (London: Geoffrey Chapman, 1966).
– *The Community of the Beloved Disciple* (New York: Paulist, 1979).
Browning, D., 'Reading Recommendations: Practical Theology', *Theological Education*, 25, 1 (1988): 83-5.
Bruce, A.B., *The Training of the Twelve* (Grand Rapids: Kregel, 1971; Orig, 1894)
Bruce, F.F., *The New Testament Documents, Are they Reliable?* (Leicester: Inter-Varsity Press, 1960).
– *The Epistle to the Galatians* (Exeter: Paternoster, 1982).
– *Acts* (New International Commentary on the New Testament; Grand Rapids: Eerdmans, 1984).
Bruffee, K.A., 'Collaborative Learning and the "Conversation of Mankind"', *College English*, 46, 7 (1984): 635-52.
Buber, M., *I and Thou* (Edinburgh: T & T Clark, 1937; German orig., 1923).
– *Between Man and Man* (London: Fontana, 1961; German orig., 1947)
– *The Knowledge of Man* (London: Allen & Unwin, 1965).
Bultmann, R., *The Gospel of John: A Commentary* (Oxford: Basil Blackwell, 1971; German orig., 1964)
Bushnell, H., 'What Christian Nurture is' in Cully, K.B. (ed.), *Basic Writings in Christian Education* (Philadelphia: Westminster, 1960): 297-309.
Butts, J.R., 'The Voyage of Discipleship: Narrative, *chreia*, and Call Story' in C. Evans and W. Stinespring (eds.), *Early Jewish and Christian Exegesis* (Atlanta: Scholars Press, 1987): 199-219.
Campbell, A.V., 'Pastoral Care: Nature of' in A.V.Campbell (ed.), *A Dictionary of Pastoral Care* (London: SPCK, 1987): 188-90.
– (ed.) *A Dictionary of Pastoral Care* (London: SPCK, 1987).
Carson, D.A., *The Farewell Discourse and Final Prayer of Jesus: An Exposition of John 14-17* (Grand Rapids: Baker, 1980).
Castle, E.B., *Ancient Education and Today* (Harmondsworth: Penguin, 1961).
Chamberlain, G.L., 'Faith Development and Campus Ministry' in J. Astley and L. Francis (eds.), *Christian Perspectives on Faith Developments: A Reader* (Grand Rapids: Eerdmans, 1992): 345-53.
Chapple, A.L., 'Local Leadership in the Pauline Churches: Theological and Social Factors in its Development, a Study based on 1 Thessalonians, 1 Corinthians and Philippians.' (Unpublished doctoral dissertation, University of Durham, 1984).
Cho, P.Y., *Successful Home Cell Groups* (Plainfield: Logos International, 1981).

Clowney, E.P., *The Message of 1 Peter* (Leicester: Inter-Varsity Press, 1988).
Clulow, V., 'A Study of Adult Students' Perceptions of Mentoring as a Support System' in S. Goodlad (ed.), *Students as Tutors and Mentors* (London: Kogan Page, 1995): 86-103.
Coe, G.A., 'The Starting Point of a Solution' in K.B. Cully (ed.), *Basic Writings in Christian Education* (Philadelphia: Westminster, 1960): 325-38.
Cohen, B. and J. Lukinsky, 'Religious Institutions as Educators' in M. Fantini and R. Sinclair (eds.), *Education in School and Nonschool Settings* (Chicago: University of Chicago Press, 1985): 140-58.
Cohen, N.H., *Mentoring Adult Leaders: A Guide for Educators and Trainers* (Malabar, Florida: Krieger, 1995).
Cole, A., *Mark* (Tyndale New Testament Commentaries; London: Tyndale Press, 1961).
Coleman, R.E., *The Master Plan of Discipleship* (Old Tappan: Revell, 1987).
Collins, A., J.S. Brown and S.E. Newman, 'Cognitive Apprenticeship: Teaching the Crafts of Reading, Writing and Mathematics' in L.B. Resnick (ed.), *Knowing, Learning and Instruction: Essays in Honour of Robert Glaser* (Hillsdale, N.J.: Lawrence Erlbaum, 1989): 453-94.
Collins, R.F., *These Things have been Written: Studies on the Fourth Gospel* (Louvain: Peters Press, 1990).
Collinson, G.E., 'The Contribution of the Sunday School Movement to Mass Elementary Schooling in England 1780-1850', *Journal of Christian Education,* Papers 90, (1987): 5-18.
Cowie, L.W., 'The first English Missions' in T. Dowley (ed.), *Eerdman's Handbook to the History of Christianity* (Grand Rapids: Eerdmans, 1977): 472-3.
Cox, A.I., *Christian Education in the Church Today* (Nashville: Graded, 1965).
Crabb, L. and D.B. Allender, *Hope When You're Hurting* (Grand Rapids: Zondervan, 1996).
Craig, W.L., 'The Historicity of the Empty Tomb of Jesus', *New Testament Studies*, 31 (1985): 39-67.
Cranfield, C.E.B., *The Gospel According to Saint Mark* (Cambridge Greek Testament Commentary; Cambridge: Cambridge University Press, 1959).
Cranton, P., *Professional Development as Transformative Learning: New Perspectives for Teachers of Adults* (San Francisco: Jossey-Bass, 1996).
Creamer, D.G. et al., *College Student Development: Theory and Practice for the 1990s* (American College Personnel Association Media Publication No.49; Alexandria, VA: ACPA, 1990).
Crehan, S.J., *The Theology of St John* (London: Darton, Longman & Todd, 1965).
Crenshaw, J.L., 'Education in Ancient Israel', *Journal of Biblical Literature*, 104, 4 (1985): 601-15.
Culligan, K., 'Toward a Contemporary Model of Spiritual Direction: A Comparative Study of St John of the Cross and Carl Rogers' in J. Sullivan, *Carmelite Studies: Contemporary Psychology and Carmel* (Washington: Institute of Carmelite Studies, 1982).
Cullmann, O., *The Johannine Circle* (London: SCM Press, 1975).
Cully, K.B. (ed.), *Basic Writings in Christian Education* (Philadelphia: Westminster, 1960).
Cully, I.V. and K.B. Cully (eds.), *Harper's Encyclopedia of Religious Education* (San Francisco: Harper & Row, 1990).
Culpepper, R.A., *The Johannine School: An Evaluation of the Johannine-School Hypothesis based on an Investigation of the Nature of Ancient Schools* (SBL Dissertation series, No 26; Missoula: Scholars, 1975): 156-70.
– 'Education' in G. Bromiley (ed.), *The International Standard Bible Encyclopedia* Vol.2 (Grand Rapids: Eerdmans, 1982).

- 'Mark 10.50: Why mention the garment?', *Journal of Biblical Literature* 10 (1982): 131-2.
- *Anatomy of the Fourth Gospel: A Study in Literary Design* (Philadelphia: Fortress Press, 1983).

Cunningham, A. and C.J. Weborg, 'Formation for "Life in the Middle"', *Journal of Supervision and Training in Ministry* 15 (1994): 144-53.

D'Angelo, M.R., 'Women in Luke-Acts: A Redactional View', *Journal of Biblical Literature* 109, 3 (1990): 441-61.

Daube, D., 'Responsibilities of Master and Disciples in the Gospels', *New Testament Studies* 19 (1973): 1-15.

Davids, P.H, *The Epistle of James* (New International Greek Testament Commentary; Exeter: Paternoster, 1982).
- 'Controlling the tongue and the wallet: Discipleship in James' in R. Longenecker (ed.), *Patterns of Discipleship in the New Testament* (Grand Rapids: Eerdmans, 1996): 225-47.

Davies, D., 'Commentary: Collaboration and Family Empowerment as Strategies to achieve Comprehensive Services' in L.C. Rigsby, M.C. Reynolds and M.C. Wang (eds.), *School-Community Connections: Exploring Issues for Research and Practice* (San Francisco: Jossey-Bass, 1995): 267-80.

Davies, M., *Rhetoric and Reference in the Fourth Gospel* (Sheffield: Journal for the Study of the Old Testament 69, 1992).

Davies, S., 'Women in the Third Gospel and the New Testament Apocrypha' in A. Levine (ed.), *"Women like this": New Perspectives on Jewish Women in the Greco-Roman World* (Atlanta: Scholars, 1991): 185-97.

Davis, R., *Mentoring: The Strategy of the Master* (Nashville: Nelson, 1991).

Delbridge, A. and J. Bernard (eds.), *The Macquarie Concise Dictionary*, (Sydney: Macquarie Library, 1988).

Delling, G., '*teleios*' in G. Kittel (ed.), *Theological Dictionary of the New Testament* Vol 8 (Grand Rapids: Eerdmans, 1972): 67-78.

Dewey, J., *Democracy and Education: An Introduction to the Philosophy of Education* (New York: Macmillan, 1916).
- *Experience and Education* (New York: Macmillan, 1938).
- 'Thinking in Education' in J. Raths, J. Pancella and J. Van Ness, *Studying Teaching* (Englewood Cliffs: Prentice-Hall, 1971).

Dillon, R.J., *From Eye-Witnesses to Ministers of the Word: Tradition and Composition in Luke 24* (Rome: Biblical Institute, 1978).

Dodd, C.H., *Historical Tradition in the Fourth Gospel* (Cambridge: Cambridge University Press, 1963).
- *The Apostolic Preaching and its Developments* (London: Hodder & Stoughton, 1970).

Donaldson, J., 'Called to Follow: A Twofold Experience of Discipleship in Mark', *Biblical Theology Bulletin* 5, 1 (1975): 67-77.

Donaldson, T.L., 'Guiding Readers – Making Disciples: Discipleship in Matthew's Narrative Strategy' in R.N. Longenecker (ed.), *Patterns of Discipleship in the New Testament* (Grand Rapids: Eerdmans, 1996).

Donnelly, J.P., 'The Jesuits' in T. Dowley (ed.), *Eerdman's Handbook to the History of Christianity* (Grand Rapids: Eerdmans, 1977): 413-4.

Dowley, T. (ed.), *Eerdman's Handbook to the History of Christianity* (Grand Rapids: Eerdmans, 1977).

Downing, F.G., 'The Social Contexts of Jesus the Teacher: Construction or Reconstruction', *New Testament Studies* 33, 3 (1987): 439-51.

Downs, P.G., 'Christian Nurture: A Comparison of Horace Bushnell and Lawrence Richards', *Christian Education Journal* 4, 2 (1983): 43-57.

Droege, T.A., 'Pastoral Counselling and Faith Development' in J. Astley and L. Francis (eds.), *Christian Perspectives on Faith Developments: A Reader* (Grand Rapids: Eerdmans, 1992): 270-83.

Dunn, J.D., *Jesus' Call to Discipleship* (Cambridge: Cambridge University Press, 1992).

Dyrness, W.A., 'Book Review of Renewal in Theological Education: Strategies for Change by Ferris, R.W.', *International Bulletin of Missionary Research* 17 (Jan 1993): 41-2.

Edersheim, A., *The Life and Times of Jesus the Messiah* (McLean: MacDonald, 1886).

Edwards, R.A., 'Uncertain Faith: Matthew's Portrait of the Disciples' in F.F. Segovia (ed.), *Discipleship in the New Testament* (Philadelphia: Fortress Press, 1985): 47-61.

Eims, L., *The Lost Art of Disciple Making* (Grand Rapids: Zondervan, 1978).

Eller, V., *The Beloved Disciple: His Name, his Story, his Thought* (Grand Rapids: Eerdmans, 1987).

Elliott, J.H., *A Home for the Homeless: A Sociological Exegesis of 1 Peter, its Situation and Strategy* (London: SCM Press, 1981).

– 'Backward and Forward "In his steps": Following Jesus from Rome to Raymond and beyond. The Tradition, Redaction, and Reception of 1 Peter 2.18-25' in F.F. Segovia (ed.), *Discipleship in the New Testament* (Philadelphia: Fortress Press, 1985): 184-208.

Engstrom, T.W., *The Making of a Christian Leader* (Grand Rapids: Zondervan, 1976).

– *The Fine Art of Mentoring: Passing on to Others what God has given to You* (Brentwood, Tennessee: Wolgemuth & Hyatt, 1989).

Eugene, T.M., 'Action-Reflection' in I.V. Cully and K.B. Cully (eds.), *Harper's Encyclopedia of Religious Education* (San Francisco: Harper & Row, 1990) 1,2.

Evans, M.J., *Woman in the Bible* (Exeter: Paternoster, 1983).

Faith Community Baptist Church, *The Cell Church is the New Wineskin*, Video recording (Singapore: Touch Resource, 1998).

Faith Community Baptist Church, *Principles of the Cell Church*, Video recording from 5th International Joint Conference on Cell Group Churches (Singapore: Touch Resource, 1996).

Fantini, M. and R. Sinclair (eds.), *Education in School and Nonschool Settings* (Chicago: University of Chicago Press, 1985).

Farley, E., *Theologia: The Fragmentation and Unity of Theological Education* (Philadelphia: Fortress Press, 1983).

– *The Fragility of Knowledge: Theological Education in the Church and University* (Philadelphia: Fortress Press, 1988).

Fee, G.D., *The First Epistle to the Corinthians* (New International Commentary on the New Testament; Grand Rapids: Eerdmans, 1987).

Fee, G.D. and D. Stuart, *How to read the Bible for all its worth: A Guide to Understanding the Bible* (Grand Rapids: Zondervan, 1982).

Feldman, K.A. and T.M. Newcomb, *The Impact of College on Students* Vol.1. (San Francisco: Jossey-Bass, 1973).

Ferguson, E., *Backgrounds of Early Christianity* (Grand Rapids: Eerdmans, 1987).

Ferris, R.W., *Renewal in Theological Education: Strategies for Change* (Wheaton: Wheaton College, 1990).

– 'Renewal of Theological Education: Commitments, Models, and the ICAA Manifesto', *Evangelical Review of Theology* 14, 1 (1990): 64-77.

– *A Candid Assessment of Ministry Education* (Unpublished paper presented at 15th Biennial

Conference of the South Pacific Association of Bible Colleges, Adelaide: 1993): 1-8.
- *Toward a Theology of Training Structures* (Unpublished paper presented at 15th Biennial Conference of the South Pacific Association of Bible Colleges, Adelaide: 1993): 1-11.
- *Toward a Theology of Training Methods* (Unpublished paper presented at 15th Biennial Conference of the South Pacific Association of Bible Colleges, Adelaide: 1993): 1-11.
- *Creative Structures for Ministry Education* (Unpublished paper presented at 15th Biennial Conference of the South Pacific Association of Bible Colleges, Adelaide: 1993): 1-5.
- *Establishing Ministry Training: A Manual for Programme Developers* (Pasadena: William Carey Library, 1995).
- 'The Future of Theological Education', *Evangelical Review of Theology* 19, 3 (1995): 248-67.
- 'The Social Context of the Renewal Problem in Theological Education: Probing beyond an Epistemology of Despair. A Rejoinder to David W. Wright', *Christian Education Journal* 15, 3 (1995): 99-104.
- 'Response to Wright Response', *Christian Education Journal* 15, 3 (1995): 108-10.

Field, B. and T. Field, *Teachers as Mentors: A Practical Guide* (London: Falmer, 1994).

Finnell, D., *Life in His Body* (Houston: Touch, 1995).

Fiorenza, E.S., *In Memory of Her: A Feminist Theological Reconstruction of Christian Origins* (New York: Crossroad, 1983).
- 'The Followers of the Lamb: Visionary Rhetoric and Social-Political Situation' in F.F. Segovia (ed.), *Discipleship in the New Testament* (Philadelphia: Fortress Press, 1985) 144-65.
- *Discipleship of Equals: A Critical Feminist Ekklesia-logy of Liberation* (New York: Crossroad, 1993).

Firebaugh, J., *Review of Beckham, W.A., The Second Reformation: Reshaping the Church for the 21st Century* (Houston: Touch, 1995) in The Small Group Network 1996 {http://smallgroups.com/reviews/coach/2ndref.htm; accessed 21 August 1998}
- *Review of Cho, P.Y. and H. Hostetler, Successful Home Cell Groups* (South Plainfield, NJ:Bridge, 1981) in The Small Group Network 1996 {http://smallgroups.com/reviews/coach/cho.htm; accessed 21 August 1998}
- *Review of Neighbour, R.W., Where do we go from here? A Guidebook for the Cell Group Church* (Houston: Touch, 1990) in The Small Group Network 1996 {http://smallgroups.com/reviews/coach/wdwgfh.htm; accessed 21 August 1998}

Fischer, K., *Women at the Well: Feminist Perspectives on Spiritual Direction* (London: SPCK, 1989).

Fitzmyer, J.A., *Luke the Theologian: Aspects of his Teaching* (New York: Paulist, 1989).

Fleddermann, H., 'The Demands of Discipleship Matt 8.19-22 par. Luke 9.57-62', in F. Segbroeck et al. (eds.), *The Four Gospels* 1992 Vol 1. (Leuven: Leuven University Press, 1992).

Flender, H., *St Luke: Theologian of Redemptive History* (London: SPCK, 1967).

Foster, C.R., *Educating Congregations: The Future of Christian Education* (Nashville: Abingdon, 1994).

Foster, R., *Celebration of Discipline* (London: Hodder & Stoughton, 1980).

Fowler, J.W., *Stages of Faith: The Psychology of Human Development and the Quest for Meaning* (San Francisco: Harper & Row, 1981).
- *Becoming Adult, Becoming Christian: Adult Development and Christian Faith* (San Francisco: Harper & Row, 1984).
- 'Perspectives on the Family from the Standpoint of Faith Development Theory' in J. Astley and L. Francis (eds.), *Christian Perspectives on Faith Developments: A Reader* (Grand Rapids: Eerdmans, 1992): 320-44.

Fowler, J.W., K.E. Nipkow and F. Schweitzer (eds.), *Stages of Faith and Religious Development: Implications for Church, Education and Society* (New York: Crossroad, 1991).
France, R.T., *Matthew* (Tyndale New Testament Commentary; Leicester: Inter-Varsity Press, 1985).
– *Matthew: Evangelist and Teacher* (Exeter: Paternoster, 1989).
Freeman, H.E., *An Introduction to the Old Testament Prophets* (Chicago: Moody Press, 1968).
Freire, P., *Pedagogy of the Oppressed* (London: Penguin, 1972).
– *Education: The Practice of Freedom* (London: Writers & Readers, 1973).
Freyne, S., *The Twelve: Disciples and Apostles* (London: Sheed & Ward, 1968).
Friend, M. and L. Cook, 'The Fundamentals of Collaboration' in *Interactions: Collaboration Skills for School Professionals* (New York: Longman, 1992).
Gangel, K.O., *Leadership for Church Education* (Chicago: Moody Press, 1970).
Gangel, K.O. and W.S. Benson, *Christian Education: Its History and Philosophy* (Chicago: Moody Press, 1983).
Garrett, J.L., *Systematic Theology: Biblical, Historical and Evangelical* Vols. 1 & 2 (Grand Rapids: Eerdmans, 1990 & 1995).
Geldenhuys, N., *The Gospel of Luke* (Grand Rapids: Eerdmans, 1979).
George, C.F., *Prepare your Church for the Future* (Grand Rapids: Fleming H Revell, 1992).
– *The Coming Church Revolution: Empowering Leaders for the Future* (Grand Rapids: Fleming H Revell, 1994).
Gerber, V., *Discipling through Theological Education by Extension* (Chicago: Moody Press, 1980).
Gibbs, E., *I Believe in Church Growth* (London: Hodder & Stoughton, 1981).
Gibson, J.B., 'The rebuke of the disciples in Mark 8.14-21', *Journal for the Study of the New Testament* 27 (1986): 31-47.
Giles, K.N., '*Imitatio Christi* in the New Testament', *The Reformed Theological Review* 28, 3 (1979): 65-73.
– 'Teachers and teaching in the church: Part 1' *Journal of Christian Education* Papers 70, (1981): 5-17.
– 'Teachers and teaching in the church: Part 2' *Journal of Christian Education* Papers 71 (1981): 52-62.
– 'The Church in the Gospel of Luke', *Scottish Journal of Theology* 34 (1981): 121-46.
– *Created Woman: A Fresh Study of the Biblical Teaching* (Canberra: Acorn, 1985).
Gill, A., 'Women Ministers in the Gospel of Mark', *Australian Biblical Review* 35 (1987): 14-21.
Gilligan, C., *In a Different Voice: Psychological Theory and Women's Development* (Cambridge, Mass: Harvard University Press, 1982).
Gish, A., *Living in Christian Community: A Personal Manifesto* (Sydney: Albatross, 1979).
Glover, R.W., 'The German Apprenticeship System: Lessons for Austin, Texas', *The Annals of the American Academy of Political and Social Science* 544 (1996): 83-94.
Goldsworthy, G., *Gospel and Wisdom* (Exeter: Paternoster, 1987).
Goffman, E., *Asylums: Essays on the Social Situation of Mental Patients and other Inmates* (New York: Doubleday, 1961).
Goodlad, S. (ed.), *Students as Tutors and Mentors* (London: Kogan Page, 1995).
Goodliff, P., 'Families at the Margins', *Encounter with God* (Scripture Union Bible notes, Apr-Jun 1995): 53-64.
Goppelt, L., *Theology of the New Testament Vol.5: The Ministry of Jesus in its Theological Significance* (Grand Rapids: Eerdmans, 1981; German orig., 1975).

Bibliography

Gordon, E.W., 'Commentary: Renewing Familial and Democratic Commitments' in L.C. Rigsby, M.C. Reynolds and M.C. Wang (eds.), *School-Community Connections: Exploring Issues for Research and Practice* (San Francisco: Jossey-Bass, 1995): 45-57.

Gordon, H., 'The Sheltered Aesthete: A New Appraisal of Martin Buber's Life' in H. Gordon and J. Bloch (eds.), *Martin Buber: A Centenary Volume* (The Negev: Ktav, 1984).

Gordon, H. and J. Bloch (eds.), *Martin Buber: A Centenary Volume* (The Negev: Ktav, 1984).

Goulder, M., 'Those Outside: Mk 4.10-12', *Novum Testamentum* 33, 4 (1991): 289-302.

Graden, J.L., J.E. Zins and M.J. Curtis (eds.), *Alternative Educational Delivery Systems: Enhancing Instructional Options for all Students* (Washington, DC: National Association of School Psychologists, 1988).

Gray, J and B. Wilcox, *Good School, Bad School: Evaluating Performance and Encouraging Improvement* (Buckingham: Open University, 1995).

Griffiths, J.G., 'The Disciple's Cross', *New Testament Studies* 16 (1970): 358-64.

Groome, T.H., *Christian Religious Education: Sharing our Story and Vision* (Melbourne: Dove, 1980).

– *Sharing Faith, a Comprehensive Approach to Religious Education and Pastoral Ministry: The Way of Shared Praxis* (San Francisco: Harper, 1991).

Guelich, R.A., *Mark 1-8:26* (Word Biblical Commentary, Vol.34A; Dallas: Word, 1989).

Gundry, R.H., 'On True and False Disciples in Matthew 8.18-22', *New Testament Studies* 40 (1994): 433-41.

Guthrie, D., *New Testament Introduction* (London: Inter-Varsity Press, 1975).

Habemas, R.T., 'Even what you don't say counts', *Christian Education Journal* 5, 2 (1984): 24-8.

Hadidian, A., *Successful Discipling* (Chicago: Moody Press, 1979).

Hahn, T., 'A Time to Learn', in J.B. Thomson, *Natural Childhood: A Practical Guide to the First Seven Years* (London: Hodder & Stoughton, 1994).

Hanks, B. and W. Shell, *Discipleship* (Grand Rapids: Zondervan, 1993).

Hanson, P.D., *The People Called: The Growth of Community in the Bible* (San Francisco: Harper & Row, 1963).

Harkness, A.G., 'Intergenerational Christian Education: Reclaiming a Significant Educational Strategy in Christian Faith Communities' (Unpublished doctoral dissertation, Murdoch University, Perth, 1996).

Hauerwas, S. and J.H. Westerhoff (eds.), *Schooling Christians: 'Holy Experiments' in American Education* (Grand Rapids: Eerdmans, 1992).

Hawryluk, M.K. and D.L. Smallwood, 'Using Peers as Instructional Agents: Peer Tutoring and Cooperative Learning', in J.L. Graden, J.E. Zins and M.J. Curtis (eds.), *Alternative Educational Delivery Systems: Enhancing Instructional Options for all Students* (Washington, DC: National Association of School Psychologists, 1988): 371-89.

Hawthorne, G.F., 'The Imitation of Christ: Discipleship in Philippians', in R. Longenecker (ed.), *Patterns of Discipleship in the New Testament* (Grand Rapids: Eerdmans, 1996): 163-79.

Held, H.J., 'Matthew as Interpreter of the Miracle Stories', in G. Bornkamm, G. Barth and H. Held, *Tradition and Interpretation in Matthew* (London: SCM Press, 1963).

Hely, A.S.M., *New Trends in Adult Education – from Elsinore to Montreal* (Paris: UNESCO, 1962).

Hengel, M., *Judaism and Hellenism Vol.1: Studies in their Encounter in Palestine during the Early Hellenistic Period* (London: SCM Press, 1974; German orig., 1973).

- *The Charismatic Leader and his Followers* (Edinburgh: T & T Clark, 1981).
- *Between Jesus and Paul* (London: SCM Press, 1983).

Henry, C.F., *Basic Christian Doctrines* (Grand Rapids: Baker, 1962).

Heywood, D., 'Christian Education as Enculturation: The Life of the Community and its place in Christian Education in the Work of John H. Westerhoff', *British Journal of Religious Education* 10 (Spr 1988): 65-77.

Hiers, R., '"Binding" and "Loosing": The Matthean Authorizations', *Journal of Biblical Literature* 104, 2 (1985): 233-50.

Hill, B.V., 'The Sanctity of the Individual as Expressed in Contemporary Thought and its Implications for Educational Theory' (Unpublished MA Hons thesis, University of Sydney, 1966).
- *Education and the Endangered Individual* (New York: Teachers' College, 1973).
- 'Toward a Conception of Morality and a Theory of Moral Education' (Unpublished Doctoral dissertation, University of Illinois, 1973).
- 'Compulsion in Education', *Journal of Christian Education* Papers 52 (1975): 39-57.
- 'Is it time we Deschooled Christianity?', *Journal of Christian Education* Papers 63 (1978): 5-21.
- *The Greening of Christian Education* (Homebush West, NSW: Lancer, 1985).
- 'Theological Education: Is it out of Practice?', *Evangelical Review of Theology* 10, 2 (1986): 174-82.
- 'The Potential of the Voluntary Christian School Student Group', *Journal of Christian Education* Papers 88 (1987): 55-63.
- *That they may Learn: Towards a Christian View of Education* (Exeter: Paternoster, 1990).
- *The Thinking Teacher: Philosophising about Education* (Perth: Murdoch University, 1992).
- 'Evaluating the School Paradigm: Curriculum for Life?' in J. Shortt and T. Cooling, *Agenda for Educational Change* (Leicester: Apollos, 1997).
- *Beyond the Transfer of Knowledge: Spirituality in Theological Education* (Auckland: Impetus, 1998).

Hillmer, M.R., 'They Believed in Him: Discipleship in the Johannine Tradition', in R. Longenecker (ed.), *Patterns of Discipleship in the New Testament* (Grand Rapids: Eerdmans, 1996): 77-97.

Hillyer, N., 'Scribe', in C. Brown (ed.), *New International Dictionary of New Testament Theology* Vol.3 (Exeter: Pasternoster, 1978): 477-82.

Hirst, P.H., 'What is Teaching?' in R.S. Peters (ed.), *The Philosophy of Education* (London: Oxford University Press, 1973).

Hirst, P.H. and R.S. Peters, *The Logic of Education* (London: Routledge & Kegan Paul, 1970).

Holman Bible, *New Revised Standard Version Bible* (Nashville: Holman, 1989).

Holmberg, B., *Paul and Power: The Structure of Authority in the Primitive Church as Reflected in the Pauline Epistles* (Philadelphia: Fortress Press, 1978).

Holt, J., 'Schools are bad places for kids', in I. Lister, *Deschooling: A reader* (London: Cambridge University Press, 1974): 39-43.

Honore, R., *Women and Mentoring: Paranoia or Schizophrenia?* Working paper No 1-1994 (Sydney: School of Management, University of Technology, 1994).

Horsley, R.A., *Sociology and the Jesus Movement* (New York: Crossroad, 1989).

Hough, M. and J. Paine, *Creating Quality Learning Communities* (Melbourne: Macmillan, 1997).

Hughes, P. and P. Bentley, *Lay Adult Christian Education: Principles and Possibilities* (Melbourne: Christian Research Association, 1991).
Hughes, P. and 'T. Blombery, *Patterns of Faith in Australian Churches: Report from the Combined Churches Survey for Faith and Mission* (Hawthorn: Christian Research Association, 1990).
Hughes, P. and S. Bond, *Making Disciples: Exploring the Evidence* (Melbourne: Uniting Education, 2000).
Hughes, P. and J. Emmett, *Making Disciples: A Survey of Christian Education in UCA Congregations* (Melbourne: Uniting Education, 2000).
Hughes, P., C. Thompson, R. Pryon and G. Bouma, *Believe it or not: Australian Spirituality and the Churches in the 90s* (Melbourne: Christian Research Association, 1993).
Hull, B., *Jesus Christ Disciple Maker* (Colorado Springs: Navpress, 1984).
Hull, J.M., *What Prevents Christian Adults from Learning?* (Philadelphia: Trinity, 1991).
Hunt, F.J. (ed.), *Socialisation in Australia* (Melbourne: Australia International, 1978).
Hunt, J.S., 'Philosophy of Adventure Education', in J.C. Miles and S. Priest, *Adventure Education* (State College, PA: Venture, 1990).
Hurding, R.F., 'Pastoral Care, Counselling and Psychotherapy', in D. Atkinson and D. Field (eds.), *New Dictionary of Christian Ethics and Pastoral Theology* (Leicester: Inter-Varsity Press, 1995).
Hurn, C.J., *The Limits and Possibilities of Schooling: An Introduction to the Sociology of Education* (Boston: Allyn & Bacon, 1978).
Hurtado, L.W., 'Following Jesus in the Gospel of Mark – and Beyond', in R. Longenecker (ed.), *Patterns of Discipleship in the New Testament* (Grand Rapids: Eerdmans, 1996): 9-29.
Iida, M., 'Adventure-Oriented Programs: A Review of Research' in E. Van der Smissen (ed.), *Research Camping and Environmental Education* Series No.11 (College of Health, Physical Education and Recreation: Pennsylvania State University Press, 1975): 219-41.
Illich, I., *Deschooling Society* (Harmondsworth: Penguin, 1973).
– 'Deschooling Society' in Bowen, J. and P. Hobson, *Theories of Education: Studies of Significant Innovation in Western Educational Thought* (Brisbane: John Wiley, 1974) 414-36.
– 'The Alternative to Schooling' in J. Bowen and P. Hobson, *Theories of Education: Studies of Significant Innovation in Western Educational Thought* (Brisbane: John Wiley, 1974): 403-13.
International Council of Accrediting Agencies for Evangelical Theological Education, 'Manifesto on the Renewal of Evangelical Theological Education', (Unpublished paper) in R.W. Ferris, *Renewal in Theological Education: Strategies for Change* (Wheaton: Wheaton College, 1990): 136-43.
Ironside, D.J., 'The Field of Adult Education: Concepts and Definitions', in C.J. Titmus (ed.), *Lifelong Education for Adults: An International Handbook* (Oxford: Pergamon, 1989): 13-18.
Ivy, S.S., 'A Faith Development/Self-Development Model for Pastoral Assessment' in J. Astley and L. Francis (eds.), *Christian Perspectives on Faith Developments: A Reader* (Grand Rapids: Eerdmans, 1992): 284-96.
Jackson, F. and K. Lake, *The Beginnings of Christianity* (Grand Rapids: Baker, 1966).
Jalongo, M.R., *Creating Learning Communities: The Role of the Teacher in the 21st Century* (Bloomington: National Educational Service, 1991).
Jeremias, J., *Jerusalem in the Time of Jesus* (Philadelphia: Fortress Press, 1969).
Jervis, L.A., 'Becoming like God through Christ; Discipleship in Romans' in R. Longenecker (ed.), *Patterns of Discipleship in the New Testament* (Grand Rapids: Eerdmans, 1996): 143-62.

Johnson, D.W. and F.P. Johnson, *Joining Together: Group Theory and Group Skills*, (Englewood Cliffs: Prentice Hall, 1982).

Johnson, D.W. and R. Johnson, 'Classroom Conflict: Controversy Versus Debate in Learning Groups', *American Educational Research Journal* 22, 2 (1985): 237-56.

Johnson, L.T., 'Friendship with the World/Friendship with God: A Study of Discipleship in James', in F.F. Segovia (ed.), *Discipleship in the New Testament* (Philadelphia: Fortress Press, 1985): 166-83.

Johnstone, P. and J. Mandruk., *Operation World: 21st Century Edition* (International Research Office: WEC International, 2001).

Jones, A., *Exploring Spiritual Direction: An Essay on Christian Friendship* (Minneapolis: Seabury, 1982).

Josephus, F., 'The Antiquities of the Jews' in *The Complete Works of Josephus* (translated by William Whiston) (Lynn: Hendrickson, 1980).

Joyce, B.R., 'Models for Teaching', in J. Raths, J. Pancella and J. Van Ness, *Studying Teaching* (Englewood Cliffs: Prentice-Hall, 1971).

Joyce, B. and M. Weil, *Models of Teaching* (Englewood Cliffs: Prentice-Hall, 1972).

Judge, E.A., *The Social Pattern of the Christian Groups in the First Century* (London: Tyndale Press, 1960).

– 'The Conflict of Educational Aims in New Testament Thought', *Journal of Christian Education* 9, 1 (1966): 32-45.

– 'The Reaction against Classical Education in the New Testament', *Journal of Christian Education* Papers 77 (1983): 7-14.

Kaiser, W.C., '*lāmad*', in R.L. Harris (ed.), *Theological Wordbook of the Old Testament* Vol.1 (Chicago: Moody Press, 1980): 480.

Kaiser, W.C., '*Talmid*' in R.L. Harris (ed.), *Theological Wordbook of the Old Testament* Vol.1 (Chicago: Moody Press, 1980): 480.

Kaldor, P., *Who Goes Where? Who Doesn't Care? Going to Church in Australia* (Sydney: Lancer, 1987).

– *First Look in the Mirror: Initial Findings of the 1991 National Church Life Survey* (Sydney: Lancer, 1992).

Kaldor, P. and R. Powell, *Views from the Pews: Australian Church Attenders Speak Out: National Church Life Survey* (Adelaide: Open Book, 1995).

Kaldor, P. et al., *Winds of Change: The Experience of Church in a Changing Australia* (Homebush West, NSW: Lancer, 1994).

– *Shaping a Future: Characteristics of Vital Congregations* (Adelaide: Open Book, 1997).

– *Build My Church: Trends and Possibilities for Australian Churches* (Adelaide: Open Book, 1999).

– *Taking Stock: A Profile of Australian Church Attenders* (Adelaide: Open Book, 1999).

Karris, R.J., 'Women and Discipleship in Luke', *Catholic Biblical Quarterly* 56, 1 (1994): 1-20.

Katz, S.T., 'A Critical Review of Martin Buber's Epistemology of I-Thou' in H. Gordon and J. Bloch (eds.), *Martin Buber: A Centenary Volume* (The Negev: Ktav, 1984).

Kealoha, A., *Trust the Children: An Activity Guide for Homeschooling and Alternative Learning* (Berkeley: Celestial Arts, 1995).

Kee, H.C., *Good News to the Ends of the Earth* (London: SCM Press, 1990).

Kebler, W.H., *Mark's Story of Jesus* (Philadelphia: Fortress Press, 1979).

– 'Apostolic Tradition and the Form of the Gospel', in F.F. Segovia (ed.), *Discipleship in the New Testament* (Philadelphia: Fortress Press, 1985): 24-46.

Kelsey, D.H., *To Understand God Truly: What's Theological about a Theological School*

(Louisville: Westminster/ John Knox, 1992).
- *Between Athens and Berlin: The Theological Education Debate* (Grand Rapids: Eerdmans, 1993).

Kidd, J.R. and C.J. Titmus, 'Introduction' in C.J. Titmus, (ed.), *Lifelong Education for Adults: An International Handbook* (Oxford: Pergamon, 1989): 23-39.

Kingdon, D.P., 'Shepherding Movement' in D.J. Atkinson and D.H. Field (eds.), *New Dictionary of Christian Ethics and Pastoral Theology* (Leicester: Inter-Varsity Press, 1995): 786.

Kingsbury, J.D., 'The Verb *akolouthein* ("to follow") as an Index of Matthew's View of his Community', *Journal of Biblical Literature* 97, 1 (1978): 56-73.
- 'The Figure of Peter in Matthew's Gospel as a Theological Problem', *Journal of Biblical Literature* 98, 1 (1979): 67-83.
- *Matthew as Story* (Philadelphia: Fortress Press, 1986).
- 'The Place, Structure and Meaning of the Sermon on the Mount' *Interpretation* 41, 2 (1987): 131-43.
- *Conflict in Mark: Jesus, Authorities, Disciples* (Minneapolis: Fortress Press, 1989).
- *Conflict in Luke* (Minneapolis: Fortress Press, 1991).

Kinsler, F.R. and J.H. Emery (eds.), *Opting for Change: A Handbook on Evaluation and Planning for Theological Education by Extension* (Geneva: Program on Theological Education, WCC, 1991).

Kistemaker, S.J., *Hebrews* (Grand Rapids: Baker, 1984).

Kittel, G. (ed.), *Theological Dictionary of the New Testament* Vol.5 (Grand Rapids: Eerdmans, 1967; German orig., 1933).

Kleinig, J., *Philosophical Issues in Education* (London: Croom Helm, 1982).

Knapp, C.E., *Creating Humane Climates Outdoors: A People Skills Primer* (Las Cruces, New Mexico: ERIC clearinghouse on Rural Education and Small Schools, 1988).

Knight, G.W., *New International Greek Commentary on the Pastoral Epistles* (Grand Rapids: Eerdmans, 1992).

Knowles, M.P., '"Christ in You, the Hope of Glory": Discipleship in Colossians' in R. Longenecker (ed.), *Patterns of Discipleship in the New Testament* (Grand Rapids: Eerdmans, 1996): 180-202.

Knowles, M.S., *Informal Adult Education: A Guide for Administrators, Leaders and Teachers* (New York: Association, 1950).
- *The Modern Practice of Adult Education: From Pedagogy to Andragogy Revised and updated* (Chicago: Follett, 1980).
- *The Adult Learner: A Neglected Species* (Houston, Gulf, 1984).

Koester, H., *Introduction to the New Testament: History, Culture and Religion of the Hellenistic Age* Vol.1 (Philadelphia: Fortress Press, 1982).

Kopas, J., 'Jesus and Women: Luke's Gospel', *Theology Today* 43, 2 (1986): 192-202.

Koperski, V., 'Luke 10,38-42 and Acts 6,1-7: Women and Discipleship in the Literary Context of Luke-Acts' in J. Verheyden (ed.), *The Unity of Luke-Acts* (Leiven: Leiven University Press, 1999) 517-44.

Kraft, R.J., 'Experiential Learning' in J.C. Miles and S. Priest (eds.), *Adventure Education* (State College, PA: Venture, 1990).

Kroeger, R.C. and C.C. Kroeger, *I Suffer not a Woman: Rethinking 1 Timothy 2.11-15 in Light of Ancient Evidence* (Grand Rapids: Baker, 1992).

Kubie, L.S., 'Are we Educating for Maturity?' in J. Raths, J. Pancella and J. Van Ness, *Studying Teaching* (Englewood Cliffs: Prentice-Hall, 1971).

Kurz, W.S., 'Kenotic Imitation of Paul and of Christ in Philippians 2 and 3' in F.F. Segovia.(ed.), *Discipleship in the New Testament* (Philadelphia: Fortress Press, 1985): 103-26.

Kvalbein, H., 'Go Therefore and Make Disciples...The Concept of Discipleship in the New Testament', *Themelios* 13, 2 (1988): 48-52.

Ladd, G.E., *A Theology of the New Testament* (Grand Rapids: Eerdmans, 1974).

Lane, W.M., *The Gospel of Mark* (New International Commentary on the New Testament; Grand Rapids: Eerdmans, 1974).

– *Hebrews 1-8* (Word Biblical Commentary, Vol.47A; Dallas: Word, 1991).

– 'Standing Before the Moral Claim of God: Discipleship in Hebrews' in R. Longenecker (ed.), *Patterns of Discipleship in the New Testament* (Grand Rapids: Eerdmans, 1996): 203-24.

Latourette, K.C., *A History of Christianity* (London: Eyre & Spottiswoode, 1954).

Laurie, S.S., *Historical Survey of Pre-Christian Education* (New York: Longmans, Green, 1907).

Lea, T.D. and H.P. Griffin, *1,2 Timothy, Titus: An Exegetical and Theological Exposition of Holy Scripture NIV Text* (Nashville: Broadman, 1992).

Leach, P., *Your Baby and You: From Birth to Age Five* (New York: Alfred Knopf, 1993).

Leavey, O.P., 'About Deschooling Christianity ...A Response to Professor Hill', *Journal of Christian Education* Papers 67 (Jul 1980): 30-44.

Lee, D.A., 'Presence or Absence? The Question of Women Disciples at the Last Supper', *Pacifica* 6 (1993): 1-20.

Leech, C.W., 'Intentional Christian Community and Education', *Journal of Christian Education* Papers 94 (1989): 33-9.

Leech, K., *Soul Friend: A Study of Spirituality* (London: Sheldon, 1977).

– *Spirituality and Pastoral Care* (London: Sheldon, 1986).

Lehman, V., 'Reflections on Thomas H. Groome: An Opportunity for Renewal in Christian Education', *Journal of Christian Education* 35, 1 (1992): 7-17.

Leichter, H.J., 'Families as Educators' in M. Fantini and R. Sinclair (eds.), *Education in School and Nonschool Settings* (Chicago: University of Chicago Press, 1985): 81-101.

Levine, A. (ed.), *"Women like this": New Perspectives on Jewish Women in the Greco-Roman World* (Atlanta: Scholars, 1991).

Lindars, B., 'Word and Sacrament in the Fourth Gospel', *Scottish Journal of Theology* 29 (1976): 49-63.

Lister, I. (ed.), *Deschooling: A reader* (London: Cambridge University Press, 1974).

Lister, I., 'The Challenge of Deschooling' in Lister, I. (ed.), *Deschooling: A Reader* (London: Cambridge University Press, 1974): 1-15.

Llovio, K., 'Toward a Definition of Christian Education: A Comparison of Richards and Westerhoff', *Christian Education Journal* 5, 2 (1984): 15-23.

Longenecker, R., *Biblical Exegesis in the Apostolic Period* (Grand Rapids: Eerdmans, 1975).

– (ed.), *Patterns of Discipleship in the New Testament* (Grand Rapids: Eerdmans, 1996a).

– 'Taking up the Cross Daily: Discipleship in Luke-Acts' in R. Longenecker (ed.), *Patterns of Discipleship in the New Testament* (Grand Rapids: Eerdmans, 1996b): 50-76.

Lotz, P.H., *Orientation in Religious Education: A Comprehensive Survey of Accomplishments, Objectives, Principles, and Methods* (New York: Abingdon, 1950).

Lovat, T.J., 'Action Research and the Praxis Model of Religious Education: A Critique', *British Journal of Religious Education* 11, 1 (1988): 30-7.

Luz, U., 'The Disciples in the Gospel According to Matthew' in G. Stanton (ed.), *The Interpretation of Matthew* (Philadelphia: Fortress Press, 1983).

MacBeath, J., (ed.), *A Question of Schooling* (London: Hodder & Stoughton, 1976).

Mackie, S.G., *Patterns of Ministry: Theological Education in a Changing World* (London: Collins, 1969).
McKenzie, B.C., *Friends in High Places: The Executive Woman's Guide* (Sydney: Business and Professional, 1995).
McFadyen, A.I., 'The Call to Discipleship: Reflections on Bonhoeffer's theme 50 years on', *Scottish Journal of Theology* 43 (1990): 461-83.
McGrath, A.E., *Christian Theology: An Introduction* (Oxford: Blackwell, 1997).
McKane, W., *Prophets and Wise Men* (London: SCM Press, 1965).
McKnight, E.V., *Post-Modern Use of the Bible: The Emergence of Reader-Orientated Criticism* (Nashville: Abingdon, 1988).
– 'Literary Criticism' in J. Green and S. McNight (eds.), *Dictionary of Jesus and the Gospels* (Leicester: Inter-Varsity Press, 1992): 473-81.
Malbon, E.S., 'Fallible Followers: Women and Men in the Gospel of Mark' *Semeia* 28 (1983): 29-48.
– 'Disciples/ Crowds/ Whoever: Markan Characters and Readers', *Novum Testamentum* 28, 2 (1986): 104-30.
– 'Texts and Contexts: Interpreting the Disciples in Mark', *Semeia* 62 (1993): 81-102.
Mallison, J., *Building Small Groups in the Christian Community* (Sydney: Renewal, 1978).
– *Growing Christians in Small Groups* (London: Scripture Union, 1989).
– *The Small-Group Leader: A Manual to Develop Vital Small Groups* (Adelaide: Openbook, 1996).
– *Two are Better than One: An Introduction to Mentoring* (Unpublished paper presented to seminar on Mentoring at Mt Pleasant Baptist Church, Perth, 12th March, 1998).
– 'Mentoring: To Make Disciples and Leaders', *Grid* (Melbourne: World Vision, Winter 1998).
– *Mentoring to Develop Disciples* (Lidcombe, NSW: Scripture Union, 1998).
Maly, E.H., 'Women and the Gospel of Luke', *Biblical Theology Bulletin* 10, 3 (1980): 99-104.
Manek,J., 'Fishers of men', *Novum Testamentum* 2 (1957): 138-141.
Manno, B.V., 'The identity of Jesus and the Christian Discipleship in the Gospel of Mark', *Religious Education* 70, 6 (1975): 619-28.
Manson, T.W., *The Teaching of Jesus* (Cambridge: Cambridge University Press, 1931).
Marshall, I.H., *The Gospel of Luke: A Commentary on the Greek Text* (Exeter: Paternoster, 1978).
– *The Epistles of John* (New International Commentary on the New Testament; Grand Rapids: Eerdmans, 1978).
– *Acts* (Tyndale New Testament Commentaries; Leicester: Inter-Varsity Press, 1980).
– *1 Peter* (Leicester: Inter-Varsity Press, 1991).
Martin, J. and R. Martin, 'What should we do with a Hidden Curriculum when we find one?' *Curriculum Inquiry* 6, 2 (1976).
Martin, R.P., *Mark: Evangelist and Theologian* (Grand Rapids: Academie, 1972).
– 'Salvation and Discipleship in Luke's Gospel', *Interpretation* 30 (1976): 366-80.
– *James* (Word Biblical Commentary, Vol.48; Waco: Word, 1988).
Matthaei, S.H., *Faith-Mentoring in the Faith Community* (Valley Forge: Trinity, 1996).
May, G.G., *Care of Mind, Care of Spirit: A Psychiatrist Explores Spiritual Direction* (San Francisco: Harper, 1992).
Maynard, A.H., 'The Role of Peter in the Fourth Gospel', *New Testament Studies* 30 (1984): 531-48.

Melbourne, B.L., *Slow to Understand: The Disciples in Synoptic Perspective* (New York: University Press of America, 1988).
Metzger, B., *A Textual Commentary on the Greek New Testament* (Stuttgart: German Bible Society, 1994).
Michaels, J.R., 'Going to Heaven with Jesus: From 1 Peter to Pilgrim's Progress' in R. Longenecker (ed.), *Patterns of Discipleship in the New Testament* (Grand Rapids: Eerdmans, 1996): 248-68.
Miles, J.C. and S. Priest, *Adventure Education* (State College, PA: Venture, 1990).
Milne, D.J.W., 'Mark: The Gospel of Servant Discipleship', *Reformed Theological Review* 49, 1 (1990): 20-9.
Minear, P.S., 'The Beloved Disciple in the Gospel of John: Some Clues and Conjectures', *Novum Testamentum* 19, 2 (1977): 105-23.
Moloney, F.J., *Woman First Among the Faithful: A New Testament Study* (Blackburn: Dove, 1984).
Moltmann-Wendel, E., *The Women Around Jesus* (New York: Crossroad, 1982).
Montefiore, H.W., *The Epistle to the Hebrews* (London: Adam & Charles Black, 1964).
Moos, R.H., *Evaluating Educational Environments* (San Francisco: Jossey-Bass, 1979).
Morris, L., *The Gospel According to John* (New International Commentary on the New Testament; Grand Rapids: Eerdmans, 1971).
– *The Gospel According to St Luke* (Grand Rapids: Eerdmans, 1974).
– *Expository Reflections on the Gospel of John* (Grand Rapids: Baker, 1986).
– *The Gospel According to Matthew* (Grand Rapids: Eerdmans, 1992).
Mosley, A.W., 'Jesus' Audiences in the Gospels of St Mark and St Luke', *New Testament Studies* 10 (1963): 139-49.
Müller, D., 'Apostle (*apostellō*)' in C. Brown (ed.), *New International Dictionary of New Testament Theology* Vol.1 (Exeter: Paternoster, 1975): 126-36.
– 'Disciple (*mathētēs*)' in C. Brown (ed.), *New International Dictionary of New Testament Theology* Vol.1 (Exeter: Paternoster, 1975): 483-90.
Munro, W., 'Women Disciples in Mark?', *Catholic Biblical Quarterly* 44, 2 (1982): 225-41.
– 'Women Disciples: Light from Secret Mark', *Journal of Feminist Studies in Religion* 8, 1 (1992): 47-64.
Murphy-O'Connor, J., 'John the Baptist and Jesus: History and Hypotheses', *New Testament Studies* 36, 3 (1990): 359-74.
Murray, J., *The Epistle to the Romans* (New International Commentary on the New Testament; Grand Rapids: Eerdmans, 1968).
Myers, C., 'The Last Days of Jesus: Mark 14.1 – 16.8, Collapse and Restoration of Discipleship', *Sojourners* 16 (1987): 32-6.
Neighbour, R.W., *Journey into Discipleship* (Memphis: Brotherhood Commission, 1974).
– *This Gift is Mine: Spiritual Gifts and How they can Build up the Body of Christ* (Nashville: Broadman, 1974).
– *Where do we go from here? A Guidebook for the Cell Group Church* (Houston: Touch, 1990).
Neighbour, R.W. and C. Thomas, *Target-Group Evangelism: Reaching People Where They Are* (Nashville: Briadman, 1975).
Neirynck, F., 'John 21', *New Testament Studies* 36 (1990): 321-36.
Nelson, C.E., *Where Faith Begins* (Richmond, Virginia: John Knox, 1967).
– 'Does Faith Develop? An Evaluation of Fowler's Position' in J. Astley and L. Francis (eds.), *Christian Perspectives on Faith Developments: A Reader* (Grand Rapids: Eerdmans, 1992): 62-76.

Nestle-Aland, von, *Computer-konkordanz zum Novum Testamentum Graece* (Berlin: Walter de Gruyter, 1980).
Newsom, C.A. and S.H. Ringe (eds.), *The Women's Bible Commentary* (London: SPCK, 1992).
Newman, B.M. and P.C. Stine, *A Translators' Handbook on the Gospel of Matthew* (London: United Bible Societies, 1988).
Nicholls, B.J., 'Role of Spiritual Development in Theological Education' *Evangelical Theological Education Today II: Agenda for Renewal* (Kenyan: Evangel, 1982) 13-25.
Nipkow, K.E., 'Stage Theories of Faith Development as a Challenge to Religious Education and Practical Theology' in J.W. Fowler, K.E. Nipkow and F. Schweitzer (eds.), *Stages of Faith and Religious Development: Implications for Church, Education and Society* (New York: Crossroad, 1991): 82-98.
Noddings, N., *Caring: A Feminine Approach to Ethics and Moral Education* (Berkeley: University of California Press, 1984).
Nyberg, D., *The Philosophy of Open Education* (London: Routledge & Kegan Paul, 1975).
O'Brien, P. and D. Peterson (eds.), *God Who is Rich in Mercy* (Homebush, NSW: Lancer, 1986).
O'Collins, G. and D. Kendall, 'Mary Magdalene as Major Witness to Jesus' Resurrection', *Theological Studies* 48 (1987): 631-46.
O'Grady, J.F., 'The Passion in Mark', *Biblical Theology Bulletin* 10, 2 (1980): 83-7.
O'Toole, R.F., *The Unity of Luke's Theology: An Analysis of Luke-Acts* (Wilmington: Michael Glazier, 1984).
- 'Luke's Message in Luke 9.1-50', *Catholic Biblical Quarterly* 49, 1 (1987): 74-89.
Ohliger, J. and C. McCarthy (eds.), *Lifelong Learning or Lifelong Schooling? A Tentative View of the Ideas of Ivan Illich with a Quotational Bibliography* (Syracuse, NY: Syracuse University Press, 1971).
Olmstead, C.E., 'Hillel 1' *World Book Encyclopedia* Vol.9 (Chicago: Field Enterprises Educational, 1976): 220.
Olsen, D.V.A., 'Making Disciples in a Liberal Protestant Church' in R. Wuthnow (ed.), *I Came Away Stronger: How Small groups are Shaping American Religion* (Grand Rapids: Eerdmans, 1994): 125-47.
Onna, van B., 'Informal Learning on the Job' in A.C. Tuijnman and M. Van der Kamp (eds.), *Learning across the Lifespan: Theories, Research, Policies* (Oxford: Pergamon, 1992).
Organization for Economic Cooperation and Development Paper, *Policies for Apprenticeship* (Paris: OECD, 1979).
Pamment, M., 'The Fourth Gospel's Beloved Disciple', *The Expository Times* 94, 12 (1983): 363-7.
Panko, S.M., *Makers of the Modern Theological Mind: Martin Buber* (Peabody, Mass: Hendrickson, 1976).
Parks, S.D., 'Young Adult Faith Development: Teaching is the Context of Theological Education' *Religious Education* 77, 6 (1982): 657-72.
- 'The North American Critique of James Fowler's Theory of Faith Development' in J.W. Fowler, K.E. Nipkow and F. Schweitzer (eds.), *Stages of Faith and Religious Development: Implications for Church, Education and Society* (New York: Crossroad, 1991): 101-15.
- 'Faith Development in a Changing World' in J. Astley and L. Francis (eds.), *Christian Perspectives on Faith Developments: A Reader* (Grand Rapids: Eerdmans, 1992): 92-106.
Parliament of the Commonwealth of Australia, *Education for Active Citizenship in Australian*

Schools and Youth Organisations: A Report by the Senate Standing Committee on Employment, Education and Training (Canberra: Australian Government, 1989).

Pascarella, E.T., P.T. Terenzini and G.S. Blimling, 'The Impact of Residential Life on Students' in C.C. Schroeder and P. Mable (eds.), *Realising the Educational Potential of Residence Halls* (San Francisco: Jossey-Bass, 1994): 22-52.

Payne, D.F., 'Education' in J.D. Douglas (ed.), *The Illustrated Bible Dictionary* Vol.1. (Leicester: Inter-Varsity Press, 1980): 413-4.

Pazdan, M.M., 'Nicodemus and the Samaritan Woman: Contrasting Models of Discipleship', *Biblical Theology Bulletin* 17, 3 (1987): 145-8.

Perkins, P., *Jesus as Teacher* (Cambridge: Cambridge University Press, 1990).

Perry, D.W. (ed.), *Homegrown Christian Education: Planning and Programming for Christian Education in the Local Congregation* (New York: Seabury, 1979).

Peterson, C., 'Adult Development at Work' in C. Peterson, *Looking Forward through the Life Span* (Sydney: Prentice Hall, 1984): 404-18.

Peterson, D.H., *Hebrews and Perfection* (Cambridge: Cambridge University Press, 1982).

Phillips, K., *The Making of a Disciple* (Eastbourne: Kingsway, 1981).

Poulton, G.A., 'A Starting Point for Non-School Education' in J. MacBeath (ed.), *A Question of Schooling* (London: Hodder & Stoughton, 1976).

Powell, M.A., *What is Narrative Criticism? A New Approach to the Bible* (London: SPCK, 1993).

Powers, B.W., 'Women in the Church: The Interpretation of 1 Tim 2.8-15', *Interchange*, 17 (1975): 55-9.

Pratney, W.A., *Doorways to Discipleship* (Minneapolis: Bethany House, 1975).

– *Handbook for Followers of Jesus* (Minneapolis: Bethany House, 1977).

Price, J.M., *Jesus the Teacher* (Nashville: Sunday School Board Southern Baptist Convention, 1946).

Priest, S., 'The Semantics of Adventure Education' in J.C. Miles and S. Priest, *Adventure Education* (State College, PA: Venture, 1990).

Pryor, J.W., *John: Evangelist of the Covenant People* (Downers Grove: Inter-Varsity Press, 1992).

Quast, K., *Peter and the Beloved Disciple: Figures for a Community in Crisis*, Journal for the Study of the New Testament, Supplement Series 32 (Sheffield: JSOT, 1989).

Rad, von G., *Wisdom in Israel* (London: SCM Press, 1972).

Raths, J., 'A Strategy for Developing Values' in J. Raths, J. Pancella and J. Van Ness, *Studying Teaching* (Englewood Cliffs: Prentice-Hall, 1971).

Raths, J., J. Pancella and J. Van Ness, *Studying Teaching* (Englewood Cliffs: Prentice-Hall, 1971).

Reimer, E., *School is Dead: An Essay on Alternatives in Education* (Harmondsworth: Penguin, 1971).

Reimer, I.R., *Woman in the Acts of the Apostles: A Feminist Liberation Perspective* (Minneapolis: Fortress Press, 1995).

Rengstorf, K.H. 'Apostolos' in G. Kittel (ed.), *Theological Dictionary of the New Testament* Vol.1 (Grand Rapids: Eerdmans, 1964; German orig., 1933): 407-45.

– 'Mathētēs' in G. Kittel (ed.), *Theological Dictionary of the New Testament* Vol.4 (Grand Rapids: Eerdmans, 1967; German orig., 1933): 415-61.

Revised Standard Version Greek-English New Testament (Grand Rapids: Zondervan, 1968).

Rhoads, D., 'Losing Life for Others in the Face of Death: Mark's Standards of Judgement', *Interpretation* 47 (1993): 358-69.

Ricci, C., *Mary Magdalene and Many Others: Women who Followed Jesus* (Tunbridge Wells: Burns & Oats, 1994).
Richards, L.O., *A New Face for the Church* (Grand Rapids: Zondervan, 1970).
– *Sixty-Nine Ways to start a Study Group and keep it Growing* (Grand Rapids: Zondervan, 1973).
– *A Theology of Christian Education* (Grand Rapids: Zondervan, 1975).
– 'The Disappearing Disciple: Why is the use of "Disciple" limited to the Gospels and Acts?', *Evangelical Journal* 10 (1992): 3-11.
Richards, L.O. and C. Hoeldtke, *A Theology of Church* (Grand Rapids: Zondervan, 1980).
Richards, L.O. and G. Martin, *A Theology of Personal Ministry: Spiritual Giftedness in the Local Church* (Grand Rapids: Zondervan, 1981).
Richmond, W.K., *Education and Schooling* (London: Methuen, 1975).
Rienecker, F., *A Linguistic Guide to the Greek New Testament: Vol.1 Matthew– Acts* (Grand Rapids: Eerdmans, 1976).
– *A Linguistic Guide to the Greek New Testament: Vol.2 Romans– Revelation* (Grand Rapids: Eerdmans, 1980).
Rigma, C., 'Discipleship: The Magnificent Mosaic', *On Being* (Apr 1989): 5-6.
Rigsby, L.C., M.C. Reynolds and M.C. Wang (eds.), *School-Community Connections: Exploring Issues for Research and Practice* (San Francisco: Jossey-Bass, 1995).
Rixon, L.D., *How Jesus Taught* (Sydney: Sydney Missionary and Bible College, 1977).
Robbins, V.K., *Jesus the Teacher: A Socio-Rhetorical Interpretation of Mark* (Philadelphia: Fortress Press, 1984).
Robertson, A.T., *Studies in the Epistle of James* (Nashville: Briadman, 1915).
Robinson, J.A.T., 'How small was the seed of the church?' in W. Weinrich, *The New Testament Age* Vol.2 (Mercer: Mercer University Press, 1984): 413-30.
Robinson, J.F., 'Book Review of Renewal in Theological Education: Strategies for Change by R.W. Ferris', *Evangelical Missions Quarterly* 27, 2 (1991): 204-6.
Robinson, W.C., 'The Quest for Wrede's Secret Messiah', *Interpretation* 27, 1 (1973): 10-30.
Ross, M.W., 'Psychotherapy as a Model for Interpersonal Dynamics in Tertiary Teaching', *Higher Education* 13 (1984): 717-29.
Rutledge, M., 'Faith Development: Bridging Theory and Practice' in J. Astley and L. Francis (eds.), *Christian Perspectives on Faith Developments: A Reader* (Grand Rapids: Eerdmans, 1992): 354-69.
Ryan, R., 'The Women from Galilee and Discipleship in Luke', *Biblical Theology Bulletin* 15, 2 (1985): 56-9.
Sanders, J.O., *Shoe Leather Commitment: Guidelines for Disciples* (Chicago: Moody Press, 1990).
Schaberg, J., 'Luke' in C.A. Newsom and S.H. Ringe (eds.), *The Women's Bible Commentary* (London: SPCK, 1992).
Scheffler, I., *The Language of Education* (Springfield: Thomas, 1960).
Schipani, D.S., *Religious Education Encounters Liberation Theology* (Birmingham, Alabama: Religious Education, 1988).
Schmitz, O., '*Parakaleō, paraklēsis* in G. Kittel (ed.), *Theological Dictionary of the New Testament* Vol.5 (Grand Rapids: Eerdmans, 1967; German orig., 1933): 773-9.
Schnackenburg, R., *The Gospel according to St John* Vols. 2 & 3 (London: Burns & Oates, 1980 & 1982).
Schneiders, I., 'Women in the Fourth Gospel and the Role of Women in the Contemporary Church' in M.W. Stibbe (ed.), *The Gospel of John as Literature: An Anthology of Twentieth-*

Century Perspectives (Leiden: Brill, 1993): 123-44.

Schroeder, C.C., 'Developing Learning Communities' in C.C. Schroeder and P. Mable, *Realising the Educational Potential of Residence Halls* (San Francisco: Jossey-Bass, 1994): 165-89.

Schroeder, C.C. and P. Mable, *Realising the Educational Potential of Residence Halls* (San Francisco: Jossey-Bass, 1994).

Schroeder, D.E., 'Faculty as Mentors: Some Leading Thoughts for Re-evaluating our Role as Christian Educators', *Christian Education Journal* 13, 2 (1993): 28-39.

Schweizer, E., *Lordship and Discipleship* (London: SCM Press, 1960).

– 'The Portrayal of the Life of Faith in the Gospel of Mark', *Interpretation* 32, 4 (1978): 387-99.

Seccombe, D.P., 'Take up your cross [Mk 8.34; Matt 10.38; 16.24; Lk 9.23; 14.27]' in P. O'Brien and D. Peterson (eds.), *God who is rich in mercy* (Homebush, NSW: Lancer, 1986): 139-51.

Segovia, F.F. (ed.), *Discipleship in the New Testament* (Philadelphia: Fortress Press, 1985).

Segovia, F.F., '"Peace I leave with you; My peace I give to you": Discipleship in the Fourth Gospel' in F.F. Segovia (ed.), *Discipleship in the New Testament* (Philadelphia: Fortress Press, 1985): 76-102.

Selvidge, M.J., 'And those who followed feared: Mark 10.32', *Catholic Biblical Quarterly* 45, 3 (1983): 396-400.

Selwyn, E.G., *The First Epistle of St Peter* (London: Macmillan, 1977).

Senior, D., *1 and 2 Peter* (Wilmington: Glazier, 1980).

Seymour, J.L., *Mapping Christian Education: Approaches to Congregational Learning* (Nashville: Abingdon, 1997).

Shackles, T., *Going Outside, Growing Inside: A look at the Relationship between Adventure Education and Religious Education* (Perth: Scripture Union, 1991).

Sharan, S., 'Cooperative Learning in Small Groups: Recent Methods and Effects on Achievement, Attitudes and Ethnic Relations', *Review of Educational Research* 50, 2 (1980): 241-71.

Shelp, E.E. and R.H. Sunderland, *The Pastor as Teacher* (New York: Pilgrim, 1989).

Shelton, R.M., 'Luke 17.1-10', *Interpretation* 31, 3 (1977): 280-5.

Sheridan, M., 'Disciples and Discipleship in Matthew and Luke', *Biblical Theological Bulletin* 3, 3 (1973): 235-55.

Sherlock, C., *Contours of Christian Theology: The Doctrine of Humanity* (Leicester: Inter-Varsity Press, 1996).

Shor, I. and P. Freire, *A Pedagogy for Liberation* (New York: Bergin & Garvey, 1987).

Shortt, J. and T. Cooling, *Agenda for Educational Change* (Leicester: Apollos, 1997).

Sim, D.C., 'Women Followers of Jesus: The Implication of Luke 8.1-3', *Heythrop Journal* 30 (1989): 51-62.

Simons, P.R-J., 'Theories and Principles of Learning to Learn' in A.C. Tuijnman and M. Van der Kamp (eds.), *Learning across the Lifespan: Theories, Research, Policies* (Oxford: Pergamon, 1992).

Simpson, J.A. and E.S.C. Weiner, *The Oxford English Dictionary* Vols.I,IV,XIV & XVII (Oxford: Clarendon Press, 1989).

Slater, T., *The Camping Book: A Guide to the Theory and Practice of Christian Camping* (Surrey Hills, NSW: ANZEA, 1976).

– *The Temporary Community: Organised Camping for Urban Society* (Sutherland, NSW: Albatross, 1984).

- *The New Camping Book: An Introduction to Christian Camping* (Sydney: Scripture Union, 1990).
Slavin, R.E., 'Cooperative Learning and Student Achievement: Six Theoretical Perspectives' in M. Maehr and C. Ames (eds.), *Advances in Motivation and Achievement: Motivation Enhancing Environments* Vol.6: 161-77.
Slee, N., 'Cognitive Developmental Studies of Religious Thinking: A Survey and Discussion with Special Reference to Post-Goldman Research in the United Kingdom' in J.W. Fowler, K.E. Nipkow and F. Schweitzer (eds.), *Stages of Faith and Religious Development: Implications for Church, Education and Society* (New York: Crossroad, 1991): 130-46.
Smith, D.M., *First, Second and Third John* (Louisville: John Knox, 1991).
Smith, K., D.W. Johnson and R.T. Johnson, 'Can Conflict be Constructive? Controversy Versus Concurrence Seeking in Learning Groups', *Journal of Educational Psychology* 73, 5 (1981): 651-63.
Smith, M., *Local Education: Community, Conversation, Praxis* (Philadelphia: Open University, 1994).
Smith, M. and T. Jeffs, *Using Informal Education: An Alternative to Casework, Teaching and Control?* (Philadelphia: Open University, 1990).
Smith, M.A., *The Church under Seige* (Leicester: Inter-Varsity Press, 1976).
Smith, P.J., 'Larry Richards' Definition of Christian Education', *Christian Education Journal* 5, 2 (1984): 5-14.
Smith, S.H., 'Bethsaida via Gennesaret: The Enigma of the Sea-Crossing in Mark 6.45-53', *Biblica* 77, 3 (1996): 349-74.
Smith, S.L., *Schooling without Schools?* (Campbelltown, NSW: Souwest, 1991).
Smith, T.B., 'Integrating Living and Learning in Residential Colleges' in C.C. Schroeder and P. Mable, *Realising the Educational Potential of Residence Halls* (San Francisco: Jossey-Bass, 1994): 241-65.
Snodgrass, K.R., 'Parable' in J. Green (ed.), *Dictionary of Jesus and the Gospels* (Downers Grove: Inter-Varsity Press, 1992): 591-601.
Snyder, H.A., *The Problem of Wineskins: Church Structure in a Technological Age* (Downers Grove: Inter-Varsity Press, 1975).
Soards, M.L., 'On Understanding Luke 22.39', *The Bible Translator* 36, 3 (1985): 336-7.
Sor, la W.S., *The Dead Sea Scrolls and the New Testament* (Grand Rapids: Eerdmans, 1972).
Standing Committee of the General Synod of the Church of England in Australia, *An Australian Prayer Book* (Sydney: Anglican Information Office, 1978).
Stanton, G., *The Interpretation of Matthew* (Philadelphia: Fortress Press, 1983).
Stein, R.H., *The Method and Message of Jesus' Teachings* (Philadelphia: Westminster, 1978).
Stevenson, J., *A New Eusebius* (London: SPCK, 1970).
Stibbe, M.W. (ed.), *The Gospel of John as Literature: An Anthology of Twentieth-Century Perspectives* (Leiden: Brill, 1993).
Stott, J.R.W., *The Epistles of John* (Tyndale New Testament Commentaries; Grand Rapids: Eerdmans, 1975).
- *The Message of Acts: To the Ends of the Earth* (The Bible Speaks Today; Leicester: Inter-Varsity Press, 1990).
Street, J.L., 'A Shared Praxis Approach', *Religious Education* 83, 2 (1988): 234-42.
Studzinski, R., *Spiritual Direction and Midlife Development* (Chicago: Loyola University Press, 1985).
Stump, J.P., 'Theological Education' in I.V. and K.B. Cully (eds.), *Harper's Encyclopedia of Religious Education* (San Francisco: Harper & Row, 1990): 647-8.

Suggit, J.N., 'The Raising of Lazarus' *Expository Times* 95, 4 (1984): 106-8.
Sullivan, J. (ed.), *Carmelite Studies: Spiritual Direction* (Washington: Institute of Carmelite Studies, 1980).
-(ed.), *Carmelite Studies: Contemporary Psychology and Carmel* (Washington: Institute of Carmelite Studies, 1982).
Talbert, C.H., 'Discipleship in Luke-Acts' in F.F. Segovia (ed.), *Discipleship in the New Testament* (Philadelphia: Fortress Press, 1985): 62-75.
Tannehill, R.C., 'The Disciples in Mark: The Functions of a Narrative Role' in W. Telford (ed.), *The Interpretation of Mark* (Philadelphia: Fortress Press, 1985): 134-57.
– 'Jesus' Ministry to the Oppressed and Excluded' in *The Narrative Unity of Luke-Acts: A Literary Interpretation 1: The Gospel of Luke* (Philadelphia: Fortress Press, 1986).
Taylor, M.J. (ed.), *An Introduction to Christian Education* (Nashville: Abingdon, 1966).
Teddlie, C. and S. Stringfield, *Schools Make a Difference: Lessons Learned from a 10-year Study of School Effects* (New York: Teachers College Press, 1993).
Tennant, M., 'Adult, Community and Non-Formal Education: The Australian Experience' in C.J. Titmus (ed.), *Lifelong Education for Adults: An International Handbook* (Oxford: Pergamon, 1989): 117-25.
Thistlethwaite, S.B. and G.F. Cairns, *Beyond Theological Tourism: Mentoring as a Grassroots Approach to Theological Education* (Maryknoll: Orbis, 1994).
Thomson, J.B., *Natural Childhood: A Practical Guide to the First Seven Years* (London: Hodder & Stoughton, 1994).
Thompson, J.W., *The Beginnings of Christian Philosophy: The Epistle to the Hebrews* (Washington: Catholic Biblical Association of America, 1982).
Thompson, M., *1-3 John* (Leicester: Inter-Varsity Press, 1992).
Thompson, M.R., *The Role of Disbelief in Mark* (New York: Paulist, 1989).
Thompson, R.J., 'Christian Moral Education: A Philosophical, Theological and Educational Foundation for Intentional Adult Moral Education in the Church' (Unpublished Master's Dissertation, Bible College of New Zealand, Auckland: 1997).
Thornton, M., *English Spirituality* (London: SPCK, 1963).
Tidball, D., *Skilful Shepherds: An Introduction to Pastoral Theology* (Leicester: Inter-Varsity Press, 1986).
Tindale, R.S. et al. (eds.), *Theory and Research on Small Groups* (New York: Plenum, 1998).
Titmus, C.J. (ed.), *Lifelong Education for Adults: An International Handbook* (Oxford: Pergamon, 1989).
Topping, K. and S. Hill, 'University and College Students as Tutors for Schoolchildren: A Typology and Review of Evaluation Research' in S. Goodlad (ed.), *Students as Tutors and Mentors* (London: Kogan Page, 1995): 13-31.
Tovey, M.D., *Training in Australia: Design, Delivery, Evaluation, Management* (Sydney: Prentice Hall, 1997).
Towner, P.H., *1-2 Timothy and Titus* (Leicester: Inter-Varsity Press, 1994).
Trainor, M., 'The Begetting of Wisdom: The Teacher and the Disciples in Matthew's Community', *Pacifica* 4, 1 (1991): 148-64.
Trocme, E., *The Formation of the Gospel According to Mark* (London: SPCK, 1975; French orig., 1963).
Tucker, A.F., 'A Training Model Integrating Spiritual Formation in Theological Education' (Unpublished Master of Theology in Missiology Dissertation, Fuller Theological Seminary, 1995).

Tuijnman, A.C. and M. Van der Kamp (eds.), *Learning Across the Lifespan: Theories, Research, Policies* (Oxford: Pergamon, 1992).

Twelftree, G., 'Discipleship in Mark's Gospel', *St Mark's Review* 141, (Aut 1990): 5-11.

Tyson, J.B., 'The Blindness of the Disciples in Mark' in C. Tuckett (ed.), *The Messianic Secret* (Philadelphia: Fortress Press, 1983).

Vallance, E., 'Hiding the Hidden Curriculum', *Curriculum Theory Network* 4, 1 (1973).

Vellanickal, M., *The Divine Sonship of Christians in the Johannine Writings* (Rome: Biblical Institute, 1977).

Verheyden, J. (ed.), *The Unity of Luke-Acts* (Leiven: Leiven University Press, 1999).

Versluis, P., *Making Disciples in the Congregation: A Guide to Christian Formation through the Process of Mentoring and the Experience of Congregational Worship* (Elkhart, Indiana: Institute of Mennonite Studies, 1995).

Waddy, M. (ed.), *Home Education in Western Australia: A Response to the School Education Bill 1997* (Unpublished materials prepared for Home Based Learning Network WA, Natural Learning Association WA and Swan Hills Homeschoolers Grapevine, Aug 1997).

Wagner, C.P., *Your Church Can Grow* (Glendale: Regal, 1976).

– *Your Spiritual Gifts Can Help Your Church Grow* (Ventura: Regal, 1979).

Wagner, M.A., 'Christian Education as Making Disciples', *Lutheran Theological Journal* 24, 2 (1990): 69-80.

Wahlde, U.C., 'Mark 9.33-50. Discipleship: The Authority that Serves', *Biblische Zeitschrift* 29, 1 (1985): 49-67.

Walker, W.G., J.E. Mumford and C. Steel, *A Glossary of Educational Terms: Usage in Five English Speaking Countries* (Brisbane: University of Queensland Press, 1973).

Wardle, D., *The Rise of the Schooled Society* (London: Routledge & Kegan Paul, 1974).

Warr, G., *You Can Make Disciples* (Waco: Word, 1978).

Watson, D., *Discipleship* (London: Hodder & Stoughton, 1981).

Watty, W.W., 'The Significance of Anonymity in the Fourth Gospel', *The Expository Times* 90, 7 (1979): 209-12.

Weigle, L.A., 'The Aim and Scope of Religious Education' in P.H. Lotz, *Orientation in Religious Education: A Comprehensive Survey of Accomplishments, Objectives, Principles, and Methods* (New York: Abingdon, 1950): 87-98.

Weil, M., B. Joyce and B. Kluwin, *Personal Models of Teaching: Expanding your Teaching Repertoire* (Englewood Cliffs: Prentice-Hall, 1978).

Weil, M. and B. Joyce, *Social Models of Teaching: Expanding your Teaching Repertoire* (Englewood Cliffs: Prentice-Hall, 1978).

Weima, J.A.D., '"How you must walk to please God": Holiness and Discipleship in 1 Thessalonians' in R. Longenecker (ed.), *Patterns of Discipleship in the New Testament* (Grand Rapids: Eerdmans, 1996): 98-119.

Weinrich, W., *The New Testament Age* Vol.2 (Mercer: Mercer University Press, 1984).

Welty, J.D., 'Achieving Curricular Objectives through Residence Halls' in C.C. Schroeder and P. Mable (eds.), *Realising the Educational Potential of Residence Halls* (San Francisco: Jossey-Bass, 1994): 70-92.

Wenham, J., *Easter Enigma* (Exeter: Paternoster, 1984).

Wentworth, W.M., *Context and Understanding: An Inquiry into Socialization Theory* (New York: Elsevier, 1980).

Westerhoff, J.H., 'What is Religious Socialisation?' in J.H. Westerhoff and G.K. Neville, *Generation to Generation* (New York: Pilgrim, 1974): 37-49.

– *Will our Children have Faith?* (East Malvern: Dove, 1976).

- *Inner Growth, Outer Change: An Educational Guide to Church Renewal* (East Malvern: Dove, 1979).
- *Building God's People in a Materialistic Society* (San Francisco: Harper & Row, 1983).,
- 'Formation, Education, Instruction' *Religious Education* 82, 4 (1987): 578-91.
- 'Fashioning Christians in Our Day' in S. Hauerwas and J.H. Westerhoff (eds.), *Schooling Christians: 'Holy Experiments' in American Education* (Grand Rapids: Eerdmans, 1992).
- *The Making of Christians: The Catechetical Process* (Unpublished manuscript, n.d.).

Westerhoff, J.H. and G.K. Neville, *Generation to Generation* (New York: Pilgrim, 1974).

Wilcock, M., *The Message of Luke* (Leicester: Inter-Varsity Press, 1979).

Wild, R.A., '"Be Imitators of God": Discipleship in the Letter to the Ephesians' in F.F. Segovia (ed.), *Discipleship in the New Testament* (Philadelphia: Fortress Press, 1985): 127-43.

Wilds, E.H. and K.V. Lottich, *The Foundations of Modern Education* (New York: Holt, Rinehart & Winston, 1961).

Wilkins, M.J., *The Concept of Disciple in Matthew's Gospel as Reflected in the Use of the Term mathētēs* (Leiden: E.J.Brill, 1988).
- *Following the Master: Discipleship in the Steps of Jesus* (Grand Rapids: Zondervan, 1992).
- 'Discipleship' in J. Green et al. (eds.), *Dictionary of Jesus and the Gospels* (Downers Grove: Inter-Varsity Press, 1992a): 182-9.

Willimon, W.H., *Acts: Interpretation, a Bible commentary for Teaching and Preaching* (Atlanta: John Knox, 1988).

Wilson, R.R., *Prophecy and Society in Ancient Israel* (Philadelphia: Fortress Press, 1980).

Witherington, B., *Women in the Ministry of Jesus: A Study of Jesus' Attitude Toward Women and their Roles as Reflected in his Earthly Ministry* (SNTS Monograph 51; Cambridge: Cambridge University Press, 1984).

Wlodkowski, R.J., *Enhancing Adult Motivation to Learn* (San Francisco: Jossey-Bass, 1990).

Wolfendale, S., *Parental Participation in Children's Development and Education* (New York: Gordon and Breach, 1983).

Wood, W.P., 'John 2.13-22', *Interpretation* 45, 1 (1991): 59-63.

Woodhead, C., *Dare to Lead: Cresting the Ideological and Political Waves* (Unpublished paper presented at the Association of Heads of Independent Schools of Australia Conference in Melbourne, 1999.)

World Book Encyclopedia Vol.9 (Chicago: Field Enterprises Educational, 1976).

World Council of Churches, *Theological Education in Europe: Report of the Consultation held in Herrnhut, German Democratic Republic on the Theme Theological Education for Ministerial Formation* (Geneva: Program on Theological Education WCC, 1980).

Wright, D.W., 'The Social Context of the Renewal Problem in Theological Education: Probing beyond the Symptoms of Failure', *Christian Education Journal* 15, 3 (1995): 87-98.
- 'A Response to Robert W. Ferris's Rejoinder', *Christian Education Journal* 15, 3 (1995): 105-7.

Wright, N.T., *Following Jesus: Biblical Reflections on Discipleship* (Grand Rapids: Eerdmans, 1994).

Wuthnow, R. (ed.), *I came away stronger: How Small Groups are Shaping American Religion* (Grand Rapids: Eerdmans, 1994).

Young, E.J., *My Servants the Prophets* (Grand Rapids: Eerdmans, 1955).

Zuck, R.B. and G.A. Getz, *Adult Education in the Church* (Chicago: Moody Press, 1970).

Zuck, R.B. and R.E. Clark, *Childhood Education in the Church* (Chicago: Moody Press, 1975).

Index

Action-reflection 4, 29, 37, 38, 42, 52-54, 58, 70-71, 73, 89, 101, 103, 123, 154, 190, 191, 210, 213, 220, 224, 230, 234, 242, 247
Adult education 9, 148, 178, 189, 192-193, 228, 231, 243
Adventure education 9, 53, 56, 151, 159, 199, 201, 234, 246
Akoloutheō 30, 31, 47, 48, 59, 65, 82, 122, 138n1
Ancient Near East 5, 8, 11-14, 19, 23, 29, 145
Apollos 111, 117, 121n19, 140n42
Apprentice 9, 11, 12, 13, 20, 23, 70, 99, 112, 116, 127, 128, 136, 145, 154-155, 159, 187, 189, 191, 196, 201, 223
Aquila 111, 121n21-24, 139n27-28, 140n42
Aristotle 13, 22n10, 25n19
Assessment 69, 87, 148, 166, 175, 180, 182, 227, 242, 247
Attitudes 9, 36, 39, 55, 99, 111, 124, 125, 150, 151, 153, 157, 158, 159, 174, 175, 176, 182, 186-188, 189, 191, 196, 198, 199, 200, 202, 207n174, 209, 214, 218, 220, 225, 226, 228, 231, 233, 244, 247
Augustine 57n18, 88, 94n48, 176n10
Australian National Church Life survey 182, 202
  1991 179-180
  1996 180-181
Australian Uniting Church Christian Education survey 181

Banks, Robert 131, 208, 226, 227, 230-234, 236n123
Baptise 55, 56, 83, 101, 110, 113, 114, 116, 117, 118, 119, 128, 246
Barnabas 108, 112, 114, 115, 116, 117, 121n19, n23, 128
Bartimaeus 31, 32
Behaviours 9, 12, 23, 55, 56, 69, 124, 126, 150, 151, 153, 158, 159, 160, 174, 175, 176, 182, 191, 202, 208, 209, 210, 212, 215, 220, 233, 244, 246
Beloved Disciple 7, 80, 82, 83, 84, 85, 88, 93n18, n24, 94n52
Bible
  colleges 188
  reading 179, 180, 245
Body of Christ 108, 171, 232, 243
Bonhoeffer, Dietrich 162
Brainwashing 146, 164n8
Buber, Martin 194, 195, 206n127, 213, 217
Buildings 118, 119, 188, 222, 242

Call, the 17, 30, 31, 32, 33, 34, 37, 39, 41, 42n5, n8, 45, 46, 47, 48, 49, 51, 52, 53, 54, 55, 60, 64, 65, 66, 67, 70, 73, 76n54, 77n77, 82, 87, 98, 100, 101, 102, 111, 125, 126, 139n19, 162, 163, 164, 169, 170, 171, 218, 220, 245
Camping 151, 197, 199
Cathedral schools 182
Cell church 9, 203, 208, 219, 222-226, 237n123, n126, n127, n128, n132, 243
Children 8, 11, 12, 19, 23, 24n9, 32, 33, 36, 37, 41, 60, 69, 72, 92n23, 101, 104, 115, 126, 131, 134, 135, 136, 137, 139n26, 140n31, n34, n36, 148, 149, 150, 158, 165n28, 169, 171, 174, 183, 184, 185, 186, 187, 188, 190, 192, 193, 194, 204n41, 205n64, 206n127, 215, 222, 234n10, 236n66, 244
Childlike 51, 101
Christian Education 6, 7, 8, 9, 108, 138, 174, 180, 183, 188, 202, 208-218, 226, 227, 236n66, 242
Christian Research Association of Australia 179
Collaborative learning 9, 37, 56, 101, 103, 112, 130, 144, 152-153, 159, 160, 188, 191, 192, 197, 200-201, 216, 221, 228, 230, 231, 232, 234, 242, 247
Communal living 13, 23, 34, 246
Community
  closed 151

learning 8, 9, 13, 16-19, 49, 102, 145, 150-152, 158, 160, 172, 189, 197, 213, 222, 228, 230, 231, 232, 233
  long-term 234
  nurturing 163, 164, 215-216, 220, 225, 226, 242
  religious 151, 160, 197, 209, 234n7
  residential 197, 198
  serving 36-37, 41, 50-51, 69-70, 89, 101, 103
  short-term 198
  temporary 151
Conflict 34, 50, 139n29, 151, 166n76, 197, 198, 199, 207n150, 234, 246
Cooperative learning 200, 201
Counselling 8, 145, 156-158, 160, 161, 189, 196, 235n57
Co-worker 128, 139n27, 140n31
Curriculum 68, 69, 112, 118, 119, 129, 146, 150, 175, 182, 183, 184, 209, 245
  hidden 146, 149, 165n11, 185, 189, 199, 204n41, 209, 225, 247

Dead Sea Scrolls 8, 21
Demonstration 4, 38-39, 54, 71-72, 89-90, 101, 191
Deschooling 153, 188
Dialogue 6, 82, 124, 184, 191, 192, 195, 213, 214, 215, 217, 235n60
Dewey, John 192-193
Discipler 4, 5, 9, 42n1, 80, 82, 85, 92, 96-98, 99, 102, 103, 107, 109, 160, 166n77, 173, 241
Discussion 4, 7, 20, 34, 38, 78n94, 117, 128, 182, 183, 184, 230

Elijah 16, 17, 22, 25n32, 71
Elisha 16, 17, 22, 25n32, 71
Encouragement 17, 52, 61, 69, 111, 116, 117, 119, 123, 125, 128, 129, 134, 135, 137, 160, 179, 182, 192, 193, 198, 223
Evaluation 7, 156, 193
Example, teaching by 5, 15, 21, 37, 39, 41, 51, 54, 69, 88, 89, 98, 111, 112, 115, 118, 120, 124, 125-126, 127, 128, 129, 135, 136, 137, 139n19, 146, 152, 155, 157, 160, 161, 170, 174, 176, 220, 230, 242

Exhortation 117, 137, 141n58, 157, 160
Experiential learning 196, 204n56
Explanation 4, 7, 30, 35, 37, 48, 78n94, 86, 90, 111, 140n42, 212
Exposition 137, 157, 160

Failure, learning through 29, 32, 33, 37, 39-41, 42, 44n43, 47, 52-54, 80, 83, 88, 93n17, 97, 100, 101, 102, 103, 112, 150, 154, 197, 216
Faith Community Baptist Church 219, 223, 226
False teaching 117, 129, 133, 140
Family 9, 10, 17, 18, 19, 21, 23, 24n9, 25n40, 30, 31, 33, 34, 35, 41, 49, 51, 52, 55, 59, 60, 61, 64, 65, 66
Fear 19, 40, 41, 53, 64, 66, 72, 77n71, 78n94, 86, 113, 169
Fellowship 12, 13, 17, 21, 66, 67, 77n73, 84, 100, 108, 110, 111, 112, 127, 132, 134, 135, 179, 182, 188, 218, 221, 237n112
Ferris, Robert 208, 226, 227-229, 231-232, 233
Fishermen 30, 33, 46, 52, 57n16, 65, 100
Formal teaching 54, 58, 66, 68-69, 73, 86-87, 101, 117, 124, 129, 135, 136, 137, 138, 148, 174, 175, 181, 183, 184, 186, 188, 212, 215, 220, 223, 224, 228, 231, 242
Freire, Paulo 191-192, 211

Great Commission 106, 108, 116
Greco-Roman 14, 32, 125
Groome, Thomas 208, 212-218, 230, 233, 235n61
Groups, small 4, 6, 51-52, 56, 98, 102, 112, 130, 132, 136, 137, 156, 180, 181, 200-201, 203, 209, 215-216, 219-226, 228, 231, 234, 236n97, 242, 243, 246

Hidden curriculum (see Curriculum, hidden)
Holistic learning 129, 130, 156, 199, 201, 214, 227, 230
Holy Spirit 38, 55, 57n18, 73, 87, 89, 91, 93n20, 98, 107, 109, 110, 119, 120, 155, 168, 170, 173, 176, 219, 241

Index 275

Home based education 150
House
  church 9, 62, 127, 129, 131, 133, 134, 139n27, 140n36, n42, n44, 156, 219, 220, 237n123
  hold 12, 117, 193, 194, 201, 220

Illich, Ivan 148, 153, 185-186, 190-191, 204n41, 207
Imitate 5, 12, 12, 14, 23, 41, 69, 110, 125, 126, 132, 139n18, n19, 162, 173
Imitatio Christi 125
Indoctrination 50, 101, 146, 164n8
Informal
  models of education 9, 145, 147, 158, 159, 178, 186, 189, 190, 200, 202, 215, 226, 232, 247
  teaching 41, 47, 111, 115, 127, 134, 148, 150, 154, 175, 208, 212, 215, 220, 231, 243
Israel, education in 14-23

Jeremiah 14, 16, 17, 18, 20
John Mark 112, 114, 115, 121n23
John the Baptist 22, 34, 71, 82, 85, 93n18, 110
Joseph of Arimathea 48, 49, 80, 81, 100
Josephus 17, 20, 22, 76n45, 96
Joshua 15, 22
Judas Iscariot 33, 47, 64, 80, 86, 92n2, 99, 121n23

Knowles, Malcolm 192-193, 201, 228

Last Supper 84
Lazarus 81, 82, 84, 87, 88, 90, 93n18, 102
Lecture 20, 183, 184
Lifelong
  education 193
  learning 47, 245
Lord's Supper 86, 222

Make disciples 3, 4, 5, 7, 9, 49, 54, 55, 56, 98, 101, 108, 110, 116, 122, 172, 212, 221, 240
Mallison, John 153, 208, 217, 220-222, 233
Martha 59, 60, 61, 62, 81, 82, 83, 84, 87, 93n19, 102

Mary Magdalene 49, 59, 74n5, n6, 81, 82, 84, 85, 88, 93n19, 102
Mary of Bethany 87, 90
Mary (mother of Jesus) 74n6, n9, 87
Mathētēs 8, 12, 13, 14, 21, 22, 30, 32, 46, 56n5, 59, 62, 67, 79, 97, 99, 107, 108, 110, 122, 132, 162, 241
Maturity 7, 22, 24, 72, 83, 89, 101, 108, 124, 127, 129, 133, 136, 138, 150, 153, 154, 155, 156, 158, 159, 160, 163, 176, 194, 195, 208, 217, 228, 229
Mentoring 8, 9, 16, 145, 154-155, 159, 189, 196, 201, 217, 219, 221, 228, 229, 231, 232
Mission teams 115, 127, 128, 130, 131, 134, 136, 159
Modelling 4, 29, 35-36, 50-51, 58, 69, 87-89, 90, 101, 108, 119, 123, 135, 153, 191, 198, 216, 217, 218, 222, 224, 225, 232, 246, 247
Monasteries 181, 199
Moses 15, 17, 21, 22, 24, 71, 72, 85

National Church Life Survey (See Australian Church Life Survey)
Neighbour, Ralph 208, 219, 222-226, 233, 236n145
Networking 145, 153, 159, 189, 222
Nicodemus 80, 81, 86, 93n19, 102

Observation 34, 38, 70, 128, 151, 154, 158, 159, 178, 220, 224, 230
Oikodomeō-teaching 124, 127, 135, 137, 138, 242, 246
Oral
  communication 4, 40, 42n1, 98, 103, 166n77
  teaching 19, 47
  tradition 19, 120n1

Partnership 30, 40, 49, 59, 62, 67, 100, 102, 112, 130, 213, 215, 217, 230
Parenting 4, 6, 144, 147, 149-150, 158, 189, 201
Pastors and pastoral care 6, 43n16, 85, 89, 91, 92, 101, 108, 112, 134, 137, 145, 156-158, 160, 172, 189, 218, 220, 221, 222, 223, 225, 237n102

Peer 150, 152, 153, 191, 196, 200, 201, 247
Persecution 40, 51, 65, 83, 110, 112, 113, 114, 116, 117, 118, 119, 121n20, 122, 126, 127, 128
Personal relationships 4, 9, 12, 15, 16, 32-33, 34, 41, 42n1, 48, 55, 66-67, 73, 79, 81, 83-84, 88, 90, 99, 100. 102, 103, 109, 112, 113-115, 117, 118, 119, 120, 122, 129, 132, 133-135, 137, 152, 157, 159, 161, 162, 164, 166n77, 168-170, 173, 175, 215, 216-217, 219, 221, 225, 231, 233, 242, 245
Praxis, shared 38, 51, 103, 191, 210, 213, 214, 215, 234n60
Preaching 4, 14, 35, 37, 61, 62, 101, 110, 112, 113, 117, 137, 174, 212, 218, 225, 235n57
Priscilla 111, 121n21,n22,n23,n24, 139,n27,n28, 140n42, 141n65
Problem solving 199, 200
Psychotherapy 8, 145, 155, 156-158, 160, 189

Questioning 21, 25n41, 38, 68, 77n83, 194, 209, 210, 226
Qumran 21, 24

Rabbi 20, 21, 26n65, 50, 60, 66, 82, 113, 128, 184
Rabbinic
  education 204n32
  movement 11, 19-21
  schools 20, 32, 48, 51
Rebuke 32, 36, 39, 40, 42, 43n19, 49, 53, 54, 56, 78n94, 101, 111, 123, 126, 133
Reflection 34, 38, 54, 70, 99, 111, 112, 129, 150, 174, 175, 180, 213, 214, 216, 225, 228, 232, 245, 246, 247
Religious education 199, 203n8, 209, 211, 212, 213, 214, 216, 217, 227, 234n42
Richards, Lawrence 107, 108, 109, 120n1, 147, 208, 209, 211-212, 215-218, 219, 220, 233, 236n66, n73, n95, 238n157
Roman Empire 3, 114, 122, 129, 140n37
Rote learning 69

Samuel 16
Saul 16

Schools
  Catholic 188
  Christian 174, 183, 186, 188
  Sunday 174, 179, 183, 185, 186, 188, 203n8, 216
  synagogue 184
Schooling 4, 12, 23, 147, 148, 150, 153, 165n11, 175, 178, 182-197, 209, 214, 217, 228, 229
  Model 3, 5, 9, 107, 118-119, 127, 138, 145, 146, 147, 153, 174, 175, 178, 182-197, 201, 202, 208, 209, 211, 215, 224, 226, 228, 231, 233, 240, 243, 244-247
Scribal training 17-18, 20
Self directed learning 150, 153
Serving community 36-37, 41, 50-52, 68-70, 89, 101, 103
Seventy, the 59, 62, 67, 70, 80, 100
Small groups, subgroups 48, 49, 55, 60, 68, 100, 102, 131
Socialisation 145, 147, 149-150, 152, 158, 189, 209, 211, 212, 213, 246
Spirit (See Holy Spirit)
Spiritual
  development 9, 115, 156, 159, 182, 189, 194, 220, 222, 225
  direction 8, 145, 155-156, 157, 158, 160, 166n61
  gifts 124, 127, 128, 130, 131, 135, 136, 137-138, 160, 163, 172, 174, 175, 210, 218, 219, 221, 222, 223, 224-225, 226, 232, 234, 241, 242, 246
Sunday Schools (See schools, Sunday)
Supervision 37, 129, 151, 154, 193, 199, 228, 233
Synagogue (See schools, synagogue)

Teams (See mission teams)
Theological
  colleges 118, 174, 185, 186
  education 7, 8, 9, 179, 181, 183, 203, 208, 226-233, 237n126, 238n149, n155, n159, 243, 247
  education by extension (TEE) 32, 43n16
Timothy 61, 114, 115, 120n12, 121n22, 123, 126, 127, 128, 129, 131, 133, 134, 138n5, 139n25, 140n34, 142, 174

Index 277

Titus 127, 128, 129, 131, 133, 134, 140n32, 142
Tutor 12, 24n1, 187, 196
Twelve, the 8, 21, 31, 32

Values 7, 9, 36, 39, 41, 55, 99, 124, 148, 150, 151, 153, 158, 159, 166n76, 168, 170, 174-176, 185, 187, 188, 189, 191, 197, 198, 199, 201, 202, 205n64, 206n144, 208, 209, 212, 214, 218, 224, 226, 227, 228, 230, 231, 235n61, 240, 243-244, 247
Verbal teaching 35, 41, 48, 69, 234n10
Voluntary group 8, 200-201

Westerhoff, John 149, 208, 209-211, 212, 215-218, 233
Wisdom movement 18-19
Women disciples 24n13, 33, 36, 59-60, 73

Young people 23, 134, 187, 194, 201, 215

Paternoster Biblical Monographs

(All titles uniform with this volume)
Dates in bold are of projected publication

Joseph Abraham
Eve: Accused or Acquitted?
A Reconsideration of Feminist Readings of the Creation Narrative Texts in Genesis 1–3

Two contrary views dominate contemporary feminist biblical scholarship. One finds in the Bible an unequivocal equality between the sexes from the very creation of humanity, whilst the other sees the biblical text as irredeemably patriarchal and androcentric. Dr Abraham enters into dialogue with both camps as well as introducing his own method of approach. An invaluable tool for any one who is interested in this contemporary debate.

2002 / 0-85364-971-5 / xxiv + 272pp

Octavian D. Baban
Mimesis and Luke's on the Road Encounters in Luke-Acts
Luke's Theology of the Way and its Literary Representation

The book argues on theological and literary (mimetic) grounds that Luke's on-the-road encounters, especially those belonging to the post-Easter period, are part of his complex theology of the Way. Jesus' teaching and that of the apostles is presented by Luke as a challenging answer to the Hellenistic reader's thirst for adventure, good literature, and existential paradigms.

2005 */ 1-84227-253-5 / approx. 374pp*

Paul Barker
The Triumph of Grace in Deuteronomy

This book is a textual and theological analysis of the interaction between the sin and faithlessness of Israel and the grace of Yahweh in response, looking especially at Deuteronomy chapters 1–3, 8–10 and 29–30. The author argues that the grace of Yahweh is determinative for the ongoing relationship between Yahweh and Israel and that Deuteronomy anticipates and fully expects Israel to be faithless.

2004 / 1-84227-226-8 / xxii + 270pp

Jonathan F. Bayes
The Weakness of the Law
God's Law and the Christian in New Testament Perspective

A study of the four New Testament books which refer to the law as weak (Acts, Romans, Galatians, Hebrews) leads to a defence of the third use in the Reformed debate about the law in the life of the believer.

2000 / 0-85364-957-X / xii + 244pp

Mark Bonnington
The Antioch Episode of Galatians 2:11-14 in Historical and Cultural Context

The Galatians 2 'incident' in Antioch over table-fellowship suggests significant disagreement between the leading apostles. This book analyses the background to the disagreement by locating the incident within the dynamics of social interaction between Jews and Gentiles. It proposes a new way of understanding the relationship between the individuals and issues involved.

2005 / 1-84227-050-8 / approx. 350pp

David Bostock
A Portrayal of Trust
The Theme of Faith in the Hezekiah Narratives

This study provides detailed and sensitive readings of the Hezekiah narratives (2 Kings 18–20 and Isaiah 36–39) from a theological perspective. It concentrates on the theme of faith, using narrative criticism as its methodology. Attention is paid especially to setting, plot, point of view and characterization within the narratives. A largely positive portrayal of Hezekiah emerges that underlines the importance and relevance of scripture.

2005 / 1-84227-314-0 / approx. 300pp

Mark Bredin
Jesus, Revolutionary of Peace
A Non-violent Christology in the Book of Revelation

This book aims to demonstrate that the figure of Jesus in the Book of Revelation can best be understood as an active non-violent revolutionary.

2003 / 1-84227-153-9 / xviii + 262pp

Robinson Butarbutar
Paul and Conflict Resolution
An Exegetical Study of Paul's Apostolic Paradigm in 1 Corinthians 9

The author sees the apostolic paradigm in 1 Corinthians 9 as part of Paul's unified arguments in 1 Corinthians 8–10 in which he seeks to mediate in the dispute over the issue of food offered to idols. The book also sees its relevance for dispute-resolution today, taking the conflict within the author's church as an example.

2006 / 1-84227-315-9 / approx. 280pp

Daniel J-S Chae
Paul as Apostle to the Gentiles
His Apostolic Self-awareness and its Influence on the Soteriological Argument in Romans
Opposing 'the post-Holocaust interpretation of Romans', Daniel Chae competently demonstrates that Paul argues for the equality of Jew and Gentile in Romans. Chae's fresh exegetical interpretation is academically outstanding and spiritually encouraging.
1997 / 0-85364-829-8 / xiv + 378pp

Luke L. Cheung
The Genre, Composition and Hermeneutics of the Epistle of James
The present work examines the employment of the wisdom genre with a certain compositional structure and the interpretation of the law through the Jesus tradition of the double love command by the author of the Epistle of James to serve his purpose in promoting perfection and warning against doubleness among the eschatologically renewed people of God in the Diaspora.
2003 / 1-84227-062-1 / xvi + 372pp

Youngmo Cho
Spirit and Kingdom in the Writings of Luke and Paul
The relationship between Spirit and Kingdom is a relatively unexplored area in Lukan and Pauline studies. This book offers a fresh perspective of two biblical writers on the subject. It explores the difference between Luke's and Paul's understanding of the Spirit by examining the specific question of the relationship of the concept of the Spirit to the concept of the Kingdom of God in each writer.
2005 / 1-84227-316-7 / approx. 270pp

Andrew C. Clark
Parallel Lives
The Relation of Paul to the Apostles in the Lucan Perspective
This study of the Peter-Paul parallels in Acts argues that their purpose was to emphasize the themes of continuity in salvation history and the unity of the Jewish and Gentile missions. New light is shed on Luke's literary techniques, partly through a comparison with Plutarch.
2001 / 1-84227-035-4 / xviii + 386pp

Andrew D. Clarke
Secular and Christian Leadership in Corinth
A Socio-Historical and Exegetical Study of 1 Corinthians 1–6

This volume is an investigation into the leadership structures and dynamics of first-century Roman Corinth. These are compared with the practice of leadership in the Corinthian Christian community which are reflected in 1 Corinthians 1–6, and contrasted with Paul's own principles of Christian leadership.

2005 / 1-84227-229-2 / 200pp

Stephen Finamore
God, Order and Chaos
René Girard and the Apocalypse

Readers are often disturbed by the images of destruction in the book of Revelation and unsure why they are unleashed after the exaltation of Jesus. This book examines past approaches to these texts and uses René Girard's theories to revive some old ideas and propose some new ones.

2005 / 1-84227-197-0 / approx. 344pp

David G. Firth
Surrendering Retribution in the Psalms
Responses to Violence in the Individual Complaints

In *Surrendering Retribution in the Psalms*, David Firth examines the ways in which the book of Psalms inculcates a model response to violence through the repetition of standard patterns of prayer. Rather than seeking justification for retributive violence, Psalms encourages not only a surrender of the right of retribution to Yahweh, but also sets limits on the retribution that can be sought in imprecations. Arising initially from the author's experience in South Africa, the possibilities of this model to a particular context of violence is then briefly explored.

2005 / 1-84227-337-X / xviii + 154pp

Scott J. Hafemann
Suffering and Ministry in the Spirit
Paul's Defence of His Ministry in II Corinthians 2:14–3:3

Shedding new light on the way Paul defended his apostleship, the author offers a careful, detailed study of 2 Corinthians 2:14–3:3 linked with other key passages throughout 1 and 2 Corinthians. Demonstrating the unity and coherence of Paul's argument in this passage, the author shows that Paul's suffering served as the vehicle for revealing God's power and glory through the Spirit.

2000 / 0-85364-967-7 / xiv + 262pp

Scott J. Hafemann
Paul, Moses and the History of Israel
The Letter/Spirit Contrast and the Argument from Scripture in 2 Corinthians 3
An exegetical study of the call of Moses, the second giving of the Law (Exodus 32–34), the new covenant, and the prophetic understanding of the history of Israel in 2 Corinthians 3. Hafemann's work demonstrates Paul's contextual use of the Old Testament and the essential unity between the Law and the Gospel within the context of the distinctive ministries of Moses and Paul.
2005 / 1-84227-317-5 / xii + 498pp

Douglas S. McComiskey
Lukan Theology in the Light of the Gospel's Literary Structure
Luke's Gospel was purposefully written with theology embedded in its patterned literary structure. A critical analysis of this cyclical structure provides new windows into Luke's interpretation of the individual pericopes comprising the Gospel and illuminates several of his theological interests.
2004 / 1-84227-148-2 / xviii + 388pp

Stephen Motyer
Your Father the Devil?
A New Approach to John and 'The Jews'
Who are 'the Jews' in John's Gospel? Defending John against the charge of antisemitism, Motyer argues that, far from demonising the Jews, the Gospel seeks to present Jesus as 'Good News for Jews' in a late first century setting.
1997 / 0-85364-832-8 / xiv + 260pp

Esther Ng
Reconstructing Christian Origins?
The Feminist Theology of Elizabeth Schüssler Fiorenza: An Evaluation
In a detailed evaluation, the author challenges Elizabeth Schüssler Fiorenza's reconstruction of early Christian origins and her underlying presuppositions. The author also presents her own views on women's roles both then and now.
2002 / 1-84227-055-9 / xxiv + 468pp

Robin Parry
Old Testament Story and Christian Ethics
The Rape of Dinah as a Case Study

What is the role of story in ethics and, more particularly, what is the role of Old Testament story in Christian ethics? This book, drawing on the work of contemporary philosophers, argues that narrative is crucial in the ethical shaping of people and, drawing on the work of contemporary Old Testament scholars, that story plays a key role in Old Testament ethics. Parry then argues that when situated in canonical context Old Testament stories can be reappropriated by Christian readers in their own ethical formation. The shocking story of the rape of Dinah and the massacre of the Shechemites provides a fascinating case study for exploring the parameters within which Christian ethical appropriations of Old Testament stories can live.

2004 / 1-84227-210-1 / xx + 350pp

Ian Paul
Power to See the World Anew
The Value of Paul Ricoeur's Hermeneutic of Metaphor in Interpreting the Symbolism of Revelation 12 and 13

This book is a study of the hermeneutics of metaphor of Paul Ricoeur, one of the most important writers on hermeneutics and metaphor of the last century. It sets out the key points of his theory, important criticisms of his work, and how his approach, modified in the light of these criticisms, offers a methodological framework for reading apocalyptic texts.

2006 / 1-84227-056-7 / approx. 350pp

Robert L. Plummer
Paul's Understanding of the Church's Mission
Did the Apostle Paul Expect the Early Christian Communities to Evangelize?

This book engages in a careful study of Paul's letters to determine if the apostle expected the communities to which he wrote to engage in missionary activity. It helpfully summarizes the discussion on this debated issue, judiciously handling contested texts, and provides a way forward in addressing this critical question. While admitting that Paul rarely explicitly commands the communities he founded to evangelize, Plummer amasses significant incidental data to provide a convincing case that Paul did indeed expect his churches to engage in mission activity. Throughout the study, Plummer progressively builds a theological basis for the church's mission that is both distinctively Pauline and compelling.

2006 / 1-84227-333-7 / approx. 324pp

David Powys
'Hell': A Hard Look at a Hard Question
The Fate of the Unrighteous in New Testament Thought
This comprehensive treatment seeks to unlock the original meaning of terms and phrases long thought to support the traditional doctrine of hell. It concludes that there is an alternative—one which is more biblical, and which can positively revive the rationale for Christian mission.
1997 / 0-85364-831-X / xxii + 478pp

Sorin Sabou
Between Horror and Hope
Paul's Metaphorical Language of Death in Romans 6.1-11
This book argues that Paul's metaphorical language of death in Romans 6.1-11 conveys two aspects: horror and hope. The 'horror' aspect is conveyed by the 'crucifixion' language, and the 'hope' aspect by 'burial' language. The life of the Christian believer is understood, as relationship with sin is concerned ('death to sin'), between these two realities: horror and hope.
2005 / 1-84227-322-1 / approx. 224pp

Rosalind Selby
The Comical Doctrine
The Epistemology of New Testament Hermeneutics
This book argues that the gospel breaks through postmodernity's critique of truth and the referential possibilities of textuality with its gift of grace. With a rigorous, philosophical challenge to modernist and postmodernist assumptions, Selby offers an alternative epistemology to all who would still read with faith *and* with academic credibility.
2005 / 1-84227-212-8 / approx. 350pp

Kiwoong Son
Zion Symbolism in Hebrews
Hebrews 12.18-24 as a Hermeneutical Key to the Epistle
This book challenges the general tendency of understanding the Epistle to the Hebrews against a Hellenistic background and suggests that the Epistle should be understood in the light of the Jewish apocalyptic tradition. The author especially argues for the importance of the theological symbolism of Sinai and Zion (Heb. 12:18-24) as it provides the Epistle's theological background as well as the rhetorical basis of the superiority motif of Jesus throughout the Epistle.
2005 / 1-84227-368-X / approx. 280pp

Kevin Walton
Thou Traveller Unknown
The Presence and Absence of God in the Jacob Narrative
The author offers a fresh reading of the story of Jacob in the book of Genesis through the paradox of divine presence and absence. The work also seeks to make a contribution to Pentateuchal studies by bringing together a close reading of the final text with historical critical insights, doing justice to the text's historical depth, final form and canonical status.
2003 / 1-84227-059-1 / xvi + 238pp

George M. Wieland
The Significance of Salvation
A Study of Salvation Language in the Pastoral Epistles
The language and ideas of salvation pervade the three Pastoral Epistles. This study offers a close examination of their soteriological statements. In all three letters the idea of salvation is found to play a vital paraenetic role, but each also exhibits distinctive soteriological emphases. The results challenge common assumptions about the Pastoral Epistles as a corpus.
2005 / 1-84227-257-8 / approx. 324pp

Alistair Wilson
When Will These Things Happen?
A Study of Jesus as Judge in Matthew 21–25
This study seeks to allow Matthew's carefully constructed presentation of Jesus to be given full weight in the modern evaluation of Jesus' eschatology. Careful analysis of the text of Matthew 21–25 reveals Jesus to be standing firmly in the Jewish prophetic and wisdom traditions as he proclaims and enacts imminent judgement on the Jewish authorities then boldly claims the central role in the final and universal judgement.
2004 / 1-84227-146-6 / xxii + 272pp

Lindsay Wilson
Joseph Wise and Otherwise
The Intersection of Covenant and Wisdom in Genesis 37–50
This book offers a careful literary reading of Genesis 37–50 that argues that the Joseph story contains both strong covenant themes and many wisdom-like elements. The connections between the two helps to explore how covenant and wisdom might intersect in an integrated biblical theology.
2004 / 1-84227-140-7 / xvi + 340pp

Stephen I. Wright
The Voice of Jesus
Studies in the Interpretation of Six Gospel Parables
This literary study considers how the 'voice' of Jesus has been heard in different periods of parable interpretation, and how the categories of figure and trope may help us towards a sensitive reading of the parables today.
2000 / 0-85364-975-8 / xiv + 280pp

Paternoster
9 Holdom Avenue,
Bletchley,
Milton Keynes MK1 1QR,
United Kingdom
Web: www.authenticmedia.co.uk/paternoster

July 2005

Paternoster Theological Monographs

(All titles uniform with this volume)
Dates in bold are of projected publication

Emil Bartos
Deification in Eastern Orthodox Theology
An Evaluation and Critique of the Theology of Dumitru Staniloae

Bartos studies a fundamental yet neglected aspect of Orthodox theology: deification. By examining the doctrines of anthropology, christology, soteriology and ecclesiology as they relate to deification, he provides an important contribution to contemporary dialogue between Eastern and Western theologians.

1999 / 0-85364-956-1 / xii + 370pp

Graham Buxton
The Trinity, Creation and Pastoral Ministry
Imaging the Perichoretic God

In this book the author proposes a three-way conversation between theology, science and pastoral ministry. His approach draws on a Trinitarian understanding of God as a relational being of love, whose life 'spills over' into all created reality, human and non-human. By locating human meaning and purpose within God's 'creation-community' this book offers the possibility of a transforming engagement between those in pastoral ministry and the scientific community.

2005 */ 1-84227-369-8 / approx. 380 pp*

Iain D. Campbell
Fixing the Indemnity
The Life and Work of George Adam Smith

When Old Testament scholar George Adam Smith (1856–1942) delivered the Lyman Beecher lectures at Yale University in 1899, he confidently declared that 'modern criticism has won its war against traditional theories. It only remains to fix the amount of the indemnity.' In this biography, Iain D. Campbell assesses Smith's critical approach to the Old Testament and evaluates its consequences, showing that Smith's life and work still raises questions about the relationship between biblical scholarship and evangelical faith.

2004 / 1-84227-228-4 / xx + 256pp

Tim Chester
Mission and the Coming of God
Eschatology, the Trinity and Mission in the Theology of Jürgen Moltmann
This book explores the theology and missiology of the influential contemporary theologian, Jürgen Moltmann. It highlights the important contribution Moltmann has made while offering a critique of his thought from an evangelical perspective. In so doing, it touches on pertinent issues for evangelical missiology. The conclusion takes Calvin as a starting point, proposing 'an eschatology of the cross' which offers a critique of the over-realised eschatologies in liberation theology and certain forms of evangelicalism.
2006 / 1-84227-320-5 / approx. 224pp

Sylvia Wilkey Collinson
Making Disciples
The Significance of Jesus' Educational Strategy for Today's Church
This study examines the biblical practice of discipling, formulates a definition, and makes comparisons with modern models of education. A recommendation is made for greater attention to its practice today.
2004 / 1-84227-116-4 / xiv + 278pp

Darrell Cosden
A Theology of Work
Work and the New Creation
Through dialogue with Moltmann, Pope John Paul II and others, this book develops a genitive 'theology of work', presenting a theological definition of work and a model for a theological ethics of work that shows work's nature, value and meaning now and eschatologically. Work is shown to be a transformative activity consisting of three dynamically inter-related dimensions: the instrumental, relational and ontological.
2005 / 1-84227-332-9 / xvi + 208pp

Stephen M. Dunning
The Crisis and the Quest
A Kierkegaardian Reading of Charles Williams
Employing Kierkegaardian categories and analysis, this study investigates both the central crisis in Charles Williams's authorship between hermetism and Christianity (Kierkegaard's Religions A and B), and the quest to resolve this crisis, a quest that ultimately presses the bounds of orthodoxy.
2000 / 0-85364-985-5 / xxiv + 254pp

Keith Ferdinando
The Triumph of Christ in African Perspective
A Study of Demonology and Redemption in the African Context
The book explores the implications of the gospel for traditional African fears of occult aggression. It analyses such traditional approaches to suffering and biblical responses to fears of demonic evil, concluding with an evaluation of African beliefs from the perspective of the gospel.
1999 / 0-85364-830-1 / xviii + 450pp

Andrew Goddard
Living the Word, Resisting the World
The Life and Thought of Jacques Ellul
This work offers a definitive study of both the life and thought of the French Reformed thinker Jacques Ellul (1912-1994). It will prove an indispensable resource for those interested in this influential theologian and sociologist and for Christian ethics and political thought generally.
2002 / 1-84227-053-2 / xxiv + 378pp

David Hilborn
The Words of our Lips
Language-Use in Free Church Worship
Studies of liturgical language have tended to focus on the written canons of Roman Catholic and Anglican communities. By contrast, David Hilborn analyses the more extemporary approach of English Nonconformity. Drawing on recent developments in linguistic pragmatics, he explores similarities and differences between 'fixed' and 'free' worship, and argues for the interdependence of each.
2006 / 0-85364-977-4 / approx. 350pp

Roger Hitching
The Church and Deaf People
A Study of Identity, Communication and Relationships with Special Reference to the Ecclesiology of Jürgen Moltmann
In *The Church and Deaf People* Roger Hitching sensitively examines the history and present experience of deaf people and finds similarities between aspects of sign language and Moltmann's theological method that 'open up' new ways of understanding theological concepts.
2003 / 1-84227-222-5 / xxii + 236pp

John G. Kelly
One God, One People
The Differentiated Unity of the People of God in the Theology of Jürgen Moltmann

The author expounds and critiques Moltmann's doctrine of God and highlights the systematic connections between it and Moltmann's influential discussion of Israel. He then proposes a fresh approach to Jewish–Christian relations building on Moltmann's work using insights from Habermas and Rawls.

2005 / 0-85346-969-3 / approx. 350pp

Mark F.W. Lovatt
Confronting the Will-to-Power
A Reconsideration of the Theology of Reinhold Niebuhr

Confronting the Will-to-Power is an analysis of the theology of Reinhold Niebuhr, arguing that his work is an attempt to identify, and provide a practical theological answer to, the existence and nature of human evil.

2001 / 1-84227-054-0 / xviii + 216pp

Neil B. MacDonald
Karl Barth and the Strange New World within the Bible
Barth, Wittgenstein, and the Metadilemmas of the Enlightenment

Barth's discovery of the strange new world within the Bible is examined in the context of Kant, Hume, Overbeck, and, most importantly, Wittgenstein. MacDonald covers some fundamental issues in theology today: epistemology, the final form of the text and biblical truth-claims.

2000 / 0-85364-970-7 / xxvi + 374pp

Keith A. Mascord
Alvin Plantinga and Christian Apologetics

This book draws together the contributions of the philosopher Alvin Plantinga to the major contemporary challenges to Christian belief, highlighting in particular his ground-breaking work in epistemology and the problem of evil. Plantinga's theory that both theistic and Christian belief is warrantedly basic is explored and critiqued, and an assessment offered as to the significance of his work for apologetic theory and practice.

2005 / 1-84227-256-X / approx. 304pp

Gillian McCulloch
The Deconstruction of Dualism in Theology
With Reference to Ecofeminist Theology and New Age Spirituality
This book challenges eco-theological anti-dualism in Christian theology, arguing that dualism has a twofold function in Christian religious discourse. Firstly, it enables us to express the discontinuities and divisions that are part of the process of reality. Secondly, dualistic language allows us to express the mysteries of divine transcendence/immanence and the survival of the soul without collapsing into monism and materialism, both of which are problematic for Christian epistemology.
2002 / 1-84227-044-3 / xii + 282pp

Leslie McCurdy
Attributes and Atonement
The Holy Love of God in the Theology of P.T. Forsyth
Attributes and Atonement is an intriguing full-length study of P.T. Forsyth's doctrine of the cross as it relates particularly to God's holy love. It includes an unparalleled bibliography of both primary and secondary material relating to Forsyth.
1999 / 0-85364-833-6 / xiv + 328pp

Nozomu Miyahira
Towards a Theology of the Concord of God
A Japanese Perspective on the Trinity
This book introduces a new Japanese theology and a unique Trinitarian formula based on the Japanese intellectual climate: three betweennesses and one concord. It also presents a new interpretation of the Trinity, a co-subordinationism, which is in line with orthodox Trinitarianism; each single person of the Trinity is eternally and equally subordinate (or serviceable) to the other persons, so that they retain the mutual dynamic equality.
2000 / 0-85364-863-8 / xiv + 256pp

Eddy José Muskus
The Origins and Early Development of Liberation Theology in Latin America
With Particular Reference to Gustavo Gutiérrez
This work challenges the fundamental premise of Liberation Theology, 'opting for the poor', and its claim that Christ is found in them. It also argues that Liberation Theology emerged as a direct result of the failure of the Roman Catholic Church in Latin America.
2002 / 0-85364-974-X / xiv + 296pp

Jim Purves
The Triune God and the Charismatic Movement
A Critical Appraisal from a Scottish Perspective

All emotion and no theology? Or a fundamental challenge to reappraise and realign our trinitarian theology in the light of Christian experience? This study of charismatic renewal as it found expression within Scotland at the end of the twentieth century evaluates the use of Patristic, Reformed and contemporary models of the Trinity in explaining the workings of the Holy Spirit.

2004 / 1-84227-321-3 / xxiv + 246pp

Anna Robbins
Methods in the Madness
Diversity in Twentieth-Century Christian Social Ethics

The author compares the ethical methods of Walter Rauschenbusch, Reinhold Niebuhr and others. She argues that unless Christians are clear about the ways that theology and philosophy are expressed practically they may lose the ability to discuss social ethics across contexts, let alone reach effective agreements.

2004 / 1-84227-211-X / xx + 294pp

Ed Rybarczyk
Beyond Salvation
Eastern Orthodoxy and Classical Pentecostalism on Becoming Like Christ

At first glance eastern Orthodoxy and classical Pentecostalism seem quite distinct. This ground-breaking study shows they share much in common, especially as it concerns the experiential elements of following Christ. Both traditions assert that authentic Christianity transcends the wooden categories of modernism.

2004 / 1-84227-144-X / xii + 356pp

Signe Sandsmark
Is World View Neutral Education Possible and Desirable?
A Christian Response to Liberal Arguments
(Published jointly with The Stapleford Centre)

This book discusses reasons for belief in world view neutrality, and argues that 'neutral' education will have a hidden, but strong world view influence. It discusses the place for Christian education in the common school.

2000 / 0-85364-973-1 / xiv + 182pp

Hazel Sherman
Reading Zechariah
The Allegorical Tradition of Biblical Interpretation through the Commentary of Didymus the Blind and Theodore of Mopsuestia
A close reading of the commentary on Zechariah by Didymus the Blind alongside that of Theodore of Mopsuestia suggests that popular categorising of Antiochene and Alexandrian biblical exegesis as 'historical' or 'allegorical' is inadequate and misleading.
2005 / 1-84227-213-6 / approx. 280pp

Andrew Sloane
On Being a Christian in the Academy
Nicholas Wolterstorff and the Practice of Christian Scholarship
An exposition and critical appraisal of Nicholas Wolterstorff's epistemology in the light of the philosophy of science, and an application of his thought to the practice of Christian scholarship.
2003 / 1-84227-058-3 / xvi + 274pp

Damon W.K. So
Jesus' Revelation of His Father
A Narrative-Conceptual Study of the Trinity with Special Reference to Karl Barth
This book explores the trinitarian dynamics in the context of Jesus' revelation of his Father in his earthly ministry with references to key passages in Matthew's Gospel. It develops from the exegeses of these passages a non-linear concept of revelation which links Jesus' communion with his Father to his revelatory words and actions through a nuanced understanding of the Holy Spirit, with references to K. Barth, G.W.H. Lampe, J.D.G. Dunn and E. Irving.
2005 / 1-84227-323-X / approx. 380pp

Daniel Strange
The Possibility of Salvation Among the Unevangelised
An Analysis of Inclusivism in Recent Evangelical Theology
For evangelical theologians the 'fate of the unevangelised' impinges upon fundamental tenets of evangelical identity. The position known as 'inclusivism', defined by the belief that the unevangelised can be ontologically saved by Christ whilst being epistemologically unaware of him, has been defended most vigorously by the Canadian evangelical Clark H. Pinnock. Through a detailed analysis and critique of Pinnock's work, this book examines a cluster of issues surrounding the unevangelised and its implications for christology, soteriology and the doctrine of revelation.
2002 / 1-84227-047-8 / xviii + 362pp

Scott Swain
God According to the Gospel
Biblical Narrative and the Identity of God in the Theology of Robert W. Jenson
Robert W. Jenson is one of the leading voices in contemporary Trinitarian theology. His boldest contribution in this area concerns his use of biblical narrative both to ground and explicate the Christian doctrine of God. *God According to the Gospel* critically examines Jenson's proposal and suggests an alternative way of reading the biblical portrayal of the triune God.
2006 / 1-84227-258-6 / approx. 180pp

Justyn Terry
The Justifying Judgement of God
A Reassessment of the Place of Judgement in the Saving Work of Christ
The argument of this book is that judgement, understood as the whole process of bringing justice, is the primary metaphor of atonement, with others, such as victory, redemption and sacrifice, subordinate to it. Judgement also provides the proper context for understanding penal substitution and the call to repentance, baptism, eucharist and holiness.
2005 / 1-84227-370-1 / approx. 274 pp

Graham Tomlin
The Power of the Cross
Theology and the Death of Christ in Paul, Luther and Pascal
This book explores the theology of the cross in St Paul, Luther and Pascal. It offers new perspectives on the theology of each, and some implications for the nature of power, apologetics, theology and church life in a postmodern context.
1999 / 0-85364-984-7 / xiv + 344pp

Adonis Vidu
Postliberal Theological Method
A Critical Study
The postliberal theology of Hans Frei, George Lindbeck, Ronald Thiemann, John Milbank and others is one of the more influential contemporary options. This book focuses on several aspects pertaining to its theological method, specifically its understanding of background, hermeneutics, epistemic justification, ontology, the nature of doctrine and, finally, Christological method.
2005 / 1-84227-395-7 / approx. 324pp

Graham J. Watts
Revelation and the Spirit
A Comparative Study of the Relationship between the Doctrine of Revelation and Pneumatology in the Theology of Eberhard Jüngel and of Wolfhart Pannenberg
The relationship between revelation and pneumatology is relatively unexplored. This approach offers a fresh angle on two important twentieth century theologians and raises pneumatological questions which are theologically crucial and relevant to mission in a postmodern culture.
2005 / 1-84227-104-0 / xxii + 232pp

Nigel G. Wright
Disavowing Constantine
Mission, Church and the Social Order in the Theologies of John Howard Yoder and Jürgen Moltmann
This book is a timely restatement of a radical theology of church and state in the Anabaptist and Baptist tradition. Dr Wright constructs his argument in dialogue and debate with Yoder and Moltmann, major contributors to a free church perspective.
2000 / 0-85364-978-2 / xvi + 252pp

Paternoster
9 Holdom Avenue,
Bletchley,
Milton Keynes MK1 1QR,
United Kingdom
Web: www.authenticmedia.co.uk/paternoster